The Monetary Theory of Production

The essays in this book are dedicated to and in honour of
Augusto Graziani

The Monetary Theory of Production

Tradition and Perspectives

Edited by

Giuseppe Fontana

and

Riccardo Realfonzo

First published 2005 by
PALGRAVE MACMILLAN
Houndmills, Basingstoke, Hampshire RG21 6XS and
175 Fifth Avenue, New York, N.Y. 10010
Companies and representatives throughout the world

PALGRAVE MACMILLAN is the global academic imprint of the Palgrave
Macmillan division of St. Martin's Press, LLC and of Palgrave Macmillan Ltd.
Macmillan® is a registered trademark in the United States, United Kingdom
and other countries. Palgrave is a registered trademark in the European
Union and other countries.

ISBN-13: 978–1–4039–3259–4
ISBN-10: 1–4039–3259–X

This book is printed on paper suitable for recycling and made from fully
managed and sustained forest sources.

A catalogue record for this book is available from the British Library.

Library of Congress Cataloging-in-Publication Data
The monetary theory of production : tradition and perspectives / edited by
    Giuseppe Fontana and Riccardo Realfonzo.
        p.   cm.
    Includes bibliographical references and index.
    ISBN 1–4039–3259–X (cloth)
    1. Money.   2. Monetary policy.   3. Economic policy.   4. Production
(Economic theory)   I. Fontana, Giuseppe, 1968–   II. Realfonzo,
Riccardo, 1964–
    HG220.A2M576 2005
    332.4′01—dc22   2004057664

10   9   8   7   6   5   4   3   2   1
14   13   12   11   10   09   08   07   06   05

Printed and bound in Great Britain by
Antony Rowe Ltd, Chippenham and Eastbourne

Contents

List of Figures	xii
List of Tables	xiii
Acknowledgements	xiv
Notes on the Contributors	xvi

Introduction: The Monetary Theory of Production   1
Giuseppe Fontana and Riccardo Realfonzo

Keynes's legacy	1
Traditions of the monetary theory of production in Keynes's time	3
The contemporary debate on the monetary theory of production	6
Overview of the book's contributions	10
Note	16
References	16

PART I   THE TRADITION OF THE MONETARY THEORY OF PRODUCTION

1 Macroeconomic Analysis and Individual Economic Rationality: Some Lessons from Wicksell, von Mises and Schumpeter   23
Richard Arena and Agnès Festré

Introduction	23
Individual economic rationality and macroeconomic analysis: Wicksell after the modern circulation approach	24
Economic rationality, circular flow and economic development in Schumpeter	27
Economic rationality, the 'evenly rotating economy' (ERE) and the 'progressing economy' (PE) in von Mises	31
Conclusion	35
References	36

2 **Monetary Economics after Wicksell: Alternative Perspectives within the Theory of the Monetary Circuit** 39
Riccardo Bellofiore

Introduction 39
Wicksell's *Interest and Prices* 40
Keynes's *Treatise on Money* 42
Schumpeter on finance, innovation and capitalist
  evolution 45
Out-of-equilibrium monetary economics before *The
  General Theory*: an assessment 47
Preliminary conclusions 50
Notes 50
References 51

3 **Lost and Found: Some History of Endogenous Money in the Twentieth Century** 53
Victoria Chick

Introduction 53
Do banks 'create credit'? 54
The deposit multiplier 57
The role of reserves 60
Conclusion 63
References 63

4 **Alternative Theories of the Rate of Interest: A Reconsideration** 67
Gunnar Heinsohn and Otto Steiger

Schumpeter's and Keynes's criticism of the
  neoclassical theory of the rate of interest:
  money *precedes* goods 67
Where does the money come from in Schumpeter's and
  Keynes's theories? 68
The 1937 debate on 'Alternative Theories of the
  Rate of Interest' 71
Own capital and collateral: the missing links in
  the theory of the rate of interest 73
The property paradigm as an alternative theory of the rate
  of interest 75
Notes 79
References 79

Contents   vii

5 An Inquiry into a Dark Mystery in the History of the
Monetary Theory of Production: What Went Wrong with
the Early Contribution of Joan Robinson   83
Alain Parguez

The Robinsonian mystery   83
Solving the mystery: one must venture beyond the veil of Joan
    Robinson's crucial concern with the classical restoration 87
At last the mystery is solved   92
Notes   93
References   93

6 Some Reflections on Changes in Keynes's Analysis
between the *Treatise* and the *General Theory*   95
Malcolm Sawyer

Introduction   95
Money in *A Treatise on Money*   95
Money in *The General Theory*   98
A Treatise versus *The General Theory*   102
Conclusion   105
Notes   106
References   106

PART II   STOCKS AND FLOWS IN THE MONETARY
          CIRCUIT

7 Single-Period Analysis: Financial Markets, Firms' Failures
and Closure of the Monetary Circuit   111
Marcello Messori and Alberto Zazzaro

Introduction   111
Profit realisation in kind   112
The financing of investment demand   115
Monetary profits and firms' failures   118
Conclusion   120
Notes   121
References   122

8 The Existence of Monetary Profits within the Monetary Circuit   125
Louis-Philippe Rochon

Introduction   125
The theory of the monetary circuit   126
The determination of profits   131

Conclusion   136
Notes   136
References   136

9 **Central Banking in a Monetary Theory of Production:**
The Economics of Payment Finality from a Circular-Flow
Perspective   139
Sergio Rossi

Introduction   139
The coexistence of central and commercial bank monies   140
The circular flow of central bank money and credit   144
Payment finality for cross-border transactions   148
Conclusion   150
Notes   150
References   151

PART III   THE MONETARY CIRCUIT AND
UNEMPLOYMENT

10 **Bank Mergers, Monopoly Power and Unemployment:**
A Monetary Circuit Approach   155
Guglielmo Forges Davanzati and Riccardo Realfonzo

Introduction   155
The monetary circuit   156
Increase in competition, bank mergers and firms'
    monopoly power   157
Monopoly power, interest rate and employment   160
Policy implications   166
Interest rate, savings and employment   167
Conclusion   169
Notes   169
References   170

11 **Circuit Theory and the Employment Issue**   173
Claude Gnos

How circuit theory accounts for the originality of Keynes's
    theory of employment   174
Circuit theory at centre stage in explaining
    unemployment   177
Conclusion   180
Notes   181
References   181

PART IV   MONEY, INFLATION AND DISTRIBUTION

12   Non-Credit Money to Fight Poverty   187
     Biagio Bossone and Abdourahmane Sarr

     Introduction   187
     Finance for growth: what works and what
          does not   188
     Finance to fight poverty: a proposal   191
     Economic effects of the NCMS   196
     Appendix I   199
     References   201

13   Towards a Non-Conventional Circuit Approach:
     Credit, Microcredit and Property Rights   203
     Lilia Costabile

     Sufia's story   204
     Conventionalism, libertarianism, welfarism, and the
          capability approach   205
     Microcredit and its reasons   210
     Microcredit and the circuit approach   213
     Notes   215
     References   215

14   Monetary Theory of Production and Disequilibrium
     Inflation   217
     Elie Sadigh

     Introduction   217
     Inflation defined only as an increase in the general
          level of prices   217
     Monetary disequilibrium inflation   220
     Consequences of disequilibrium inflation   222
     Conclusion   226
     Note   226
     References   226

PART V   MONETARY CIRCULATION AND ECONOMIC
          POLICY

15   What is Wrong with the Euro Area Monetary Model?   231
     Philip Arestis and Malcolm Sawyer

     Introduction   231
     Theoretical underpinnings of the EMU model   231
     Institutional framework   233

The monetary theory of production view   234
Effectiveness of interest rate changes   236
Conclusions   241
Notes   242
References   242

16 **Circulation Approach and Applied Economics: Monetary
    Duality in Cuba**   243
    Ghislain Deleplace

    The issue of monetary duality   244
    The specificity of the Cuban monetary regime   247
    Viability and stability of monetary duality
       in Cuba   249
    Conclusion   254
    Notes   255
    References   255

17 **Lessons from Asset-Based Financial Systems with
    Zero-Reserve Requirements**   257
    Marc Lavoie

    Zero-reserve requirements at the Bank of Canada   259
    The operations of the settlements system   260
    The determination of the overnight interest rate   261
    The case of the American financial system   264
    Conclusion   266
    References   267

18 **Interest Rates, Interest Spreads and Monetary Circulation:
    Theoretical Framework and Empirical Implications for
    Macroeconomic Performance**   269
    Mario Seccareccia

    Introduction   269
    Brief historical digression: Wicksell's model of
       monetary circulation and some original insights
       from Robinson to Nell   270
    Financial implications of the interest spread: Graziani's
       analytics   271
    Real interest rates, debt and macroeconomic performance:
       some further Grazianian insights   273
    Some empirical insights on the effects of changes in interest
       spreads and real interest rates   275

Conclusion   283
References   283

Appendix: Augusto Graziani's Selected Publications   285

Index   288

List of Figures

9.1 The circular flow of central bank money in the
     interbank market   144
9.2 The two circuits of central bank money   145
9.3 Bilateral and multilateral credit operations between banks   146
9.4 The real flows of a central bank's monetary circuit   147
9.5 The circular flow of international central bank money   149
10.1 The monetary circuit   157
10.2 Interest rate, prices and employment   163
10.3 Interest rate, productivity and employment   165
12.1 Flow of funds in the circuit model   189
12.2 Flow of funds in the NCMS   196
16.1 Pattern of circulation without private resources in dollars   250
16.2 Pattern of circulation with private resources in dollars
     totally spent in dollars   251
16.3 Pattern of circulation with private resources in dollars
     partly spent in dollars   252
18.1 Interest spreads: deviations from HP trend   277
18.2 Interest spread and growth in short-term business credit   278
18.3 Interest spread and real GDP growth   279

List of Tables

9.1   The result of a payment between two clients of
      distinct banks   142
9.2   Central bank money as the means of interbank settlements   143
12.1 The balance sheet of a DCI   192
15.1 Effects of monetary policy change   238
15.2 Impact of changes in interest rates   239
15.3 Effects of 1 percentage point increase in interest rate
      sustained for 2 years   241
18.1 Regression results: rate of growth of business
      short-term credit correlated with interest spread and
      real long-term rates   280
18.2 Regression results: rate of growth of real gross domestic
      product correlated with interest spread and real
      long-term rates   281
18.3 Granger causality tests: interest spread and real GDP growth 283

Acknowledgements

This book contains the proceedings of an international conference entitled 'The Monetary Theory of Production: Tradition and Perspectives' held in honour of Augusto Graziani at the Faculty of Economic and Business Sciences (SEA), University of Sannio (Benevento, Italy), on 2003, December 5 and 6. All over the world, scholars of the monetary theory of production (hereafter MTP) acknowledge that some of the most important contributions to this field of research come from the work of Augusto Graziani. He is the most prominent Italian scholar of MTP. This book is dedicated to him as an acknowledgment of the great intellectual debt and personal gratitude that economists owe him. His writings have been a constant reference point for the contributors to this book, for those who took part in the conference as chairs and discussants, and for many other scholars, who for various reasons could not play a part in this event. We are confident that Graziani's present and future work will push the frontiers of MTP even further.

The editors would like to thank all the scholars who took part in the conference, not only the authors of the papers included in this book, but also those who gave an important contribution as chairs or discussants: Piero Barucci, Piero Bini, Emiliano Brancaccio, Maurizio Caserta, Duccio Cavalieri, Guglielmo Chiodi, Marina Colonna, Carlo D'Adda, Marcello De Cecco, Stefano Figuera, Alberto Giacomin, Adriano Giannola, Carlo Giannone, Marco Guidi, Bruno Jossa, Ferruccio Marzano, Carlo Panico, Roberto Panizza, Giovanni Pavanelli, Neri Salvadori, Eugenio Zagari and Gennaro Zezza. The editors are grateful to the head of the SEA, Ennio De Simone, and colleagues at the University of Sannio for continuous encouragement and support in the organisation of the conference. They are also very grateful to those who worked towards the successful outcome of the conference: Emiliano Brancaccio, Guido Tortorella Esposito, and Carmen Vita as well as the members of the Cooperativa Risorse. The editors would also like to express appreciation to the Società Italiana degli Economisti (SIE) and the Associazione Italiana per la Storia del Pensiero Economico (AISPE) for sponsoring the conference, and to the Banca d'Italia, Camera di Commercio di Benevento, Ente Provinciale per il Turismo di Benevento, Istituto Banco di Napoli Fondazione, Istituto Italiano per gli Studi Filosofici, and Provincia di Benevento for their financial support.

The editors are grateful to Philip Arestis, Emiliano Brancaccio, Guglielmo Forges Davanzati, Sergio Rossi, Malcolm Sawyer and Eric Tymoigne for comments on an earlier draft of the Introduction. The usual disclaimer applies. Last, but not least, the final corrections to the book were made when

Giuseppe Fontana was a visiting research scholar at the School of Economics, University of New South Wales (UNSW), Sydney (Australia). He would like to express appreciation to the members of the School of Economics, and to Peter Kriesler in particular, for providing a stimulating and pleasant working environment.

GIUSEPPE FONTANA
RICCARDO REALFONZO

Notes on the Contributors

Richard Arena (arena@idefi.cnrs.fr) is Professor of Economics at the University of Nice-Sophia Antipolis, France. He is also President of the European Society of the History of Economic Thought. His main research interests concern the history of economic analysis, the economics of knowledge and business cycle theory. He has edited several books on the history of economic thought, including studies of Marshall, Keynes, Schumpeter and Sraffa.

Philip Arestis (arestis@levy.org) is University Director of Research at Cambridge University, and Institute Professor of Economics at the Levy Economics Institute. He is the author of several books and articles. His current research interests include the causes of unemployment and the obstacles to the achievement of full unemployment, and the relationship between finance and growth, as well as work on Keynesian macroeconomics.

Riccardo Bellofiore (riccardo.bellofiore@unibg.it) is Professor of Economics at the University of Bergamo, Italy. In English he has edited: *Marxian Economics: A Reappraisal*, 2 vols (Palgrave, 1998); *Global Money, Capital Restructuring and the Changing Patterns of Labour* (1999); (with Piero Ferri) *Financial Keynesianism and Market Instability* and *Financial Fragility and Investment in the Capitalist Economy*, both on Minsky's economic legacy (2001); (with Nicola Taylor) *The Constitution of Capital. Essays on Volume I of Marx's Capital* (Palgrave).

Biagio Bossone (bbossone@worldbank.org) is Executive Director to the World Bank for Italy, Portugal, Greece, Malta, Albania, San Marino and Timor Leste, and Associate Director at the Banca d'Italia. His research has focused on money and banking, international finance, and financial sector policy. Bossone has been a member of several international groups and task forces dealing with preparation of the European Monetary Union and with G10 central banking issues. Bossone holds doctoral and postdoctoral degrees in economics and economic policy from the Università degli Studi di Palermo and Northeastern University.

Victoria Chick (uctpa98@ucl.ac.uk) is Emeritus Professor of Economics at University College London. She has held visiting posts at the Reserve Bank of Australia, McGill University and the Universities of Southampton, Aarhus, Louvain, Catania, Burgundy (Dijon) and California at Berkeley and at Santa Cruz. She has published four books: *The Theory of Monetary Policy* (1973 and 1977); *Macroeconomics after Keynes: A Reconsideration of The General Theory*

(1983); *On Money, Method and Keynes: Selected Essays of Victoria Chick* (P. Arestis and S.C. Dow, eds, Macmillan, 1992); *Recent Developments in Post-Keynesian Economics* (ed., with P. Arestis, 1992), and articles on monetary theory and policy, methodology and the economics of Keynes. She has served on the Council and Executive Committee of the Royal Economic Society and on the Editorial Boards of several journals. She was a member of the Governing Bodies of UCL and the University of London.

Lilia Costabile (costabil@unina.it), is Professor of Economics at the University of Naples. Her research interests include economic theory (with special emphasis on the economics of institutions, the economics of labour markets, and Keynesian economics) and the history of economic thought. She has published her work both in books (for some of which she has also been the editor) and in journals (for example, *The Economic Journal, The Cambridge Journal of Economics, Australian Economic Papers, Economia Politica, Rivista Italiana degli Economisti*).

Ghislain Deleplace (ghislain.deleplace@univ-paris8.fr) is Professor of Economics at the University of Paris 8–Saint-Denis. His main interests are the history of monetary theory and the history of the metallic-standard monetary regimes. He has co-authored *Private Money and Public Currencies* (1994), co-edited *Money in Motion: The Post Keynesian and Circulation Approaches* (1996), and he is the author of *Histoire de la Pensée Économique: du 'Royaume Agricole' de Quesnay au 'Monde à la Arrow-Debreu'* (1999).

Agnès Festré (festre@idefi.cnrs.fr) is Assistant Professor at the University of Nice-Sophia Antipolis. She belongs to the department IODE (Institutions, Organization and Economic Dynamics) of the GREDEG research group. Her research interests include monetary and business cycle analysis in both a historical and theoretical approach, economics of knowledge and related issues such as the role of beliefs in economic activity and history of economic thought.

Giuseppe Fontana (gf@lubs.leeds.ac.uk) is Senior Lecturer in Economics at the University of Leeds (UK) and Associate Professor at the University of Sannio (Italy). He is secretary of the Post Keynesian Economics Study Group (PKESG). His research interests are in the areas of macroeconomics, monetary economics, history of economic thought and methodology. He has recent publications in the *American Journal of Economics and Sociology, Cambridge Journal of Economics, Journal of Post Keynesian Economics, Metroeconomica, Revue d'Economie Politique and the Scottish Journal of Political Economy*. His latest publication is *Money, Uncertainty and Time: Essays in the Post Keynesian Tradition (2004)*.

Guglielmo Forges Davanzati (forges@cds.unina.it) is Associate Professor of History of Economic Thought at the University of Lecce (Italy). His field of research includes the post-Keynesian theory of income distribution, theories on wage bargaining and the functioning of the labour market in historical perspectives, issues on ethics and economics. He has published three books and several papers on these subjects, these papers having appeared in Italian and English in international journals.

Claude Gnos (claude.gnos@u-bourgogne.fr) is Associate Professor of Economics at the University of Burgundy and Director of the Center for Monetary and Financial Studies in Dijon, France. He is the author of *L'Euro* (1988) and *Les Grands Auteurs en économie* (2000), and co-editor of *Post Keynesian Principles of Economic Policy* (with L.-P. Rochon). He has also published a number of articles on monetary economics, circuit theory, European integration, and the history of economic thought in refereed journals and books.

Gunnar Heinsohn (gheins@uni-bremen.de) is Professor of Social Sciences at Universität Bremen, Germany. He has published some 20 books and over 500 articles on the property foundations of the economy and on the history and theory of money, population, genocide, education, civilisation, and chronology. In a German encyclopedia on impulse giving treatises in the history of economic thought, three of his books have been reviewed out of 500. He is founder and president of the Raphael-Lemkin-Institut at Universität Bremen, an institution for research on genocide. His property theory of interest and money, developed with Otto Steiger (*Eigentum, Zins und Geld*, 1996; English edition 2005), has been recognized as one of the five most important explanations of money in the Museum of Money in History of the Deutsche Bundesbank.

Marc Lavoie (mlavoie@uottawa.ca) is Professor in the Department of Economics at the University of Ottawa, where he started teaching twenty-five years ago. He has written five books, among which *Macroéconomie: Théorie et Controverses Postkeynésiennes* (1987), *Foundations of Post-Keynesian Economic Analysis* (1992) and *L'économie Postkeynésienne* (2004). He has been the co-editor, with Mario Seccareccia, of a book on the works of Milton Friedman (1993) and of *Central Banking in the Modern World: Alternative Perspectives* (2004), as well as being an associate editor of the *Encyclopedia of Political Economy* (1999). Lavoie has been a visiting professor at the Universities of Bordeaux, Nice, Rennes, Dijon, Grenoble, Limoges, Paris-Nord as well as Curtin University in Perth (Australia).

Marcello Messori (Messori@uniroma2.it) is Professor of Economics at the University of Rome 'Tor Vergata'. His current fields of research are the empirical analysis of the evolution of the Italian banking system, and the macroeconomic impact of credit rationing. He has also written several papers on the history of economic analysis and on the monetary sequence. Amongst his more recent publications, there are: 'Financial constraints and unemployment equilibrium', *Quaderni Ceis*, 2003, n. 191, pp. 1–51 (with G. Cesaroni); and 'Credit and money in Schumpeter's theory', in *Money, Credit and the Role of the State*, edited by R. Arena and N. Salvadori (2004), pp. 173–198.

Alain Parguez (alain.parguez@neties.com) is Professor of Economics at the University of Franche-Comté, Besançon (France) and is associated with the Economics Department at the University of Ottawa. He has worked extensively on developing a genuine general theory of capitalism, which is a monetary production economy, which he labelled the Theory of the Monetary Circuit. He has written extensively on monetary policy, crisis theory and economic policy, including many articles on the impact of austerity measures, which he believes are the cause of world crises. Parguez was the editor of *Monnaie et Production* from 1984 to 1996, and has written numerous articles and books. He is currently writing a book on the General Theory of the Monetary Circuit and its economic policy implications.

Riccardo Realfonzo (realfonzo@unisannio.it) is Professor of Theories and Methods of Political Economy at the University of Sannio, Italy. He is Secretary of the Italian Association for the History of Economic Thought (AISPE). His research interests are the theory of monetary circuit, the theory of distribution, Marxian economics and the history of economic analysis. His publications include *Money and Banking: Theory and Debate (1900–1940)* (Elgar, 1998), several papers in international journals (such as *Review of Political Economy, Economie Appliquée, International Journal of Political Economy, History of Economics Review, History of Economic Ideas*) and he has contributed chapters in various books. He has also edited several books about Italian monetary theory and the labour market.

Louis-Philippe Rochon (lprochon2003@yahoo.com) is Assistant Professor of economics at Laurentian University, Canada. He is the author of numerous articles, books and edited books on post-Keynesian economics, theory and policy. Among his books are *Credit, Money and Production: An Alternative Post-Keynesian Approach, Credit, Interest Rates and the Open Economy: Essays on Horizontalism, Dollarization: Lessons from Europe and the Americas, Studies in Modern Theories of Money, Théories monétaires post keynésiennes* and *Keynesian Economic Policies*. He has published in the *Journal of Post Keynesian Economics*, the *Review of Political Economy, Metroeconomica*, the *European Journal of the History of Economic Thought* and the *Journal of Economic Issues*. His interests include post-Keynesian economics, monetary theory and policy and globalization.

Sergio Rossi (sergio.rossi@unifr.ch) is Assistant Professor of Economics at the University of Fribourg and at the University of Lugano, Switzerland. His research interests are in the area of monetary macroeconomics (theory and practice). His recent publications include *Money and Inflation* (2001, reprinted 2003), *Modern Theories of Money* (2003), as well as 'The enlargement of the euro area: what lessons can be learned from EMU?' (*Journal of Asian Economics*, 2004).

Elie Sadigh (elie.sadigh@u-bourgogne.fr) is Maître de Conférences at the Université de Bourgogne. His research interests lie in economical analysis. He is the author of several books including: *La Théorie Économique Dominante* (1998); *Principes de l'Économie Salariale* (1999); *Du Libéralisme ou de la Loi du plus fort à l'Économie Politique* (2001); *Valeur, Prix et Capital* (2002); *Etude Économique et gÉopolitique du Développement* (2003); *Plein-emploi, Chômage* (2003).

Abdourahmane Sarr (ASarr@imf.org) is an economist with the International Monetary Fund. He holds a PhD in Economics from George Washington University. He is the author of several publications in the *International Monetary Fund Working Paper* series.

Malcolm Sawyer (mcs@lubs.leeds.ac.uk) is Professor of Economics, University of Leeds, formerly Professor of Economics at the University of York. He is managing editor of the *International Review of Applied Economics* and managing co-editor of *International Papers in Political Economy*. He is editor of the series *New Directions in Modern Economics* and has been an elected member of the Council of the Royal Economic Society. He is the author of numerous books, the most recent being (with P. Arestis) *Re-examining Monetary and Fiscal Policies in the Twenty-first Century* (forthcoming) and edited collections (the most recent being *The UK Economy*, 16th edition, 2004). He has published over 150 articles and chapters, and the most recent include 'Employer of last resort: could it deliver full employment and price stability?', *Journal of Economic Issues*, December 2003, pp. 881–908 and 'The NAIRU, aggregate demand and investment', *Metroeconomica*, vol. 53, no.1, pp. 66–94.

Mario Seccareccia (mseccare@uottawa.ca) is Professor of Economics at the University of Ottawa, Canada, as well as Lecturer at the Labour College of Canada. He is the author of numerous journal articles and chapters of books in the areas of monetary economics, history of economic thought, labour economics and Canadian economic history. Among his most recent publications, there are two co-edited volumes: *Dollarization: Lessons from Europe and the Americas* (with L.-P. Rochon) (2003) and *Central Banking in the Modern World: Alternative Perspectives* (with M. Lavoie, 2004) He is also editor of the *International Journal of Political Economy*.

Otto Steiger (osteiger@uni-bremen.de) is Professor of Economics Emeritus at Universität Bremen, Germany. He has published some 10 books and over

250 articles on the property foundations of economy, macroeconomics, development economics and monetary theory, the history and theory of population, and the history of economic thought. In a German encyclopedia on impulse giving treatises in the history of economic thought, out of 500 books reviewed, two are his. He has been invited four times by the Swedish Academy of Sciences to nominate candidates for the Nobel Prize in the economic sciences. His property theory of interest and money, developed with Gunnar Heinsohn (*Eigentum, Zins und Geld*, 1996; English edition 2005), has been recognised as one of the five most important explanations of money in the Museum of Money in History of the Deutsche Bundesbank.

Alberto Zazzaro (albertoz@dea.unian.it) is Professor of Economics at the Università Politecnica delle Marche (Italy) where he teaches macroeconomis and regulation of financial markets. He has published articles in the areas of monetary theory, banking, industrial organization, law and economics, regulation and economic growth. Some recent articles include 'Bank's inefficiency and economic growth: a micro-macro approach' (*Scottish Journal of Political Economy*, 2001, with R. Lucchetti and L. Papi), 'The enigma of medieval craft guilds' (with. M.R. Carillo in N. Salvadori (ed.), *Old and New Growth Theories*, (2003), 'How heterodox is the heterodoxy of monetary circuit theory?' (in L.-P. Rochon and S. Rossi (eds), *Modern Theories of Money*, (2003) 'Should courts enforce credit contracts strictly?' (*Economic Journal*, forthcoming).

Introduction: The Monetary Theory of Production

Giuseppe Fontana and Riccardo Realfonzo

Keynes's legacy

On 10 October 1932 Keynes resumed the Michaelmas term at King's College in Cambridge with a new title for his lectures; namely, 'The Monetary Theory of Production'. At around that time, Keynes used the same title for a contribution to a Festschrift for Arthur Spiethoff (Keynes, 1933). In this short paper Keynes discusses the difference between a real-exchange economy and a monetary economy, the distinction being that in the latter, but not in the former, money plays an essential role in the determination of the aggregate level of output and employment. According to Keynes, the lack of understanding of this non-neutral role of money is at the root of many problems in economics. In particular, the failure of the economic discipline to provide satisfactory explanations and solutions to real world problems, such as economic crises, is due to the lack of a theory for a monetary economy; what Keynes termed a monetary theory of production (MTP):

> In my opinion the main reason why the problem of crises is unsolved, or at any rate why this theory is so unsatisfactory, is to be found in the lack of what might be termed a *monetary theory of production*. The distinction which is normally made between a barter economy and a monetary economy depends upon the employment of money as a convenient means of effecting exchanges – as an instrument of great convenience, but transitory and neutral in its effect. It is regarded as a mere link between cloth and wheat... It is not supposed to affect the essential nature of the transaction from being, in the minds of those making it, one between real things, or to modify the motives and decision of the parties to it. Money, that is to say, is employed, but is treated as being in some sense *neutral*... That, however, is not the distinction which I have in mind when I say that we lack a monetary theory of production. An economy, which uses money but uses it merely as a neutral link between transactions in real things and real assets and does not allow it to enter into motives or decisions,

1

might be called – for want of a better name – a *real exchange economy*. The theory which I desiderate would deal, in contradistinction to this, with an economy in which money plays a part of its own and affects motives and decisions and is, in short, one of the operative factors in the situation, so that the course of events cannot be predicted, either in the long period or in the short, without a knowledge of the behaviour of money between the first state and the last. And it is this which we ought to mean when we speak of *a monetary economy*. (Keynes 1933, pp. 408–9; italics in original)

A similar plea for an MTP is also part of the surviving early drafts of *The General Theory of Employment, Interest and Money* (Keynes, 1979). In these drafts Keynes explains the difference between the classical theory and his theory in terms of three alternative theoretical representations of the economic system, namely a 'real-wage economy', a 'neutral economy', and a 'money-wage economy' (Fontana and Gerrard, 2002).

A 'real-wage economy' is a barter economy. In the 'real-wage economy' the factors of production are rewarded by allocating in agreed proportions the actual outcome of their cooperative efforts. Thus a 'real-wage economy' is also a cooperative economy. If, however, the factors of production receive their agreed share of output in monetary units rather than *in specie*, then the economic context of behaviour is better termed a 'neutral economy'. A 'neutral economy' is an economy in which money exists but where the use of money is allowed only for purposes of transitory convenience. This means that the existence of money does not affect economic behaviour in any essential way. The 'neutral economy' thus behaves in the same way as the 'real-wage economy'. For this reason Keynes rejects both conceptualisations of the economic system, and suggests replacing them with an analysis of a 'money-wage economy'. In making this suggestion Keynes refers to a pregnant observation made by Karl Marx; namely, that there are two different forms of economic systems, the C-M-C economy and the M-C-M' economy (Keynes, 1979, p. 81). The former is a 'neutral economy'. Money is present but only for the purpose of facilitating the exchange of goods and services. Money does not have any relevant impact on economic behaviour. Money does not affect the starting, evolution and final outcome of the economic process. By contrast, in the M-C-M' economy money plays an essential role, in the sense that, on one side, firms cannot produce commodities without bank finance and, on the other side, production and exchange activities are undertaken in order to achieve monetary returns (Graziani, 1997; Bellofiore *et al.*, 2000; Bellofiore and Realfonzo, 2003). In the M-C-M' economy, the allocative process is a means of achieving monetary ends rather than the monetary process being the means of achieving allocative ends. According to Keynes, it is the M-C-M' economy that provides a realistic description of modern economic systems. The economic context of behaviour in the M-C-M' economy is made by entrepreneurs hiring factors of production, mainly workers, for a money income. For this reason the M-C-M' economy can also be termed a 'money-wage economy'. More importantly, in the M-C-M' economy there is no mechanism to ensure that the exchange value of the money income of the owners of the factors of production is always equal in aggregate to the proportion of real output that could have been the factor's share in the C-M-C economy (Keynes, 1979, p. 78). According to Keynes, fluctuations in effective demand are the major factor explaining the difference between the two terms. For this reason Keynes suggests developing a theory, in his own words an MTP, in which money affects motives and decisions of economic agents both in the short and the long period.

As argued by Graziani (1992, pp. 43–89), Keynes's point of view was anything but isolated in the twentieth-century debate. Quite the contrary, it was part of a long tradition in economics. Before and after Keynes, dissatisfaction with the lack of an MTP had been expressed by many economists all over the world. The next two sections look briefly at these different contributions to the MTP.

Traditions of the monetary theory of production in Keynes's time

Before Keynes's work, the main contributions to the MTP came from Knut Wicksell, Joseph Alois Schumpeter, and Dennis Robertson (Realfonzo, 1998). There is no doubt that the twentieth-century debate over the model of an authentically monetary economy had been triggered by Wicksell's book *Interest and Prices* (1898). The original aim of Wicksell was to criticise the quantity theory of money, and in particular the hypothesis of an exogenous money supply. In chapter 9 section B of the book Wicksell presents the famous pure credit model with a wage fund. In his model the money supply is endogenous, and the economy is described as a sequential process where bank finance is essential to firms in order to start production. Wicksell's pure credit model was later developed by the Stockholm School of Myrdal, Lindahl, Ohlin, Lundberg.

The second great pre-Keynesian supporter of the MTP was Schumpeter. He was critical of the neoclassical theory. As argued by Graziani (1981), Schumpeter wanted mainly to show that the Walrasian approach had too limited a field of application, the static, and that it offered no theoretical explanation for the rate of profit and the rate of interest. For this reason, in the dynamic analysis contained in *The Theory of Economic Development* (1912) Schumpeter formulates a theory of money as a social institution, a theory of the bank as the creator of money, and a new theory of distribution.

However, the heterodox scholar that had the greatest influence on Keynes was Robertson. In *Banking Policy and the Price Level* (1926), Robertson maintained that the neoclassical theory generated the model of a barter or cooperative economy that was of no use for the study of modern economies. For this reason he suggested creating the alternative model of a 'wage and money system' incorporating the characteristics of the 'actual world [where] decisions about the scale of output and about the purchase of new instruments are made, not by cooperative groups, but by the members of a relatively rich employing class, who hire the services of relatively poor wage-earners and give them orders which can on the whole be effectively enforced' (Robertson, 1926, p. 19).

Setting aside the specific contributions by Wicksell, Schumpeter, and Robertson, several scholars made important contributions to the development of the MTP, and in particular to the following topics (Realfonzo, 1998):

1 *The debate on chartalism.* According to the supporters of chartalism, the neoclassical Mengerian theory of money as a commodity had to be rejected in favour of a theory of money as a pure symbol. In their view, as G.F. Knapp, the main exponent of this approach, wrote 'money is a creature of law. A theory of money must therefore deal with legal history ... First and foremost [money] frees us from our debts towards the State, for the State, when emitting it, acknowledges that, in receiving it, it will accept this means of payment' (1924 [1905], pp. 1 and 52). This point of view was taken up by K. Helfferich and F. Bendixen, among others.

2 *The debate on nominalism.* The nominalists agreed with chartalists' criticism of the neoclassical theory of the nature of money. According to nominalism, however, money was not a creation of the State but – to use Schumpeter's words (*Das Wesen des Geldes*, 1970 [but written at the beginning of the 1930s]) – a 'social institution', the result of a social convention. In their view money was not the outcome of a State imposition but the result of a social custom. Besides Schumpeter and Wicksell (with the members of the Stockholm School) other advocates of this approach were A. de Viti de Marco (1934 [1898]); H. Withers (1930 [1909]); M. Fanno (1912); W.G.L. Taylor (1913); L.A. Hahn (1920); L. Lugli (1937); and A. Dahlberg (1938).

3 *The theory of the bank as creator of money.* The contributions to this theory were extremely numerous and led to a strong criticism of the basic neo-classical idea of banks as pure financial intermediaries as well as of the neoclassical developments of the theory of the bank deposit multiplier. According to the theory of banks as creators of money (which was strongly linked to nominalism), the bank is an agent that transforms assets that are not money (as a simple promise of reimbursement) into claims on itself that are money. The neoclassical idea that deposits make loans was reversed into the thesis that loans make deposits. According to this approach, bank credit potential is theoretically unlimited: 'the limit to the credit which the bank can grant ... cannot be fixed ... payments on credit can reach any amount, however great' (de Viti de Marco, 1934

[1898], p. 47). Besides the three main supporters of the MTP and de Viti de Marco, developments in this direction are to be found in J.L. Laughlin (1903) and the whole American School of qualitative credit theory; H.J. Davenport (1964 [1908]); H. Withers (1930 [1909]); M. Fanno (1912, 1992 [1932–34]); W.G.L. Taylor (1913); L.A. Hahn (1920); R. McKenna (1929) and the Midland Bank School; E. Mireaux (1930); R.L. Garis (1934); H. Meulen (1934); L. Lugli (1937); and A. Dahlberg (1938).

4 *The endogenous nature of the money supply.* As explained by Graziani (2003a, pp. 48–57), the criticism of the theory of banks as financial intermediaries was strictly linked with the rejection of the neoclassical theory of the exogenous money supply (and to the criticism of the quantity theory of money). Many scholars stressed both the incompleteness of the neoclassical monetary theory (it did not explain how money is introduced into the economy) as well as their dissatisfaction with the assumption of a constant quantity of money over time. The critics of the orthodox approach maintained that money was introduced into the economy in order to finance production and, for this reason, the quantity of money in circulation was mainly linked to the level of production and employment. Many scholars proposed a theory according to which money supply was demand driven. Together with Wicksell and Schumpeter the main advocates of this point of view were de Viti de Marco (1934 [1898]); Laughlin (1903) and the American School of qualitative credit theory; H. Withers (1930 [1909]); M. Fanno (1912; 1992 [1932–34]); L.A. Hahn (1920); D. Robertson (1926); H. Meulen (1934); and L. Lugli (1937).

5 *The evolutionary approach to the development stages of money and banking.* According to this approach, by passing through a series of stages the bank has been transformed from pure financial intermediary into an agent that creates money. This idea was mainly proposed by de Viti de Marco (1934 [1898]). In the literature one can also find the thesis according to which money was transformed, in the course of history, from commodity money (money as a good) into a pure symbol (money as a symbol). A supporter of this view was A. Dahlberg (1938).

6 *The monetary circuit.* Some of the pre-Keynesian scholars put forward an interpretation of the working of capitalist economies in terms of a monetary circuit (Graziani, 1992; Realfonzo, 1998). According to these scholars, the working of the economic system must be described as a sequential process, characterised by successive phases whose links form a circuit of money. In their view, the monetary circuit opens with banks' decision to grant the financing requested by firms (creation of money); then firms can buy inputs and produce commodities; finally, firms sell commodities and securities to households and repay the banks (destruction of money). The best analysis of the working of the monetary circuit can be found again in Wicksell (1962 [1898]) and Schumpeter (1959 [1912]); but also in Fanno (1912, 1992 [1932–34]) and Robertson (1926).

The contemporary debate on the monetary theory of production

In the years around the middle of the twentieth century, scholars paid less attention to the MTP (with relevant exceptions, such as the Italian debate on the financing of the war and the later contributions by J. Le Bourva). However, since 1984 we have seen the flourishing of a complex body of writings in the tradition of the MTP. The focus of these writings has been the credit nature of money in modern economies (Graziani, 2003a, ch. 1) and, among other things, its implication for policy making (Wray, 1998). One of the main tenets defended by this literature is the idea that money is a social convention and fulfils the need for a standard of value in which contractual obligations for the organisation of production and exchange transactions are made (Dow and Smithin, 1999). The roles of money as a final means of payment and as a store of wealth are then easily derived from that function, once it is acknowledged that economic agents interact in an environment subject to fundamental uncertainty (Fontana, 2000). As to its origin, Graziani (2003a, pp. 64–6) has explained that money is considered a by-product of the normal working of the economic mechanism. Its supply arises as a result of the creation of new bank liabilities within the income generating process (Cencini, 1988; Moore, 1988; Rossi, 2003). Since the process of creation of money lies within the economic system rather than in the independent discretionary action of the central bank, this view has been labelled 'endogenous money theory' to distinguish it from the exogenous money theory of the monetarist school (e.g. Cottrell, 1986).

Unfortunately, this positive flourishing of writings has been combined with growing doubts and deep tensions between scholars contributing to the tradition of MTP (Graziani, 2003a, ch. 1). Whereas most of these scholars share a critical view of the traditional Walrasian approach to money, they seem to disagree on the way forward for the construction of an alternative theory of money. As a result of these disagreements a variety of labels have been created to differentiate the plurality of recent contributions to the MTP.

At the most general level, a distinction has been made between the so-called circuitist school and the Post Keynesian school (e.g. Deleplace and Nell, 1996). The former considers money essentially in its role of final means of payment whereas the latter focuses on the role of money as a store of wealth (Graziani, 1996). This flow versus stock definition of money in part also explains the preferences of circuitists and Post-Keynesians regarding Keynes's writings. Circuitists found in *A Treatise on Money* (1930) and the 1937–39 post-*General Theory* articles the main source of inspiration for their work. By contrast, Post-Keynesians like Hyman Minsky and Paul Davidson mainly refer to *The General Theory* (1936). Of course, this is a very broad distinction that does not do justice to the subtleties of the contributions made by members of these two different schools. The distinction is only presented here as a way of making sense of a separation often maintained in the literature. A noteworthy exception is Marc Lavoie, who has worked in both traditions and indeed has recently refused to be labelled as a member of either of these two schools (Rochon and Rossi, 2003, p. xxxix). As for Keynes's writings, it is also important to point out that what really differentiates *A Treatise on Money* (1930) from *The General Theory* (1936) is the formal method and the specific purpose of the analysis (Fontana, 2003a). Keynes always had in mind a close connection between theoretical analysis and historical events. In 1930, Keynes was mainly concerned with the instability of market economies, the ups and downs that characterise the economic process. Output and employment were seen moving around some norm, and he aimed at explaining the causal mechanism behind these movements. By 1936, however, he felt that the actual problem was not with fluctuations around a norm but with the norm itself. Persisting mass unemployment was the practical interest and, for the sake of getting his solution across, he was content to set aside some of his most brilliant though highly heterodox ideas. This is an important link between *A Treatise* and *The General Theory*. It represents a driving force for a continuist interpretation of Keynes's two major books (Graziani, 1991; Forges Davanzati and Realfonzo, 2004) and a main reason for having a more constructive view of the circuitist and Post Keynesian contributions to the MTP (Fontana, 2000).

A second-tier classification has then been made between different views within the circuitist school and the Post Keynesian school. Following Graziani (1994, 1995), in the circuitist school it is necessary to distinguish at least two main groups. There is a Dijon-Fribourg group, whose leader is Bernard Schmitt (1966, 1972, 1984), and a second group following the teaching of Alain Parguez (1975) and Augusto Graziani (1995, 2003a). Besides the leaders of the two groups, relevant contributions to the theory of monetary circuit have come from scholars such as R. Bellofiore, B. Bossone, L. Costabile, A. Cencini, S. Figuera, G. Forges Davanzati, G. Fontana, C. Gnos, M. Lavoie, M. Messori, F. Poulon, R. Realfonzo, L.-P. Rochon, S. Rossi, E. Sadigh, M. Seccareccia and others. As Graziani explains, all these scholars reject methodological individualism, maintain an endogenous money theory, describe the working of the economy through a sequential analysis, and refuse the marginal theory of income distribution (Graziani, 2003a, pp. 16–32). However, while the Schmitt school develops an independent general theory, Graziani's and Parguez's approach is more linked to the Post Keynesian view, particularly with those scholars who have always stressed the monetary essence of the economy such as Davidson, Kaldor, Minsky, Moore and Weintraub.[1]

As for the monetary contributions of the Post Keynesian school, the separation has been made, and sometimes fiercely defended (e.g. Rochon and Vernengo, 2001), between the accommodationist or horizontalist view and the structuralist view (Pollin, 1991). Both views are critical of the exogenous money theory of the monetarist school, but they disagree about the degree of endogeneity of the stock of money in modern economies. More precisely, the debate between horizontalists and structuralists can be summarised in terms of the assumptions describing the behaviour of monetary authorities in the reserve market, the behaviour of banks in the credit market, and the behaviour of different holders of bank deposits in the financial market. The differences between the horizontalist and structuralist approaches have recently been presented in terms of the distinction between a single-period analysis and a continuation analysis (Fontana, 2003b). The former is at the heart of the horizontalist view and is based on the assumption that the state of expectations of economics agents is given and constant. The single-period horizontalist analysis is a simple but very effective attempt to explain, for example, the price-maker and quantity-taker behaviour of monetary authorities in the reserve market, and of banks in the credit market. By contrast, a continuation analysis allows for shifts in the general state of expectations of economic agents. Continuation analysis is the basic feature of the structuralist view. It builds on the simple and stable functional relationships of the single period analysis to allow for the possibility that, over the business cycle, central banks may, for example, adopt new monetary stances or banks may revise price and non-price credit conditions (e.g. Wray, 1990; Palley, 1994; and Dow, 1997). Similarly, continuation analysis explains the way changes in interest rate differentials reconcile the preferences of the final holders of newly created deposits, that is, wage earners, with the preferences of the initial recipients of newly created deposits, namely firms (Arestis and Howells, 1996; Lavoie, 1999; Dalziel, 2001).

Finally, a new classification has recently been introduced by Lavoie in order to separate the work of neo-chartalists from that of post-chartalists, the difference residing for him in the way the financial relationship between government and the banking system is described. According to Lavoie, the post-chartalists defend the view that, as in the case of private firms, the treasury needs to borrow from private banks in order to pay for its purchases. Government expenditure or deficit is thus financed by sales of government bonds to banks (Rossi, 2001, pp. 97–105). By contrast, Lavoie maintains that for neo-chartalists government expenditure or deficit is financed by drawing cheques from the government account at the central bank and selling bonds to the monetary authorities in order to replenish the government account. For this reason, Lavoie concludes that whether government expenditure is financed by selling Treasury bills to private banks or to monetary authorities is simply a question of institutional arrangements, and it makes no difference to the final requirements of the banking system (Lavoie, 2003, pp. 525–8). However, the description of the neo-chartalist view on which these conciliatory conclusions rest is not fully congruent with core theoretical propositions put forward by key proponents of the neo-chartalist view. For instance, Wray has long argued that treasury bills are never issued to pay for government expenditures but rather to drain excess reserves in order to maintain a positive overnight lending interest rate (Wray, 1998, pp. 85–9). In other words, neo-chartalists would take issue with the causal ordering of the process of government spending and bonds sales (Mosler and Forstater, 1999; Bell, 2000; Tcherneva, 2001).

Prima facie this great diversity of contributions to MTP may appear to have undermined the claim of scholars working in MTP to provide an alternative, coherent theoretical framework to the Walrasian approach to money. Against this suggestion and the increasing proliferation of labels, this chapter maintains that in recent years, among scholars who deal directly or indirectly with MTP, it has become increasingly clear that a reasonably common body of doctrine has been built up. More importantly, this body of doctrine, which would now benefit from some systematisation, constitutes the basis – the new starting point – of future developments in MTP. Therefore, this chapter suggests the following set of propositions as the building blocks of new research in MTP:

1 *An awareness of the method of research.* More or less explicitly, participants in the debate over MTP reject methodological individualism (which holds that economic analysis must start from the study of the perfectly rational behaviour of an abstract individual agent) in favour of the historical-social methods of analysis. This means that in MTP literature, the analysis is carried out in macroeconomic terms. It has also been theorised that there must be a search for the macroeconomic foundations of microeconomics. In other words, the study of individual behaviour is always subordinate to the macro approach.

2 *The theory of endogenous money.* All scholars contributing to MTP agree that a fundamental step in the construction of a theoretical model alternative to the neoclassical-Walrasian analysis of money involves a theory of the endogenous nature of the money supply. This leads these authors to converge on at least two points: (a) money does not have a commodity nature but is a pure symbol; namely, money is a bank liability; (b) the money supply is demand driven (this aspect was originally discussed in relation to Keynes's finance motive, e.g. Graziani, 1987).

3 *A preference for sequential analysis.* In different ways, advocates of MTP reject the simultaneous logic of general equilibrium analysis. They consider (some authors explicitly, others less so) the need for analysing the successive phases of the economic process. All of them agree on the issue that 'time matters' in MTP.

4 *The role of effective demand.* Supporters of MTP basically agree on the criticism of Say's Law, concluding that *laissez faire* does not automatically generate full employment equilibrium. They believe, like Keynes, that effective demand determines the level of economic activity and the volume of employment.

5 *The role of fundamental uncertainty.* Proponents of MTP focus on the incompleteness of information and the role of fundamental uncertainty.

For this reason they do not favour the use of the rational expectations hypothesis in their work.

6 *An encompassing view of the different functions of money.* There is now widespread awareness among the contributors to MTP that a complete theory of money should reconcile the analysis of money as a flow with the analysis of money as a stock. This distinction is usually presented in terms of the analysis of money as a final means of payment and money as a liquid store of wealth.

7 *A non-marginalist theory of income distribution.* The marginalist theory of income distribution is unanimously rejected in favour of a Kaleckian–Keynesian analysis of income distribution. The analysis of the labour market is generally carried out – following Keynes's teaching – by stressing that, in the labour market, bargaining concerns only money wages and consequently there may be a difference between the *ex ante* real wage (expected by workers) and the *ex post* real wage (the actual real wage).

8 *A separation of the money market from the financial market.* There is debate over the relation between the money market and the financial market. Starting with the seminal contributions of Graziani (1984, 1987) a series of recent contributions converge in pointing out that there is a hierarchy between the two markets: the money market is the 'place' where firms obtain the initial finance, while in the financial market firms can only recover some of the liquidity previously injected into the circular flow of income (final finance or funding).

With regard also to the general principles of political economy there are some elements on which there is agreement on:

1 the need for the government to support aggregate demand by means of an expansionary fiscal policy;
2 the wisdom of setting a low cost of money on the part of the monetary authorities (although the level of investment – and therefore of aggregate demand – does not depend solely on the interest rate but also on profit expectations);
3 a need for better balance than in current policy debate between the issue of full employment and price stability, together with the rejection of employment policies based exclusively on the growing flexibility of the labour market.

Overview of the book's contributions

This book is divided into five parts plus an Appendix listing a selection of Augusto Graziani's most important publications. Part I is devoted to the tradition of MTP. It contains six chapters dealing with the different historical origins of MTP. The first chapter is a joint contribution by Richard Arena and Agnès Festré. The authors question the lack of contributions on structural change in MTP. Drawing on the monetary contributions of Schumpeter and von Mises, Arena and Festré speculate that this lack may be due to the neglected role of individual economic rationality in the modern contributions to MTP. The second chapter is written by Riccardo Bellofiore and deals with some controversial issues concerning the monetary contributions by Wicksell, Keynes and Schumpeter. Bellofiore shows that these authors are part of MTP as they all stressed the role of money as initial finance for the commencement of the economic process. He concludes his historical journey by arguing that further contributions to MTP lie in the evolutionary analysis of the dynamics of capitalism along Schumpeterian and Marxian lines. The topic of the creation of money is the driving force of the third chapter, written by Victoria Chick. The chapter is a *tour de force* on the struggle for, and loss of, the concept of endogenous money from English-language textbooks (and some treatises or monographs). Chick shows how the accepted wisdom in the profession has changed over time. From the 1930s to the 1960s there was a widespread acceptance of the notion of bank credit as the origin of the bulk of the money supply, but by the late 1970s the monetarist idea of the money base multiplier had conquered the hearts and minds of the majority of economists. Of course, there were exceptions and important institutional differences. For instance, it seems that in the United Kingdom the money base multiplier approach was never fully embraced. What is certain, however, is that the notion of endogenous money is not part of today's accepted wisdom in the economic profession. If that were not bad enough, Chick warns that there are also some real risks in rediscovering economic ideas that were once very popular. There is a sort of hysteresis in the development of ideas, and for good or bad the rediscovery of endogenous money may be tainted by the distortions of the past. This is an important lesson for participants in the current debate between the horizontalist and structuralist interpreters of the endogenous money view. A concern with Schumpeter's and Keynes's contributions to MTP is behind the fourth chapter contributed by Gunnar Heinsohn and Otto Steiger. The authors look at Schumpeter's and Keynes's criticisms of the neoclassical theory of money and interest rates, suggesting that both criticisms fell short of properly distinguishing between possession and property, the difference being that the former is restricted to the physical use of goods and resources while the latter refers to claims to intangible non-physical capacities like borrowing and lending. With that distinction in mind, Heinsohn and Steiger qualify Schumpeter's and Keynes's views that money is created *ex nihilo* by arguing that intangible titles to property rather than the possession of physical goods give rise to money. Chapter 5, written by Alain Parguez, is an attempt to qualify recent claims that Joan Robinson is a genuine precursor of MTP. The focus of the enquiry is book IV of *The Accumulation of Capital* (Robinson, 1956), including chapters 23 and 24. Parguez acknowledges that these chapters contain important propositions for the construction of MTP, but he is quite explicit about Robinson's position toward MTP. Robinson was too stubborn a proponent of the real long-run analysis to devote any serious attention to the construction of MTP. Paraphrasing her colleague Richard Goodwin, she was a real-woman not a money-woman. Chapters 23 and 24 must thus be considered as a missed opportunity, a road never taken, rather than the beginning of a long-standing contribution to MTP. Part I ends with a chapter by Malcolm Sawyer on changes in Keynes's analysis of money and interest rates between *A Treatise on Money* and *The General Theory*. Sawyer subscribes to the view that the two books are substantially different, and the retention of the monetary analysis of *A Treatise* may have precluded Keynes from reaching some of the conclusions of *The General Theory*. He goes to some lengths to quote Keynes in explaining how the *natural rate* of interest in *A Treatise* came to be replaced by the *neutral rate* of interest in *The General Theory*, where the latter rate is a special restricted case of the former. The interest rate that preserves equality between the rate of saving and the rate of investment is, in *A Treatise* terms, the *natural rate* of interest. However, if there is such rate, which is significant and unique, it is the rate corresponding to the level of effective demand that is consistent with full employment. This is the *neutral rate* of interest in *The General Theory*. According to Sawyer, in *A Treatise* Keynes accepted the existence of a neutral rate of interest that could be achieved by the central bank's manipulation of the market rate of interest. However, by the time he wrote *The General Theory*, Keynes accepted a market-determination theory of interest rates, namely the theory of liquidity preference, and for this reason the role of achieving a full employment level in the economy was left to the autonomous components of the aggregate demand function.

Part II is devoted to the issue of stocks and flows within the circuitist contributions to MTP. It starts off with Chapter 7, jointly written by Marcello Messori and Alberto Zazzaro on the realization of monetary gross profits in the monetary circuit approach. The issue at stake is that in traditional MTP the flow of new means of payment introduced in the economy at the beginning of any given period is, at most, sufficient for firms to pay their initial debts back to banks. How could we then account for the existence of monetary profits or for the monetary payment of bank interest in modern economies? Several contributions have been put forward in the past to solve this intricate question. Messori and Zazzaro review these contributions only to find them unsatisfactory. For this reason they propose an alternative solution to the issue of the realisation of monetary gross profits, namely the failure and market exit of a number of firms and banks as a standard condition for the normal working of the economy. The issue of the realisation of monetary gross profits is also the topic of Chapter 8 by Louis-Philippe Rochon. In this case the proposed solution is the separation of the production circuit from the investment circuit. At the beginning of each monetary circuit, firms borrow money against variable and fixed production costs, but Rochon assumes that at the end of the economic process – that is, the production circuit – firms pay back debts against variable costs only. Rochon's argument is that firms are allowed to cancel debts against fixed production costs over a long time horizon, what he calls a multi-period investment circuit. Thus, in any given production circuit a new flow of money, equal to the monetary value of fixed and variable capital, is created but only a proportion of the monetary value of the fixed capital produced is reimbursed. The positive difference between the initial flow of money and the final reimbursement of firms' debt allows for the existence of monetary profits and for the monetary payments of bank interest in the monetary circuit. Finally, Chapter 9, contributed by Sergio Rossi, deals with the creation and destruction of means of payment at the interbank level. The chapter focuses on the nature and role of central bank money as a final means of payment between banks in a closed-economy framework. Suggestions are also made for expanding the analysis to cross-border transactions. Rossi's analysis confirms the endogeneity of the supply of central bank money in a variety of circumstances, including the case in which the monetary authorities carry out the separate but often conflated functions of money-purveying and credit-purveying agents.

Part III deals with the problem of unemployment within MTP. Chapter 10, by Guglielmo Forges Davanzati and Riccardo Realfonzo, analyses the effects of changes in the market structure of the banking sector on unemployment. Forges Davanzati and Realfonzo argue that one of the effects of bank mergers is an increase in bank monopoly power and a consequent rise in the cost of borrowing, which, via colluding behaviour of firms, gives rise to a reduction of employment. In order to stop this mechanism, Forges Davanzati and Realfonzo suggest increasing the degree of competition in the banking and business sectors, increasing public expenditure and regulating the labour market. Chapter 11 is written by Claude Gnos and discusses an original circuit-ist analysis of unemployment. The chapter is presented as an attempt to build an alternative analysis to the imperfectionist theory of unemployment proposed by mainstream economists. The contribution is offered in the spirit of close collaboration and mutual support to the Post Keynesian analysis of unemployment based on the theory of decision making under uncertainty (Davidson, 1972). Drawing on Keynes's theory of unemployment, Gnos argues that the principle of effective demand does not deny the existence of markets or the role of supply and demand in determining prices. He nevertheless maintains that, among other things, the principle of effective demand shows the implications for the labour market of an asymmetric relationship between employers and employees. The former but not the latter have access to bank credit, the level of employment is determined by employers' decisions regarding the process of capital formation.

Part IV deals with two main economic problems of our times; namely, the issue of income distribution in low income countries and the problem of inflation. Chapter 12, by Biagio Bossone and Abdourahmane Sarr, is an attempt to use MTP for the purpose of overcoming the lack of internal demand caused by inadequate levels of bank credit in low income countries. MTP shows how banks enable a monetary production economy to function and grow by creating and allocating bank loans to support demand and production. Unfortunately, high credit and liquidity risks due to under-developed financial infrastructures, inadequate collateral, weak contract enforcement, and low participation in payment systems mean that banks play a limited role in the fight for a decent standard of living in low income countries. Bossone and Sarr propose a solution to this problem by reforming the way money is created. They suggest replacing a lending based system with a gift-to-demand depositors based system. In the latter system, newly created liquidity should stimulate the demand for the output of firms, which in turn should finance further production through retained earnings. Bossone and Sarr suggest that in this way the new credit arrangements resolve the problem of credit risks and encourage broader participation in the payment system, thereby reducing liquidity risks. Finally, Bossone and Sarr maintain that, if appropriately designed, the new credit arrangements could help growth and reduce poverty in low income countries without creating high levels of inflation. Poverty, and the possibility of overcoming it through the credit channel along the lines set by MTP, is also the topic of Chapter 13, written by Lilia Costabile. The chapter starts by recalling the story of Sufia Begum, a woman in Bangladesh during the terrible famine of the early 1970s. Sufia's job with a merchant hardly offers her the means for a decent standard of living. She is too poor to obtain credit. For this reason, Sufia has no choice but to enter a debt-credit relationship with the merchant, thereby perpetrating her state of deprivation. Costabile assesses Sufia's story through the spectacles of alternative streams of economic and philo-sophical thought; namely, conventionalism, libertarianism, welfarism and the capability theory of Amartya Sen. Costabile favours capability theory, because it offers the most sensitive approach to the issue of social justice and to the removal of absolute and relative deprivation. On these grounds, she argues that the credit channel as discussed in MTP should be used to reform the banking system, allowing millions of individuals in Sufra's conditions to get out of disadvantageous relations with employers. Finally, Chapter 14, by Elie Sadigh, deals with another major problem of our economies, namely inflation. Sadigh dismisses both the monetarist and traditional Keynesian explanations of inflation, and replaces them with a monetary disequilibrium analysis of inflation along the lines of Bernard Schmitt's work (1975). Sadigh concludes by suggesting a reform of the banking system in order to remove the heavy social costs produced by inflation.

Part V is devoted to the use of MTP for policy purposes. It contains four chapters providing a critical evaluation of the macroeconomic performance of modern economies. Chapter 15, by Philip Arestis and Malcolm Sawyer, deals with the theoretical framework underpinning the economic policies of those European countries that are part of the European Monetary Union (EMU). Arestis and Sawyer show that the monetary policy of the EMU is based on the so-called 'new consensus' model, which restates the classical dichotomy between the real and the monetary sector of the economy, the long-run neutrality of money, and the relevance of Say's Law. At a more institutional level, they find that the creation of the European Central Bank (ECB) and its links with other European Union bodies are consistent with the 'new consensus' model. After reviewing recent empirical research on the effects of interest rate changes in the EMU and other major countries, Arestis and Sawyer raise serious doubts about the effectiveness of monetary policy in responding to economic recession and in controlling inflation. For this reason they reject the 'new consensus' model, and recommend that economic policies at EMU level should be reformulated in accordance with MTP. Monetary policy should thus aim at economic growth and high levels of employment alongside the control of inflation, and should be complemented by an appropriate fiscal policy. Economic policies or, more precisely, the viability and stability of the monetary regime in Cuba are the topic of Chapter 16, by Ghislain Deleplace. The Cuban economy is characterised by the use of two currencies (the US dollar and the 'national peso'), two domestic exchange rates (one for firms and one for households), two exchange regimes (one fixed and one floating), two productive sectors (the 'emerging' sector and the 'traditional' sector), two types of property in these sectors (public property and private property), two domestic markets for goods (one in dollars and one in 'national pesos'), two price regimes (an administrative regime and a market-based regime), two banking sectors (one for firms and one for households), and two ways for households to get access to the dollar (one legal and one illegal). Using MTP, Deleplace reviews this duality of the Cuban economy and the intricate policy implications that derive from it. He forecasts monetary instability for the Cuban economy because of the depreciation of the national currency vis-à-vis the dollar. Another economic system, that of Canada, is the main topic of Chapter 17, contributed by Marc Lavoie. Canada, and in part also the USA, has gone through important institutional changes in the last decade. Lavoie assesses these changes in the light of one of the main propositions of MTP, namely the endogeneity of the stock of money. His main contention is that the endogeneity of money is a well accepted proposition for overdraft financial systems like France or Italy but it is rejected for asset-based financial systems like Canada or the USA. For this reason Lavoie goes to great pains to describe the new zero-reserve requirement system at the Bank of Canada, as well as the operation of the settlement system and the determination of the overnight interest rate in Canada. He shows that the supply of high-powered money in Canada is just as fully endogenous as it is in France or Italy. From this perspective, asset-based financial systems are not dissimilar from overdraft financial systems. Short-term interest rates are the exogenous variable under the control of the monetary authorities. Monetary aggregates are not, and cannot be, controlled by monetary authorities. Some of Canada's key economic features are also a concern of Chapter 18, written by Mario Seccareccia. In MTP great attention is usual paid to the role of interest rate spreads. Changes in the difference between loan and deposit rates are understood to affect, via changes in the flows of the overall level of expenditure, the final level of output and employment in an economy. However, little empirical research has been offered in support of this proposition since the 1970s. Seccareccia tries to fill in this gap in MTP by looking at some empirical measures of interest rate spreads in G7 countries and their effects on macroeconomic performance. Especially for the case of Canada, he provides evidence relating the behaviour of output growth and business debts to changes in interest rate spreads, suggesting that the topic deserves much more attention than is generally accorded in economic literature.

Note

1. In their edited book, Rochon and Rossi (2003) maintain a clear separation between the different circuitist views, and their introductory remarks – together with Realfonzo (1999, 2003) – are a useful starting point for interested readers.

References

Arestis, P. and Howells, P.G.A. (1996) 'Theoretical reflection on endogenous money: the problem with "convenience lending"', *Cambridge Journal of Economics*, 20(5), pp. 539–51.

Bell, S. (2000) 'Do taxes and bonds finance government spending?', *Journal of Economic Issues*, 34, pp. 603–20.

Bellofiore, R., Forges Davanzati, G. and Realfonzo, R. (2000) 'Marx inside the Circuit. Discipline Device, Wage Bargaining and Unemployment in a Sequential Monetary Economy', *Review of Political Economy*, 12(1), pp. 403–17.

Bellofiore, R. and Realfonzo, R. (2003) 'Money as Finance and Money as Universal Equivalent: Re-reading Marxian Monetary Theory', in L.-P. Rochon and S. Rossi (eds), *Modern theories of Money: The Nature and Role of Money in Capitalist Economies* (Cheltenham and Northampton: Edward Elgar,) pp. 198–218.

Cencini, A. (1988) *Money, Income and Time* (London and New York: Pinter).

Cottrell, A. (1986) 'The endogeneity of money and money-income causality', *Scottish Journal of Political Economy*, 33(1), pp. 2–27.

Dahlberg, A. (1938) *When Capital Goes on Strike. How to Speed up Spending* (New York and London: Harper).

Dalziel, P. (2001) *Money, Credit and Price Stability* (London and New York: Routledge).

Davenport, H.J. (1964 [1908]) *Value and Distribution. A Critical and Constructive Study* (New York: Kelley).

Davidson, P. (1972) *Money and the Real World* (London: Macmillan).

Deleplace, G. and Nell, E. (eds) (1996) *Money in Motion: The Post Keynesian and Circulation Approaches* (London and New York: Macmillan and St. Martin's Press).

de Viti de Marco, A. (1934 [1898]) *La funzione della banca* (Torino: Einaudi).

Dow, S.C. (1997) 'Endogenous money', in G.C. Harcourt and P.A. Riach (eds), *A 'Second Edition' of The General Theory* (London and New York: Routledge), 2, pp. 61–78.

Dow, S.C. and Smithin, J. (1999) 'The structure of financial markets and the "first principles" of monetary economics', *Scottish Journal of Political Economy*, 46(1), pp. 72–90.

Fanno, M. (1912) *Le banche e il mercato monetario* (Rome: Athenaeum), (English translation of the second part: M. Fanno, *The Money Market*, New York, St. Martin's Press, 1995).

Fanno, M. (1992 [1932–34]) *Teoria del credito e della circolazione* (Naples: Edizioni Scientifiche Italiane).

Fontana, G. (2000) 'Post Keynesians and Circuitists on money and uncertainty: an attempt at generality', *Journal of Post Keynesian Economics*, 23(1), pp. 27–48.

Fontana, G. (2003a) 'Keynes's *A Treatise on Money*', in J.E. King (ed.), *Elgar Companion to Post Keynesian Economics* (Cheltenham and Northampton: Edward Elgar), pp. 237–41.

Fontana, G. (2003b) 'Post Keynesian approaches to endogenous money: a time framework explanation', *Review of Political Economy*, 15(3), pp. 291–314.

Fontana, G. and Gerrard, B. (2002) 'The monetary context of economic behaviour', *Review of Social Economy*, 60(2), pp. 243–62.

Forges Davanzati, G. and Realfonzo, R. (2004) 'Towards a "continuist" interpretation of Keynes: Labour Market Deregulation in a Monetary Economy', paper presented at the Conference of the European Society for the History of Economic Thought, Treviso, 26–29 February 2004.

Garis, R.L. (1934) *Principles of Money, Credit and Banking* (New York: Macmillan).

Graziani, A. (1981) 'Introduction' to J.A. Schumpeter, *Il processo capitalistico* (Turin: Boringhieri) (Italian edition of Schumpeter's *Business Cycles*).

Graziani, A. (1984) 'Moneta senza crisi', *Studi economici*, 24, pp. 3–37.

Graziani, A. (1987) 'Keynes's Finance Motive', *Économies et Sociétés* (Série 'Monnaie et Production', 4), 21(9), pp. 23–42.

Graziani, A. (1991) 'Nuove interpretazioni dell'analisi monetaria di Keynes', in J. Kregel (ed.), *Nuove interpretazioni dell'analisi monetaria di Keynes* (Bologna: il Mulino), pp. 15–42.

Graziani, A. (1992) *Teoria economica. Macroeconomia* (Naples: ESI), 4th edn.

Graziani, A. (1994) *La teoria monetaria della produzione* (Arezzo: Banca dell'Etruria, Collana Studi e Ricerche).

Graziani, A. (1995 [1989]) 'The Theory of the Monetary Circuit', in M. Musella and C. Panico (eds), *The Money Supply in the Economic Process: a Post Keynesian Perspective*, (Aldershot and Brookfield: Edward Elgar), pp. 516–41.

Graziani, A. (1996) 'Money as Purchasing Power and Money as a Stock of Wealth in Keynesian Economic Thought', in G. Deleplace and E. Nell (eds), *Money in Motion. The Post Keynesian and Circulation Approaches* (London: Macmillan), pp. 139–54.

Graziani, A. (1997 [1986]) 'The Marxist Theory of Money', *International Journal of Political Economy*, 27(2).

Graziani, A. (2003a) *The Monetary Theory of Production* (Cambridge University Press).

Graziani, A. (2003b) 'Finance Motive', in J.E. King (ed.), *Elgar Companion to Post Keynesian Economics* (Cheltenham and Northampton: Edward Elgar), pp. 142–5.

Hahn, L.A. (1920) *Volkswirtschaftliche Theorie des Bankkredits* (Tübingen: Mohr).

Keynes, J.M. (1930) *A Treatise on Money* (London: Macmillan), in J.M. Keynes, *The Collected Writings of J.M. Keynes*, vols v–vi (London: Macmillan, 1971).

Keynes, J.M. (1933) 'A Monetary Theory of Production', in J.M. Keynes, *The Collected Writings of J.M. Keynes*, vol. XIII (London: Macmillan, 1973), pp. 408–11.

Keynes, J.M. (1936) *The General Theory of Employment, Interest and Money* (London: Macmillan), in J.M. Keynes, *The Collected Writings of J.M. Keynes*, vol. VII (London: Macmillan, 1973).

Keynes, J.M. (1979) 'Towards the General Theory', in J.M. Keynes, *The Collected Writings of J.M. Keynes*, vol. XXIX (London: Macmillan), pp. 35–160.

Knapp, G.F. (1924 [1905]) *The State Theory of Money* (London: Macmillan).

Laughlin, J.L. (1903) *The Principles of Money* (London: Murray).

Lavoie, M. (1999) 'The credit-led supply of deposits and the demand for money: Kaldor's reflux mechanism as previously endorsed by Joan Robinson', *Cambridge Journal of Economics*, 23(1), pp. 103–13.

Lavoie, M. (2003) 'A primer on endogenous credit-money', in L.-P. Rochon and S. Rossi (eds), *Modern Theories of Money: The Nature and Role of Money in Capitalist Economies* (Cheltenham and Northampton: Edward Elgar), pp. 506–43.

Lugli, L. (1937) *Che cosa è il credito?* (Milan: La Prora).

McKenna, R. (1929) 'Credit and Currency', address delivered before the Royal Institution of Great Britain, 4 May 1928, Cambridge, MA, Harvard Economic Society.

Meulen, H. (1934) *Free Banking: an Outline of a Policy of Individualism* (London: Macmillan).

Mireaux, E. (1930) *Les miracles du crédit* (Paris: Editions des portiques).

Moore, B.J. (1988) *Horizontalists and Verticalists: the Macroeconomics of Credit Money* (Cambridge University Press).

Mosler, W. and Forstater, M. (1999) 'A general framework for the analysis of currencies and commodities', in P. Davidson and J. Kregel (eds), *Full Employment and Price Stability in a Global Economy* (Cheltenham and Northampton: Edward Elgar), pp. 166–77.

Palley, T.I. (1994) 'Competing views of the money supply process: theory and evidence', *Metroeconomica*, 45(1), pp. 67–88.

Parguez, A. (1975) *Monnaie et macroéconomie: théorie de la monnaie en déséquilibre* (Paris: Economica).

Pollin, R. (1991) 'Two theories of money supply endogeneity: some empirical evidence', *Journal of Post Keynesian Economics*, 13(3), pp. 366–96.

Realfonzo, R. (1998) *Money and Banking: Theory and Debate (1900–1940)* (Cheltenham and Northampton: Edward Elgar).

Realfonzo, R. (1999) 'French Circuit School', in P.A. O'Hara (ed.), *Encyclopedia of Political Economy* (London and New York: Routledge), 1, pp. 375–8.

Realfonzo, R. (2003) 'Circuit Theory', in J.E. King (ed.), *Elgar Companion to Post Keynesian Economics* (Cheltenham and Northampton: Edward Elgar), pp. 60–5.

Robertson, D.H. (1926) *Banking Policy and the Price Level* (London: King).

Robinson, J. (1956) *The Accumulation of Capital* (London: Macmillan).

Rochon L.-P. and Rossi, S. (eds) (2003) *Modern Theories of Money: The Nature and Role of Money in Capitalist Economies* (Cheltenham and Northampton: Edward Elgar), pp. 339–59.

Rochon, L.-P. and Vernengo, M. (eds) (2001) *Credit, Interest Rates and the Open Economy: Essays on Horizontalism* (Cheltenham and Northampton: Edward Elgar).

Rossi, S. (2001) *Money and Inflation: A New Macroeconomic Analysis* (Cheltenham and Northampton: Edward Elgar) (repr. 2003).

Rossi, S. (2003) 'Money and banking in a monetary theory of production', in L.-P. Rochon and S. Rossi (eds), *Modern Theories of Money: The Nature and Role of Money in Capitalist Economies* (Cheltenham and Northampton: Edward Elgar), pp. 339–59.

Schumpeter, J.A. (1959 [1912]) *The Theory of Economic Development* (Cambridge, MA: Harvard University Press).

Schumpeter, J.A. (1970) *Das Wesen des Geldes* (Göttingen: Vandenhoeck & Ruprecht).

Schmitt, B. (1966) *Monnaie, salaires et profits* (Paris: Presses Universitaires de France) (repr. Albeuve: Castella, 1975).

Schmitt, B. (1972) *Macroeconomic Theory: A Fundamental Revision* (Albeuve: Castella).

Schmitt, B. (ed.) (1975) *Théorie unitaire de la monnaie, nationale et internationale* (Albeuve: Castella).

Schmitt, B. (1984) *Inflation, chômage et malformations du capital* (Paris: Economica).

Taylor, W.G.L. (1913) *The Credit System* (New York: Macmillan).

Tcherneva, P. (2001) 'Money: a comparison of the Post Keynesian and orthodox approaches', *Oeconomicus*, IV, pp. 109–214.

Wicksell, K. (1962 [1898]) *Interest and Prices* (New York: Kelley).

Withers, H. (1930 [1909]) *The Meaning of Money* (New York: Dutton).

Wray, L.R. (1990) *Money and Credit in Capitalist Economies: the Endogenous Money Approach* (Aldershot and Brookfield: Edward Elgar).

Wray, L.R. (1998) *Understanding Modern Money: the Key to Full Employment and Price Stability* (Cheltenham and Northampton: Edward Elgar).

Part I

The Tradition of the Monetary Theory of Production

1
Macroeconomic Analysis and Individual Economic Rationality: Some Lessons from Wicksell, von Mises and Schumpeter

Richard Arena and Agnès Festré*

Introduction

The purpose of this contribution is to investigate the problem of the room attributed to individual economic rationality by circulation approaches. The expression 'circulation approaches' here refers to an analytical framework in which income distribution, production and exchange activities cannot be simultaneously implemented on interdependent markets but are organized according to a given logical and chronological order which implies the pre-eminence of the *production* of commodities and of the existence of the means of payment that permit the *circulation* of these commodities (Arena, 1985, p. 47; see also Deleplace and Nell, 1996). Our investigation will not privilege however the modern versions of these approaches (see Graziani 2003a, ch.1). We will instead utilise the works of some economists of the past, namely, Knut Wicksell, Josef Schumpeter and Ludwig von Mises. The reason of the choice of these three authors is that their respective contributions to economic analysis belong to what Leijonhufvud called the 'Wicksell Connection theories' (Leijonhufvud, 1981, p. 132). In this context, Schumpeter's and von Mises's theories of money and economic progress appear to be two possible extensions of Wicksell's original work. Our view is that, by contrast with Wicksell's economic theory, they both give an essential role to individual economic rationality. Our explanatory conjecture on this contrast is that the place afforded to individual rationality is directly related to the stress put by Schumpeter's and von Mises's contributions on the necessity of building a

* The authors would like to thank all the participants at the conference 'Monetary Theory: Tradition and Perspectives' in honour of Augusto Graziani, Benevento (Italy), University of Sannio, 5–6 December 2003. Special thanks to Marco Guidi, the discussant of this paper.

true theory of economic dynamics. If this conjecture proves to be correct, it will be possible to reconsider the place of individual economic rationality within the analytical framework of circulation approaches in the light of the process of transition from static to dynamic analysis. The chapter is divided into four parts. The first section recalls how the modern 'circulation approaches' consider the problem of the compatibility between economic individual rationality and macroeconomic analysis, and how this problem emerged in Wicksell's original theory of a pure credit economy. The second section focuses on the transition from Schumpeter's circular flow to economic development, and shows how it is directly related to the problem of economic rationality. The third section shows that von Mises's conception of economic progress emphasises the importance of consumers' and producers' individual behaviours. In the last section, we finally draw some conclusions from our previous investigation of Wicksell's, Schumpeter's and von Mises's works, and confront them with the developments of the modern circulation approach.

Individual economic rationality and macroeconomic analysis: Wicksell after the modern circulation approach

Modern contributions to the circulation approach have never focused on individual economic rationality. One could attribute this relative silence to the fact that individual economic behaviours do not matter within the framework of the modern circulation approach. However, a more thorough examination of the different contributions belonging to the theory of the monetary circuit rather shows some substantial disagreement between the different economists belonging to this analytical tradition. Lavoie, for instance, characterises what he calls the 'post-classical paradigm' as a 'form of holistic approach or of organicism' (Lavoie, 1992, p. 10). This means that:

> Although individual choices are not necessarily denied, they are severely constrained by the existing institutions, social economic classes, social norms and social pressure and even macroeconomic events. Individual behaviour is interdependent. The social context places an important role in the manner beliefs are formed. Institutions embody values to which an individual is habituated. Individuals can influence and are influenced by their social environment. (Lavoie, 1992, p. 10)

In our view, in spite of what Lavoie pretends, his conception appears to be rather an intermediate or a conciliatory position between individualism and holism. This interpretation seems to be confirmed by his defence of the notion of 'procedural' against 'substantive' rationality and by the importance he attributes among the 'foundations of post-Keynesian economic analysis' to the respective theories of choice (see Lavoie, 1992, ch. 2) and of the firm (see Lavoie, 1992, ch. 3).

Graziani's view seems to be more anti-individualistic than that of Lavoie. Referring to some criticisms of neo-classical analysis outside the modern circulation approach, he notes:

> Most if not all of these criticisms do not reject the individualistic approach typical of neo-classical theory. On the contrary, according to circuit theorists, so long as this approach is preserved, the fundamental limits of neo-classical theory are not overcome. The first and most important of those limits, according to circuit theorists, is that any theory based on an individualistic approach is necessarily confined to microeconomics and is unable to build a true macroeconomic analysis. (Graziani, 2003a, p. 18)

In Graziani's view, this does not mean that there is no space at all attributed to economic individual behaviours within the context of the circulation approach. However, what this quotation implies is that individual behaviours are always submitted to macroeconomic independent laws. In a recent paper, Graziani observes that, within the circulation approach,

> the individual behaviour is only considered in a second stage; it is derived from macroeconomic conditions and has to be considered as the behaviour that agents ought to adopt in order to ensure the durability of the current economic system. (Graziani, 2003b, p. 124)

Graziani's conception means that economic behaviour can never be the *primum mobile* of economic activity or dynamics. Macroeconomic analysis is assumed to be based on its own independent foundations and it can only compel macroeconomic behaviours. Therefore, the idea of microfoundations of macroeconomic analysis has to be discarded whatever its rationale (economic aggregation or social interaction) may be.

Finally, Cencini's standpoint is even less individualistic and more holistic than that of Graziani. It consists of a complete denial of any form of microfoundation and leads Cencini to criticise Post Keynesian and circuit theorists, noting that:

> They are unable to get entirely rid of the microfoundations and to provide an analysis in which the monetary 'structure' is completely independent from the agents' behaviour. Asserting that the agents' behaviour must be compatible with the structure of the system in order that it could be perpetuated [see Graziani, 2003b] amounts to identify the monetary structure with a system of rules that economic agents are free to accept or to reject. Actually, the 'structure' which depends on macroeconomics is a set of laws that imposes upon agents. (Cencini, 2003, p. 224)

These three examples are sufficient to show that, if there is a general agreement among circuit theorists to reject the notion of microfoundation as it is currently used in standard microeconomics, the disagreement on the reasons for this rejection points out the absence of a clear justification of the necessary neglect of individual economic rationality within the circulation approach. As we noted in the introduction of this contribution, our conjecture is that an investigation in the field of the history of economic analysis can help to shed some light on these issues. This investigation will naturally begin with Wicksell since, as Graziani noted,

> under a strictly chronological criterion, the first description of a monetary circuit is found in Knut Wicksell's rightly celebrated monograph on *Interest and Prices*. (Graziani, 2003a, p. 1)

Various interpretations of Wicksell's monetary theory are provided within the literature. In spite of the puzzling orthodox interpretation of Patinkin, it is clear that more and more authors consider Wicksell as one of the main forerunners of the circulation approach (see, for instance, Nell, 1967; Chiodi, 1983; Realfonzo, 1998; and Graziani, 2003a). This is not surprising. On the one hand, Wicksell's conception of the circular flow is close to the classical scheme of reproduction and its sequential organisation: as Quesnay and James Mill before him, Wicksell refers to a 'year' defined as a period during which expectations, production and market transactions succeed before giving birth to a new economic period. On the other hand, Wicksell distinguishes various groups of economic agents, each of whom has a role to perform in the period in order to permit the reproduction and perpetuation of the economic system. What is striking is that, in Wicksell, this role seems to be perfectly independent from any economic individual rationality. However, one could hardly consider that Wicksell consciously preferred methodological holism to individualism. One must not actually forget that, as Menger or Walras, he always mentioned that entrepreneurs were profit maximizers (for instance, Wicksell, 1965 [1898], p. 131). Moreover, Wicksell provided a rational reformulation of the Austrian capital theory in terms of marginal productivity. He formulated an assumption of maximisation of the net yield, which required that the investment period could extend in all cases to a point where any further extension would involve an increase in marginal productivity less than that which would be achieved by a corresponding extension elsewhere. Therefore, it is clear that the reason for his neglect of individual economic rationality is not related in any way to an illusory hostility towards methodological individualism. In our view, it rather lies in the static nature of his economic analysis: in a stationary state such as the one characterised by Wicksell, the prevailing constraint is the macroeconomic necessity of simple reproduction and this constraint leaves little space for taking individual economic behaviours into account.

On the one hand, one must not forget that, according to Uhr, one of the most informed commentators of Wicksell's economic theory,

> It is evident that Wicksell's models left much to be desired. The main difficulty with them was that they were too near-static in nature, and that the economy confined to producing only consumption goods, left no room for introducing changes in the structure of capital or in the length of the period of investment. (Uhr, 1960, p. 245; see also Lindahl, 1969, p. 43)

This is the consequence of the fact that Wicksell predominantly focused on monetary theory and, therefore, chose the context of a stationary state to facilitate his analytical project. Wicksell's cumulative process is prevalently monetary and if, during the second year of the process, the productivity of capital is increased, it is exogenously determined and the mere reason for this increase is to permit the emergence of a positive gap between the natural and the monetary rate. One must remember that, at the beginning of the cumulative process, productive factors are fully employed. Therefore, this positive gap only creates a *tendency* to the increase of the national output and does not imply an *actual* variation. If the cumulative process may terminate in a crisis of hyperinflation or deflation, it is clear that the maladjustment it may generate in production, in the capital structure and with respect to employment and income distribution are on the whole ignored by Wicksell.

On the other hand, as Boianovsky (1995) recently wrote, Wicksell was aware of the opposition between static and dynamic analysis in economics and realised that he was unable to make a contribution to the dynamic process. This is why he limited his analysis to stationary states and uniform growth paths (Boianovsky, 1995, pp. 378–83). As Boianovsky (1995, p. 376) again noted, Wicksell even expressed his doubts concerning the possible project of building a business cycle theory.

We would therefore be inclined to conclude that the reason why the role given to individual economic rationality is so limited in Wicksell's analysis is that his natural analytical framework corresponded to a stationary or a steady state, which implies that agents' transactions are entirely submitted to the necessity of the reiteration of their initial endowments and of the perpetuation of the current production techniques. Our argument is however incomplete. We need now to show that 'neo-Wicksellian' authors who introduced economic progress in their analytical framework were compelled to attribute a substantial role to individual economic rationality.

Economic rationality, circular flow and economic development in Schumpeter

Schumpeter mentioned Wicksell as one of the major economists who exerted an influence on the elaboration of his monetary theory. This is not surprising.

Wicksell's theory of a pure credit economy is very close to his own theory of the circular flow and, after Wicksell, Schumpeter is certainly one of the economists from the beginning of the twentieth century who attributed great importance to the role of credit in market economies. Schumpeter's concept of the circular flow describes the reproductive process of an economy (see, for instance, Schumpeter, 1956 [1917–18], pp. 151–2), which fits well with what elsewhere he calls 'the classic scheme of the economic process' in a stationary state, belonging to the conception of '*advance economics*' (Schumpeter, 1954, pp. 554 and 564–5). As in Wicksell, Schumpeter's circular flow appears to be a monetary circuit and, within this context, money has only one role to perform, namely to allow monetary transactions (Schumpeter, 1934, pp. 52–3). It is therefore analysed by Schumpeter as a 'claim ticket' and 'receipt voucher' recognised by every agent in the economy as socially valuable. Moreover, Schumpeter characterises the role of agents in production and exchange activities and in the distribution of income in the circular flow as the result of the functions they perform within socio-economic classes, as in the Wicksellian macroeconomic scheme.

However, individual economic rationality is not absent from the Schumpeterian approach to the circular flow, and this is a crucial difference that we will note between the Wicksellian and the Schumpeterian conceptions. One of the reasons which convinced Schumpeter to take individual economic rationality into account, even within the analysis of the circular flow, is related to the dynamic problem of the stability of general equilibrium. Schumpeter indeed rejected the Walrasian theory of tâtonnement and instead tried to explain an empirical tendency to equilibrium by employing the concept of 'routine' (Schumpeter, 1934, pp. 8–9; 84). From this perspective, Schumpeter reinterpreted the Walrasian conception of rationality as a hedonistic–static mode of behaviour, arguing that, in this sense, it was of limited validity. It could be defined as the rationality of firm owners who prefer to minimise their efforts to attain their ends and, therefore, to rely on routinised modes of behaviour. It is therefore striking to see that, in Schumpeter's view, the notion of circular flow is compatible with *adaptive* behaviours based on routines as well as with *optimal* behaviours based on cost-minimising. Moreover, we noted that, in the Wicksellian circular flow, individual economic rationality played a very limited role in the theory. These observations confirm the fact that the framework of a stationary state does not imply that some substantial role has to be left to individual economic rationality. We have now to investigate if this is still the case when we enter into the realm of economic dynamics.

How did Schumpeter cope with these issues when he left the theory of the circular flow for the theory of economic development? The answer is already contained in *Das Wesen des Geldes* and in the first German edition of the *Theory of Economic Development*. Schumpeter here distinguishes between two types of 'egoism' (1908, pp. 86–7): we have already seen that 'hedonistic egoism' describes adaptive/routine-minded or Walrasian/rational behaviour, whereas the notion of 'energetic egoism' is reserved to describe an active and 'voluntaristic' behaviour based on a different kind of rationality (see Santarelli and Pesciarelli, 1990, pp. 684–7; and Arena, 1992, pp. 132–5).

While these terms disappeared from Schumpeter's subsequent writings, mainly to allow him to avoid the charges of 'sociologism' or 'psychologism' levelled at him, he implicitly held on to the distinction, transforming it into a methodological device. As we already noted, this device allowed him to retain Walrasian rationality as a specific form of behaviour valid only in the limited context of static or stationary economic states.

This reinterpretation of the Walrasian type of economic behaviour has to be related to Schumpeter's more general conception of economic rationality. According to the author, human motives are never strictly individual. Rather, they are always embedded in a social context and related to the historical circumstances under which they have emerged. From this point of view, two main concepts are essential.

On the one hand, following Wieser's conception of economic sociology, Schumpeter argues that, whatever the social environment, men are always divided into two categories: leaders and followers (see Arena and Gloria-Palermo, 2001; Arena and Dangel-Hagnauer, 2002; Arena and Festré, 2002; Arena and Romani, 2002). It should, however, be noted that Schumpeter does not regard leaders as superior or 'great men' (Schumpeter 1951 [1927], pp. 216). They are not in possession of special intellectual qualities that would lead them to play a pre-eminent social role. Nor do they have a conscious concept of social optimality that they would strive to put into practice (*ibid.*). Rather, '[w]e are content to say that social leadership means to decide, to command, to prevail, to advance. As such it is a special function, always clearly discernible in the actions of the individual and within the social whole' (*ibid.*, p. 217). Schumpeter regards followers as playing a more passive role in that they are the mere recipients of leaders' decisions, acting to diffuse them. They can reinforce these decisions and contribute to their social generalisation through the adoption of imitative behaviour or the manifestation of trust. But they can also resist them, slowing down the process of diffusion or sometimes even preventing the mechanisms of social diffusion from working.

On the other hand, however, social leadership is not independent from the historical context in which it appears. If we consider, for instance, the context of market economies, entrepreneurs appear to be the economic and social leaders. The excess energy that characterised the leaders of ancient societies based on aristocratic hierarchies and military objectives now turns into what Schumpeter calls 'energetic' – as opposed to 'hedonistic' – rationality or egoism. (Schumpeter 1951, [1919], p. 90). It is channelled into the introduction of innovations, such as new products or new productive techniques. These innovations do not result from exogenous shocks or endogenous mechanisms of technology creation generated by firm managers or owners.

Rather, they are introduced by what Schumpeter called 'New Men' (Schumpeter, 1939, p. 96). However, innovations do not last forever. Gradually, they are diffused throughout the economic system and transformed into routines or 'habitual economic methods' (Schumpeter, 1934, p. 8). As they come to prevail, these individual routines and the resulting network of social rules or norms eventually produce the 'institutional patterns' that pervade the markets and influence the internal organisation of the firm.

The previous developments show why and how, in the Schumpeterian framework, economic dynamics cannot be conceived without institutional change defined in a broad sense; namely, involving changes in social norms and values *as well as individual economic rationality*. This, of course, explains why the analysis of the evolution of forms of productive organisation received such considerable attention in his writings, albeit in the context of his discussion of entrepreneurship, of capitalism's tendency to 'trustification', or of their respective impact on innovations.

From the very start, therefore, Schumpeter's theory of dynamics requires important conceptual changes to the economist's toolbox and, in particular, the introduction of a new type of economic agent – the entrepreneur, as well as a new type of rationality – energetic rationality. The theory of economic dynamics does not thus involve any kind of 'evolutionary' belief or assumption. Instead, what it implies is a new approach, based on the combination of history with economic theory. However, building a theory of economic dynamics also implies changes within the conceptual foundations of economic analysis. For instance, one will need to explain structural changes, such as those made possible by the generalisation of credit or associated with the changes in income distribution (Schumpeter, 1908, p. 619). Consequently, the study of dynamics cannot be reduced to the analysis of the conditions of convergence towards some predetermined 'dynamic' or 'long-run equilibrium'.

All the preceding developments enlighten Schumpeter's conception of individualism. For Schumpeter, the task of the social scientist is to study both individual particularities *and* their context as defined by social stratification in conjunction. The importance of social classes for societal analysis derives from a number of reasons. First, '[t]he class membership of an individual is a primary fact, originally quite independent of his will.' (Schumpeter, 1951 [1919], p. 143). Secondly, path-dependency is an undeniable fact of social reality and must therefore be taken into account by the social scientist (Schumpeter, 1951 [1919], pp. 144–6). Finally, in any given society, social classes correspond to specific social functions:

> Every class, in other words, has a definite function, which it must fulfill according to its whole concept and orientation, and which it actually does discharge as a class and through the class conduct of its members. Moreover, the position of each class in the total national structure depends, on the one hand, on the significance that is attributed to that

function, and, on the other hand, on the degree to which the class successfully performs the function. (Schumpeter, 1951 [1927], pp. 179–80)

However, what follows from this is not an outright rejection of methodological individualism since:

[t]he ultimate foundation on which the class phenomenon rests consists of individual differences in aptitude. What is meant are not differences in an absolute sense, but differences in aptitude with respect to those functions which the environment makes 'socially necessary' – in our sense – at any given time; and with respect to leadership, along lines that are in keeping with those functions. (Schumpeter, 1951 [1927], p. 210)

Rather, both self-interest and class interest coexist in every given society (Schumpeter, 1951 [1919], p. 34). The relative importance of individual motivation, on the one hand, and class interests, on the other, differs according to the type of society under investigation. While in 'traditional economies... the economy is the concern of the whole group or at least is subject to a super-individual system' (Schumpeter, 1954 [1918], p. 18), in the case of pure economics, the individualist approach is essential, in particular since social organisation is included in the data.

Finally, the crucial importance given by Schumpeter to economic dynamics also implies some analytical consequences on the role of credit in market economies. In contrast to Wicksell's approach, Schumpeter's theory does not primarily limit the role of credit to the circulation of the national income but relates it to the emergence of innovations. In a production economy, to carry out new technical combinations firms must invest, and this investment must, in turn, be financed (Schumpeter, 1934, p. 71). This means that monetary and financial institutions are among those that must exist as a matter of 'logical priority' (Schumpeter, 1939, p. 114) to render the emergence of the entrepreneur feasible. Thus, the existence of a banking system based on credit allows entrepreneurs to employ new means of production without these having to be transferred a priori from existing industries to innovative ones (ibid., p. 114). These institutions are not simply forms of social organisation. They also take the form of new behavioural rules, what Schumpeter called 'the attitudes of the public mind' (Schumpeter, 1950, p. 135). For these two reasons, they are finally an essential ingredient in Schumpeterian economic dynamics (Festré, 2002a).

Economic rationality, the 'evenly rotating economy' (ERE) and the 'progressing economy' (PE) in von Mises

Ludwig von Mises is often presented as an inheritor of Wicksell (see, for instance, Seccareccia, 1990; Laidler, 1991; Bellofiore, 1998; Festré, 2002b;

Leijonhufvud, 1981) even if this affiliation is sometimes underestimated in the literature. However, in contrast to Schumpeter, von Mises did not really accept Wicksell's conception of the circular flow. On the one hand, his analytical framework was much larger than the Wicksellian stationary economy since he provided a dynamic framework of the working of a market economy. On the other hand, he gave a crucial role to individual economic rationality.

Von Mises's conception of 'statics' is found in *Human Action* where the author contrasts the case of an 'Evenly Rotating Economy' (ERE) with the case of a 'Progressing Economy' (PE). The case of an ERE is an instance of 'imaginary construction', because it describes an economy where any factor of change and the time element are abstracted (von Mises, 1996 [1949], p. 261). This shows that von Mises does not subscribe to the representation of a circular flow for describing a stationary or static economy. According to him, the only purpose of this 'imaginary construction' is to permit the introduction of the various factors of change that are necessary in order to build an dynamic analytical framework:

> In reality there is never such a thing as an evenly rotating economy. However, in order to analyse *the problems of change in the data and of unevenly and irregularly varying movement*, we must confront them with a fictitious state in which both are hypothetically eliminated.... *This so-called state method is precisely the proper mental tool for the examination of change.* There is no means of studying the complex phenomena of action other than first to abstract from change altogether, then to introduce an isolated factor provoking change, and ultimately to analyse its effects under the assumption that other things remain equal. (von Mises, 1996 [1949], pp. 247–8, emphasis added)

From this viewpoint, von Mises's conception of statics is not far from that of Schumpeter. As we have seen, Schumpeter's circular flow is mainly intended to provide a basic framework in which successive factors of qualitative change are later introduced in order to deal with economic development.

By contrast, a PE is characterised by an 'unevenly and irregularly varying movement'. It corresponds to 'an economy in which the per capita quota of capital invested in increasing' (von Mises, 1996 [1949], p. 294), the capacity for savings increases and, eventually, the ratio between the value of present goods and future goods is modified in favour of the latter (von Mises, 1980 [1924], p. 386). In the meanwhile, on the production side, 'the range of entrepreneurial activities includes, moreover, the determination of the employment of the additional capital goods accumulated by new savings' (*ibid.*, p. 295). These new investments in production goods generate an increase in the total amount of income, which is obtained either by modifications of consumers' preferences or by the occurrence of technical innovations (*ibid.*, p. 297).

From this perspective, and in compliance with the so-called method of counterfactuals (see Gunning 1998) or of *argumentum a contrario*, von Mises rigorously envisages the various elements of change – or what he calls the 'catallactic functions' (*ibid.*, p. 251) – that characterise economic dynamics. A first factor of change is entrepreneurial activity. Von Mises indeed introduces the figure of the 'entrepreneur-promoter' defined as a 'pacemaker', or as 'the one who has more initiative, more venturesomeness, and a quicker eye than the crowd, the pushing and promoting pioneer of economic improvement' (*ibid.*, p. 255).

Furthermore, the 'entrepreneurs–promoters' are endowed with specific behavioural features that are directly related to the necessity of perceiving and exploiting any change in economic data:

> *changes in the data are first perceived only by a few people and that different men draw different conclusions in appraising their effects.* The more enterprising and brighter individuals take the lead, others follow later. (von Mises, 1996 [1949], p. 328, emphasis added)

It remains, however, that promoters' awareness and their ability to recognise potential conflict with cost-minimizing or routine-minded behaviour. Von Mises indeed points out that:

> [a] prospective entrepreneur does not consult the calculus of probability which is of no avail in the field of *understanding*. He trusts his own ability to understand future market conditions better than his less gifted fellow men. (von Mises, 1996 [1949], p. 299, emphasis added).

Moreover, although von Mises champions radical subjectivist individualism (see Festré, 2002a), he does not however conceive individuals as being living '*in abstracto*' (von Mises, 1996 [1949], p. 46). The man is always inserted into a socio-cultural context that influences his subjective choices. In this perspective, it is interesting to emphasise that the figure of the 'common man' radically contrasts with the one of the 'promoter': Common men, indeed, only adapt to the ideas and beliefs of individuality that they inherit from the past and/or from their environment:

> [the common man] does not himself create his ideas; he borrows them from other people. His ideology is what his environment enjoins upon him . . . Common man does not speculate about the great problems. With regard to them, he relies upon other people's authority, he behaves as 'every decent fellow must behave', he is like a sheep in the herd. (von Mises, 1996 [1949], p. 46)

The distinction between 'promoters' and 'ordinary men' is important for our purpose. It permits us to explain the diffusion of novelty by means of a social process of imitation. In other terms, common men follow 'shared' habits or routines that they may modify only if they are convinced that the promoters will improve their well-being (von Mises, 1996 [1949], p. 47). This approach, in terms of shared individual beliefs, appears coherent. Von Mises utilises it in order to analyse the functioning of the market. The latter is not 'a place', 'a thing', or a 'collective entity' (von Mises, 1996 [1949], p. 257). It is a 'process' allowing the compatibility between 'value judgements' and individual behaviours (*ibid.*). In this framework, the 'promoter–entrepreneur' plays a leading role; speculative awareness and behaviour turned to the discovery of new opportunities, is critical (*ibid.*, p. 329), especially since he is in the last resort submitted to the 'sovereignty of the consumers' (*ibid.*, p. 269).

The concept of the 'sovereignty of the consumer' emphasises a second factor of novelty that permits us to understand why changes in consumers' preferences constitute a major component of dynamic analysis in von Mises. It also implies the existence of some hierarchical organisation in the operation of the market, according to which the causality goes from the demand to the productive side. This is no surprise if one has in mind Menger's analysis and knows how this strongly influenced von Mises. From Menger's perspective, subjective evaluations of the final product (first-order goods) by consumers tend to be reflected in the prices of the higher-order goods (production goods) that contribute to its completion. Under these circumstances, entrepreneurs are compelled to satisfy consumers' (von Mises, 1996 [1949], pp. 269–70). The pre-eminence of consumers reaches all the domain of market economic activity. They, in fact, determine the prices of all factors of production as well as the income of every member of the market economy (*ibid.*, p. 271).

Finally, a PE is characterised by the existence of 'true' money. According to von Mises, there is indeed no conceivable form of money in the imaginary construction of an ERE:

> [I]ndirect exchange and the use of money are tacitly implied. But what kind of money can that be. In a system without change in which there is no uncertainty whatever about the future, nobody needs to hold cash. Every individual knows precisely what amount of money he will need at any future date. (von Mises, 1996 [1949], p. 249)

Von Mises then concludes that 'money is necessarily a "dynamic factor"' and that 'there is no room left for money in a "static" system' (*ibid.*, p. 249).

By contrast, in an economy of 'unevenly and irregularly varying movement', money performs an essential role by rendering economic calculation possible: the currency is a 'tool of action' because 'prices in currency are the only vehicle of economic calculation' (*ibid.*, p. 201) and 'monetary calculation is the guiding star of action' (*ibid.*, p. 210). Credit also contributes to the dynamics of the economy. We indeed know that capital accumulation implies an extension of the period of production and that this necessity can take various forms (von Mises, 1980 [1924], p. 400). The increase of credit by banks constitutes one of these forms, in accordance with the various versions of the Austrian theory of money and business cycles.

Our re-lecture of Mises's theory of economic dynamics provides a new opportunity to contrast his views with those of Schumpeter (Festré, 2002b). However, these differences do not conceal the substantial analogies between both contributions. We stressed particularly how, in both cases, the consideration of individual economic rationality was a key for the construction of their dynamic analyses. It is therefore time to draw some conclusions from these results with respect to the modern versions of the circulation approach.

Conclusion

We offer three conclusions from our investigation of the respective contributions of Wicksell, Schumpeter and von Mises to the circulation approach:

(i)   The Wicksellian theory of the circular flow is founded on the concept of stationary state in spite of the existence of a cumulative process and of a gap between the two rates of interest, which is allowed by an increase in productivity. The concept of stationary state is so demanding logically that the type of individual economic rationality hardly plays a role in the analysis of the circular flow.

(ii) The Schumpeterian theory of the circular flow is also founded on the concept of stationary state. For Schumpeter, this state is compatible with an adaptive type of behaviour based on the notion of routine as well as an optimal type of behaviour based on the principle of cost-minimizing. This observation confirms that the concept of stationary state leaves very limited space to individual economic rationality. Quite the contrary, the investigation of the *Theory of Economic Development* shows that individual economic rationality plays a crucial role in the construction of Schumpeter's economic dynamics.

(iii) Von Mises's interpretation of the Wicksellian circular flow leads to a theory of the market process. The introduction of dynamic phenomena, such as changes in consumers' preferences or technical progress, into this theory implies individual economic rationality to be taken into account. Even if von Mises's economic dynamics substantially differ from Schumpeter's, the rationality assumptions that form the foundation of both approaches are similar; namely, based on the distinction between leaders and followers.

These reasons are insufficient to prove that the consideration of individual economic rationality is necessary if true economic dynamics (as structural change) are to be introduced in the circulation approach. They however constitute some serious clues in favour of this conclusion. Further work has still to be done in this direction. However, previous developments are sufficient for reviving the old and nagging question of the role of individual economic rationality in the circulation approach and, especially, in its modern versions. The three conclusions mentioned indeed suggest a conjecture: are not the difficulties related to the introduction of a true dynamic analysis in the modern versions of the circulation approach (Arena, 1988) the price to be paid for the absence of individual economic rationality? From the works of B. Schmitt, the founder of the modern version of this approach, to the time of writing, this introduction has proved to be uneasy. No true theory of business cycles or structural change seems to have emerged from the modern versions of the circulation approach. If our conjecture is correct, the road to a possible solution to this question, as suggested by history of economic analysis, is to take individual economic rationality into account within the circulation approach. In this perspective, an essential analytical choice has still to be made: modern circulation theorists are not compelled either to choose the theory of substantial rationality favoured by modern mainstream economists or to accept the aggregation method of connecting micro and macroeconomic levels. This contribution is nothing more than an incentive for open discussion of these issues.

References

Arena, R. (1985) 'Circulations, revenu et capital: théorie monétaire et tradition non quantitative', in R. Arena, A. Graziani and J. Kregel (eds), *Production, Circulation et Monnaie* (Paris: Presses Universitaires de France), pp. 47–73.

Arena, R. (1988) 'Moneta, Capitale e circolazione: problemi e un tentativo di artiolazione teorica', in M. Messori (ed.), *Moneta e Produzione* (Turin: Scientifica Einaudi).

Arena, R. (1992) 'Schumpeter after Walras: "économie pure" or "stylised facts"?', in T. Lowry (ed.) *Perspectives on the History of Economic Thought*, vol. VIII, Aldershot: Edward Elgar.

Arena, R. and Dangel-Hagnauer, C. (eds) (2002) *The Contribution of Joseph Schumpeter to Economics: Economic Development and Institutional Change* (London: Routledge).

Arena, R. and Festré, A. (2002) 'Connaissance et croyances en économie: l'exemple de la tradition autrichienne', *Revue d'Economie Politique*, 112(5), pp. 635–57.

Arena, R. and Gloria-Palermo, S. (2001) 'Evolutionary themes in the Austrian Tradition: Menger, Wieser and Schumpeter on Institutions and Rationality', in Pierre Garrouste and Stavros Ioannides (eds), *Evolution and Path Dependence in Economic Ideas: Past, Present* (Aldershot: Edward Elgar).

Arena, R. and Romani, P. (2002) 'Schumpeter on Entrepreneurship', in R. Arena and C. Dangel-Hagnauer (eds), *The Contribution of Joseph Schumpeter to Economics: Economic Development and Institutional Change* (London: Routledge), pp. 167–83.

Bellofiore, R. (1998) 'Between Wicksell and Hayek: Mises' Theory of Money and Credit Revisited', *The American Journal of Economics and Sociology*, 57(4), pp. 531–78.

Boianovsky, M. (1995) 'Wicksell's business cycle', *The European Journal of the History of Economic Thought*, 2(2), pp. 315–411.

Cencini, A. (2003) 'Micro, macro et l'analyse du circuit', in P. Piégay and L.-P. Rochon (eds), *Théories Monétaires Post Keynésiennes* (Paris: Economica).

Chiodi, G. (1983) *La teoria monetaria di Wicksell* (Rome: La Nuova Italia Scientifica).

Deleplace, G. and Nell, E. (eds) (1996) *Money in Motion. The Post-Keynesian and Circulation Approaches* (New York: Macmillan).

Festré, A. (2002a) 'Innovation and business cycles', in R. Arena and C. Dangel-Hagnauer (eds), *The Contribution of Joseph Schumpeter to Economics: Economic Development and Institutional Change* (London: Routledge), pp. 127–45.

Festré, A. (2002b) 'Money, banking and dynamics: two Wicksellian routes from Mises to Hayek and Schumpeter', *American Journal of Economics and Sociology*, 61(2), pp. 439–80.

Graziani, A. (2003a) *The Monetary Theory of Production* (Cambridge University Press).

Graziani, A. (2003b) 'Microéconomie et macroéconomie: à qui la priorité?', in P. Piégay and L.-P. Rochon (eds), *Théories Monétaires Post Keynésiennes* (Paris: Economica).

Gunning, J.P. (1998) 'The Logical Concept of Equilibrium', Free Web space and hosting – cafeprogressive.com, November 17.

Laidler, D. (1991) 'The Austrians and the Stockholm School: Two failures in the development of modern economics', in L. Jonung (ed.), *The Stockholm School of Economics Revisited* (Cambridge University Press).

Lavoie, M. (1992) *Foundations of Post-Keynesian Economic Analysis* (Aldershot: Edward Elgar).

Leijonhufvud, A. (1981) *Information and Coordination: Essays in Macroeconomic Theory* (New York: Oxford University Press).

Lindahl, E. (1969) 'Wicksell's life and work', in Knut Wicksell, *Selected Papers on Economic Theory* (New York: Augustus M. Kelley).

Mises, L. von (1912) *Theorie des Geldes und der Umlaufsmittel* (Munich and Leipzig: Duncker & Humblot).

Mises, L. von (1980 [1924]) *The Theory of Money and Credit* (Indianapolis: Liberty Classics).

Mises, L. von (1996 [1949]) *Human Action: A Treatise on Economics*, 4th edn by Bettina Bien Greaves (Fox & Wilkes).

Nell, E.J. (1967) 'Wicksell's theory of circulation', *Journal of Political Economy*, 75(4), pp. 386–94.

Realfonzo, R. (1998) *Money and Banking. Theory and Debate 1900–1940* (Aldershot: Edward Elgar).

Santarelli, E. and Pesciarelli, E. (1990) 'The emergence of a vision: the development of Schumpeter's theory of entrepreneurship', *History of Political Economy*, 22(4), pp. 677–96.

Schumpeter, J.A. (1908) *Das Wesen und der Hauptinhalt der theoretischen Nationaloekonomie*, 2nd edn (Berlin: Duncker & Humblot).

Schumpeter, J.A. (1934) *Theory of Economic Development* (Cambridge, MA: Havard University Press).

Schumpeter, J.A. (1939) *Business Cycles*, 2 vols (New York: McGraw-Hill).

Schumpeter, J.A. (1942) *Capitalism, Socialism and Democracy* (New York: Harper).

Schumpeter, J.A. (1950) *Capitalism, Socialism and Democracy*, 3rd edn (London: Allen & Unwin).

Schumpeter, J.A. (1951 [1919]) 'Zur Soziologie der Imperialismen', *Archiv für Sozialwissenschaft und Sozialpolitik*, 46, pp. 1–39. (Trans. into English as 'The sociology of imperialisms' in Schumpeter (1951)).

Schumpeter, J.A. (1951 [1927]) 'Die sozialen Klassen im ethnisch homogen Milieu', *Archiv für Sozialwissenschaft und Sozialpolitik*, 57, (1927) pp. 1–67. (Trans. into English as 'Social classes in an ethnically homogeneous environment', in Schumpeter (1951)).

Schumpeter, J.A. (1951) *Social Imperialism and Classes*, P. Sweezy (ed.) (New York: Augustus M. Kelley).

Schumpeter, J.A. (1954 [1918]) *History of Economic Analysis* (London: Allen & Unwin).

Schumpeter, J.A. (1956 [1917–18]) 'Das Sozialprodukt und die Rechenpfennige: Glossen und Beitrage zur Geldtheorie von Heute', *Archiv für Sozialwissenschaft*, XLIV, pp. 627–715. (Trans. into English by A.W. Marget as 'Money and the Social Product', *International Economic Paper*, 6 (1956)).

Schumpeter, J.A. (1970) *Das Wesen des Geldes*, F.K. Mann (ed.) (Göttengen: Vandenhoeck & Ruprecht).

Schumpeter, J.A. (1991) *The Economics and Sociology of Capitalism*, R. Swedberg (ed.) (Princeton University Press).

Seccareccia, M. (1990) 'The Two Faces of Neo-Wicksellianism during the 1930s: The Austrians and the Swedes', in D. Moggridge (ed.), *Perspectives in the History of Economic Thought*, IV (Aldershot: Edward Elgar).

Uhr, C.G. (1960) *Economic Doctrines of Knut Wicksell* (University of California Press).

Wicksell, K. (1965 [1898]) *Interest and Prices* (New York: M. Kelley).

Wicksell, K. (1967 [1906]) *Lectures II: Money* (New York: M. Kelley).

2
Monetary Economics after Wicksell: Alternative Perspectives within the Theory of the Monetary Circuit

Riccardo Bellofiore

Introduction

Augusto Graziani's main theoretical contribution has been the development of the theory of the monetary circuit. This contemporary approach has its roots in the monetary heterodoxy of the end of the nineteenth century and the first thirty years of the twentieth century. Graziani's theoretical enterprise has never divorced positive contributions to economic thought from an appraisal of past theories and authors. His position is highly original. Usually, two conflicting visions are held. The first move backwards from modern theories to older antecedents, on the assumption that the former are a progress relative to the latter because either they have overcome prior errors or encapsulated the partial truth sedimented by past developments. It is a continuist view. The second is a discontinuist view, stressing paradigm shifts, advancing no pretence that formal refinements mean that the older views are wrong or outdated. The door is then open to conflict among different viewpoints in contemporary theorising.

Graziani, as the first approach, looks at the history of economic analysis starting from an assessment of the present state of economic science. At the same time, as with the second vision, he underlines the plurality of competing economic theories, asking different questions. This novel methodological perspective may be better evaluated by looking at two of Graziani's propositions. The first is his individuation of monetary macroeconomics as an area, whereas the mainstream, both neoclassical and Keynesian, has been seen to be inadequate. The second is that past unorthodox theories very often are themselves problematic, so that a reconstruction of past authors is needed. The two propositions together press for questioning the authors of the past from the open issues of the present.

Working with this method, Graziani has been led to stress the divide between the individualistic, non-monetary, static and equilibrium paradigms on the one hand, and the holistic, monetary, dynamic and disequilibrium paradigms on the other. Among these latter, Graziani has chosen to privilege those authors who proposed an analysis of capitalism as a monetary production economy. The crucial notion of money here refers to its purchasing power, not merely as means of payment but primarily as 'finance'. The banking system's credit creation allows the firm's sector to shape the real structure of the economy, and define income distribution. The main reference is therefore to Wicksell, Schumpeter and Keynes's *Treatise on Money*. In the following, I shall look at Graziani's theory of the monetary circuit from this history of economic analysis window.[1]

Wicksell's *Interest and Prices*

In Wicksell, Graziani finds the first author who clearly bases his picture of the monetary economy on the need for firms to finance production in a non-commodity money view. *Interest and Prices* is the first crystal clear exposition on how money enters into the capitalist process, and opens up a line and a debate that will influence monetary theory for more than three decades. In particular, in the pure credit economy the money stock is entirely determined by the credit granted by banks to firms, and is not of a given magnitude.

Wicksell's model, however, has specificities that are abandoned by Graziani. The agents in the economy comprise the sector of merchant capitalists (traders or shop-keepers) who are owners of at least part of the output of the previous period bought from firms at the end of the last circuit. Merchant capitalists are in fact offering the 'wage fund' to workers. This stock of finished commodities is at the same time the real saving available at the end of the previous circuit and, as in the Smith–Ricardo tradition, is the real counterpart of the investments of the current circuit. Workers immediately spend their money wage at the beginning of the 'year', thus transforming the real saving into money saving. Banks' loans to firms then become merchant capitalists' deposits. The same thing may be said in this way: bank loans are identical to the money value of investment, bank deposits are identical with money savings. Another point is that the interest paid by banks on deposits is the same as they gain on loans, so the banks do not earn any net proceeds. Finally, the economy is stationary and in full employment. In this setting, at the end of the period, when merchant capitalists have to buy the output from firms, the money they receive from banks is augmented exactly by the same amount firms owe to banks on their debt in excess of capital. These are all aspects we no longer find in Graziani's model.

What seems more relevant in Graziani's reading of Wicksell, because it influences his further positive and historiographic positions, are the following elements:

1 The distinction between 'equilibrium' and 'disequilibrium' positions. In equilibrium, the natural, or real, rate of return on production processes is the same as the monetary, or bank, rate of interest. Merchant capitalists buy from firms the total amount of final output, investment is equal to saving since bank finance is equal to the deposits collected at the end of the last period, the price level is stable, the marginalist rules of distribution are confirmed with 'capital' and labour being paid according to their marginal product. In disequilibrium, the natural rate may be higher or lower than the monetary rate. Let us concentrate on the case where the real rate is greater than the bank rate. Entrepreneurs will gain a positive profit at the expense of savers (merchant capitalists). The demand for finance will rise in the next period. Banks have no difficulty whatsoever in satisfying the higher demand, and investment exceeds savings (their credit supply is supposed to be horizontal). Cumulative inflation plus dynamic instability set in, with the positive divergence between the two rates being reproduced period after period and no built-in automatic self-adjusting mechanism.

2 The equality between the two rates happens by chance, since the monetary rate is fixed by banks in a discretionary way and the real rate is inherently unstable. Equilibrium as characterised by the equality between the two is turned thereby into a merely 'ideal' reference point, and 'disequilibrium' is depicted as the 'normal' situation – banks have no possibility whatsoever of knowing the natural rate beforehand. Note that from the point of view of the firms–banks relationship in both situations, firms are able to meet their liabilities with banks. Final finance is equal to initial finance, and all the money created by banks is destroyed. In the equilibrium position, firms are achieving neither profits nor losses, which is contrary to what happens in the disequilibrium position. Note also that there is no reason for equilibrium to be unique. Moreover, and most relevant, if and when by chance it is reached, equilibrium is seen as an unstable point of rest. No 'gravitation' theory is meaningful in this perspective.

3 With Wicksell's organised banking system, the so-called 'capital market' disappears. Real capital goods are not 'borrowed and lent', but 'bought and sold'. What matters is how the money to produce or buy them is created, and its 'price'. The rate of interest becomes a wholly monetary magnitude.

4 All the above points descend from the situation that Wicksell clearly sees; that, rigorously speaking, all money, including metallic money, is credit money, and more specifically bank credit money. The analytical starting point, the most basic model, in the inquiry about a 'true monetary economy' is the one portraying a pure credit system. It is the presence of bank money that severs the real rate of return from the loan rate of interest, makes the capital market a fiction and gives way to disequilibrium as the normal situation.

Thus Wicksell is not only the author who puts forward the principle of endogenous money proper to a pure-credit setting with no self-adjustment mechanism, the essential role he plays for Graziani comes from the fact that Wicksell was the first to introduce the theme – and the term – of 'forced savings' in a reasoning directly framed with references to macro 'agents' in monetary production economy. If there are some people who receive fixed money incomes, or if an effect of the positive difference between the natural and the monetary rates of interest on the 'capitalisation' expected from 'intermediate goods' is allowed into the model, then inflation has real effects. The dynamics of distribution and accumulation depend therefore on the balance of power between the conflicting social groups. A quote from Wicksell here is most astonishing and revealing. In other words, as Graziani says, the hypothetical agreement between firms and banks can bring about a lengthening of the 'average period of production', thus originating extra-profits at the expense of consumers.

Keynes's *Treatise on Money*

These real effects, however, do not seem to be necessary in the Wicksellian model. Though in Wicksell, banks grant credit only to producers and not also to workers, and though forced savings is a definite possibility, many points in his pure credit model seem too ad hoc or underdeveloped. To name just a few: the stickiness of the price level within the period when a positive divergence between the two rates happens; the exogeneity of the determination and dynamics of both rates; the absence of feedbacks of inflation on the real rate (except in the event that the natural rate falls because of the declining marginal productivity of capital – in which case, unfortunately, a readjustment mechanism to disequilibrium is at work in neoclassical fashion). The effects of inflation on the structure of production and distribution are left outside the main thrust of the argument.

These criticisms are implicit in Graziani's writings. What is explicit are other objections against neoclassical developments out of Wicksell. Graziani argues against the possibility of maintaining the thesis that the real wages are paid in advance of production with productive resources getting their marginal rewards at the end of the same period, and with investments redefined as newly produced capital goods. In fact, in his own model Graziani integrates Wicksell's approach to the circulation of money with an ex post real wage – that is, the real wage is eventually determined on the commodity market after production at the end of the period, and the 'macro' setting is implicitly or explicitly framed as a two-goods economy. This, of course, looks very similar to Keynes's *Treatise on Money*. And this latter work very clearly provides a way out from some of Wicksell's limitations to which I have referred.

The characteristics of Keynes's book (1930) that make it useful to Graziani's questioning in monetary macroeconomics are the following:

1 The real effects and non-neutrality of bank endogenous money are inevitably associated with the temporal articulation of the circuit in a three-agents model with only banks, firms, and workers, without the wage-fund sold by the traders. Here, not only initial finance is needed to pay the money wage bill both for producing the consumption goods and the investment goods sector. In this author – differently than in Wicksell – the allocation of the total labour employed is autonomously decided by the firm sector, and the real wage is given as an actual magnitude ex post, when firms sell 'available goods' to workers on the commodity market. This creates an explicit hierarchical structure between the choices of social groups. Wage-earners, whatever the sector in which they are hired, may decide whether to consume or save their money income. Meanwhile, but in total independence, entrepreneurs decide in what proportions to produce the two categories of output. Workers' real consumption is therefore dominated by entrepreneurs' choices about the structure of production.

2 The two-goods framework is prolonged in the so-called Keynes's dual theory of prices. The price of consumption goods is the one clearing the market, and may comply or not with consumers' choices. As a consequence, if there is excess investment, there will be 'commodity inflation' and 'forced savings'. Inflation does not spring from an increase in the quantity of money in circulation, but on firms' propensity to invest being higher than workers' propensity to save. The price of new capital goods, on the contrary, is not fixed on the market but depends on the relationship between the desire of the public to hold saving deposits and the amount of savings that the banking system is willing and able to create. If the former exceeds the latter, the price of securities will tend to rise; conversely, it will fall. The key variables in this case are the expectations of future returns and the rate of interest.

3 The financial market in Keynes has a much larger and more crucial role than in Wicksell. It is the market allowing firms to recover the liquidity lost because consumer expenditure is less than the money income that workers receive (as wage or interest) from firms. The conditions for final finance to be equal to initial finance is that all money savings are spent on buying securities. It is therefore incorrect to see in the financial market the place where investment demand is financed.

4 The above conclusions explain why Keynes in the 1930s has no readjustment mechanisms. There is no reason why a change in the price of consumption goods would be automatically corrected by a change in the other direction in the price of investment goods. Let us assume that

savings exceed investments, and that the degree of bearishness and the amount of saving deposits created by banks are given. The resulting 'disequilibrium' between savings and investments produces losses that may be financed by selling securities to savers, and also through a reduction in entrepreneurs' idle balances. If savings fall short of investments, the disequilibrium in the consumption goods sector corresponds to extra-profits, which, added to voluntary savings, may explain a steady price in the cost of investment goods.

5 In this view there is no longer any identity between bank loans and investments on the one hand, and bank deposits and savings on the other. It is therefore plainly inconceivable to propose that banks should lend only what they have collected as deposits so that the equality between investments and savings is preserved.

All these are points of departure either from Wicksell or from the neoclassical reading of Wicksell. At the same time, a lot of the Wicksellian scaffolding is still in place, and it is essential to reach the desired results. Let me remind two of these elements: the distinction between equilibrium and disequilibrium situations, with disequilibrium being the norm, and the independence of the real rate of return.

What is clear, however, is that once more it is not (mainly) the principle of endogenous (bank) money as 'finance' driven by demand to be completely decisive for Graziani; and even less so the 'horizontalism' of the simpler model. What is decisive, rather, is the 'power of the banks', and the consequent 'power of producers' concerning the composition of output, such that these two 'macro' agents are the 'active' subjects jointly determining the real structure of the economy. Keynes's *Treatise* is a most interesting instance of these self-reinforcing, though conflictual, powers of the two social groups within the capitalist class, linked by a complex relation of functionality and rivalry. It is interesting because in the book (commodity-) inflation and forced savings may be imposed on households even without any increase in bank credit flows.

Let us start, for simplicity's sake, from a stationary reproduction equilibrium, with the wage level, the number of workers employed and the propensity to consume taken as given. Initial finance and the value of income are thereby unchanged period after period. It is enough that entrepreneurs decide to reduce the share of (the unchanging total) employment going to produce what is put on sale to workers – and then the cost of production of the sector producing 'available goods' – in favour of the sector producing what firms have decided to keep for themselves. If this happens, given consumption demand, and because of the reduced supply, the price of available goods will rise and extra-profits will be gained in the sector.

Schumpeter on finance, innovation and capitalist evolution

The encounter between Graziani and Schumpeter seems to be the most natural. The reasons are straightforward. Schumpeter, like Keynes, provides reasons for the differential distribution of money as purchasing power, but these reasons go well beyond not only Wicksell's but also those of Keynes. They pertain to capitalism as an intrinsically dynamic economy, based on endogenous technical change, and then on intra-capitalist competition as a struggle to gain extra profits and the creation of an inner tendency to the diversification of the rate of profits. Bank financing of entrepreneurs provides the essential monetary complement of innovation, because it is the vehicle for a squeeze of the purchasing power of managers producing along the circular flow lines. In his theory of economic development, Schumpeter in fact wants, at the same time, to endogenize both the bank rate of interest and the real rate of return, and to explain how bank finance is the condition of possibility of, and the screening device for, entrepreneurial action. Disequilibrating forces leading to structural instability are thus located within the very fabric of capitalism.

A short review of the Schumpeterian system will confirm this. For Schumpeter, technological change in the capitalist process is incessant but discontinuous. It is propelled by the entrepreneurial introduction of new combinations, which may be implemented only thanks to bank-credit creation. The entrepreneurial introduction needs to be backed by bank-credit creation because the 'circular flow' – where agents follow routine behaviour – is characterised by no unused resources, no profits, no interest, no savings. Economic processes merely reproduce themselves on the same scale with constant flows. The picture would not be radically altered if we substituted a stationary equilibrium for an equilibrium growth path. Though production takes time and needs to be financed, since production processes are synchronised, each supply finds its own demand at the expected prices just covering money costs. Bank-credit repeatedly circulates the same amount of money. The monetary details may be neglected in order to have a full grasp of the real aspects of the economy. Money is therefore interpreted only as a 'receipt voucher' of past production. As a consequence, potential entrepreneurs do not have available to them the purchasing power to command the productive resources required to implement new combinations.

However the banking system, as Wicksell showed, may advance finance without any need to be constrained by the amount of reserves. Money now shows itself to be also, and primarily, a 'claim ticket' on resources. The justification of finance to innovation ex novo in the last instance comes from the higher quantity and quality of future production allowed by innovative behaviour. Banks, says Schumpeter, are the 'social accountants' of the capitalist system. More than that: finance to innovation is the differentia specifica of the present economic system, characterised also by the private ownership of the means of production and by the private production for the market. It is entrepreneurial activity that inevitably leads to the endogenous and non-uniform increase in the money supply and, without bank finance, private ownership in a market system would be a brake to economic development. Since innovations are financed by a new inflow of money and then new purchasing power, the demand for labour and for other productive resources increases; and so do prices, because credit creation to entrepreneurs is granted before they contribute to the stream of goods.

This inflation is not only or mainly an increase in the general level of prices, it is rather, and essentially, a change in the relative structure of prices. This change was not at the core of Wicksell's thought, and has a different nature than the relative variation in prices stressed by Keynes in 1930 because it now mainly affects producers. Indeed, it is only thanks to this – at first limited, but later generalised – revolution in relative prices that entrepreneurs are able to carry out 'new combinations'; that is, to produce new things or the same thing by a different method. Thus, the outcome of bank financing is that 'new' entrepreneurs gain access to resources because 'old' managers of traditional firms suffer a squeeze in their purchasing power. Forced savings of workers and households, on the contrary, though likely, may be absent, and, in any case, this is secondary relative to the fundamental role of transferring resources from 'old' to 'new' producers. According to Schumpeter, when this partial disequilibrium becomes general, innovative activity comes to a halt because uncertainty on the future system of quantity and prices is too high and the calculation of costs and receipts of innovations is impossible. Prosperity turns into depression, bank finance collapses, deflation ensues. The economic system once again approaches a different circular flow – where profits and interests tend to disappear, and whose structure we now know to be determined exactly by the prior non-equibirum dynamics ruled by dynamic competition.

What strikes home in Graziani's reading of Schumpeter is this; on the one hand, it is clear that Schumpeter's picture of capitalism as driven by entrepreneurial action fulfils Graziani's 'vision'. Loans make deposits. Money as purchasing power is the lever of qualitative change. Firms' sovereignty over the structure of production wins over consumer sovereignty. The short-term money rate of interest fixed by banks during development is a wholly monetary and conventional phenomenon, and is a tax on entrepreneurial profit. The accumulation of capital is an unbalanced, out-of-equilibrium process that cannot be divorced from technical change – investments cannot be divorced from innovations introduced by entrepreneurs. On the other hand, he affirms that in Schumpeter there is no place for any notion of equilibrium, the dominant tendency is not (also, and periodically) towards the annihilation but (always, and exclusively) to the differentiation of the rate of profits, capitalism is perpetually in the flux of change. In this reading, the similarity with Wicksell is clear. In a nutshell, the similarity is in the fact that Graziani reads Schumpeter's couple circular flow/capitalist develoment as the analogue of Wicksell's couple equilibrium/ disequilibrium, again with the capitalist development depicted as the normal situation, thus underplaying the succession of phases in evolutionary dynamics of the *Theory of Economic Development* and *Business Cycles*. Schumpeter is read in continuity with Wicksell's technical picture of the monetary economy, the break is in the 'vision' rather than in the 'analysis'. Schumpeter's theoretical aim – namely, to explain the internal and discontinuous path of innovation and development within capitalism – seems to be put outside the analytical core of the theory of the monetary circuit. This seems to be confirmed by the fact that Graziani in some places suggests that the connection between bank finance and innovators is just a normative rule expressing Schumpeter's neoclassical remnants, rather than an integral part of his perspective.

Out-of-equilibrium monetary economics before *The General Theory*: an assessment

Graziani's re-reading of these authors goes against the dominant inter-pretations. For all of the authors in the heterodox monetary tradition, in the actual working of the capitalist economy, agents in the market do not have equal power. Bankers and innovators or firms enjoy a command over real resources, whereas wage-earners negotiate their money wage and may decide only how to spend it.

As for Wicksell, Graziani contrasts starkly with Patinkin, who looks at Wicksell as the forerunner of the real balance effect. Gold standard is the reference model. An exogenous change in the money stock automatically originates movements in reserves, and then banks variation in the loan rate. The disequilibrium is automatically sorted out by either an internal or an external drain of metallic money. Patinkin's perspective goes against the twin facts that for Wicksell, first, disequilibrium arises because of the instability of the real rate and, second, the pure credit system with endogenous money is the general case. Though Graziani does not commit himself to a particular view about which rate is the prime mover, he is clear on the second point, so that the banking system can finance inflationary processes without inner limits, no risks of insolvency, no liquidity problems. The presence of reserve requirements on legal tender just introduces institutional constraints, but we know that their stringency may be very much weakened by banks expanding in step or granting each other reciprocal credit at clearing. Of course, the instability of the real rate makes Patinkin's reading of Wicksell wrong, even outside the pure credit model: a point that it is relevant in order to understand the different paths taken by Schumpeter, on the one hand, and by von Mises–Hayek on the other. An interesting puzzle is understanding the position of von Mises and Hayek relative to this Wicksellian monetary heterodoxy. According to Realfonzo (1998), the Austrians criticised the quantity theory in the rigid bank deposit multiplier version, but they endorsed a flexible deposit multiplier approach. An exogenous variation in base money brings about an expansion in reserves, and bank credit rises more than that because of the presence of surrogates: but the only real money is commodity money, fund collecting precedes loans, and – most importantly – the multiplication of deposits that is responsible for the trade cycle cannot go on forever since the growing demand for finance goes against banks' inability to expand the credit granted to firms. The main reason would be that the reserve ratio of individual banks, and of the entire banking system, decreases, and banks are more and more illiquid. This reading cannot be accepted, since von Mises clearly thought that Wicksell's extreme case of a single bank and of a 'pure credit system', in which there is no limit to the amount of credit the bank(s) can create, is anything but unrealistic: on the contrary, it is representative of the working of a modern monetary economy. It is true, of course, that in von Mises's view, money growth, leading to an inflationary spiral and an unjustified lengthening of the period of production, cannot go on undisturbed. The reaction, however, does not arise from the constraints banks encounter in the creation of credit. Rather, it comes from the agents' spending decisions, which, in the final phase of the cycle, bring about a rise in the price of consumption goods relative to capital goods. The rise in this relative price shows the entrepreneurs that, during the boom, the real structure of production has moved against consumption and in favour of investment despite individual preferences. The clash between the structure of production and consumers' preferences therefore enforces the liquidation of firms undertaken on the basis of the false signal given by excessively low money rates of interest. If the banks unite to try to resist this adjustment by keeping the loan rate below the real rate, they can safely do so, without encountering any liquidity constraint. But if they persist in injecting ever greater inflationary doses of money, the monetary system quickly undoes itself.[2]

Relative to Keynes, the novelty of Graziani's reading is radical. It amounts to the rebuttal of the widespread opinion according to which Keynes's heresy is only to be found in *The General Theory*. Along these lines, after the Great Crash of 1929–32, Keynes's aim was to explain involuntary unemployment as an equilibrium position in a fully competitive market economy with flexible prices. To reach this result, the function of money that is crucial is that of being a store of value: money as the most convenient form of wealth owing to uncertainty. Graziani is convincing in showing that this interpretation underplays the fact that the 1936 book has to be seen as a step within a much longer process of departure from orthodoxy that Keynes undertook before the First World War. The true break was *A Treatise on Money* and, I think, the historical watershed is the Great War. Endogenous creation of bank money is already there in Keynes, in 1911–3. Even the gold standard was, for him, not an automatic but a managed system. But it is the autonomous power of entrepreneurs, thanks to bank finance, to decide the level and composition of output and employment that marks the break with the Marshallian legacy. One problem, however, remains. The positive side of Graziani's reading is that it is faithful to Keynes's Introduction to *The General Theory*, where the Cambridge economist insists that the new book should be read against the background of the *A Treatise on Money* analysis of banking and money. The negative side is that Graziani's ingenious attempt to conciliate the 'given' stock of money in 1936 with the creation and administration of bank credit flows in 1930 makes the determination of employment levels (and then involuntary unemployment) something exogenous.

Regarding Schumpeter, I have already hinted that Graziani is stretching this author too far to meet the straightjacket of the Wicksell–Keynes line. The spontaneous and incessant introduction of innovations by entrepreneurs is discontinuous for the Austrian economist. Since entrepreneurs, backed by bank credit, appear in clusters, capitalist development exhibits a cyclical pattern. Entrepreneurial action gives way to the 'prosperity' phase, in which innovations emerge, which then turns into the 'depression' phase, a lapse of time during which the system adapts to creative destruction. The cyclical process of capitalistic development sets off from a 'neighborhood of equilibrium' near the circular flow. The first innovators lessen the social resistance to novelty and force a restructuring of firms still working along traditional lines, thereby inducing a wave of secondary innovations, and are followed by imitators. The economic system cannot adapt gradually to qualitative change and moves further away from equilibrium. The partial disequilibrium introduced by entrepreneurs cannot but degenerate into a general disequilibrium marked by a radical upsetting of the price and quantity system, by growing uncertainty, and thus by the impossibility of calculating costs and receipts from 'doing new things'. As entrepreneurial action and dynamic competition decline, adaptive behaviour and static competition take the field. The economic system once more approaches a new circular flow, where profit and interest disappear.

Graziani's aversion to shaping Schumpeter's theory of economic development, giving the circular flow more than a logical role, can be understood as a reaction against those interpretations, such as the one by Napoleoni, who saw prosperity as just a short-term deviation around the trend given by the Walrasian general economic equilibrium. This may give the impression that, in the end, consumer sovereignty reigns. In fact, Schumpeter's approach breaks with mainstream theorising, virtually on each step of the argument. The same circular flow from which economic development originates is shown to be the outcome of previous waves of entrepreneurial action made possible by credit creation, and it is structurally unstable. On the one hand, the system will once again come to approach a new equilibrium after the boom, but only as a transient and temporary resting point. On the other hand, after a while prosperity necessarily causes a slackening of entrepreneurial action. The long run is nothing but a sequence of short period positions, the trend is conditioned by cyclical movements.

Preliminary conclusions

This chapter has shown how fruitful Graziani's journey into the history of economic analysis has been. His theoretical glasses have opened up new ways to read the authors of the past, and have made his theoretical model richer. The power of the firm sector is the outcome of their privileged access to bank credit, resulting in producers' sovereignty, under the constraint of the conflict among social groups. This conclusion, however, may be reached only in a macroeconomic inquiry where money is finance to production and the basic model is in terms of pure credit.

A few problems have emerged. The main ones are that structural change is assumed rather than explained, and that the possibility and mechanism of readjustment to disequilibrium are not discussed in detail. Indeed, this may be coherent for a perspective – such as the one favoured by some French authors – strictly opposing a 'monetary' approach from any value theory, a position that Graziani has never explicitly endorsed.

However, if the survey I have produced has some meaning, it shows that an alternative view concerning the circulation of money is a necessary, but insufficient, ingredient in order to break from orthodox conclusion. It must be integrated with an evolutionary perspective on capitalist dynamics along Schumpeterian – and may be, Marxian – lines.

Notes

1. In the following, I will have mainly in mind the interpretation of the monetary theories of production put forward by Graziani in his macroeconomics textbook (Graziani, 2002), and the way he refers to Wicksell, Schumpeter and Keynes in his recent book on the theory of the monetary circuit (Graziani, 2003). See also Bellofiore (1985, 1992).

2. This interpretation is confirmed by this von Mises quote criticizing Wicksell: 'But if we start with the assumption, as Wicksell does, that only fiduciary media are in circulation and that the quantity of them is not legislatively restricted, so that the banks are entirely free to extend their issues of them, then it is impossible to see why rising prices and an increasing demand for loans should induce them to raise the rate of interest they charge for loans. Even Wicksell can think of no other reason for this than that since the requirements of business for gold coins and bank-notes becomes greater as the price level rises, the banks do not receive back the whole of the sums they have lent, part of them remaining in the hands of the public; and that the banks reserves are consequently depleted while the total liabilities of the

banks increase; and that this must naturally induce them to raise their rate of interest. *But in this argument Wicksell contradicts the assumption that he takes as the starting-point of his investigation.* Consideration of the level of its cash reserves and their relation to the liabilities arising from the issue of fiduciary media cannot concern the hypothetical bank that he describes. He seems suddenly to have forgotten his original assumption of a circulation consisting exclusively of fiduciary media, on which assumption, at first, he *rightly* laid great weight' (von Mises, 1971, pp. 267–8). On all this, and on Hayek's position, cf. Bellofiore (1998).

References

Bellofiore, R. (1985) 'Money and Development in Schumpeter', *Review of Radical Political Economics*, no. 1–2, pp. 21–40. Also in John Cunningham Wood, (ed.), *Joseph Alois Schumpeter: Critical Assessments*, IV (London: Routledge, 1991), pp. 371–94.

Bellofiore, R. (1992) 'Monetary Macroeconomics before *The General Theory*. The circuit theory of money in Wicksell, Schumpeter and Keynes', *Social Concept*, no. 2, pp. 47–89.

Bellofiore, R. (1998) 'Between Wicksell and Hayek. Mises' *Theory of Money and Credit* Revisited', *American Journal of Economics and Sociology*, October, pp. 531–78.

Graziani, A. (2002) *Teoria economica: Macroeconomia*, 5th edn, Naples: ESI.

Graziani, A. (2003) *The Monetary Theory of Production* (Cambridge University Press).

Keynes, J.M. (1975) *The Treatise on Money*, 2 vols, *The Collected Writings of John Maynard Keynes* (London: Macmillan).

Mises, L. von (1971) *The Theory of Money and Credit* (New Haven: Yale University Press) [Theorie des Geldes und des Umlaufsmittel, Munich and Leipzig: Duncker & Humblot, 1912; 2nd edn, 1924; 3rd edn, 1953].

Realfonzo, R. (1998) *Money and Banking*, (Aldershot: Edward Elgar).

Schumpeter, J.A. (1934) *The Theory of Economic Development. An Enquiry into Profits, Capital, Credit, Interest and the Business Cycle* (Cambridge, MA: Harvard University Press [From the 2nd German edn, *Theorie der wirtschaftlichen Entwicklung. Eine Untersuchung über Unternehmergewinn, Kapital, Kredit, Zins und den Konjunkturzyklus*, Leipzig: Dunker & Humblot, 1912].

Schumpeter, J.A. (1939) *Business Cycles* (Philadelphia, PA: Porcupine Press).

Wicksell, K. (1936) *Interest and Prices* (London: Macmillan) [*Geldzins und Güterpreise*, Jena: G. Fischer, 1898].

3
Lost and Found: Some History of Endogenous Money in the Twentieth Century

Victoria Chick

Introduction

This chapter started in an airport waiting room. I happened on Tim Congdon, and we talked about Keynes's monetary theory while we waited for our flight. The conversation brought into sharp focus an idea that had been festering in the back of my mind for some little time: that I had been brought up to take the endogenous generation of money (deposits) by banks for granted; why was it necessary for the modern theory of endogenous money to re-invent the concept? But Tim had been given a very different understanding. An informal survey of other economist friends of roughly his age (currently (2003) around the age of fifty), showed a pretty uniform experience of having been taught that 'the central bank provides money and the banks multiply it', as Roger Backhouse (in conversation) succinctly characterised the money-base theory of the money supply. Clearly something had happened somewhere between the time of my under- and post-graduate education in the late 1950s–early 60s to theirs some 15 years later.

Schumpeter (1954, pp. 1110–17) gives the impression that endogenous money was well understood in Germany (and even more so in England) by the 1930s at the latest and should have been understood by the end of the nineteenth century (perhaps he thought this because he understood it so well himself: Schumpeter, 1912). (See also Ellis, US treatise, 1934, pp. 395–7.) So why did that understanding disappear? This paper reconstructs some of the story of the struggle for, and loss of, the concept of endogenous money. To this end I have examined a number of monetary textbooks, these being the repository of accepted wisdom, as well as some treatises or 'monographs'. I have explored only English-language texts. Since both banking institutions and ways of thinking differ between countries, especially in the early years covered here, I shall systematically indicate the origin of sources in the text, even for famous works. I have also been limited by time to a very quick examination of a somewhat unsystematic and incomplete selection from the open shelves of the LSE library. This work then should be seen as asking what I hope is an interesting question and providing some preliminary evidence rather than giving a definitive answer.

No definite time-line emerged. This is to be expected, given that old doctrines are so persistent in economics. The work is further complicated by the fact that there are many strands to the endogenous-money story, and by the fact that very subtle differences of language and emphasis are involved. But a general drift can be discerned, from widespread acceptance of bank credit as the origin of the bulk of the money supply in the 1930s to the 1960s, to the emergence of the money-base story in the 1970s. Also, in the 1970s banks began to be portrayed as but one class of financial intermediary; later still they were analysed as multiproduct firms. In the first case, no amount of later questioning whether banks are 'special' is going to remove that first impression of banks 'lending on' deposits, which our forebears fought so hard to dispel. And in the second, the importance to the story of the monetary quality of deposits is fatally obscured, as is the distinction between the individual bank and the system as a whole.

That is where the story is going, but the story begins with metallic money, the question of a monetary standard and the role of money in the determination of prices and the exchange rate. There are texts on money from the nineteenth century – even, in one case, the twentieth – that do not even mention banks (e.g. F.A. Walker, 1891, US text; Nogaro, 1927, translated from a French text, 1924). The first step is recognising deposits as money. At the time of writing we take for granted that deposits are money, so it is surprising how late full recognition was in coming. Then came the distinction between primary and secondary or derivative deposits, which has now virtually disappeared. The main part of the story is the deposit multiplier, which begins as the hard-won core of the concept of endogenous money and ends up the villain of the piece. This transformation is connected to a progressive formalisation of the money multiplier, in which the emphasis in earlier literature on bank behaviour tends to be replaced with something mechanical, and to the role ascribed to reserves, which are seen first as a limit to expansion, then as the means of control, and finally as the cause of multiplicative expansion. The transition to an exogenous-money theory is then complete.

The rest of the chapter will explore the evolution of three key elements of endogenous-money theory: the mechanism of generating deposits by banks' acquisition of assets, the multiplicative expansion of bank lending, and the role of reserves. These are not easy to disentangle and the chronology is sometimes upset.

Do banks 'create credit'?

This conventional formulation of our key question is, on the face of it, rather odd. I once wrote (1973) that of course the answer was yes: creating credit – that is, making loans – was the nature of banks' business: a point that is surely uncontroversial. I was really complaining against a misleading use of language. Until perhaps the 1940s, deposits were not thought to be 'money proper' (Keynes, UK treatise, 1930, vol. 1, ch. 2; Hart, US text, 1948, p. 10) or 'common money' (Robertson, UK text, 1928) or 'actual money' (Dowrie, US text, 1936, p. 114), where these terms meant notes and coin. As late as 1948, Hart insisted that bank deposits are only near-money! Everyone knows the title of Hawtrey's famous (UK) treatise, *Currency and Credit* (1919): by credit he means bank deposits, whereas it should refer to advances, on the other side of the banks' balance sheets. Currie (US treatise, 1934) chides him and others for this use of language. The same confusion is found today (Wray, 1990; users of the currently fashionable term credit-money, a compound noun fusing two disparate components). It is true that bank deposits are a credit extended by depositors to banks, and that deposits arise from credit extended to borrowers by banks; but now that deposits are included in the definition of money, the terminology can only be confusing. 'The two things originate in the same transaction, but they are quite separate' (Crowther, UK text, 1940, p. 45). But we know what is meant and can examine the issue: whether loans and investments give rise to deposits or the opposite, that expansion of assets is constrained by the prior receipt of deposits.

A single credit transaction

Crowther indicates his scepticism about bank money creation by enclosing 'creation' in inverted commas throughout. His difficulty is that deposit money is not a real thing but only the banks' debt. However, he replies to those who deny 'creation' with 'two answers, one theoretical, one practical'. The theoretical answer is, as we have known since Phillips (US treatise, 1920), that one must think of the system as a whole, though this is getting ahead of our story. The practical answer appeals to the fact that there exists a far greater volume of deposits than the amount of cash. 'If the banks do not "create" their deposits, where can [they have] come from?' (Crowther, p. 50).

Something from nothing?

The path from fact to explanation, however, was far from smooth. Humphrey (1987) reminds us that 'Crowther's Fact' was understood by the eighteenth century (he cites John Law, Bishop Berkeley, Alexander Hamilton). But its implications were persistently denied as late as the 1930s, notably by Edwin Cannan, whose 'cloakroom rule' was, however, challenged each time it appeared (Laidler, 1999, p. 89; for a review of the letters between Cannan and Keynes, see Skidelsky, 1995). An earlier, symptomatic but more ambiguous passage is found in Laughlin (US treatise, 1903): under a heading that asserts that 'Banks do not "coin credit" ' we have this text: 'Clearly enough, banks cannot make something out of nothing; they cannot create wealth, or money, out of an intangible thing. The operations of legitimate banking are always ultimately based on salable goods, or property; if they are not so based, the operations cease to be legitimate and are purely speculative' (p. 116).

Positive and normative considerations are confused in this passage: Laughlin protests that, since creating something out of nothing would not be a good thing, it does not happen. He does not actually deny the fact that bank lending creates deposits, for he names two sources of the origin of deposits, receipt of cash and a discount operation (primary and derivative deposits, though he does not use those terms). And he accepts Crowther's Fact: '[A] medium of exchange, based on commercial assets and therefore perfectly elastic, is here with us, active, efficient, performing a mass of exchanges out of all proportion to the work of bank notes' (p. 120). There is, however, no multiplier analysis. His alliance of money with real wealth probably stems from thinking about metallic money, though this was Crowther's sticking point too, long after metallic money had disappeared. The question of whether (bank) money is net wealth continues (Gurley and Shaw, 1960; the deeply confused Pesek and Saving, 1967; Ahmed, 1970 and later issues of *Oxford Economic Papers*). Ahmed's question was asked again more recently (Weil, 1991) but, as with an examination question, the answer has now changed.

'Creation' or 'lending on'?

One is led to wonder about ideas in the air in England, for Withers (1909), writing not that long after Laughlin, 'speaks boldly about the manufacture of money' (Schumpeter, 1954, p. 1111). 'But', Schumpeter continues, 'this should not have surprised anyone. Yet it was considered a novel and some-what heretical doctrine.' Withers cites no one on this point. Did he know the work of Pennington and Torrens (see the discussion of Humphrey in the next section) or H.D. Macleod (1855–6), all of whom recognised derivative deposits much earlier?

Schumpeter (1954, p. 1115, n. 7) refers to Macleod's failure to achieve recognition, owing partly to his manner of writing and partly to his offending Marshall, which limited his job prospects and the penetration of his ideas. They certainly disagreed on banking: Marshall (1887, quoted in Humphrey, 1987, p. 7) speaks of 'what part of its deposits a bank could lend'. And in *Money, Credit and Commerce* (1923, p. 200, n. 2), he deplores 'the fraud committed by the Bank of Amsterdam in lending its deposits'. Later in the same footnote it becomes clear he is thinking of bullion deposited for safekeeping; that is, in terms of Stage 1 banking (Chick, 1986). Despite this, he played a role in the development of the deposit multiplier! (see below).

Once the causal priority of loans and investments was widely understood, many writers devised clever ways to counter the natural instinct of their readers to think in terms of banks 'lending on' cash deposited with them. This instinct stems either from thinking in terms of an obsolete stage of bank development (Marshall's error) or from applying the personal experience of depositing cash, without thinking that the cash came from another deposit – that is, from thinking microeconomically about a systemic question. (The word 'deposit' encourages this instinct.) Prather (US text, 1937), though confusingly he states in a section heading that 'Depositors provide most of the funds used by bankers' (p. 233), redeems himself with 'A bank does not lend money; it merely lends its credit' (p. 247). Or Curtis and Townshend (UK text, 1937, pp. 32–3): 'Deposits are not something a bank *has*, but something it *owes*.... The picture ... of the banks receiving money from their depositors for "safekeeping", and lending some of this money out to others and buying investments with the rest is very far from the truth ... This fact about banking is so peculiar that even many bankers fail to recognise its truth.'

Whittlesey (US text, 1948) perhaps handles the matter most brilliantly. He distinguishes three types of lending, which overlap historically: lending one's own money, lending other people's money (intermediation), and 'lending money that is created as a part of the process of lending it'. The latter – somewhat dangerously phrased – he considers 'the very essence of deposit banking' (pp. 102–4). He takes as examples of the three types, respectively, shareholders subscribing capital to a new bank, the deposit of cash (a primary deposit) which the bank then invests in government bonds, and a businessman asking to open an account in exchange for some bills. Thus the difficult matter of the third type of lending is placed immediately in contrast to the types of lending most commonly understood. The even more unnerving example, something (a deposit) exchanged for nothing more than a promise of future repayment, is missing.

By 1940, Crowther could speak of 'Every loan creates a deposit' as an 'old banking maxim' (p. 43) and in 1948 Hart (US text) wrote that the disagreement over whether banks could create credit 'had faded' (p. 63). This sense of security for 'loans create deposits' causality goes through until the 1970s. Harrod (UK text, 1969) calls it a 'well-known aphorism' (p. 33). Perhaps it has become too much of a catchphrase, for now it is often not stressed that the same consequence follows from bank purchases of securities.

The deposit multiplier

So far we have only discussed causality in the case of a single transaction. The quantitative importance of the derivative deposit depends on the deposit multiplier. Phillips (US treatise, 1920) and Crick (UK article, 1927) may be the classic references in the development of the idea of the bank credit multiplier, but according to Humphrey (1987), the struggle to explain Crowther's Fact with adequate theory took place over nearly a century. He finds several stages and key authors. Pennington (UK memorandum, 1826) understood the connection between lending, the redeposit of cash and a mutiplicative effect; Torrens (UK letter, 1837) discussed the limits of the process, focusing on the cash reserve; Joplin (UK letter, 1841) dealt with expansion in a multibank system; Marshall set the matter out algebraically in the margin of a book published in 1877 and a verbal account was published in 1887 (UK memorandum); and Davenport (US text, 1913) saw the importance of distinguishing between a monopoly bank and a bank in competition with others (for references in this paragraph, see Humphrey). (Laidler, 1999, p. 89, also mentions Giffen.) The importance of Phillips is that he brought all these considerations together into a coherent whole.

In the literature of the 1930s and 1940s the question of credit creation is usually phrased as a debate between bankers and economists, the bankers taking the view that they can only lend what has previously been lent to them, and the economists converted to the credit-creation view. Examples of bankers are Walter Leaf, Chairman of the Westminster Bank (UK text, 1926, p. 102): 'The banks can lend no more than they can borrow [in the form of their deposits] . . . for the banks are strictly limited in their lending operations by the amount which the depositor thinks fit to leave with them'; and Reginald McKenna, Chairman of the Midland Bank and former Chancellor of the Exchequer (UK, 1925, p. 94): 'the bank merely stands as an intermediary between the depositor and the borrower'. But the categories were not watertight: Crick was also at the Midland Bank and refers to the contrary view of his Chairman, and Cannan, who sided with the bankers, was Professor at LSE.

Phillips saw his main point as the distinction between a single bank and a banking system: the single bank's lending is constrained by its deposits, but the system as a whole is not so constrained. 'The accepted statements of banking theory, with scarcely an exception [he cites Davenport 1913] have made no such distinction' (p. 32). This distinction reconciles the perceptions of bankers with what became the majority view: that the system as a whole has the power to expand multiplicatively. Crick achieves nearly the same immediate objective – demonstrating the multiplier – but uses a system of five banks of equal size (the structure of UK banking at the time), where the redeposit ratio is bound to be high. Thus, he blurred the distinction between an individual bank and the system. The deposit multiplier is the first demonstration, to my knowledge, of the fallacy of composition in economics and the first example of truly macro or systemic perspective.

Phillips is cited in Keynes's *A Treatise on Money* (1930), as is Crick. Keynes makes a contribution which has not been widely exploited: he argues that, in a closed banking system that settles without cash, 'there is no limit to the amount of money which the banks can safely create, *provided that they move forward in step*' (p. 23, italics in original). The standard exposition takes the multiplier through successive steps. With the unrealistic assumption of cashless settlement relaxed, the 'in-step' scenario, so consonant with the idea of waves of optimism and pessimism, has the advantage of eliminating the dynamic question of how quickly the cash returns to the bank that initiated the expansion. This question was raised by Crick and again by Angell and Ficek (US article, 1933); it is a source of residual disbelief in the deposit multiplier (Ivor Pearce in conversation) for, if the lag is long enough, the initial expansion will have to be reversed because of the cash lost through clearing, and no multiplier will occur. I have found two exceptions to the sequential multiplier. H.M. Smith (US text, 1968, p. 60) speaks of 'simultaneous expansion', and Peterson and Cawthorne (US text, 1941, p. 336) search for the 'limits to which the banks, acting in unison, may increase their deposits by means of loans and investment expansion'. Neither gives an algebraic analysis, and neither cites Keynes.

After Phillips, textbooks explicitly distinguished between what an individual bank could do and what a monopoly bank or the system as a whole could do, though for some there is still no multiplier (Shaw, US text, 1950 – indeed there is very little on banks – strange for the co-author of Gurley and Shaw, 1960). Banker resistance is reported in Meigs (US text, 1972): Maisel, a member of the FRS Board of Governors, is reported (p. 158) as saying (1969) that the credit multiplier is naive. But Meigs counters this (p. 159) with a statement from *The Federal Reserve: Purposes and Functions* (1959, p. 27): 'the issuance of a given amount of high powered money by the Federal Reserve may generate a volume of ordinary money which is several times as large.' (For references, see Meigs.) The latter is an early statement of money-base theory. Note that 'ordinary money' is now bank deposits.

What starts the multiplier off?

I have only found two exceptions to the rule that the multiplier is started off either by a primary deposit or a change in reserves: L.B. Thomas (1979) starts with a new loan, without saying that the bank concerned must decide to become less liquid – and he ends up with a money-base theory anyway, and Sause (US text, 1966) starts with new paid-in capital providing cash. Those that start with a change in reserves are Frazer and Yohe (US text, 1966); Kent (US text, 1966); Meigs (US text, 1972); Marshall and Swanson (US text, 1974); Goldfeld and Chandler (US text, 1981); and Struthers and Speight (UK text, 1986). Early texts are more careful than later ones to outline the various sources of cash to the banking system as a whole (Bernstein (US text, 1935); Curtis and Townshend (UK text, 1937); Thomas (US text, 1964); Harrod (UK text, 1969)), but there are later examples as well: Boughton and Wicker (US text, 1975); Klein (US text, 1982). Bernstein explains the following sources of net primary deposits: a change in the public's desired cash holdings, gold imports, an issue of currency, and a central bank purchase of financial assets or the granting of a reserve credit. These details help the reader both to understand that constraints on individual banks and the system of banks differ and to move away from the notion that banks are entirely reliant on the central bank for their supply of cash reserves.

Much more dangerous, especially when the sources of cash to the banking system as a whole are not explained, are those texts that start with a primary deposit (Chandler (US text, 1948); Mills and Walker (Australian text, 1952); Shapiro *et al.* (US text, 1968); Auerbach (US text, 1985); Scott (Singapore text, 1995)). Only Chandler, in the third edition, adds the appropriate caveat, 'It was perhaps injudicious to begin with this case, for it may reinforce popular misconceptions' (1959, p. 89). Auerbach starts his multiplier with 'In comes John Jones with a $1000 deposit' (p. 154), powerfully supporting inappropriate microeconomic thinking.

The role of reserves

It was understood from the beginning that the expansion of bank credit and deposits was limited by the banks' need to redeem deposits for cash on demand. At the time of writing most texts focus on the cash reserve, but many writers took a far more comprehensive view. Laughlin's new treatise (US, 1931) is, by modern standards, very radical. He stated that as the Federal Reserve System had evolved, it was 'no longer intelligent to insist that credit is limited by cash reserves' but rather by assets (vol. 2, p. 726). (I am not clear what developments he had in mind; I should have thought the development of 'broad, deep and resilient' asset markets was more to the point.) Bernstein echoes the point in weaker form: all bank assets are reserves, but cash has a special significance. Curtis and Townshend (1937) match Laughlin: 'What limits the banks' power to lend is ... their own power to obtain cash at need' (p. 33). Few have followed their lead.

For both Crick (1927) and Sayers (UK text, 1st edn 1939), the role of the central bank as the ultimate supplier of cash is very strong. Sayers, like Crick, does not use the distinction between the individual bank and the system. Perhaps the English banking system was so close-knit and oligopolistic that it would have seemed artificial for him to do so, or perhaps, like Agger (US text, 1918), of whose book Phillips complained, he overestimated the powers of an individual bank. He starts with the observation that the banks keep very close to their chosen ratio of cash reserves to deposits, though the ratio is not fixed by law or even by long tradition (p. 34). The banks do this by substituting between advances and investments but always staying 'fully loaned up', in the American phrase. The fact that they maintain a fixed cash ratio 'means that they hand over to [the central bank] the responsibility of determining the volume of deposits... [I]f the central bank can control the supply of cash and allow for the public's demand for cash for circulation, the volume of bank deposits is absolutely determined' (p. 35). Crick (1927, pp. 52–3) agrees: 'the volume of bank cash is determined, over relatively short periods, not by the public, nor by the joint stock banks, not merely by gold movements, but ultimately by the actions of the Bank of England' (p. 43), which is able though open market operations to counteract changes from other sources. Crowther (1940, p. 45) and Hawtrey (1950, p. 90) concur.

Sayers's 6th edition (1964) reflects the institution of a liquid assets ratio comprising assets readily discountable by the Bank of England, thus neutralising the cash ratio. Liquid assets became 'the effective constraint' on but not the 'determinant of the creation of' deposits (p. 40). Sayers was less confident that the Bank could control the distribution of liquid assets between the banks and other holders.

From constraints to instruments of control to initiating cause

Non-UK authors are more varied in their interpretation. American authors focus, first on the constraints on bank expansion and drift toward consideration of control. Eventually the Fed is given a causal role. For Dowrie (US text, 1936, p. 132) reserves 'serve as a guide or warning signal with respect to the expansion of deposits'. Mills and Walker (Australian text, 1952) acknowledge the role of reserves and the cash/deposit ratio but assert that there is no general rule for credit expansion: its determinants are complex (p. 34). Peterson and Cawthorne (US text, 1941, p. 336) spell out some of those complexities. Their list of constraining factors includes the amount of reserves, the cash/deposit preferences of the public, the size of bank, loan policy and the demand for credit. The language of limitation is found as late as 1978 (Hanson, US text). The list of factors is progressively narrowed to focus on central bank control through reserves.

The emphasis on control may be related to American monetary history, including the debate over the right to issue money and experience of banking abuses: it is the latter that led them to make reserve ratios (plural because they differ for different classes of bank) legal requirements, while in most of Europe until comparatively recent times, the matter was left to the bankers (Dowrie, US text, 1936, p. 122; Chandler, 1948, p. 178; see also Robertson, 1922). The creation of assets which count as money has (rightly) always aroused anxiety, though in Britain the Bank of England, at least between Bagehot (1873) and the secondary banking crisis of 1974, has been widely trusted to limit bank expansion.

Barger (US text, 1964) declares that a central bank is necessary if paper money is to succeed (which gives pause for thought, considering that the US ran a paper currency long before the Fed was established in 1913). Frazer and Yohe (US text, 1966, p. 28) already declare their special interest in 'actions by the Federal Reserve to provide or extinguish reserves'. Ritter and Silber in their 1st edition (US text, 1970) speak of deposits being controlled by the Fed; in a subsequent edition (1977) this becomes 'constrained', reversing the general trend as does Cochran (US text, 4th edition, 1979), who stresses the monetary base but mentions other factors. Goldfeld and

Chandler (US text, 1981); Mishkin (US text, 1986); and King (US text, 1987) all give primacy to the Fed.

The algebraic expression of the deposit multiplier is by the 1970s routine, and both the behavioural content and the qualifications found in earlier literature have virtually vanished. Indeed, Goodhart's criticism of the multiplier (UK text, 1975, pp. 129–36) is precisely its mechanical nature and its lack of behavioural content, but it was not always thus. The deposit multiplier has become the money multiplier, $M = mH$. See P.F. Smith (US text, 1978) for one example, but they are everywhere. The stage is set for the central bank to be seen not just as controller but as the prime cause of monetary change. In monetarist thought, following Friedman and Schwartz (1963) – or Meade (UK article, 1934)! – changes in the money supply are regularly analysed in terms of the volume of high powered money, the cash/deposit ratio, and the reserve ratio, with a strong preponderance of attention to the first and last of these: Meigs, 1972; Kaufman (US text, 1973). Monetarism places responsibility for money solely on the monetary authorities by asserting their control over high-powered money and assuming that the two ratios are either constant or highly predictable. This is the position, for example, of Newlyn (UK text, 1971).

Bucking the trend

Of course, this trend provoked dissent. Tobin, in his famous article (US, 1963), attacks the assumption that money can be unambiguously demarcated from non-money, the corollary that banks are significantly different from other financial intermediaries, and the primacy given to reserves in the multiplier story. He objected to the assumption in the mechanical multiplier that banks were always fully and exactly loaned up, and to the lack of behavioural content generally. He proposes, in contrast, a theory of the supply of deposits based on the balance between expected revenue from assets and the cost of attracting and holding deposits. That sounds entirely reasonable, but begs the question of whether the reserve 'constraint' is binding or not. Indeed, he suggests, as others do later, that the fractional reserve is the *reason* for multiple expansion. Compare this to the earlier English literature.

Central bank control of high-powered money

In the 1950s in the UK, the Bank of England promoted the doctrine of supplying cash on demand from the public. In the 1960s, it nominated the interest rate as its target variable (as it always had been, indeed). Thus, it came to be understood that the Bank either would not or could not control the supply of cash and therefore could not control the money supply. Two other developments also subverted the 'monetarist multiplier', as it had become. The first was the idea that the lender-of-last-resort function could (and should) be used more widely and that therefore the banks, when they 'overlent', could force the Bank to provide the cash that the banks needed – called, in the USA, the 'reverse causation' argument (Lombra and Torto, US article, 1973). The second was the recognition that the banks' refusal to buy government securities could force the Bank to buy them, thus providing reserves (Hall, UK treatise, 1983). Meigs (1972) titled his chapter 10 'High powered money out of control'.

Conclusion

The rediscovery of the wheel may produce something very like the original: function demands it. But rediscovery in economics is like history: ideas do not quite repeat themselves. There is a kind of hysteresis – the 'new' idea is influenced by the distortions of the recent past, so that the original is difficult to recover. In any case, few plaudits are given for pure rediscovery, but originality scores highly. By the time the idea is rediscovered, institutions and behaviour have changed, so that simple recovery is not really what is needed. It is my hope, however, that this exploration of some history of three key ideas in endogenous-money theory will shed some light on the rediscovery in which we have all been engaged since the early 1980s.

In particular, I draw the following conclusion: The idea that bank asset-expansion is chiefly responsible for determining the money supply – a point on which all 'second-wave' endogenous-money theorists agree – was at one time widely accepted. It was lost in favour of the money-base theory through very subtle changes of emphasis and language. Partly through excessive formalisation of the multiplier and partly through reinterpreting cash reserves from a limitation on banks to an instrument of control, the multiplier came to support the monetarist project. (I have not even mentioned the effect of IS-LM in macroeconomics in support of this, but the influence is profound.) Recognition of the multiple sources of cash to the banking system and the importance of secondary reserves have given way to a simple relation between central-bank money and bank money: $M = mH$. Hence, some modern endogenous-money theorists may have argued for a passive central bank in reaction. An elastic supply of high-powered money may indeed reflect the facts and be defended on those grounds (see Lavoie, this volume), but there is no need to adopt it on the grounds that the money-base theory is the only alternative.

References

Agger, E.E. (1918) *Organized Banking* (New York: Holt).
Ahmed, S. (1970) 'Is Money Net Wealth?', *Oxford Economic Papers*, 22, pp. 357–61.
Angell, J.A. and Ficek, K.F. (1933) 'Expansion of Bank Credit', *Journal of Political Economy*, 41, pp. 1–32 and 152–93.
Auerbach, R.D. (1985) *Money, Banking and Financial Markets* (New York: Macmillan).
Bagehot, W. (1873) *Lombard Street* (London: P.S. King).
Barger, H. (1964) *The Management of Money* (New York: Rand McNally).

Bernstein, E.M. (1935) *Money and the Economic System* (Chapel Hill: University of North Carolina Press).

Boughton, J.M. and Wicker, E.R. (1975) *The Principles of Monetary Economics* (Homewood, IL.: R.D. Irwin).

Chandler, L. (1959) *The Economics of Money and Banking*, 3rd edn (New York: Harper). First US edn 1948.

Chick, V. (1977) *The Theory of Monetary Policy* (2nd edn, Oxford: Blackwell) (1st edn, London: Gray-Mills, 1973).

Chick, V. (1986) 'The Evolution of the Banking System and the Theory of Saving, Investment and Interest', *Économies et sociétés*, Cahiers de l'ISMEA, Paris, Série 'Monnaie et Production', 3, pp. 111–26.

Cochran, J.A. (1979) *Money, Banking and the Economy*, 4th edn (New York: Macmillan).

Crick, W.F. (1927) 'The Genesis of Bank Deposits', *Economica*, 7, pp. 191–202. (Repr. in F.A. Lutz and L.W. Mints, (eds) *Readings in Monetary Theory* (New York: Blakiston, 1951).) Page references to reprint. [Keynes (1930) and Schumpeter (1954) both give Crick's initials as F.W. He appears as W.F. in the original source.]

Crowther, G. (1940) *An Outline of Money* (London: Thomas Nelson).

Currie, L. (1934) *The Supply and Control of Money in the United States* (Cambridge, MA: Harvard University Press).

Curtis, M. and Townshend, H. (1937) *Modern Money* (London: Harrap).

Davenport, H.J. (1913) *The Economics of Enterprise* (New York: Macmillan).

Dowrie, G.W. (1936) *Money and Banking* (New York: Wiley).

Ellis, H.S. (1934) *German Monetary Theory, 1905–1933* (Cambridge, MA: Harvard University Press).

Frazer, W.J. and Yohe, W.P. (1966) *An Introduction to the Analeptics and Institutions of Money and Banking* (Princeton: Princeton University Press, 1966).

Friedman, M. and Schwartz, A. (1963) *A Monetary History of the United States, 1867–1960* (Princeton University Press for NBER).

Goldfeld, S.M. and Chandler, L.V. (1981) *Economics of Money and Banking* (New York: Harper & Row).

Goodhart, C.A.E. (1975) *Money, Information and Uncertainty*, 1st edition (London: Macmillan).

Goucher, D.J. (1990) *The Monetary and Financial System* (London: Chartered Institute of Bankers).

Gurley, J.G. and Shaw, E.S. (1960) *Money in a Theory of Finance* (Washington: Brookings Institution).

Hall, M.J.B. (1983) *Monetary Policy since 1971* (London: Macmillan).

Hanson, J.L. (1978) *Monetary Theory and Practice*, 6th edn (Plymouth: Macdonald & Evans).

Harrod, R.F. (1969) *Money* (London: Macmillan).

Hart, A.G. (1948) *Money, Debt and Economic Activity* (New York: Prentice-Hall).

Hawtrey, R.G. (1919) *Currency and Credit*, 1st edn (London: Longmans) (4th edn 1950).

Humphrey, T.M. (1987) 'The Theory of Multiple Expansion of Deposits: What it is and Whence it Came', Federal Reserve Bank of Richmond *Economic Review*, pp. 3–11.

Kaufman, G.C. (1973) *Money, the Financial System and the Economy* (Chicago: Rand McNally).

Kent, R.P. (1966) *Money and Banking*, 5th edn (New York: Holt, Rinehart & Winston).

Keynes, J.M. (1930) *A Treatise on Money* (London: Macmillan).

King, D. (1987) *Banking and Money* (Sevenoaks: Edward Arnold).

Klein, J.J. (1982) *Money and the Economy*, 5th edn (New York: Harcourt Brace).
Laidler, D. (1999) *Fabricating the Keynesian Revolution* (Cambridge University Press).
Laughlin, J.L. (1903) *The Principles of Money* (New York: Scribner).
Laughlin, J.L. (1931) *Money, Credit and Prices*, 2 vols (Chicago: University of Chicago Press).
Lavoie, M. this volume.
Leaf, W. (1999) *Banking* (London: Williams & Norgate, 1926) (Reissued Routledge).
Lombra, R. and Torto, R. (1973) 'Federal Reserve "Defensive" Behavior and the Reverse Causation Argument', *Southern Economic Journal*, 40, pp. 47–55.
Macleod, H.D. (1855–6) *Theory and Practice of Banking* (London: Longmans).
Marshall, A. (1965 [1923]) *Money, Credit and Commerce* (New York, Kelley).
Marshall, R.H. and Swanson, R.B. (1974) *The Monetary Process* (Boston: Houghton Mifflin).
McKenna, R. (1925) 'Commodity Prices and the Gold Standard', in R. McKenna (ed.) *Post-war Banking Policy: A Series of Addresses* (London: Heinemann, 1928), pp. 88–103.
Meade, J.E. (1934) 'The Amount of Money and the Banking System', *Economic Journal*, 44, pp. 77–83.
Meigs, A.J. (1972) *Money Matters* (New York: Harper & Row).
Mills, R.C. and Walker, E.R. (1952) *Money*, 13th edn (Sydney: Angus & Robertson).
Mishkin, F.S. (1986) *The Economics of Money, Banking, and Financial Markets* (Boston: Little, Brown).
Newlyn, W.T. (1971) *Theory of Money* (Oxford University Press).
Nogaro, B. (1927) *Modern Monetary Systems* (London: P.S. King).
Pesek, B.P. and Saving, T.R. (1967) *Money, Wealth and Economic Theory* (New York: Macmillan).
Peterson, J.M. and Cawthorne, D.R. (1941) *Money and Banking* (New York: Macmillan).
Phillips, C.A. (1920) *Bank Credit* (New York: Macmillan).
Prather, C.L. (1937) *Money and Banking* (Chicago: Business Publications).
Ritter, L.S. and Silber, W.S. (1970) *Money*, 1st edn (New York: Basic Books) (3rd edn, 1977).
Robertson, D.H. (1928) *Money*, 3rd edn (London: Nisbet).
Sause, G.G. (1966) *Money, Banking and Economic Activity* (Boston: D.C. Heath).
Sayers, R.S. (1939) *Modern Banking*, 1st edn (Oxford University Press) (6th edn, 1964).
Schumpeter, J.A. (1934 [1912]) *The Theory of Economic Development*, trans. R. Opie (Cambridge, MA: Harvard Economic Studies) (First published in German, 1912).
Schumpeter, J.A. (1954) *A History of Economic Analysis* (London: Allen & Unwin).
Scott, R.H. (1995) *Money, Financial Markets and the Economy* (Singapore: Prentice-Hall).
Shapiro, E., Solomon, E. and White, W.L. (1968) *Money and Banking* (New York: Holt, Rinehart & Winston).
Shaw, E.S. (1950) *Money, Income and Monetary Policy* (Chicago: R.D. Irwin).
Skidelsky, R. (1995) 'J.M. Keynes and the Quantity Theory of Money', in M. Blaug *et al.*, *The Quantity Theory of Money: from Locke to Keynes and Friedman* (Cheltenham: Edward Elgar).
Smith, H.M. (1968) *The Essentials of Money and Banking* (New York: Random House).
Smith, P.F. (1978) *Money and Financial Intermediaries* (Englewood Cliffs: Prentice-Hall).
Struthers, J. and Speight, H. (1986) *Money: Institutions, Theory and Policy* (London: Longmans).
Thomas, L.B. Jr (1979) *Money, Banking and Economic Activity* (Englewood Cliffs: Prentice-Hall).

Thomas, R.G. (1964) *Our Modern Monetary System*, 4th edn (Englewood Cliffs: Prentice-Hall).

Tobin, J. (1963) 'Commercial Banks as Creators of "Money"', in D. Carson, (ed.) *Banking and Monetary Studies* (Homewood, IL: R.D. Irwin).

Walker, F.A. (1981) *Money* (New York: Macmillan).

Whittlesey, C.R. (1948) *Principles and Practice of Money and Banking* (New York: Macmillan).

Withers, H. (1909) *The Meaning of Money* (London: Smith, Elder).

Weil, P. (1991) 'Is Money Net Wealth?', *International Economic Review*, 32, pp. 37–53.

Wray, L.R. (1990) *Money and Credit in Capitalist Economies* (Aldershot: Edward Elgar).

4
Alternative Theories of the Rate of Interest: A Reconsideration*

Gunnar Heinsohn and Otto Steiger

> We now know that it is not enough to think of the rate of interest
> as a single link between the financial and industrial sectors of the
> economy; for that really implies that a borrower can borrow as
> much as he likes at the rate of interest charged, *no attention being
> paid to the security offered*. (Hicks 1980–1, p. 153, n. 11, our emphasis)

Schumpeter's and Keynes's criticism of the neoclassical theory of the rate of interest: money *precedes* goods

The view of money as a special good was so deeply burnt into economic thought after neoclassical theory had stormed the universities of the Western world for forty years that, in 1911, a trailblazer like Joseph Schumpeter was required to inform a learned public that the entrepreneur, 'before he requires any goods whatsoever, he requires ... money, and which is not based upon goods already produced' (1911, pp. 102 and 112).

A quarter of a century later, in 1936, John Maynard Keynes analysed Schumpeter's discovery from the viewpoint of the distinction between savings and investment, developing the notion that credit by the banking system allows investment without previous savings and that savings only occur as a result of the increase in income due to an increase of investment (1936, p. 82 f.)[1]: 'No one can save without acquiring an asset, whether it be cash or a debt or capital-goods; no one can acquire an asset which he did not previously possess, unless *either* an asset of equal value is newly produced *or* someone else parts with an asset which he previously had' (p. 81 f.).

---

*This chapter is a late 'thank you' to Augusto Graziani for being the first economist who published a very early version of our theory in English, see Heinsohn and Steiger 1983. Later, he (1997, p. 160) emphasised that, without adhering to every detail of our approach to interest and money, it discusses a fundamental weakness not only of the orthodox theories of money, but also of the more heterodox ones that, like the circulation approach, are not so far from ours.

Keynes differed from Schumpeter, however, by recognising more clearly that one cannot have money disconnected from savings goods without fully replacing the neoclassical time preference theory of the rate of interest as determined by savings and investment.

Keynes moved away from such a physical view towards a monetary theory of interest. Schumpeter, on the other hand, was not keen to develop a truly alternative theory disconnected from goods by focusing on 'the creation of new purchasing power created *out of nothing*' (p. 73, our emphasis). He replaced only the neoclassical time preference of the creditor for consumption goods as the cause of interest by a time preference of the borrower – his famous 'innovative entrepreneur' – for out-of-nothing money. Schumpeter argued that its instantly available purchasing power means that 'the possession of a sum of money is a means of obtaining a bigger sum. On this account, and to this extent, a present sum will be normally valued more highly than a future sum. Therefore, present sums of money... will have a value premium, which also leads to a price premium. *And in this lies the explanation of interest'* (p. 190).

For Schumpeter, the expected rate of profit is the decisive and sole determinant of the rate of interest. Thus, the goods resulting from his entrepreneur-driven, profit-seeking development would not only suck up temporary 'credit inflation' caused by 'uncovered bank-note[s]' (p. 109) but also provide the so far unaccounted surplus for paying interest. All this, however, could only be achieved, as long as the 'out of nothing' notes would be exclusively 'placed at the entrepreneur's disposal' (p. 108), and not be given to consumers who should only borrow traditional commodity money or coins, that is, an already existing 'quantity of metal money' (p. 106). Otherwise, Schumpeter observes, 'credit inflation for consumptive purposes' (p. 110) would occur.

How can Schumpeter seriously speak of two different types of money? Because to him only precious metal coins are money proper whereas money notes are 'credit instruments' or 'bank means of payment for redemption' (p. 112 f.). Thus, he confuses the note of a bank of issue, the banknote, with so-called 'credit money' created by banks that cannot issue such notes themselves. He does not understand that every banknote is created in a credit contract but that it must never be confused with this contract. The latter only establishes a claim to redeem banknotes (cf. Stadermann and Steiger, 2001, pp. 312–14; and see 2005).

Where does the money come from in Schumpeter's and Keynes's theories?

In Schumpeter's discussion of the creation of money collateral is explicitly considered. After all, he uses the image of creating credit as a process of minting out property:

Some kind of security... makes it much easier for him [the entrepreneur] in practice to obtain credit. But it does not belong to the nature of the thing in its purest form... It follows then that the statement that credit as it were *'coins property'* is not a sufficient formulation of the matter.... The frequent foundation... upon some kind of collateral only eliminates the insecurity which otherwise exists, but does not alter the fact that there is no new supply of products corresponding to the new demand for products proceeding from it (1911, p. 100 f., our emphasis).

Schumpeter fully understands that the pledging of collateral has nothing to do with activating goods that otherwise would lay idle. Since, however, he does not distinguish a property title from a possession title, he does not comprehend what it is that is offered when collateral is pledged. Therefore, Schumpeter's view of the possible role of collateral in the creation of money nearly ends in a revival of the classical real bills doctrine by which bills of exchange as 'credit means of payment' (Schumpeter) are indeed based on already existing goods. We will, however, see (pp. 75–8) that in a credit contract the debtor only pledges the property side of his assets as collateral whereas he continues undisturbed with the possession side of the very same assets; that is, continues the right to use its returns. We will also see that prospective entrepreneurs may simply not want to pledge as collateral what they 'may happen to own' (1911, p. 106) because they prefer the yield accruing of property unburdened and free. This immaterial yield we have termed 'property premium'. Thus, only a possession may lay idle whereas a property either yields property premium or employs it in collateralisation. Schumpeter's dictum of new purchasing power created 'out of nothing', thus, is not so much a witty point but a clever evasion of answering the question of where money comes from in the first place.

Schumpeter's ignorance of collateral makes him look for other restrictions in the money creating process. He identifies them in the innovative entrepreneur's possible failure to pay interest and to redeem his debt. In this case, Schumpeter states, 'the banker intervenes with purchasing power drawn from the circular flow, for example with money saved by other people' (1911, p. 113). This is a funny view of the operations of a bank. He does not understand that a banker has to cover his debtor's bad loans with his equity in case the insolvent has not pledged collateral. Even more bewildering is Schumpeter's proposal that the banker may pay the loss with his liabilities to his clients. In short, a bank lending against no collateral will endanger its own solvency (cf. Stadermann and Steiger, 2001, p. 314; and see 2005b).

Keynes was not prepared to settle with two different types of money – banknotes for the producer and metal money for the consumer. Yet, he was certainly looking for something akin to Schumpeter's 'uncovered' money. Like the latter, however, he eventually had to leave unanswered the question as to how such money was created. Terms like 'banking system' or the public being willing or unwilling to 'release cash' (Keynes, 1937b, p. 667) hide his perplexity rather than enlighten the problem. However, formulations like 'existing cash' (p. 665) and 'new cash provided by the banks' (p. 665) or 'supply of hoards' (Keynes, 1937a, p. 250) and a 'revolving fund which can be used over and over again [and which]...does not absorb or exhaust any resources' (p. 247) undoubtedly underline Keynes's dismissal of neoclassical liquid resources in favour of a money that exists '*before* the investment takes place, that is to say, before the corresponding saving has taken place' (p. 246). Still, by relegating the creation of such money to 'business, banking and personal techniques and habits' (Keynes, 1938, p. 233) we do not understand this process any better.

At the heart of Keynes's view of money in *General Theory* lies his idea that it is a link between the known presence of the economy and its uncertain future (1936, p. 293). This means that money is not merely a means of exchange and a measure of value but is first of all an asset held and preferred over all others. Keynes uses a broad definition of money including not only central bank money but also banking deposits up to three months and treasury bills. This mix of money and (short) debts weakens his most promising distinction between 'money of account' and 'money proper' in *Treatise* (1930a, p. 3). Money of account comes into existence along with debt contracts and 'price lists'. Money proper can only exist in relation to the former. At the same time, however, Keynes, as a follower of Georg Friedrich Knapp (1905), holds that money proper is always 'State money' (1930a, p. 6).

Keynes knows that private debt titles, which may be used to discharge liabilities and which he calls 'bank money', must not be confused with money proper (Keynes, 1930a, p. 6). However, when the state declares his debt titles as an acceptable discharge of a liability, they become a particular kind of bank money – a species of money proper that he terms 'representative' or state money: 'A particular kind of bank money is then transformed into money proper which we may call representative money. When, however, what was merely a debt has become money proper, it has changed its character and should no longer be reckoned as a debt, since it is of the essence of a debt to be enforceable in terms of something other than itself' (p. 6).

The flaw in this reasoning is threefold (cf. Stadermann and Steiger, 2001, p. 289 f.; and see 2005b): (i) Keynes confuses the mutual clearing of debt titles with a substitution of debts for money proper. However, the former do not substitute the latter, instead clearing is substituted for the payment of money; (ii) Keynes also confuses debt titles offered by a creditor with debt titles offered by a debtor. Only the former may use the title as a substitute for the payment in money proper, while for the latter the title is a possibility to loan money; (iii) in his discussion of 'bank money', Keynes lumps together a variety of claims that must be clearly distinguished. 'Bank money' does not only comprise bills of exchange and cheques – with which debtors bring claims against themselves into circulation – but also banknotes, which are claims against the bank of issue. Keynes does not see that the central bank's creation of money through buying debt titles from its counterparty commercial bank deals with titles that are not issued by this very debtor. Yet, the commercial bank in its role as creditor to the issuer of such eligible titles has to guarantee them with its own capital to achieve access to the central bank.

The 1937 debate on 'Alternative Theories of the Rate of Interest'

Though Keynes's groping in the dark as to the creation of money is only too obvious, his opponents in the famous debate on 'Alternative Theories of the Rate of Interest' in the *Economic Journal* of 1937 and elsewhere immediately after the publication of *General Theory* – John Hicks (1936), Bertil Ohlin (1937a and 1937b), Ralph Hawtrey (1937a and 1937b) and Dennis Robertson (1937 and 1940) – never took him to task for his aberrance. Rather, they could see nothing new in his monetary theory of interest.

Therefore, economic theory has lost almost seven decades – or nearly a century after Schumpeter's first bold moves in 1911 – because the protagonists of the new thinking had something fundamental in common with the defenders of the old faith: a stunning lack of understanding the creation of money and of methodological rigour to formulate a satisfactory theory of interest. These shortcomings gave the neoclassical theory of interest a new lease to life.

Keynes's theory of the rate of interest was formulated as the liquidity preference theory of interest. It attacked the neoclassical explanation of interest as determined by savings and investment that he himself had still adhered to in *Treatise*. In *General Theory*, his point was that the rate of interest can never be a reward for savings because savings, with income being a variable, are the result of investment and not its source. The rate of interest arises only after the choice out of a given income between consumption and saving – fundamental in the neoclassical explanation – has been made. It arises out of the choice for the form in which savings are held; that is, between 'bank money' or interest-bearing debt titles: 'The rate of interest is not the "price" which brings into equilibrium the demand for resources to invest with the readiness to abstain from present consumption. It is the "price" which equilibrates the desire to hold wealth in the form of cash with the available quantity of cash' (Keynes, 1936, p. 167).

The desire to hold cash Keynes has termed 'its *liquidity-premium*' (p. 226, our emphasis). The rate of interest, therefore, is a materialisation of this premium. The actual rate of interest is determined by the quantity of money supplied exogenously by the 'banking system' and so on in conjunction with liquidity preference.

The flaw in Keynes's explanation of the rate of interest out of giving up the liquidity premium on money is twofold: (i) most fundamentally, the choice between 'bank money' and debt titles simply presupposes the existence of money. Keynes does not recognize that the rate of interest arises already with the creation of money proper; that is, *before* it can be given up (Heinsohn and Steiger, 1996, pp. 194–205; and see 2000, 496); (ii) not only debt titles but also 'bank money' bears a rate of interest, although a lower one (Stadermann and Steiger, 2001, p. 301 f., and see 2005b).

Other than Keynes, Schumpeter never bothered about the basic question of economics[2] as to the loss of a creditor that has to be compensated by interest. People are ready to lend money 'provided they get a premium which more than compensates them for the disturbance which the lending of sums held for definitive purposes must entail'. This explanation reflects Keynes's belief in a 'revolving fund' where fixed liquid resources are borrowed and where 'it is impossible with a given money sum to obtain a greater money sum' (Schumpeter, 1911, p. 189). Therefore, he leaves us in the dark as to why banks demand interest for money created 'out of nothing'. After all, they do not suffer a 'disturbance'.

Schumpeter's and Keynes's discovery – that money lent for new investment must not be confused with neoclassical loans of money, which are loaned resources in monetary form – was never understood in the 1937 debate. The critics rather felt that Keynes – with his seductive terms 'loanable funds' or 'liquid resources' – had made a fine, though involuntary, contribution to a better formulation of the neoclassical theory of interest: 'Thus I remain of the opinion that Mr. Keynes' apparatus and the "loanable funds" apparatus are not "radically opposed to one another" ' (Robertson, 1937, p. 432).

Keynes's loanable funds are always a stock of money that is not related whatsoever to resources or – in Robertson's disapproving words – for Keynes there seems to be 'no connection between idle money and the process of saving' (Robertson, 1937, p. 428). Keynes's critics, however, perceived of loanable funds as mainly a supply of resources – 'a certain agent of production' (Robertson, 1937, p. 428). The loanable funds contain: (i) current savings; (ii) liquidation of past savings; (iii) net dishoardings of cash balances; and (iv) net additional bank loans – the emphasis being on the first and third items. Hoards are defined as resources held in the form of money. Investment not financed by resources saved must be financed by dishoarding of resources held; that is, out of an already existing money stock.

In the discussion on Keynes's and Robertson's theories of interest, the latter was helped by Keynes's assertion in *General Theory* that 'liquidity preference', the desire to hold cash, would be absent in a 'static society' or in one 'in which no one feels any uncertainty about future rates of interest' (Keynes, 1936, p. 208). This explanation of the phenomenon of interest out of the uncertainty of its future rate can be regarded as an alternative theory to Keynes's liquidity premium theory of the rate of interest. Robertson ridiculed the 'uncertainty' explanation as a 'bootstrap' theory that leaves the neoclassical theory unharmed. 'Thus, the rate of interest is what it is because it is expected to become other than it is; if it is not expected to become other than it is, there is nothing left to tell us why it is what it is. The organ which secretes it has been amputated, and yet it somehow still exists – a grin without a cat... If we ask what ultimately governs the judgements of wealth-owners as to why the rate of interest should be different in the future from what it is to-day, we are surely led straight back to *the fundamental phenomena of Productivity and Thrift'* (Robertson, 1940, p. 25; our emphasis).[3]

The modern version of Robertson's loanable funds theory of interest assumes that saving is directed wholly to the purchase of securities and that investment is financed entirely by issuing securities (Horwich, 1997, pp. 400b–404a). In the simplest formulation of the model as a stock-flow-equilibrium, both stock and flow markets are in equilibrium at the same real rate of interest: (i) the flow market of real savings and investment on the one side; and (ii) the stock markets of (a) the demand and supply for real money balances, and (b) the demand and supply for existing securities. An increased demand for investment in this model is regarded as an increased demand for loanable funds. If this is not matched by current savings, it must lead to an excess flow supply of securities, which in turn leads to a fall in their price and rise in their yield. This rise in the rate of interest induces holders of the existing stock of assets to hold more securities and fewer cash balances. With total output fixed, the general price level rises and the real money balances fall until the rate of interest rises to its new, higher 'natural' level as determined by (existing) savings and (increased) investment or 'the forces of thrift and productivity' (Horwich, 1997, p. 403b).

Own capital and collateral: the missing links in the theory of the rate of interest[4]

In accordance with Schumpeter and Keynes – but in contradiction to the latter's neoclassical and neo-Keynesian opponents – we still have to understand the money preceding goods or savings because these masters simply obscured it. Our key of understanding is provided by our distinction between *possession* and *property*, which the entire economic profession to the time of writing has failed to make the starting point of the analysis of what turns a mere reproduction system into an economy.[5] This judgement may sound high-nosed. Yet, as has recently been vindicated by one of the most eminent scholars of the theory of property rights or new institutional economics, Harold Demsetz (1998, p. 144a), 'Although our theoretical ideas about capitalism have improved as mainstream economics developed, they have never matured into a theory of capitalism'. Demsetz himself, however, cannot identify the very core of property rights: 'They designate the owner as that person or group, as compared to others, that exercises the most important subset of exclusive, alienable, and presumptive rights. There is no easy way to generalize "important subset"' (p. 146a). His failure is due to the confusion of possession rights with property rights. The former are restricted to the physical use of goods and resources whereas true property rights are claims that entitle their holders to the intangible, non-physical capacities: (i) to burden in issuing money against interest; (ii) to encumber as collateral for obtaining money; (iii) to alienate by sale and lease; and (iv) to enforce by law.

We focus on the employment of property as own capital and collateral because – with the notable exception of James Steuart (cf. Stadermann and Steiger, 2001, pp. 45–86; and see 2005a) – the most obvious property rights of burdening and encumbrance have escaped all schools of economic thought, albeit the simple existence of at least collateral has not gone entirely unnoticed in mainstream economics. The most comprehensive compendium of our discipline, *The New Palgrave Dictionary of Economics* of 1987, carries no entry on 'collateral'. An independent entry on this term was first introduced in *The New Palgrave Dictionary on Money and Finance* of 1992 (Kanatas, 1992, pp. 381a–83a), thereby living up to our motto above (Hicks's, 1980–81) that an explanation of the rate of interest must pay attention to the securities involved. Kanatas's entry makes clear that collateral has eventually been noticed because neoclassical assumptions about market exchange of goods are in obvious contradiction to phenomena in the credit market. Until the 1980s the credit market was analysed as a market for goods; that is, the price on the credit market, the rate of interest, is determined solely by demand and supply of credit. In the 1937 debate with Keynes, it was Bertil Ohlin who most vigorously took this position. 'The truth is that the price of 3 per cent bonds – and thus the long term rate of interest – is fixed on the bond market by the demand and supply curves in the same way as the price of eggs or strawberries on a village market.... The rate of interest is the price of credit, and is governed by the supply and demand *curves* in the same way as commodity prices' (Ohlin, 1937b, pp. 424 and 427).

First in 1981, Joseph Stiglitz, founder of the New Keynesian credit rationing school, rediscovered the importance of collateral for understanding the credit market. Although his explanation is not as straight forward as it should be, Stiglitz's ideas can be formulated as follows. In the market for goods, an excess demand is, indeed, met in the short run by an increase of prices, and in the long run by a rise of supply induced by the short run rise in prices leading to a reduction of prices. In the credit market, however, an increase of demand met by a rise in its price, the rate of interest, would lead to the problem that interest is only a promised price. Other than the supplier of goods, the creditor has to take into account that the ability of the debtor to repay the loan is directly correlated to the levels of the rate of interest promised. When the debtor is unable to refund the loss, the profit of the creditor is diminished. Supposedly, this risk is circumvented by 'credit rationing' (Stiglitz and Weiss, 1981, especially pp. 393–5; and see Jaffee and Stiglitz, 1990, p. 854), which requires a ranking of debtors according to their creditworthiness. As Stiglitz assumes the existence of a principal–agent problem between the creditor and the debtor (so called 'asymmetric' information) the necessary information for creditworthiness is provided by information on the assets potential debtors can pledge as collateral. However, Stiglitz, not looking at collateral as a property title, does not understand that, without collateral, there would be an asymmetric distribution of *risk* between the contract partners – a risk of loss that cannot be ruled out by symmetric information. Even with perfect information about the debtor, the creditor cannot do without the debtor's securities. Otherwise the creditor would risk his own capital as soon as the debtor is unable to fulfil his obligations. Since rationing to market principles, it leaves New Keynesians uneasy. After all, there is no systematic place for credit rationing in their theory of free market exchange, because the physical use of collateral is not exchanged but stays with the debtor. Because of this most uncomfortable fact, New Keynesians simply concede that there is 'little definitive evidence on the relative economic importance of the ... explanations regarding collateral' (Kanatas, 1992, p. 382b).

The property paradigm as an alternative theory of the rate of interest

Economists' bewildering failure to distinguish possession and property and the neglect of collateral and own capital are due, according to Gunnar Heinsohn and Otto Steiger (1996; and see 2000),[6] to a more common failure to distinguish between the character of goods and resources in different societal structures. Three distinctive systems of material reproduction are known in history. They are: (i) custom-based communities (tribes) controlled by reciprocity; (ii) feudal reigns or lord ships (including state socialism) controlled by command; and (iii) property-based societies controlled by interest and money – the only system that with due right can be labelled an economic system. While in the two former systems only possession exists as the de facto right physically to use a good or resource, in the latter property exists as the de jure right to burden, to encumber, to sell to lease and to enforce *in addition* to possession, thereby making it a de jure right too. Only in the property-based system there exist two types of return: (i) the return of the physical use of the possessed goods and resources (which now are commodities and assets; see below); that is, a material yield; and (ii) the return of the title to the property of the commodities and assets, which is an immaterial yield. The latter yield is the starting point for understanding an economic system and one we label 'property premium' (1996, p. 15; and see 2000, p. 67).

A title to property never comes naturally. It can only be brought about by a legal act, which by definition is intangible and initially does not alter the possession state of resources. However, as a property title resources are transformed into saleable and rentable and, therefore, valuable, assets – in the same way as property rights turn mere goods into commodities. As soon as property is created – indeed ex nihilo – it carries the unearned property premium. This premium – it has to be stressed time and again – does not derive from the physical use of assets. Nor does it accrue from some pre-existing money.

What is the meaning of property premium? It is a non-physical yield of security inherent to assets. It allows proprietors of the assets to enter credit contracts and is a measure of the potential of private[7] individuals to become a creditor or debtor. While only unburdened property is a free asset, burdening turns the asset into a 'liability' that, however, is not necessarily encumbered. An unburdened asset entails the capacity of a creditor to issue notified titles to his property, his own capital; that is, to act like a credit bank of issue creating money notes. An unencumbered asset entails the capacity of a debtor to borrow the money notes by pledging titles to his property as collateral, thereby not only burdening but also encumbering it.

In principal, every proprietor can issue anonymised claims against his property that take the form of transferable documents or notes to be redeemable in the issuer's property because otherwise they would not be accepted or circulate. However, in the evolution of money, both in antiquity and early modern times, only those creditors survived as issuers of money-notes who, as solvent proprietors with a high ratio of own capital, established strong credit banks.

By burdening and, therefore, blocking property in the money issuing contract, the credit bank gives up immaterial property premium in exchange for a specified amount of the same type of titles promised by its debtor: the rate of interest. The debtor, in addition to this promise, has to secure the refunding of the loan by the pledging of collateral. Thereby, his property premium is turned into liquidity premium attached to the money-notes he receives. The collateralised property of the debtor must be at least equal in value to the notes loaned to him. The notes are neither state debt titles transformed into 'representative money' (Keynes), nor given resources in monetary form (Robertson *et al.*), nor out-of-nothing money created endogenously in a loan contract in which collateral is not essential (Schumpeter).

As long as the debtor fulfils his obligations, the bank is not allowed to touch the collateral; that is, by using it for redemption of its notes. This has to be done by the bank's own capital. Therefore, interest is not only a compensation for the credit bank's loss of property premium but stands simultaneously for the fact that the latter does not gain the debtor's property premium.

This is why interest is demanded by the credit bank and why it is paid by its debtor. In other words: why only loaned money-notes or liabilities of a debtor carry interest and money notes per se or 'liabilities' of a creditor none. James Steuart (1767, II, p. 132; our emphasis) has named the difference between both types of liabilities the '*advantage of circulation*'. Stadermann and Steiger (2001, p. 69) have brought out this advantage as follows: '*Debtors pay interest because only the bank* [of issue] *is able to let the debtor keep the possession side of his collateral and* [at the same time] *guarantees its property side.'* The credit bank cannot help but to establish its own standard at the very moment it issues notes or money proper. Therefore, Keynes (1930a, p. 3) was right in his insistence that money proper can only exist in relation to a standard of measurement, the money of account. This standard must reckon the issued notes in terms of an abstract unit necessary for denominating their amount in the debt contract in which they are created. It must not be confused with a standard of measurement that is derived from a standard physical good as unit of account or *numéraire* as in neoclassical theory.

In the neoclassical model of a barter economy, the commodity chosen as unit of account is assigned the price 1 (one) and serves, thereby, as the nominal anchor for the prices of all other goods. However, this anchor can only help to express their exchange ratios or relative prices. In the truly monetary economy based on property, the credit bank does not need a commodity selected as a nominal anchor. Instead it issues – denominated in its money of account – money notes as anonymised claims to its assets as property, but never to the assets as possession. Uno actu with the credit bank's setting a money of account by granting a loan, all property titles receive prices in this standard and are, thereby, nominal or money prices.

The creation of money cannot be separated from the process of loaning it to a proprietor-debtor. Thus, both the issuing of money-notes and the establishment of a loan contract occur uno actu. Money is created in a credit contract but is not itself a credit.[8] Interest settled in this contract goes to the credit bank who, by issuing notes redeemable in the net worth of its property – its own capital – has lost property premium which must be compensated. The money-notes go to the debtor who also has lost property premium but who, at the same time, not only has gained the borrowed money-notes' liquidity premium but, in addition, preserved his right to use the possession side of the collateral pledged to the credit bank.

Our thesis, that property has to be blocked temporarily for the issue of money, also pertains to the case of 'non-redeemable money' in the modern two-stage banking system, where the bank of issue is the central bank as the monopoly issuer of money and the debtor its counterparty commercial bank. However, as distinct from a one-stage banking system, with competing private credit banks as issuers of money, in the two-stage banking system any holder of the central bank's notes – the non-bank public – at the time of writing is no longer allowed to redeem them. This right is restricted to the counterparty of the central bank, the commercial bank, who redeems the money loaned when it refunds its credit.

In the two-stage banking system, the commercial bank can give up the money loaned – lose its liquidity premium – by loaning it at another, higher rate of interest than that paid to the central bank. It goes without saying that Keynes's liquidity premium or monetary theory of the rate of interest overlooks the rate of interest charged by the central bank. The latter exists before liquidity premium can be transformed into interest charged by the commercial bank. Therefore, Keynes's explanation of the rate of interest is one step short.

In the money-creating contract, creditor and debtor retain their material possessions, whose immaterial property titles are pledged to guarantee the circulation of money (by the creditor) and to collateralise the contract (by the debtor). Both continue with their possessions' capacity to earn a material yield that exists beyond their property side; that is, the immaterial yield of property premium. Therefore, goods are never transferred in a loan contract as the neoclassical theory of the rate of interest suggests.

On the other hand, the money transferred in these contracts is not a special good as emphasized by Keynes in his discussion of the particular characteristics of money in chapter 17 of *General Theory*. According to his view, money differs from other goods only insofar as both its elasticity of production and its elasticity of substitution goods are nearly equal to zero. However, Keynes's characterisation of money completely fails to recognise its role in the property-based economy. Money's low elasticity of production is a necessary condition for money to be accepted in contracts. For this, it is necessary that money is brought into circulation only against the market rate of interest and good securities, and not by arbitrary issue. And its low elasticity of substitution is a necessary consequence of the denomination of all contracts in the money of account, since money alone is able to finally dissolve the contracts and cannot, therefore, be replaced by goods.

We now understand that money proper is never created ex nihilo from the viewpoint of property titles that – albeit no material things – must always exist before money can come into existence. Schumpeter's paradox that money obviously precedes goods can now be solved. Not a physical good but intangible titles to property give rise to money, thereby safeguarding the pre-existence of money over commodities. Keynes's idea that an entrepreneur needs money in a credit contract, and not savings out of real income as neoclassical theory of interest still assumes at the time of writing, was right but lacked substantiation.

We also see that Schumpeter's creditor does not create money out of nothing but out of giving up property premium. Furthermore, we understand why Keynes's creditor can only give up his liquidity premium for interest because he deals with money already created. It is the property premium lost in this process that bestows liquidity premium on money. The property premium can only be understood when burdening and encumbrance – as property titles temporarily parted with and as a possession titles not parted with – is seen as the core of the money creation process. While Schumpeter at least hinted at the idea of collateral, Keynes – not unlike the adherents to the neoclassical theory of interest – did not even bother to consider collateral as a possible source of understanding interest. The distinction between possession and property evaded both of them entirely.

Notes

1. A reference to Schumpeter's discussion (1911, p. 156 of the revised 2nd German edition of 1926 = 108 f. in the abridged English translation of 1934) is not found in *General Theory* but in *Treatise* (Keynes, 1930a), p. 154, n. 1.
2. Keynes had stated this question as follows: 'The question why capital is scarce, is...best regarded as being, in the long run, the same question as why the rate of interest exceeds zero' (1934, p. 456).
3. Forty years later, a prominent Keynesian in no uncertain terms put Keynes's theory to rest: 'Robertson was consistently right on every aspect of the interest rate controversy between himself and Keynes and Keynes' Cambridge followers....I believe it [the liquidity preference theory of interest] to be theoretically unsound, empirically false, and practically dangerous' (Leijonhufvud, 1981, pp. 171, n. 58, and 195; and see 2003, p. 10).
4. This section draws on Heinsohn and Steiger, 2005.
5. Elsewhere, we have shown in detail that economists from the classical school to the modern theory of property rights always mean possession and its physical use when they speak of property. The focus is on collective versus private use of resources identified with collective versus private property (Heinsohn and Steiger, 1996; and see 2000).
6. Meanwhile, Hernando de Soto (2000, pp. 56 and 218) has recognised the striking similarity between his and our theory in explaining economic activity and, furthermore, accepted our property foundation of money. However, while we distinguish between possession and property, de Soto's dichotomy is between 'informal' or de facto rights to property and 'formal' or de jure rights to property, thereby missing that de jure rights to property transform de facto rights to possession into de jure rights too.
7. Private in the Latin sense of the word; that is, without interference by power relations.
8. Of course, money can also be created by buying property titles outright. But in such a case, the problem arises that to control the circulation of money, titles have regularly to be sold outright. This is nothing but a poor imitation of the credit issue of money, which automatically guarantees the reflux of money as, for example, in the form of bills of exchange, the preferred methods of central banks in former times. The credit issue of money, especially as nowadays in the form of repurchase agreements, also has the advantage for the issuing bank that the risk of the titles to depreciate is with its counterparty debtor, the notes receiving commercial bank, while in outright transactions it stays with the central bank as the creditor of the loan.

References

Demsetz, H. (1998) 'Property Rights', in *The New Palgrave Dictionary of Economics and The Law* (London: Macmillan), III, pp. 144–55.
Graziani, A. (1997) Review of G. Heinsohn and O. Steiger, *Eigentum, Zins und Geld. Ungelöste Rätsel der Wirtschaftswissenschaft*. Reinbek: Rowohlt Verlag, 1996, *European Journal of the History of Economic Thought*, 4, pp. 158–60.
Hawtrey, R.G. (1937a) 'Alternative Theories of the Rate of Interest: Three Rejoinders III', *Economic Journal*, 47, pp. 436–43.
Hawtrey, R.G. (1937b) *Capital and Employment* (London: Longman).

Heinsohn, G. and Steiger, O. (1983) 'Private Property, Debts and Interest, or the Origin of Money and the Rise and Fall of Monetary Economies', *Studi economici*, 30 (21), pp. 3–56.

Heinsohn, G. and Steiger, O. (1996) *Eigentum, Zins und Geld: Ungelöste Rätsel der Wirtschaftswissenschaft* (Reinbek: Rowohlt (3rd edn Marburg: Metropolis, 2004; revised English version: *Property, Interest and Money: Foundations of Economic Theory*, London: Routledge, 2005, forthcoming).

Heinsohn, G. and Steiger, O. (2000) 'The Property Theory of Interest and Money', in J. Smithin, (ed.), *What Is Money?* (London: Routledge), pp. 67–100 (Reprint, with corrections and additions, in G.M. Hodgson, (ed.), *Recent Developments in Institutional Economics*, Cheltenham: Edward Elgar, 2003, pp. 484–517).

Heinsohn, G. and Steiger, O. (2005) 'Own Capital and Collateral: the Missing Links in the Theory of the Rate of Interest', in O. Steiger (ed.), *Property Rights, Creditors' Money and the Foundations of the Economy* (Marburg: Metropolis, forthcoming).

Hicks, J.R. (1936) 'Mr. Keynes' Theory of Employment', *Economic Journal*, 46, pp. 238–53.

Hicks, J.R. (1980–81) 'IS–LM: An Explanation', *Journal of Post Keynesian Economics*, 3, pp. 139–54.

Horwich, G. (1997) 'Loanable-Funds Doctrine', in D. Glass, (ed.), *Business Cycles and Depressions: An Encyclopedia* (New York: Garland), pp. 400–4.

Jaffee, D.M. and Stiglitz, J. (1990) 'Credit Rationing', in B.M. Friedman and F.H. Hahn (eds), *Handbook of Monetary Economics* (Amsterdam: North-Holland), II, pp. 837–88.

Kanatas, G. (1992) 'Collateral', in *The New Palgrave Dictionary of Money and Finance* (London: Macmillan), I, pp. 381–3.

Keynes, J.M. (1930a) *A Treatise on Money. Volume 1: The Pure Theory of Money* (1930), in *The Collected Writings of John Maynard Keynes*, V (London: Macmillan, 1971).

Keynes, J.M. (1930b) *A Treatise on Money. Volume 2: The Applied Theory of Money* (1930), in *The Collected Writings of John Maynard Keynes*, VI (London: Macmillan, 1971).

Keynes, J.M. (1934) 'The Propensity to Invest', in *The Collected Writings of John Maynard Keynes*, XIII: *The General Theory And After. Part I: Preparation* (London: Macmillan, 1973), pp. 450–6.

Keynes, J.M. (1936) *The General Theory of Employment, Interest and Money*, in *The Collected Writings of John Maynard Keynes*, VII (London: Macmillan) 1973.

Keynes, J.M. (1937a) 'Alternative Theories of the Rate of Interest', *Economic Journal*, 47, pp. 241–53.

Keynes, J.M. (1937b) 'The "Ex-Ante" Theory of the Rate of Interest', *Economic Journal*, 47, 663–9.

Keynes, J.M. (1938) 'Mr. Keynes on "Finance" ', *Economic Journal*, 48, as quoted in *The Collected Writings of John Maynard Keynes*, XIV: *The General Theory and After. Part II: Defence and Development* (London: Macmillan, 1973), pp. 229–33.

Knapp, G.F. (1905) *The State Theory of Money*, abridged translation from the 4th German edition of 1923 (London: Macmillan, 1924).

Leijonhufvud, A. (1981) 'The Wicksellian Connection: Variations on a Theme', in his *Information and Coordination: Essays in Macroeconomic Theory* (New York and Oxford: Oxford University Press), pp. 131–202.

Leijonhufvud, A. (2003) 'The Long Swings in Economic Understanding', *Discussion Papers of the Dipartimento di Economica di Università degli Studi di Trento*, 3.

Ohlin, B. (1937a) 'Some Notes on the Stockholm Theory of Savings and Investment II', *Economic Journal*, 47, pp. 221–40.

Ohlin, B. (1937b) 'Alternative Theories of the Rate of Interest: Three Rejoinders I', *Economic Journal*, 47, 423–7.

Robertson, D.H. (1936–37) 'Some Notes on Mr. Keynes' General Theory of Employment', *Quarterly Journal of Economics*, 51, pp. 168–91.

Robertson, D.H. (1937) 'Alternative Theories of the Rate of Interest: Three Rejoinders II', *Economic Journal*, 47, 428–36.

Robertson, D.H. (1940) 'Mr Keynes and the Rate of Interest', in his *Essays in Monetary Theory* (London and New York: Staples Press), pp. 1–38.

Schumpeter, J.A. (1911) *The Theory of Economic Development: An Inquiry into Profits, Capital, Credit, Interest, and the Business Cycle*, slightly abridged translation of the revised 2nd German edition of 1926 (Cambridge, MA: Harvard University Press), 1934.

Soto, H. de (2000) *The Mystery of Capital: Why Capitalism Triumphs in the West and Fails Everywhere Else* (London: Bantam Press).

Stadermann, H.-J. and Steiger, O. (2001) *Allgemeine Theorie der Wirtschaf – Erster Band: Schulökonomik*, (Tübingen: Mohr Siebeck).

Stadermann, H.-J. and Steiger, O. (2005a) 'James Steuart and the Theory of the Monetary Economy', in J. Backhaus (ed.), *The Founders of Modern Economics: The Maastricht Lectures in Political Economy* (Cheltenham: Edward Elgar), forthcoming.

Stadermann, H.-J. and Steiger, O. (2005b) 'John Maynard Keynes and the Theory of the Monetary Economy', in J. Backhaus (ed.), *The Founders of Modern Economics: The Maastricht Lectures in Political Economy* (Cheltenham: Edward Elgar), forthcoming.

Steuart, J. (1767) *An Inquiry into the Principles of Political Œconomy: Being an Essay on the Science of Domestic Policy in Free Nations* (London: A. Millar & T. Cadell, I–II) (Reprint Düsseldorf: Verlag Wirtschaft und Finanzen, 1993).

Stiglitz, J. and Weiss, A. (1981) 'Credit Rationing in Markets with Imperfect Information', *American Economic Review*, 71, pp. 393–410.

5
An Inquiry into a Dark Mystery in the History of the Monetary Theory of Production: What Went Wrong with the Early Contribution of Joan Robinson

Alain Parguez

The Robinsonian mystery

In their introduction to the book in honour of Augusto Graziani, Arena and Salvadori (2004) emphasise his paramount contribution to the rehabilitation of history of economic thought. For too many years since the advent of so-called 'mainstream-orthodox economics', studying great economists of the past (before the advent) has been jeopardised by two interwined commitments. On one hand, it is scorned by mainstreamers because it is a waste of time to be interested in pre-scientific writers. They could only be saved if it could be proven that there are some neoclassical roots helping their reinterpretation within the framework of some standard model. On the other hand, it has been progressively turned into a pure historical field of research without any impact on the building of a positive alternate scientific programme that is to be substituted for the mainstream economics. History of economic thought has become the 'refuge' for dissenters who disagree with orthodoxy but, for whatever reason, believe that conceiving a true general theory, free from the methodological and ideological somewhat hidden postulates of mainstreamers, is beyond the possibility of the human mind. From both those perspectives, the search for a genuine precursor of contemporary Monetary Theory of Production (MTP) would be a vain or academic exercise. Both are denied by Graziani's (2003) specific interpretation of the history of economic thought. It is to be fully integrated into the progressive elaboration of the general theory of positive economies. Its sole and self-sufficient justification is to discover how economics of pre-advent times endeavoured to venture beyond the veil of illusion in their search for the fundamental and objective laws of the economic system. As long as the possibility of a general theory is not rejected from the start, its core propositions cannot have been ignored by those economists who desperately strived to find what exists beyond the veil of mere facts and ideological rhetoric. Building a general theory of positive economics requires a tremendous effort to doubt the whole world of 'appearance'. It is a long-term commitment, a genuine Cartesian Meditation in search for the economic 'Cogito'.

So much is to be learned from the efforts of those doubters of olden times, and more from their failure to escape fully from the snare of the Cartesian Genie: the search for precursors that should perfectly fit the positive research programme. To be qualified as a genuine precursor of MTP, an economist of the past must comply with three principles:

1 Of course, either he (she) never explicitly referred to MTP, at least in its ultimate (at least relative to the present time) aspect, or MTP was not the explicit major concern of his (her) exploration;
2 Notwithstanding 1, it is possible to discover some (at least) core propositions of MTP in his (her) work, without any dubious attempt to rewrite it;
3 That part of his (her) work must not be inconsistent with what was the main concern of his (her) work. This means that 2 cannot be just some side issue of the work fully contradicted by the core of the work.

The search for precursors started after the inception of contemporary MTP. It aimed at discovering some explicit or remote roots in the economics of Keynes. I now believe that the search failed because, as shown in 1, those roots do not exist in *The General Theory* (Parguez, 2002); it is highly dubious that they could be found in *A Treatise* (there could be some hint of 2 but it does not comply with 3); and finally, I am not convinced that sound MTP roots had been sowed in the post General Theory writings. At least it cannot be denied that a tremendous energy is required to turn Keynes into a precursor, which is tantamount to the violation of principle 3.

Abstracting from later efforts to discover MTP roots in Kalecki or Post Keynesian economics, and indeed from attempts to find roots in Marx, which I addressed in Parguez (2004), there must remain one obvious precursor that perfectly fits principles 1, 2 and 3, Joan Robinson herself, because of her major contribution to economic theory *The Accumulation of Capital* (1956). Her candidacy to the dignity of a true precursor has been sustained by Lavoie (1999), Rochon (1999), Gnos and Rochon (2003). They refer to book IV of *The Accumulation of Capital* (AOC), including chapters 23 and 24. Their claim was somewhat of a surprise for most (if not all) former readers (including myself) of AOC, for whom Joan Robinson was remembered for her crucial contribution to the debunking of the production function and her life-long attempt to build an alternate real framework unveiling the fundamental long-run laws ruling the real structure of capitalism. So shocking was the revelation of Joan Robinson as a precursor that it could have been triggered by another revelation, Sraffa as a precursor! One could argue that Joan Robinson had already been praised for her contribution to monetary theory but who praised her and for what? She was honoured by Hahn who obviously ignored MTP and had only in mind her analyses of choice between assets as if she were some precursor of Tobin portfolio choice theory.[1] It seems that one cannot doubt the defence of Joan Robinson's advocates, who successfully prove by their careful exegesis of the text that she had discovered the most crucial aspects of MTP. They assume that chapters 23 and 24 fit the three precursor's principles which lead them to the fundamental proposition:

> Joan Robinson is the sole genuine precursor of MTP. Not the least painful work of interpretation is required to prove her discovery.

Herein lies one of the darkest mysteries of the history of economic thought: how can we explain that half a century was spent in seeking precursors that could not be, while the Robinsonian discovery was ignored and fell into obscurity? The mystery goes deeper, and it is much more agonizing. There had been one reader of AOC who discovered the Robinsonian contribution to MTP and proved that she was 'The' precursor. This bold advocate was Augusto Graziani (1989) in his contribution to a collective book dedicated to Joan Robinson. Let us therefore emphasise the core propositions of chapters 23 and 24 which, according to Graziani's defence (all references are from AOC), embody MTP, at least its Italian version:

1 Without money, no capitalist economy (and no economy beyond its Robin's aspect p. 25) can exist;
2 In a genuine positive economy, money exists in the abstract aspect of notes created by banks at the request of firms having to spend to acquire the labour force to be invested in the ongoing production process;
3 Chapter 23 relies on the explicit distinction between initial and final finance. Initial finance is the amount of notes firms instantaneously invest in the payment of the wage bill, which must be dubbed the wage-bill postulate. Final finance is the amount of notes that goes back to firms out of the sale of their output or the sale of bonds to savers;
4 Joan Robinson explains the banks rate by the fundamental quasi-hierarchical relationship between firms and banks. Firms have to pay an interest on the borrowed notes, which can be deemed exogenous relative to conventional portfolio choices. Bank rate is fully independent of the Keynesian preference for liquidity;
5 The distinction between notes and deposits is quite explicit. Joan Robinson is straightforward: the issue of new deposits is the outcome of savers' desire for liquidity. Deposits reflect a debt of banks to savers. They are a component of saving because they are part of final finance;[2]

6 What matters for firms is the rate of profit accounted by the ratio of net profits to newly borrowed money.[3] She therefore rejects as irrelevant any effort to compute a rate of profit relative to some meaningless stock of capital;

7 The true role of competition in the capitalist economy is to impose some minimum targeted rate of profit that is changing over time and is perfectly exogenous relative to the market mechanism. Being the motive of production, it must be a component of the price structure imposed by firms in the opening stage of the monetary circuit;

8 Chapter 23 explicitly addresses both the possibility for firms to pay interest and the impact of interest on net profits. Were banks not net profit motivated, or if they spent their whole net profit to acquire equipment, interest on notes would be neutral relative to firms' net profit; but 'banks are a specific class of capitalists' (p. 227), therefore they target net profits that could be exceeding banks' investment in equipment goods. Herein is her answer to Graziani's future problem: how banks' net excess profits relative to their investment could be recycled? Firms are obliged to sell new bonds to banks, which accounts for the rise in their net wealth. She has also discovered that interest paid on deposits is both a source of income and a constraint on banks' ability to exact net profits.

For both Joan Robinson (1956) and Augusto Graziani (1988), the ultimate proof of essentiality of money – what explains why capitalism cannot be a non-monetary economy – is that saving cannot be the source of finance for firms' accumulation of wealth. Joan Robinson is adamant in the debunking of the leading role of thriftiness in chapter 24:

> It is necessary to guard against the confusion of thinking of rentiers thriftiness as providing finance for investment ... This confusion came to surface in connection with the saving campaign during the war ... Its purpose was to induce the public to refrain from consumption not to provide funds (p. 276).

She therefore reached the same theory of profits as Graziani, since both rely, with some generalisation accounting for interest payments, on the wage-bill postulate for initial finance, profits are directly exacted for firms as a whole in real terms (Parguez, 2004) they account for the value in money units of the share of output available for firms' accumulation minus firms' increased indebtness. The growth of firms' debt is determined by desired saving or thriftiness; therefore Joan Robinson's quotation means that thriftiness is an obstacle to investment because it is generating a fall in the rate of profit below its required level.[4] In such a context, it can be proven that the share of labour invested into production for accumulation is determined by the required rate of profit (Parguez, 2004).

It is now the time to confront a new mystery: how can we explain that Graziani's defence remain ignored for so many years by precursor-seekers?

Solving the mystery: one must venture beyond the veil of Joan Robinson's crucial concern with the classical restoration

Joan Robinson had always been straightforward in her critical assessment of Keynes's desperate efforts to convince orthodox economists by integrating a large number of orthodox components in *General Theory*. Keynes was therefore responsible for all attempts (present and future) to integrate his theory into a 'more general' version of neoclassical economics. She was indeed right: Hicks's LS–LM model and its future progeny are already ensconced in *General Theory* as long as we address its most conventional aspects (theory of money, investment function, etc.). There are indeed genuine 'revolutionary' aspects but they are hidden beyond the fog of debates with mainstreamers on their own grounds (the convoluted definition of involuntary unemployment is a perfect example).

In her preface to AOC, Joan Robinson goes further by reproaching Keynes for his life-long obsession with the short-run, which prevented a genuine debunking of the neoclassical economics core. This core is enshrined in the (very) long-run theory of production and accumulation relying on a major 'tool', the production function, and its twin the concept of a perfectly known stock of capital. On one hand, she was again right, there is no genuine theory of production in *General Theory* and it is mostly a short-run view of the economy (with scant exceptions, chapter 12, for instance). On the other hand, she gives us a clue that could help to solve the mystery by explicitly emphasising that her concern is the (very) long-run laws of capitalism, the very ones that must replace the false mainstream own long-run theory. Herein lies our inquiry. Is it true that chapters 23 and 24 comply with the three precursor principles?

They comply with the first principle

According to Joan Robinson, the MTP they address is not the major concern of her inquiry. Both only appear in the third part of the book, which addresses the short-run aspects of capitalist economy. There is more; they follow a chapter dealing with the impact of uncertainty. In her preface, she explains without any ambiguity that the volume must be read as the sequel of the debunking of the neoclassical production function. Having proven the logical fallacy of the production function, it is now time to prove that it is possible to build an alternate framework embodying the most fundamental laws ruling the (very) long-run course of capitalist economy. Herein lies the core of the book, which is addressed by book II (pp. 63–173), while chapter 23 is quite short (pp. 225–36). The very logical structure of the volume is enough to reveal the role of the MTP model in Joan Robinson's theoretical programme:

1   It is not essential for the ultimate debunking of neoclassical economics. What is the necessary and sufficient logical condition is that part II, in some way the logical end of AOC, could have been the last page of book II.
2   What could have fogged the understanding of the most careful readers is that book II only deals with the pure real aspects of capitalist economy. I could not find any hint to the monetary structure of economy. The long-run theory of accumulation in book II is no more monetary than Sraffa's own reconstruction of the theory of production! I think that one should venture further in this comparison: both are convinced that mainstreamers were so uninterested in money that it was useless to attack them on this ground. Both believed that mainstream economics' fortress was its long-run theory of accumulation, which ignored money. Both therefore decided to occupy the real long-run field by proving that it was perfectly possible to build a logical real long-term theory free from any contradiction. Searching themselves for precursors, they decided to strive to restore classical economics in its Ricardian aspect.
3   The short-term matters because according to Joan Robinson herself:

'Everything that happens in an economy happens in a short period and every decision that is taken is taken in a short period' (pp. 100–1). But she is quite adamant; discovering the long-run real laws does matter because they operate through the short-run factors: 'This does not mean that all our elaborate analysis of golden-ages and quasi golden-ages has been a waste of time, for the long-run period influences we have been considering are working themselves out through the fog of uncertainty in which short-term period develops, though there cannot be situations in which they are seen with any great precision' (p. 192). It means that the MTP model can only be properly understood through its subordinate relationship with the real long-term. On one hand, whatever firms' short-term plans, the monetary structure is ruled by those long-term real laws as if they were some invisible hand. The quotation above could even lead the reader to the false conclusion that the MTP model is nothing but some veil fogging the real laws. On the other hand, the MTP factor is to be interpreted as an obstacle to the operation of real laws preventing the convergence on a golden-age path: 'Within the limit set by the technical surplus lies the inflation barrier, which operates through the mechanism of interest rates. Within this may lie a limit due to overcautious and clumsily operated banking policy which keeps investment lower than it is necessary to avoid inflation. Within this is the limit set up by the energy of entrepreneur that involves a complex of technical human and financial influence' (p. 243)

Since the concept of an inflation barrier stems from the long-term real theory, there is no doubt that MTP only matters as a cause of the automatic inability to attain the equilibrium long-term path. One could be tempted to draw from this quotation a somewhat shocking conclusion: thanks to a shrewd monetary policy (or other state interventions), one could neutralise the disturbing role of money and nothing could henceforth hinder the supremacy of real long-term laws.

They comply with the second principle with three major and significant exceptions

Since the proof of the second principle has already been spelled out, let us address three exceptions that could fog search for a precursor:

1 The first is the outcome of the logical structure of the volume. Chapters 23 and 24 come just after book III, devoted to 'the evolution of an economy in which uncertainty prevails'. Stricto sensu it could mean that uncertainty is the existing condition of money, which would turn Joan Robinson into a precursor not of MTP but of the Davidsonian school. Such an exegetical interpretation would contradict the whole MTP because it has always emphasised that the essentiality of money as initial finance is fully independent of the degree of uncertainty (or unknowability) firms and banks have to fight with. It can only be properly interpreted relative to the dominant book II world, in which there is obviously no uncertainty and where money is irrelevant. We cannot escape from the conclusion that Joan Robinson is not a precursor of Davidson because firms do not need notes just to compensate for unknowability. But notwithstanding her adamant denial of the confusion of money with liquidity preference, she does not seem to accept that money could exist in the context of a world with firms more or less free from the threat of uncertainty.

We could go deeper, the priority of book III reveals her conception of uncertainty, (and her theory of time). The Robinson certainty (or degree of certainty) has nothing to do with individual capitalists' behaviour. It is a purely objective concept that can only be defined in the long-term real tranquil universe where time, as such, does not matter because it is perfectly frozen. From this neutral theory of time stems a logical conclusion: even though firms could be certain to achieve their goals by taking the right wagers on the future, uncertainty still rules since we are outside the realm of frozen time.

2 The second exception lies in the Robinsonian ambiguity relative to the problem of the realisation of profits. It has been proven that, by virtue of the intrinsic logic of her MTP model (the wage-bill postulate), she is obliged to reach the same conclusion as the Graziani school: for firms as a whole, net profits cannot be exacted in money and be a part of final finance. They

are directly exacted in kind as the share of output on which wage-earners have no right (no more than banks).

Notwithstanding this logical constraint, there are some hints in chapter 23 to the possibility of firms catching profits as part of final finance (and also in chapter 24). It seems to be a consequence of banks' own payments of salaries (and interest). 'The entrepreneur's total profits over any period are equal to their own investment plus expenditures of the bankers' (p. 227). But she adds: 'Since the latter is equal to interest paid to banks, net profits are equal to net investment' (*ibid.*).

Now, our motivated precursor-seeker could be lost, as chapter 23 becomes a maze. Even if we maintain the assumption of a full recycling of banks' receipts, what exactly does the last part of the quotation mean? It could be interpreted in terms of profits as a source of finance – but how could they exist at all?

3   At last, there is a third exception already put forward by Graziani. Both in chapters 23 and 24, the creation of new notes is interpreted as an addition to the stock of money as notes not only for individual entrepreneurs but also for entrepreneurs as a whole. 'When employment is increasing (or the wage-rate rising) the entrepreneurs are paying out every week more than they received from last week, so that the entrepreneurs – taken as a whole – are continuously increasing their indebtness to the banks and the circulation increases as required' (*ibid.*).

By identifying the creation of new notes and the growth of the wage-bill, Joan Robinson suddenly becomes a precursor of future Post Keynesian monetary theory (Parguez and Seccareccia, 2000) while contradicting a crucial proposition of MTP. In his passionate defence, Graziani argues that it is a legacy of her inability to break-up with Keynes once and for all. It could make sense but our precursor-seeker is now more and more puzzled; a straightforward interpretation of the quotation leads to a rather stunning conclusion: assuming a stationary economy, notes would never have been paid back to banks and there would be an eternal stock of money contradicting the ephemerality theorem she seems to endorse elsewhere.

They do not comply with the third principle

The MTP of chapters 23 and 24 is so strange, relative to the core, that one must accept that it cannot be reconciled with it. There exists an absolute contradiction between the dominant real core and the MTP chapters which now appear as nothing other than some side or 'marginal' issue playing no part at all in the debate with mainstream economics.

The proof of this contradiction stems from the following four propositions:

1   Again, notwithstanding the defence raised by Graziani, the MTP model cannot be discovered either in the former writings of Joan Robinson on

dealing with monetary theory or in her later contributions. At least, I cannot find it in her celebrated essay 'The Rate of Interest' (1952), which is so close to Keynes's own theory that it emphasises the major role of portfolio choice. I cannot find it in her article 'Own Rates of Interest' (1961) and I was quite surprised when I reread *Economic Heresies*. There is not the slightest reference to chapters 23 and 24 in the part devoted to monetary theories. There is just one exception discovered by Graziani, her *Exercises in Economic Analyses* (1960), in which she explains what must be the right definition of the rate of profit. From their perspective, chapters 23 and 24 must be viewed as an exception, a way she tried but abandoned because, in my interpretation, she understood that it could lead her too far from her major route to the reconstruction of economics.

2   It was the way of restoring classical economics, and money has no part to play in this restoration. There are some quotations in book I of AOC that support this proposition; they are so puzzling that they must upset the precursor-seeker and indeed their interpretation is not obvious. They appear in chapter 3 devoted to the meaning of money.

First, a reference to Pigou: 'One of the purposes of economic theory is to look through the veil of money' (p. 25); 'The economist however has to be purchasing-power conscious' (*ibid.*).

Contrary to the man of deeds thinking in terms of money, the economist must look beyond the veil; it is the condition for existence of economy as a science – but there is more to come:

'Though it is impossible to imagine a non-monetary capitalist economy, it is an instructive exercise to imagine an economy in which the various functions of money are carried by different vehicles: debts are settled and payments made in nails, values are expressed in ounces of silver, wage contracts are made in wheat. Employers pay a worker by hoarding him a quantity of wheat' (p. 27).

Indeed, at the beginning of book IV on finance, Joan Robinson explains that 'our economy has evolved (we will assume beyond the stage of paying weekly wage-bills in nails). Certain highly respected banks have been established which cater for the monetary need' (p. 226) because the nail system is obviously a logical impossibility that cannot make sense whatever the stage of the capitalist economy. Both quotations cannot be reconciled with the MTP core, especially the reference to Pigou. It only makes some sense by reference to the dominant real restored classical system. The men of deeds live in the veil and they must be veiled so as not to be turned into speculators. The men and women of science dare to look beyond the veil, classical tools help them to be free from the fog of money. What are they discovering beyond the fogging veil, the beautiful rule of long-run real laws that do not depend on the men of deeds. Herein is the explanation of the absolute supremacy of that long-term which could be the true reality, the hidden 'essence' of society. Relying on such a neo-Kantian metaphysical ontology is tantamount to restoring the neutrality of money and a commodity view of money (the strange nail model).

3 The ontological supremacy of the real long-run explains why Joan Robinson could never reach the conclusion that money was truly essential. Had she drawn this conclusion, she would at once have discovered that the neoclassical production function was falling apart. It has been now fully proven (Graziani, 2003; Parguez, 2004) that in the MTP world, no neoclassical production function can be defined, which at once solves the problem of 'capital'. She ignored this route because had she done otherwise, going back to classical economics would have been meaningless.

4 Ultimately, her ontological interpretation of the long-run explains why she devoted most of her writing to the debate with neoclassical economics on their own preferred ground, the real long-term bereft of monetary fog. She became the advocate of the alternative vision of the economy beyond the veil; she was more and more close to Sraffa and his school, and henceforth all was lost. She never went back to her former MTP model because it was absolutely impossible to reconcile it with the controversies in the theory of capital. It is quite interesting that in his review of those controversies, Harcourt (1972) does not even mention AOC. Maybe he thought that it included components that were too strange relative to true hard theory.

At last the mystery is solved

What has been proven is that Joan Robinson is not a true precursor, and she is not the precursor of contemporary MTP. It is therefore logical that chapters 23 and 24, some dissident part in a complex work, were utterly alien to the fundamental issues addressed by this work, fell into oblivion and could therefore be ignored by readers only interested in Ricardian restoration. Graziani's wonderful defence could not convince the court of history, maybe because the best advocate cannot win when her client pleads 'guilty', excepting a dubious agreement with the court. Graziani himself did not strive to prove that chapters 23–24 were self-sufficient from Joan Robinson's perspective. In the guise of conclusion, I am convinced that she would have refused the dignity of precursor and would have rejected her advocates. Never in her life-long efforts to reconstruct economics has she denied her ontological theory of the long-run, while since its inception MTP adamantly rejected such a metaphysical view; herein is the ultimate explanation of the mystery. Returning to Graziani's defence of the history of economic thought, Joan Robinson's failure teaches us a useful lesson: it is nothing but a vain exercise to restore long-run Ricardian economics in some desperate attempt to debunk neoclassical economics.

Questions remain: Are there other genuine precursors of MTP? Is the very notion of the quest for the precursor sensible? In this contribution, I do not want to answer these fundamental questions. However, another comes to mind: Is not any economist endowed with imagination and scientific boldness his or her own precursor?

Notes

1. Hahn's interpretation is quoted by Rochon (1999).
2. The crucial distinction between money (notes) and deposits (savings borrowed by banks) is a cornerstone of the so-called Schmittian School.
3. Graziani refers to Robinson (1960) to support this explicit rejection of a rate of profit defined in terms of a stock of capital. It is also logically implied by the short-term part of AOC, including chapters 23 and 24 (for example p. 224).
4. Joan Robinson's quotation proves that those who extol the virtue of thriftiness refer to a war economy or to a pure command economy (of which the war economy is an aspect). For a full proof of the adverse impact of thriftiness over investment, see Parguez (2003–2004).

References

Arena, R. and Salvadori, N. (2004) 'Introduction' to *Money, Credit and the Role of the State. Essays in honour of Augusto Graziani* (London: Ashgate).

Gnos, C. and Rochon, L.-P. (2003) 'Joan Robinson and Keynes on Money, Relative Prices and the Monetary Circuit', *Review of Political Economy*, 15(4).

Graziani, A. (1989) 'Money and Finance in Joan Robinson's works', in *The Economics of Imperfect Competition, Joan Robinson and Beyond*, George Feiwel (ed.) (New York University Press), 22, pp. 613–30.

Graziani, A. (2003) *The Monetary Theory of Production* (Cambridge University Press).

Harcourt, G. (1972) *Some Cambridge Controversies in the Theory of Capital* (Cambridge University Press).

Lavoie, M. (1999) 'The credit-led supply of deposits and the demand for money: Kaldor's reflux mechanism as previously endorsed by Joan Robinson', *Cambridge Journal of Economics*, 23, pp. 103–13.

Parguez, A. (2002) 'Victoria Chick and the Theory of the Monetary Circuit: An enlightening debate', *Money, Macroeconomics and Keynes*, I, Philip Arestis, Meghnad Desai and Sheila Dow (eds) (London: Routledge) pp. 49–67.

Parguez, A. (2003) *The Tragedy of Disciplinary Fiscal Economics or Back to the Ancient Regime*, paper presented at the 29th annual conference of Eastern Economic Association, New York, February 2003.

Parguez, A. (2004) 'The Solution of the problem of profits', in *Money, Credit and the Role of the State. Essays in honour of Augusto Graziani*, Richard Arena and Neri Salvadori (eds) (Ashgate: London), pp. 263–76.

Parguez, A. and Seccareccia, M. (2000) 'The credit theory of money: a circuit approach', in John Smithin (ed.), *What is Money?*, London: Routledge, pp. 101–23.

Robinson, J. (1952) *The Rate of Interest and Other Essays* (London: Macmillan).

Robinson, J. (1956) *The Accumulation of Capital* (London: Macmillan).

Robinson, J. (1960) *Exercises in Economic Analyses* (London: Macmillan).
Robinson, J. (1961) 'Own Rates of Interest', *Economic Journal*, 71, pp. 596–600.
Robinson, J. (1971) *Economic Heresies* (New York: Basic Books).
Rochon, L.-P. (1999) *Credit and Production: An Alternative Post-Keynesian Approach* (Cheltenham: Edward Elgar).

6
Some Reflections on Changes in Keynes's Analysis between the *Treatise* and the *General Theory*

Malcolm Sawyer

Introduction

This chapter explores some of the differences in the treatment of money and interest rates by Keynes in *A Treatise on Money* (hereafter TM) (Keynes, 1930) and in *The General Theory of Employment, Interest and Money* (hereafter GT) (Keynes, 1936). The analysis of money is much more extensive in TM than in GT, and it could be argued that the treatment of money in GT is relatively brief (e.g. it does not discuss banks in any detail) because it was not necessary to repeat the lengthier treatment of TM (and Keynes assumed his readers knew TM).

The argument here is rather different; namely, that the treatments of money and of interest rate in the two books are substantially different and that retention of the approach of TM would have precluded Keynes from reaching some of the conclusions of GT. Thus, it is not a matter of having explored the details of money and banking in one book, which are then built on in a subsequent book.

This chapter has two main themes. The first concerns the nature of the change in the treatment of money between TM and GT, along with some suggestions as to the consequences of the changes which occurred. The second theme is to consider the key role attributed to money in GT as a cause of unemployment, and to discuss whether the bank money approach of TM would support that role.

Money in *A Treatise on Money*

Keynes began TM by acknowledging that money 'comes into existence along with debts, which are contracts for deferred payment and ... offers of contracts for sale or purchase' (Keynes, 1930, p. 3). He distinguished between state money and bank money, and viewed 'current money' as being based on both state money and bank money. However, he argued that the use of bank money is now so dominant that much less confusion will be caused by treating this as typical and the use of other kinds of currency as secondary, than by treating State money as typical and bringing in bank money as a subsequent complication. The latter practice, which has outstayed the facts, leads to insufficient emphasis being placed on some of the most typical features of modern money, and to its essential characteristics being treated as anomalous or exceptional. (Keynes, 1930, pp. 28–9)

In TM, Keynes distinguished between the types of money held to satisfy what would later be termed the transactions and precautionary motives (labelled in TM as a cash deposit) and the type of money held to satisfy the speculative motive (labelled as a savings deposit):

A cash deposit [which consist of income deposits and business deposits] roughly corresponds to what Americans call demand deposits and we call current accounts; and a savings deposit to what Americans call time deposits and we call deposit accounts. A savings deposit also corresponds to what used to be called in theories of money, which were started with primary reference to a commodity money, the use of money as a 'Store of Value'. But the correspondence is not exact. (Keynes, 1930, p. 32)

Skidelsky argues that

Books I and II [of *Treatise*] introduce three important ideas. The first is that the deposit-creating power of the banking system gives it complete control over a community's credit conditions. There is a circular flow of income in and out of the banking system, all the active (bank-created) deposits flowing back into the system as passive (customer-created) ones. The banking system's cash reserves are never run down, so there is no limit to the amount of credit it can create. Secondly, Keynes distinguishes between income and business deposits held for the purpose of making current payments on the one hand, and savings deposits held for the purpose of making investments on the other. Thirdly, he discusses the plurality of price levels and the question of which one most accurately measures the purchasing power of money. (Skidelsky, 1992, p. 320)

However, it is suggested that a narrow measure of money (such as M1) is appropriate when money is considered as a medium of exchange. It is 'cash deposits' (that is, roughly the measure of money M1) along with its velocity of circulation which appeared in the 'quantity theory equation' along with nominal output.

Keynes (1930) mentioned the payment of a positive rate of interest on both current account and deposits accounts. 'Increasingly, banks allow interest on the average of a customer's current-account in excess of an agreed minimum' (vol. 1, p. 37). Short-term interest rates often move in line with bank rate, particularly as banks have agreed to pay depositors at a rate defined in relationship to the official bank rate and loans bear a 'more or less fixed relationship to the bank rate' (cf. vol. 2, p. 366). The long-term rate, which is seen as relevant for investment decisions, bears some relationship with the short-term rates. Keynes (1930, p. 316) noted that short-term rates of interest have an influence on long-term rate which is 'much greater than anyone who argued on the above lines would have expected'.

Keynes developed two fundamental equations designed to explain the movement of prices, and as an elaboration of the mechanisms by which monetary policy influenced prices. In particular, it suggested that the rate of interest played a key role in the determination of the price level.

The two fundamental equations were:

$$P = E/O + (I' - S)/R \tag{1}$$

where P is price level of consumption goods, E is money income, I' cost of production of investment, S savings, R consumption goods purchased and O total output of goods.

$$\Pi = E/O + (I - S)/O \tag{2}$$

where Π is the price level of output as a whole and I the value of investment goods (which differs from the costs of production).

Profits which were defined in terms of excess of revenue over costs (including a 'normal' rate of return) were shown (p. 124) to be equal to the difference between I and S.

The particular significance of these fundamental equations here concerns the link between the rate of interest and the price level.

Following Wicksell, it will be convenient to call the rate of interest which would cause the second term of our fundamental equation to be zero the *natural rate* of interest, and the rate which actually prevails the *market rate* of interest. Thus the natural rate of interest is the rate at which saving and the value of investment are exactly balanced, so that the price level of output as a whole (Π) exactly corresponds to the money rate of the efficiency earnings of the factors of production. Every departure of the market rate from the natural rate tends, on the other hand, to set up a disturbance of the price level by causing the second term of the second fundamental equation to depart from zero.

We have, therefore, something with which the ordinary quantity equation does not furnish us, namely, a simple and direct explanation why a rise in the bank rate tends, in so far as it modifies the effective rates of interest, to depress price levels. (Keynes, 1930, p. 139)

If the economy were operating where savings are not equal to investment (as defined by Keynes), then inflation or deflation will result. It is (implicitly) assumed that investment and savings are interest rate sensitive and that a unique positive 'natural rate' of interest exists. Hence, deflation or inflation arise from a failure of the central bank to set the correct level of the rate of interest.

The focus of TM is on the determination of, and movements in, the price level. 'The conditions for the equilibrium of the purchasing power of money require that the banking system should so regulate its rate of lending that the value of investment is equal to savings' (Keynes, 1930, p. 137). There is little discussion on the level of output or employment, though it is implicit that fluctuations in the price level correspond with fluctuations in output. However, a rise in the bank rate means that 'a state of unemployment may be expected to ensue, and to continue, until the rise in bank rate is reversed or, by a chance, something happens to alter the natural rate of interest so as to bring it back to equality with the new market rate' (p. 184).

We can summarise the key features of the discussion of money and interest rates in TM as being:

(i)   inflation/deflation is driven by the difference between the market rate of interest and the 'natural rate', and that equality between the two would yield savings equal investment;
(ii) money is seen as largely bank money, and a distinction drawn between a narrow money (current accounts) held as 'cash deposits' and a broader money (deposit accounts) held as 'savings deposits';
(iii) interest payments may be made on bank deposits, and hence money is (or can be) an interest bearing asset;
(iv) unused overdraft facilities are a liability of the banking system and form available purchasing power.

Money in *The General Theory*

In Keynes (1936), the stock of money is treated as one of the 'givens' of the economy along with the wage-unit. Treating something as given for the purposes of an analysis is not the same as postulating that it is forever a constant or remains unchanged. But it does mean that within the analysis it is assumed that there are no significant feedbacks between the variable treated as given and the rest of the economy. Although there are rather few quotes that can be used to directly support that money is treated as exogenous, the general interpretation of money in GT has been along those lines.[1] Treating the stock of money as given does not indicate what are the forces that would lead to a change in the stock of money, and it does not necessarily mean that the stock of money is exogenously determined by the government or the central bank (cf. Dow, 1997).

It is clear that the analysis of Keynes was based on a given stock of money, which means that feedbacks between the real side of the economy (notably investment) and the stock of money are overlooked. Keynes argued that 'we can *sometimes* regard our *ultimate* independent variables as consisting of... (3) the quantity of money as determined by the actions of the *central bank*' (Keynes, 1936, pp. 246–7; emphasis added). There may be some ambiguity in this statement, but it is suggestive that the stock of money is taken as given, and indeed can be set by the central bank (which precludes independent actions of the banking system). The dependent variables are the volume of employment and the national income measured in wage units, and are determined by the independent variables including the stock of money. This then precludes the feedback of, for example, investment expenditure on loans and thereby on bank deposits and the stock of money.

A number of features stand out in Keynes's treatment of money in GT. Keynes employed a broad definition of money; that is, one that included all financial assets which had a fixed nominal price, and that would be held as part of a wealth portfolio. But money was, in effect, treated as having a zero rate of interest. No mention was made of unused overdraft facilities that could be used to satisfy the transactions and precautionary motives.

Keynes proceeded as follows:

> Let the amount of cash [sic] held to satisfy the transactions- and precautionary motives be M_1, and the amount held to satisfy the speculative-motive be M_2. Corresponding to these two compartments of cash, we then have two liquidity functions L_1 and L_2. L_1 mainly depends on the level of income, whilst L_2 mainly depends on the relation between the current rate of interest and the state of expectation [sic]. Thus
>
> $$M = M_1 + M_2 = L_1(Y) + L_2(r)$$
>
> where L_1 is the liquidity function corresponding to an income Y, which determines M_1, and L_2 is the liquidity function of the rate of interest r, which determines M_2. (Keynes, 1936, pp. 199–200)

The three motives for holding money are fused together to give an overall demand for money.

Keynes viewed the demand for money as a store of wealth as arising from uncertainty over the future. In the absence of such uncertainty, no one would hold money as it was a barren asset.

Our desire to hold money as a store of wealth is a barometer of the degree of our distrust of our own calculations and conventions concerning the future...the possession of actual money lulls our disquietude. (Keynes, 1936, p.187)

Money provides liquidity and becomes a haven in times of mounting uncertainty. Money considered as a store of wealth is seen as a (often *the*) major cause of unemployment.

Unemployment develops...because people want the moon; – men cannot be employed when the object of desire [i.e. money] is something which cannot be produced and the demand for which cannot be readily choked off. There is no remedy but to persuade the public that green cheese is practically the same thing and to have a green cheese factory [i.e. a central bank] under public control. (Keynes, 1936, p. 235)

It is the hoarding of money rather than of other financial assets that is viewed as generating difficulties for employment levels. In GT, money differs from other financial assets in that the stock of money is constant whereas other financial assets can be created by (or on behalf of) firms who wish to borrow to finance investment.

Keynes (1936, pp. 230–1) gave two major characteristics of money as having a zero or low elasticity of production ('money...cannot be readily produced'), and a zero or low elasticity of substitution ('this follows from the peculiarity of money that its utility is solely derived from its exchange value': 'as the exchange value of money rises there is no tendency to substitute some other factor for it').

Thus, not only is it impossible to turn more labour on to producing money when its labour-price rises, but money is a bottomless sink for purchasing power, when the demand for it increases, since there is no value for it at which demand is diverted...so as to slop over into a demand for other things. (Keynes, 1936, p. 231)

The combination of these properties means that an upward shift in liquidity preference would shift demand towards money that cannot be readily produced. Thus, these two essential properties of money are viewed as laying at the heart of the causes of unemployment.

In GT, Keynes spoke of money as an asset which 'yields little or no interest' (Keynes, 1936, p. 168), and representations of GT have treated money as yielding a zero rate of interest. He later argued that

it is a recognized characteristic of money as a store of wealth that it is barren; whereas practically every other form of storing wealth yields some interest or profit. Why should anyone outside a lunatic asylum wish to use money as a store of wealth? (Keynes, 1937c)

In GT, there is no mention of the rate of interest on money (or bank deposits or loans), and *the* (money) rate of interest is aligned with the rate of interest on bonds. The rate of interest on money is taken as effectively zero, and hence the rate of interest on bonds is both an absolute rate of interest and a relative (to that on money) rate of interest. Treating the rate of interest on money as zero may have been a reasonable approximation to the experience of the 1930s, though it runs counter to Keynes's discussion in TM. But in doing so, the rate of interest was not only assumed to be constant (at zero) for the specific analysis, but also it could not be changed to another level in subsequent analysis. Liquidity preference (interacting with the given stock of money) sets the rate of interest on bonds and in doing so sets the *absolute* level of the rate of interest. The substitution between bonds and money that could be viewed as influencing the relative rates of return on bonds and money is translated into setting the absolute rate of interest. It is the absolute rate of interest that is relevant for investment and other decisions.

The introduction of the concept of liquidity preference in the context of a given money supply gives an alternative view on the determinants of the rate of interest. It permits the rate of interest to be determined in the market (through the interplay of the demand for and given supply of money) and to be set at a rate that is incompatible with the equality between savings and investment occurring at full employment.

In GT, Keynes explicitly rejects the idea of a unique 'natural rate' of interest, and in effect argues that there is a 'natural rate' of interest corresponding to each level of effective demand that would bring savings and investment into balance. Keynes argued that in TM:

I defined what purported to be a unique rate of interest, which I called the *natural rate* of interest – namely, the rate of interest which, in the terminology of my *Treatise*, preserved equality between the rate of saving (as there defined) and the rate of investment...I had, however, over-looked the fact that in any given society there is, on this definition, a *different* natural rate of interest for each hypothetical level of employment. And, similarly, for every rate of interest there is a level of employment for which the rate is the 'natural' rate, in the sense that the system will be in equilibrium with that rate of interest and that level of employment. Thus it was a mistake to speak of *the* natural rate of interest or to suggest that the above definition would yield a unique value for the rate of interest irrespective of the level of employment. I had not then understood that, in certain conditions, the system, could be in equilibrium with less than full employment. (Keynes, 1936, pp. 242–3)

It is also the case that a shift in the state of confidence and expectations leading to a shift in the investment schedule would lead to a shift in the 'natural rate' of interest:

> If there is any such rate of interest, which is unique and significant, it must be the rate which we might term the *neutral* rate of interest, namely, the natural rate in the above sense which is consistent with *full* employment, given the other parameters of the system; though this rate might be better described, perhaps, as the *optimum* rate. (Keynes, 1936, p. 243)

The above gives us, once again, the answer to the question as to what tacit assumption is required to make sense of the classical theory of the rate of interest. This theory assumes either that the actual rate of interest is always equal to the neutral rate of interest in the sense in which we have just defined the latter, or alternatively that the actual rate of interest is always equal to the rate of interest which will maintain employment at some specified constant level. If the traditional theory is thus interpreted, there is little or nothing in its practical conclusions to which we need take exception. The classical theory assumes that the banking authority or natural forces cause the market-rate of interest to satisfy one or other of the above conditions. (Keynes, 1936, pp. 243–4)

In GT, the stock of money is treated as given and the rate of interest on money is taken as zero. The rate of interest on bonds arises from liquidity preference considerations and the equality between the demand for and the stock of money, and this rate of interest is generally not compatible with the equality of savings and investment at full employment.

A Treatise versus *The General Theory*

The emphasis in TM is on the analysis of bank money, whereas in GT the stock of money is taken as given with little mention of banks. Although TM says relatively little about the process of loan creation and the links with investment expenditure, it does (chapter 2) indicate how the banking system can expand through loan creation and the limitations on that expansion. It also links loans with deposit creation, and the 'elasticity' of money is recognised, along with the existence of unused overdraft facilities. In GT, there is an absence of discussion on the availability of loans and overdrafts and how investment is financed, though this is rectified to some degree in Keynes (1937b) where he wrote that

> the transition from a lower to a higher scale of activity involves an increased demand for liquid resources which cannot be met without a rise

in the rate of interest, unless the banks are ready to lend more cash or the rest of the public to release more cash at the existing rate of interest. (p. 668)

But

this [overdraft system] is an ideal system for mitigating the effects on the banking system of an increased demand for ex-ante finance... Thus to the extent that the overdraft system is employed and unused overdrafts ignored by the banking system, there is no superimposed pressure resulting from planned activity over and above the pressure resulting from actual activity. (p. 669)

It follows that, if the liquidity-preferences of the public (as distinct from the entrepreneurial investors) and of the banks are unchanged, an excess in the finance required by current ex-ante output... over the finance released by current ex-post output will lead to a rise in the rate of interest; and a decrease will lead to a fall. I should not have previously overlooked this point, since it is the coping-stone of the liquidity theory of the rate of interest. (Keynes, 1937b, p. 667)

In TM, changes in the price level can be seen as driven by the difference between savings and investment, but that in turn rests on the difference between the market rate of interest and the 'natural' rate of interest. The market rate of interest is something of a misnomer in that the actual rate of interest cannot be said to be market determined in that the central bank through the bank rate influences (if not determines) the actual rate of interest. In the short run then, the rate of interest is set by the central bank but it is assumed to fluctuate around the 'natural rate of interest'. In GT, a liquidity preference view of the rate of interest is adopted with the rate of interest (on bonds) set by the interaction of the demand for and supply of money. However, this interest rate on bonds could be said to be market determined, and the central bank discount rate gets little no mention in GT.[2] In particular, nothing is said on the relationship between the rate of interest on bonds and the central bank discount rate. In TM, the central bank is viewed as setting the key interest rate, and other interest rates would be determined in relation to that key rate. Factors such as liquidity preference would then influence the structure of interest rates. In GT, there is barely a mention of the central bank interest rate, the rate of interest on money is treated as zero, and liquidity preference determines not only relative interest rates but also the absolute level of interest rates.

In GT, money is more broadly defined rather as in TM (except that overdraft facilities are not included in GT). In GT, the various motives (transactions, precautionary and speculative) for holding money are fused together into a single demand for an entity labelled money. Hence, a change in one motive (e.g. the speculative) has to be accommodated by changes in the other motive (e.g. transactions) in the context of a given stock of money. In TM, the motives for holding money (under different names) are kept separate, and each of the motives is linked with a particular type of money.

In chapter 14 of GT, Keynes discussed the 'classical theory of the rate of interest'. He argued that although this was 'something upon which we have all been brought up', it was difficult 'to discover an explicit account of it in the leading treaties of the modern classical school' (p. 175). There were two aspects of Keynes's discussion that are relevant here. First, there had been

> the idea that whenever an individual performs an act of saving he has done something which automatically brings down the rate of interest, that this automatically stimulates the output of capital, and that the fall in the rate of interest is just so much as is necessary to stimulate the output of capital to an extent which is equal to the increment of saving; and further that this is a self-regulatory process of adjustment which takes place without the necessity for any special intervention or grandmotherly care on the part of the monetary authority. (p. 177)

Whatever the accuracy of this assessment with regard to the classical authors (whom Keynes cites extensively in the appendix to chapter 14 of GT), it could be said that in the context of the TM, the Central Bank could play this role of 'grandmother' (as might be appropriate for the 'Old Lady of Threadneedle Street'), and ensure that the rate of interest was such that savings and investment were in balance.

Second, Keynes, in effect, said that since savings and investment depend on both the rate of interest and the level of income, any discussion of savings and investment determining the rate of interest without consideration of the level of income was incomplete. However, a full employment 'natural rate' of interest can be defined (as indeed Keynes did with the label of 'neutral rate'), and an equilibrium outcome obtained from the equality between savings and investment. However, that 'neutral rate' of interest shifts as the investment schedule shifts with the state of expectations.

In that light, it could be said that in TM the relative attractiveness of various forms of wealth serves to influence the relative returns on those forms of wealth, with a base that rests on the central bank discount rate (bank rate in the context of TM). Whilst the rate of return on cash is zero, the rate of interest on bank deposits can be above zero (as indicated by Keynes), and influenced by the central bank discount rate. The degree of 'bearishness' then serves to determine the rates of return relative to the central bank discount rate. The rate of interest on a specific asset then depends on the central bank discount rate and the degree of 'bearishness' relevant for that asset. In GT, with the central bank discount rate largely forgotten, the 'base' interest rate becomes the zero rate of interest on money. Liquidity preference then sets the rate of interest on bonds relative to the rate of interest on money, and hence the absolute rate of interest on bonds. This rate of interest on bonds is further assumed to be the rate of interest relevant for the funding of investment (or at least that that rate of interest bears a fixed relationship with the rate of interest on bonds).

Conclusion

If interest rates could adjust such as to ensure that savings and investment are equal at a full employment level of income, there would be no essential demand deficiency problem. In TM, Keynes accepted that idea in the sense that he postulated the existence of a (unique) 'natural rate' of interest that would equate savings and investment. His concern, as expressed in the fundamental equations, was with the inflationary/deflationary consequences of a difference emerging between the market rate of interest (set by the central bank) and the 'natural rate' of interest. In GT, he dismissed the usefulness of the 'natural rate' of interest, but he did define a 'neutral rate' of interest which would indeed equate savings and investment at full employment income. Inflation or deflation can arise through lack of knowledge of the central bank as to the 'natural rate' of interest, through incompetence on the part of the central bank, or through foreign exchange market considerations which preclude the setting of domestic interest rates at the 'natural rate'. In GT, Keynes could be seen to have adopted a quite different view of the determination of the rate of interest with the focus on market-determined interest rates arising from liquidity preference considerations. In effect, the 'neutral rate' of interest may not be reached though (in the absence of the liquidity trap) a sufficient increase in the stock of money would reduce the interest rate set in the market to the 'neutral rate'.

The bank money approach espoused by Keynes in TM has some similarities with the endogenous money approach which Post Keynesians have widely adopted. Viewed in that light, the question arises as to why the central bank cannot or does not set the key discount rate around the 'neutral rate' of interest. It could be argued that Keynes had to find some mechanism that prevented that happening and did so in the form of a given money stock and liquidity preference.

Keynes in GT did not treat savings as interest rate sensitive but did treat investment as sensitive to interest rates. In that context, the question arises as to why the central bank cannot set its discount rate at a level that equates savings and investment at full employment. Several answers suggest themselves including: the savings and investment schedules do not intersect at a positive rate of interest, foreign exchange considerations preclude it and lack of knowledge and expertise on part of the central bank. The alternative approach is to deny any significant interest rate sensitivity of savings and investment.

It has also been argued here that liquidity preference may help to explain relative interest rates in the context of bank money but does not explain the absolute level which rests on the central bank discount rate. An increase in liquidity preference may change the structure of interest rates but does not unambiguously shift them up or down. Further, in a bank money environment, an increase in liquidity preference can be accommodated by some increase in money (bank deposits).

Notes

1. There are some quotes however, such as

   in the case of money, however – postponing, for the moment our consideration of the effects of reducing the wage-unit or of a deliberate increase in its supply by the monetary authorities – the supply is fixed. (Keynes, 1936, p. 230)

   We must consider whether these conclusions are upset by the fact that, even though the quantity of money cannot be increased by diverting labour into producing it, nevertheless an assumption that its effective supply is rigidly fixed would be inaccurate. In particular, a reduction of the wage-unit will release cash from its other uses for the satisfaction of the liquidity-motive; whilst, in addition to this, as money-values fall, the stock of money will bear a higher proportion to the total wealth of the community. (Keynes, 1936, pp. 231–2)

2. Keynes (1936, p. 205) stated that

   corresponding to the quantity of money created by the monetary authority, there will, therefore, be *cet. par.* a determinate rate of interest or, more strictly, a determinate complex of rates of interest for debts of different maturities.

   But he then continued to consider

   the extent to which the price of debts as fixed by the banking system is 'effective' in the market. (p. 206)

References

Dow, S. (1997) 'Endogenous money', in G.C. Harcourt and P.A. Riach (eds) *A 'Second Edition' of The General Theory* (London: Routledge), pp. 61–78.

Keynes, J.M. (1930) *A Treatise on Money* (London: Macmillan) (page references refer to *The Collected Writings of John Maynard Keynes*, volumes V and VI, London: Macmillan).

Keynes, J.M. (1936) *The General Theory of Employment, Interest and Money* (London: Macmillan).

Keynes, J.M. (1937a) 'Alternative theories of the rate of interest', *Economic Journal*, 47, pp. 241–52.

Keynes, J.M. (1937b) 'The ex-ante theory of the rate of interest', *Economic Journal*, 47, pp. 663–9.

Keynes, J.M. (1937c) 'The general theory of employment', *Quarterly Journal of Economics*, 51, pp. 209–23.

Keynes, J.M. (1979) *The Collected Writings of John Maynard Keynes: The General Theory and After A Supplement*, vol. XXIX, (edited by Donald Moggridge) (London: Macmillan).

Skidelsky, R. (1992) *John Maynard Keynes: The Economist as Saviour* (Harmondsworth: Penguin) (page references to the Penguin edition, 1995).

Part II
Stocks and Flows in the Monetary Circuit

7
Single-Period Analysis: Financial Markets, Firms' Failures and Closure of the Monetary Circuit*

Marcello Messori and Alberto Zazzaro

Introduction

The seminal contributions of Augusto Graziani (1982; 1984) to the monetary theory of production make it clear that the realisation of monetary gross profits of firms at the macroeconomic level represents the most intricate and awkward puzzle in the circuit approach. The analytical reason for this puzzle is simple: assuming a single macro period, isolated from those that precede and follow it, and a private pure credit economy, closed to foreign exchanges, the quantity of means of payment introduced into the economy at the beginning of the period coincides with the total debt of firms and with the wage bill; hence the total monetary revenues realised by the set of firms at the closure of the period will at most be equal to their initial debt and cannot account either for the existence of monetary profits or for the monetary payment of bank interest.[1]

Faced with this arithmetic difficulty, some circuit theorists have admitted the impossibility of the monetary realisation of profits and bank interest at the macroeconomic level, preferring to conclude that the two variables are realised in kind (see Graziani, 1984). As we argue in our second section, this 'solution' constitutes an analytical expedient which, while satisfying a criterion of formal consistency, renders the debt contract between banks and non-financial firms indeterminate and calls into question even the separation between these two sets of agents. Other authors, instead, have sought to overcome the puzzle of profits by enriching the monetary circuit model. Within this line of research, a promising assumption is that bank loans for working capital are supplemented by bank loans for investment demand

* We wish to thank Riccardo Bellofiore, Duccio Cavalieri, Mauro Gallegati, Adriano Giannola, Marc Lavoie, Alain Parguez, Domenico Scalera and Gennaro Zezza for comments and criticisms.

(Parguez, 1980; Seccareccia, 2003).[2] Although it has the merit of realism, this solution is unsatisfactory since it does not consider that bank loans for investment demand must be repaid inclusive of interest. Hence, as we argue in our third section, the introduction of long-term financing for investment demand allows the monetary realisation of profits and the monetary payment of bank interest by the set of firms within the single period, but it also causes a stock of long-term debt that grows in aggregate from period to period until it necessarily flows into a 'Ponzi finance' macroeconomic regime (Minsky, 1977).

In this chapter, we propose a radical change of perspective. In our view, to achieve a rigorous explanation of the formation of monetary profits, the implicit notion of equilibrium normally used in the monetary circuit has to be abandoned. This usual notion of equilibrium rests on two conditions: (a) the means of payment created and introduced into the system at the beginning of each period must be destroyed at its closure; (b) the expectations of firms and banks related to sales, revenues and savings collection through financial markets must be fulfilled (De Vroey, 1988; Graziani, 1988 and 1990). These two conditions are incompatible with the realisation in money of profits within the single period. Profits obviously constitute firms' income. If monetary profits were not spent at the closure of the circuit-period in which they are generated, even a propensity of workers to consume equal to 1 would not be sufficient to destroy the means of payment introduced into the system and to realise the expectations of the whole set of firms and banks; hence equilibrium conditions (a) and (b) would not be fulfilled. Conversely, if monetary profits (inclusive of monetary interest) were realised and spent during the same period, equilibrium conditions (a) and (b) would be satisfied (see Graziani, 1992); however, the monetary form of profits and interest would be a mere veil for their determination in real terms.

Building on an observation of Graziani (1984, 1994), in the fourth section we argue that the solution of the profits paradox in the monetary circuit requires the bankruptcy of some firms and banks in the normal working of the economy. This, however, implies abandoning the notion of equilibrium defined by conditions (a) and (b) in favour of a vaguer but more consistent notion of equilibrium defined as systemic order (see Zazzaro, 2003).

Profit realisation in kind

Graziani (1984) offers a simple model of the monetary circuit which analyses the transactions and the corresponding market equilibria in the opening and closing phases of a given period. Consider a period *t*, isolated from other periods and characterised by relations between macroeconomic aggregates.[3] This period is divided into three phases: the opening phase, where transactions are carried out in the credit and labour markets; the production phase, which gives rise to output; and the closing phase, where transactions are carried out in the goods markets and the debtor positions in the credit market are wound up. Assume that the only monetary means present in the economic system are those introduced by the banks at the beginning of the period. In the opening phase, the aggregate of households offers labour units to the set of firms in exchange for the exogenously determined monetary wage (*w*). The aggregate of firms decides the quantity to be produced of both the composite consumer good (*C*) and the composite capital good (*I*) and – given the technical coefficients of production of the two sectors – purchases the consequent amount of labour units ($N = N_C + N_I$) by means of bank credit. The aggregate of banks makes available the finance required by the set of firms ($L = L_C + L_I$), designing single-period (short-term) standard debt contracts.

In the closing phase, the aggregate of workers–consumers utilises all or part of the income received earlier in order to acquire the quantity of the composite consumer good produced and sold by the aggregate of firms. With these monetary revenues, the aggregate of firms settles (part of) its debts to the aggregate of banks, and internally exchanges the amount of the composite capital good produced so as to renew capital endowment in the two sectors. The aggregate of banks realises the debt contract by receiving the principal and interest or, in case of default, by receiving firms' monetary revenues; thus, the banking system destroys (part of) the means of payment put into the economic system at the opening of the period.

The monetary revenues obtained by the subset of firms producing the composite consumer good are:

$$R_C = p_C C = cw(N_C + N_I) = cL \tag{1}$$

where p_C denotes the equilibrium price of the composite consumer good, and *c* the average propensity to consume.

If the amount of savings of the aggregate of workers–consumers is smaller than the wage bill for the production of the composite capital good, $(1-c)L < wL_I$, the subset of firms supplying the consumption good obtains monetary profits gross of interest (gross profits) equal to:

$$\pi_C = (cN - N_C)w = cL - L_C \tag{2}$$

Firms have also produced the composite capital good and borne the related cost. At the closure of the period, they must therefore internally redistribute the amount of that good and the monetary receipts of the consumer good sector. In principle, this redistribution may follow different criteria. Assuming that the economic system operates in a situation of equilibrium and perfect competition, Graziani (1984) supposes that the amount of the composite capital good must be divided between the two sectors in proportion to the monetary production costs (net of interest) borne by them. This allocation criterion makes it possible to set an 'accounting' price p_I for the composite investment good:

$$P_I = \frac{CL_I}{I} \frac{L}{L_C} \tag{3}$$

The revenues from the production of the composite capital good and the composite consumer good are therefore given by the sum of a monetary flow and a share of the new capital goods measured for accounting purposes in monetary units:

$$R_I = cL_I + \left(1 - \frac{L_C}{L}\right)P_I I \tag{4}$$

$$R_c = cL_C + \frac{L_C}{L}P_I I \tag{5}$$

As a consequence, the gross profits of the two sectors are partly formed by the new composite capital good measured for accounting purposes in monetary units:

$$\pi = \underbrace{\left(1 - \frac{L_C}{L}\right)P_I I - (1-c)L_I}_{\pi_I} + \underbrace{\frac{L_C}{L}P_I I - (1-c)L_C}_{\pi_c} = P_I I - (1-c)L \tag{6}$$

For the sake of simplicity, let us assume that the propensity to consume of the aggregate of workers is equal to 1; then expression (6) shows that the gross profits of the aggregate of firms, which are in kind even if computed in money, coincide with the amount of the capital good produced. It follows that the monetary revenues of the aggregate of firms are strictly sufficient to repay the principal L. In order to wipe out their debt with the banks, the aggregate of firms must therefore pay the interest in the form of a share of the capital good produced. Repayment of the debt closes all the markets and leads to the destruction of the bank means of payment introduced into the system at the beginning of the period.

However, the fact that gross profits are determined in kind and that the interest paid is a share of the capital goods produced creates various analytical problems at the closure of the period. Here, we shall only emphasise the three most important (see Messori, 1988).

First, the fact that revenues and profits are not realised through market transactions but by a reallocation of the composite capital good between the two productive sectors makes it impossible to distinguish the part of the amount of the capital goods that will constitute the new desired capital endowment at the beginning of the following period from any part of these goods that might constitute an undesired stock. To avoid this difficulty, one could assume that the aggregate of firms decides the level of activity in each period on the basis of the criterion of full utilisation of its capital stock. In this case, however, the gross profits in kind are maximised when the ratio of the capital goods produced to total current production tends to 1, so that the role of consumption and the market itself would be destined to disappear.

Secondly, if interest must be paid in kind, the banking system will appropriate a share of the composite capital good; and to keep these goods from turning into an undesired stock, in the subsequent period banks will have to start up a non-financial business. This, however, would raise doubts about the separation between the aggregate of banks and the aggregate of non-financial firms, which is a crucial feature of any model of the monetary circuit. Thirdly, the quantitative amount of interest as a share of the composite capital good produced is indeterminate. The debt contract concluded between the aggregate of banks and the aggregate of firms at the opening of the period, establishes both the size of the loan and the monetary amount of interest thereon. This implies that the aggregate of firms is formally in default. Therefore, there is no reason for the aggregate of banks to agree to determine its share of the composite capital good on the basis of an 'accounting' price established within the aggregate of firms, without any evaluation by the market.

The financing of investment demand

Given the difficulties stemming from the realisation of profits and interest in kind, we now seek to arrive at a purely monetary definition of these two variables, pursuing an apparently obvious solution to the paradox of profits: a second injection of means of payment in order to finance the demand for the composite capital good. Let us distinguish the set of firms as producers of the capital and consumption goods and as purchasers of the composite capital good. Assume that the firms as purchasers order a given amount of the composite capital good at the opening of period t, and that as producers of that good they realise their output in the second phase of the same period. These decisions are made on the basis of an expectation regarding the market price of the composite capital good (p_{ml}), which will be realised at the end of the period.[4]

Since the exchange of the capital good at the closure of the period is based on market demand and supply, the purchasing firms will have to hold an amount of means of payment equal to the monetary value of the exchange. However, firms have no purchasing power beyond the monetary amount equal to the short-term debt they have to repay to the banks. Therefore, in order to translate the investment orders into an effective investment demand, the aggregate of firms requires new long-term bank financing (F).

Assume that the banking system grants the financing requested by firms at an interest rate r_F which, for simplicity, does not influence either the investment orders or the actual demand for investment. We have:

$$F_D = F_S \, (r_F) \equiv F \tag{7}$$

where: $F_D = p_{ml}I$ indicates the amount of long-term financing demanded by the purchasing firms and F_S the amount supplied by the aggregate of banks.

At the closure of period t the subset of firms that produced the composite consumer goods obtains a gross monetary profit equal to L_I; and the subset of firms that produced the composite investment good obtains a gross monetary profit equal to $p_{ml}I - L_I$. It follows that, at the closure of period t after honouring the short-term debt contract, the aggregate of firms holds a stock of means of payment equal to $p_{ml}I - r_L L$ against an interest-bearing long-term debt equal to $p_{ml}I$.

This result generates a paradox. The aggregate of firms would behave irrationally if it did not use the non-interest-bearing monetary stock to reduce its own long-term debt, on which it must pay a positive interest rate (r_F). But if a portion $p_{ml}I - r_L L$ of the bank financing disbursed in the third phase of period t were repaid in the same phase, that portion would contradict the essential characteristics of whatever debt contract: (i) a gap between the time the loan is made and its repayment, (ii) the consequent positive probability that at least some borrowers will default at the maturity of the contract, and (iii) the associated setting of a positive interest rate by the lender. We can escape this paradox by assuming that the subset of firms producing the composite consumer good utilises its net monetary profits to self-finance part of its own investment demand; and that the subset of firms–purchasers producing the composite capital good behaves in similar fashion with regard to the net monetary profits arising from the production and sale of that good. All the other assumptions made remaining unchanged, the long-term financing required by the aggregate of firms becomes thus equal to:

$$F = p_{ml}I - (\pi_I - r_L L_I) - (\pi_C - r_L L_C) \tag{8}$$

Inserting expression (8) in Graziani's (1984) model, and assuming $c = 1$, we obtain:

$$\pi_C = L_I \tag{9}$$

$$\pi_I = p_{ml}I - L_I \tag{10}$$

$$\pi = \pi_C + \pi_I = p_{ml}I \tag{11}$$

Finally, substituting expressions (9) and (10) in (8), we can quantitatively specify the amount of the long-term financing requested by the aggregate of firms–purchasers:

$$F = r_L L \tag{12}$$

During the closing phase of period t, F allows the two subsets of producing firms to realise their investment demand and their monetary profits and to settle their short-term bank debt in monetary form. However, the aggregate of firms still has a bank debt that will mature at the end of period $t+n$ (with $n>0$). To be honoured, this long-term debt will require payment of a monetary amount of interest equal to $r_F r_L L$ at the end of every period between $t+1$ and $t+n$, and repayment of the principal at the end of $t+n$. Hence, our analytical framework must be extended over more than one period. This extension shows that the introduction of long-term debt raises a problem of financial sustainability. The aggregate of firms accumulates a stock of long-term debts that grows from period to period until it necessarily flows into an ultra-speculative or 'Ponzi' macro-financial regime (Minsky, 1977).

To be more precise, let us assume that in each period $t+j$ ($j=0$, $1,\ldots$, $n,\ldots$) firms obtain the long-term loans required to realise their planned investment orders. For the sake of simplicity, let us also assume that the investment orders as well as the short-term interest rate remain unchanged from period to period and that all the long-term loans have a duration of two periods.[5] This means that the financing demanded and obtained at the closing phase of $t+j$ must be repaid in the third phase of $t+j+2$. Therefore, if we consider the generic period n, the amount of long-term loans requested by firms is equal to:

$$F_{t+n} = F + r_{F_{t+n-1}} F_{t+n-1} + (1 + r_{F_{t+n-2}}) F_{t+n-2} \tag{13}$$

Substituting recursively for F_{t+n-1} and F_{t+n-2} in (13), and considering that n is an even number we have:[6]

$$F_{t+n+1} = F\Big\{ 1 + (1 + r_{F_{t+n}})(1 + r_{F_{t+n-1}})[1 + (1 + r_{F_{t+n-2}})(1 + r_{F_{t+n-3}}) \times$$

$$\ldots$$

$$\times [1 + (1 + r_{F_{t+3}})(1 + r_{F_{t+2}})[1 + (1 + r_{F_{t+1}})(1 + r_{F_t})]]]\Big\} \tag{14}$$

On the reasonable assumption that r_F is not decreasing with the amount of total demand for long-term financing, it follows that after a certain number of periods the aggregate of firms will be forced to borrow in order to settle its old debts and to pay bank interest. Extending the duration of the loans contracted by firms in the closing phase of each period can distance the period at which a similar situation will happen. However, at some point the aggregate of firms will have to borrow from the banking system, not only to finance part of its own current investment demand but also to repay the amount of its long-term debt falling due and pay the accrued interest on the long-term debt which has not yet fallen due. As is well known after Minsky (1977), this means that firms will find themselves in an ultra-speculative Ponzi financial position, a position that creates situations of financial instability that result in the bankruptcy of the borrowers and lenders involved.

The problem is that, in our case, the agents involved are the aggregate of firms and the aggregate of banks so that the working of the economy would be characterised by the 'production of debts by means of debts' and its prospects for growth would be compromised by intrinsic and insoluble contradictions. Such a portrayal of the working of the economy is analytically unsatisfactory and empirically unrealistic if extended to the macroeconomic level; moreover, it is not compatible with the monetary circuit theory's representation of the working of capitalism. This last representation is instead influenced by analytical models that portray capitalist development as a process based on innovative processes, the financing of these processes, the resulting structural imbalances and dynamic adjustments (see Schumpeter, 1912 and 1939). The implication for the present purposes is that a subset of firms is destined to exit the market, especially during cyclical downturns, because of crushing debt or rampant losses; but that, at the same time, another subset of firms is able to reap the fruit of innovation by temporarily realising positive monetary profits. In this framework, the aggregate of firms does not produce 'debts by means of debts'. If debt is used to launch and complete successful innovative processes, it constitutes a temporary premise for realising profits; only if it serves as a stopgap to ward off crises does it signal the bankruptcy of firms (Messori, 2004).

Monetary profits and firms' failures

The main limitation of the multi-period framework developed in the previous section derives from having introduced insufficient elements of heterogeneity among firms; in particular, we have assumed that firms are all equally profitable. However, as Graziani (1984) also acknowledges, this assumption conflicts with the stringent logic of the monetary circuit: when long-term borrowing is excluded, within the single period some firms can realise monetary profits and can pay interest in money only if other firms suffer an equivalent amount of monetary losses.[7] In this section, we present a framework of monetary circuit in which we distinguish profitable from failing firms.[8] This new division permits the determination of profits and interest in monetary form without falling into an unsustainable Ponzi macroeconomic regime. It does, however, create new elements of economic instability.

Let us consider a single period. Suppose that the economy consists of a very large number of firms (Q), each endowed with a technology for producing a qualitatively different consumption good. The N workers–consumers are interested in the variety of products. However, not all of the goods supplied by firms enjoy their preference. For the sake of simplicity, suppose that the wage bill disbursed – and wholly spent within the period – is allocated in equal parts for the purchase of a number of goods denoted by q (with $q < Q$). It follows that each firm has a probability $\theta = q/Q$ of selling the amount of good it produced, while each of Q firms has a probability $\varphi = 1 - \theta$ of not obtaining any receipts and hence failing. If we assume for simplicity's sake that the production technology is the same for all the firms, the quantity of the specific consumption good produced by firm i ($i = 1, 2, \ldots, Q$) is equal to $C_i = aN/Q$. For the q firms that are able to sell their goods, the equilibrium price is equal to $p = w/\theta a$, while their net monetary profits are given by:

$$\pi = \left[\frac{1}{\theta} - (1 + r_L)\right]\frac{wN}{Q} \tag{15}$$

Expression (15) shows that firms will be able to realise their profits in money only if the number of successful firms q is less than $Q/(1 + r_L)$. Moreover, the profits of each successful firm increase as the number of these firms decreases and, until the percentage of bankruptcies becomes too high, even the share of national income appropriated by the aggregate of firms is positively correlated with the number of firms' bankruptcies.[9] Expression (15) also shows that as the loan interest rate increases, the minimum share of failing firms that assures successful firms earning positive monetary profits must increase.

Assume that banks compete *à la* Bertrand in the credit market, and that in equilibrium they set the loan interest rate at such a level that their expected profits are zero. Therefore, if the interest rate on deposits is *zero*, and if θ^e denotes the percentage of firms that the banks expect to succeed, the loan interest rate must be equal to $r_L = \dfrac{1}{\theta^e} - 1$. Substituting this latter expression in (15), then the successful firms can realise their profits in money only if the banks are optimistic in evaluating their probability of success, or, more precisely, only if $\theta^e > \theta$. In this case, however, the profits of the bank with a portfolio of customers representing the average quality of firms (i.e., with a portfolio consisting of θ firms that will succeed and $1 - \theta$ firms that will fail) are negative. Of course, if the successful firms are not distributed evenly among the banks, one or more banks may obtain profits. However, given that $\theta^e > \theta$, the banking system as a whole must make losses. This implies that profits for some firms go along not only with the losses for other firms, but also with losses for the banks that financed them. This in turn implies that, if the monetary profits of the firms that borrow from the loss-making banks are to be truly cashed, it will be necessary to rely on an interbank market and/or a last-resort lender to prevent these banks from failing.

Conclusion

The introduction of bankruptcy into the framework of the monetary circuit has at least three consequences that open up possible lines of research. First, the realisation of profits and interest in money is unavoidably associated with the failure of a number of firms and banks. This means that a monetary economy cannot work without public and private institutions that guarantee its stability and orderly operations: a central bank that pumps liquidity into the economy and acts as last-resort lender, an interbank market that acts as stabiliser averting automatic transformation of business failures into bank failures, bankruptcy legislation, and a state that stabilises and integrates private investment demand.

Second, since the realisation of profits in money is linked to the bankruptcy and market exit of a certain number of firms, in the economy there is a stock of money that no longer represents a debt of the corporate sector to the banking system but is a debt within the banking system (which may include the central bank). In other words, at any instant part of the money held by firms and households is a net financial asset for these two groups of agents. It follows that self-financing becomes one of the channels through which production can be realised; that is, it is an initial source of financing and not only a final form of financing, contrary to what is commonly asserted in the theory of the circuit.

Lastly, the existence of monetary profits forces us to abandon the concept of equilibrium that characterises the theory of the circuit. As De Vroey (1988) and Graziani (1988) recall, that concept requires that two conditions be satisfied: (a) the money originating from banks at the opening phase of each period must be completely destroyed at its closure, (b) the expectations of firms concerning the sales of the goods produced and the expectations of banks concerning the repayment of the loans granted must be fully realised. Evidently, if monetary profits derive from the bankruptcy of part of the firms financed at the opening of the circuit, both conditions cannot be satisfied. Hence, realisation of the expectations of all the individual economic agents cannot be one of the conditions for stability of a monetary economy. For that matter, Keynes himself wrote: 'it is probable that the actual average results of investments, even during periods of progress and prosperity, have disappointed the hopes which prompted them' (Keynes, 1936, p. 150).

The implication is that within the framework of the monetary circuit the *microeconomic* notion of equilibrium implicitly contained in conditions (a) and (b) – the accounts of all economic agents (banks, firms and workers) break even – must be abandoned in favour of a *macroeconomic* notion of equilibrium: the economic system is in equilibrium when it works in an orderly fashion; that is, when explosive recessionary or expansionary trends are not developing within it. Plainly, reference to a notion of equilibrium as systemic order introduces an element of greater indeterminacy into the analysis.[10] However, this choice is consistent with the theoretical formulation of the monetary circuit and removes analytical inconsistencies and paradoxes. Above all, it accords with common experience, which tells us that 'it is an outstanding characteristic of the economic system in which we live that, whilst it is subject to severe fluctuations in respect of output and employment, it is not violently unstable' (Keynes, 1936, p. 249).

Notes

1. The monetary realization of profits and the monetary payment of bank interest would not be a problem, if one assumed that two or more overlapping circuits coexist in each period and the economy has an infinite duration (Dupont and Reus, 1989; MacKinnon and Smithin, 1993) or if one gave up macroeconomic aggregation (De Vroey, 1988). However, as Rochon (2005) also recognizes in his contribution to present volume, to give full coherence to the circuit theory it is necessary to explain the existence of the aggregate monetary profits within the single period.

2. Other explanations of the aggregate monetary profits are built on the hypothesis that the velocity of circulation of credit-money is increasing and endogenous (Schmitt, 1984), or that firms and banks anticipate the formation of their profits and spend them in advance (De Vroey, 1988; Renaud, 2000), or that legal tender is introduced into the circuit through public-sector expenditure (Graziani, 1985). For a comprehensive review of the different solutions to the puzzle of profits offered within the monetary circuit approach, see Dupont and Reus (1989) and Parguez (2004).

3. A micro-founded monetary circuit model in line with Graziani's macro-model has been proposed by Bossone (2001).

4. Given the model's assumptions (see above, section 2), the expected and effective prices of goods will coincide.

5. This is the most simplified assumption permitting the composite capital good to be identified with fixed capital and not only with circulating capital; and, as Hicks shows (1965, chs. 3, 4 and 6), the treatment of fixed capital is essential to moving from the single-period to the multiperiod analysis.

6. For the analytical derivation of (14), see Messori and Zazzaro (2004).

7. This is also one of the main features of Schumpeter's recession phase in his two-phase cycle (see Schumpeter, 1912 and 1939). The old productive units which are unable to imitate the innovations introduced in the prosperity phase, make losses and fail (creative destruction process: Schumpeter, 1942); in the meantime, innovators and imitators obtain their expected and temporary monetary profits and can transfer the amount of means of payment (principal and interest) due to the banks (see Messori, 2004).

8. In this section, we only outline the model which is developed in Messori and Zazzaro (2004).

9. Namely, it is easy to show that the ratio of aggregate profits to aggregate income increases if $\varphi < (1 + 2r_L)/2(1 + r_L)$ holds (see Messori and Zazzaro, 2004).

10. On close inspection, a notion of macroeconomic equilibrium similar to that proposed here is present in Graziani (1994), who notes that if money is to be an empirically observable variable in equilibrium it will be necessary to admit that there exists a 'normal' amount of firms' debt to banks. However, there remains a

fundamental difference between our approach and Graziani's. Since the failure of firms is not part of his model, Graziani states that the existence of a money stock is explained by the fact that workers do not use all their income in the real or financial markets; hence money still constitutes a financial liability for firms. In our approach, the money stock is created through the realization of monetary profits, and thus constitutes a net financial asset for the set of surviving firms.

References

Bossone, B. (2001) 'Circuit theory of banking and finance', *Journal of Banking and Finance*, 25 (5), pp. 857–90.

De Vroey, M. (1988) 'Il circuito della moneta: due interpretazioni', in M. Messori (ed.), *Moneta e produzione* (Torino: Einaudi), pp. 215–45.

Dupont, F. and Reus, E. (1989) 'Le profit macroéconomique monétaire', *Economie Appliquée*, 42(1), pp. 87–114.

Graziani, A. (1982) 'L'analisi marxista e la struttura del capitalismo moderno', in *Storia del marxismo. Vol. IV: Il marximo oggi* (Torino: Einaudi).

Graziani, A. (1984) 'Moneta senza crisi', *Studi Economici*, 39(24), pp. 3–37.

Graziani, A. (1985) 'Monnaie, intérêt, dépense publique', *Economies et Sociétés* (Série 'Monnaie et Production'), 19 (2), pp. 87–114.

Graziani, A. (1988) 'Il circuito monetario', in M. Messori (ed.), *Moneta e produzione* (Torino: Einaudi), pp. XI–XLIII.

Graziani, A. (1990) 'The theory of monetary circuit', *Economies et Sociétés* (Série 'Monnaie et Production'), 24(7), pp. 7–36.

Graziani, A. (1992) 'Production and distribution in a monetary economy', in H. Brink (ed.), *Themes in Modern Macroeconomics* (London: MacMillan), pp. 98–114.

Graziani, A. (1994) *La teoria monetaria della produzione* (Arezzo: Banca Popolare dell'Etruria e del Lazio, Studi e Ricerche).

Hicks, J.R. (1965) *Capital and Growth* (Oxford University Press).

Keynes, J.M. (1936) *The General Theory of Employment, Interest and Money*, in *The Collected Writings of John Maynard Keynes*, VII (London: MacMillan), 1973.

MacKinnon, K. and Smithin, J. (1993) 'An interest rate peg, inflation and output', *Journal of Macroeconomics*, 15(4), pp. 769–85.

Messori, M. (1988) 'Agenti e mercati in uno schema periodale', in M. Messori (ed.), *Moneta e produzione* (Torino: Einaudi), pp. 285–330.

Messori, M. (2004) 'Credit and money in Schumpeter's theory', in R. Arena and N. Salvadori (eds), *Money, Credit and the Role of the State. Essays in Honour of Augusto Graziani* (Aldershot: Ashgate), pp. 175–200.

Messori, M. and Zazzaro, A. (2004) 'Monetary profits within the circuit: Ponzi finance or *mors tua, vita mea*?', *Quaderni di Ricerca*, 200, Università Politecnica delle Marche.

Minsky, H.P. (1977) 'The financial instability hypothesis. An interpretation of Keynes and an alternative to "standard" theory', *Nebraska Journal of Economics and Business*, 16 (1) (Reprinted in H.P. Minsky, *Inflation Recession and Economic Policy*, Brighton: Wheatsheaf Books, 1982.)

Parguez, A. (1980) 'Profit, épargne, investissement: éléments pour une théorie monétaire du profit', *Economie Appliquée*, 43(2), pp. 425–55.

Parguez, A. (2004) 'The solution of the paradox of profits', in R. Arena and N. Salvadori (eds), *Money, Credit and the Role of the State. Essays in Honour of Augusto Graziani* (Aldershot: Ashgate), pp. 257–70.

Renaud, J.F. (2000) 'The problem of the monetary realization of profits in a post Keynesian sequential financing model: two solutions of the Kaleckian option', *Review of Political Economy*, 12(3), pp. 285–303.

Rochon, L.-P. (2005) 'The existence of monetary profits within the monetary circuit', in the present volume.

Schmitt, B. (1984) *Inflation, chômage et malformations du capital* (Albeuve: Castella; and Paris: Economica).

Schumpeter, J.A. (1926 [1912]) *Theorie der wirtschaftlichen Entwicklung*, 2nd edn (München und Leipzig: Duncker & Humblot). (Engl. edn, *The Theory of Economic Development*, New York: Oxford University Press, 1934).

Schumpeter, J.A. (1939) *Business Cycles: A Theoretical, Historical and Statistical Analysis of the Capitalist Process*, 2 vols (New York: McGraw-Hill).

Schumpeter, J.A. (1942) *Capitalism, Socialism, and Democracy* (New York: Harpers & Brothers).

Seccareccia, M. (2003) 'Pricing, investment and the financing of production within the framework of the monetary circuit: Some preliminary evidence', in L.-P. Rochon and S. Rossi (eds), *Modern Theories of Money. The Nature and Role of Money in Capitalist Economies* (Cheltenham: Edward Elgar), pp. 173–97.

Zazzaro, A. (2003) 'How heterodox is the heterodoxy of monetary circuit theory? The nature of money and the microeconomics of the circuit', in L.-P. Rochon and S. Rossi (eds), *Modern Theories of Money. The Nature and Role of Money in Capitalist Economies* (Cheltenham: Edward Elgar), pp. 219–45.

8
The Existence of Monetary Profits within the Monetary Circuit*

Louis-Philippe Rochon

Introduction

The many writings of Augusto Graziani have had a large influence on a generation of younger economists who have taken his writings to heart. In my own case, I have been seduced by many of his ideas on the monetary circuit including his perceptive analysis of initial and final finance. In this chapter, I would like to turn to a topic that has raised considerable debate and on which Professor Graziani had much to contribute.

The existence of monetary profits at the macroeconomic (aggregate) level has always been a conundrum for theoreticians of the monetary circuit. If money is created from bank credit, how can we explain profits if firms borrow just enough to cover wages that are simply spent on consumption goods and returned to firms to extinguish their initial debt? Indeed, not only are firms unable to create profits, they also cannot raise sufficient funds to cover the payment of interest. In other words, how can M become M'?

Several explanations can be identified that attempt to explain the existence of aggregate monetary profits, none I feel very satisfactory. Yet, all these models pose a certain problem and challenge. The purpose of this chapter is to offer a review of each approach as well as a criticism, and then present an alternative explanation that rests on current financing and credit practices of firms, consistent with the theory of the monetary circuit, Post Keynesian economics and the real world. It rests on the dynamic nature of bank lending, which is at the heart of the theory of the monetary circuit, as well as the notion that firms borrow both short-term and long-term credit. In essence, the theory of the monetary circuit must be able, in its simplest form, to explain the existence of aggregate profits, as well as sectoral profits.

*The author would like to thank the following for their comments: Claude Gnos, Alain Parguez, Sergio Rossi, Mario Seccareccia and Alberto Zazzaro. The usual disclaimers apply.

The first section will give a brief overlook of the main arguments of the monetary circuit. The second section discusses some of the attempts at explaining profits, and presents an approach that will undoubtedly be criticized, for such is the nature of this delicate subject. Because of space considerations, this chapter can at best sketch out the main lines of the problem, but does not allow me to go into great detail.

The theory of the monetary circuit

The theory of the monetary circuit is a sequential approach to money and macroeconomics that allows economists to analyse the real world in a methodical way. In a sense, it organises our thoughts around the complexities of causal relationships, and allows us to see clearly the relevant features of a monetary capitalist economy of production. It implies a specific sequence of irreversible events and relies on the creditworthiness of both firms and banks, where the theory of effective demand and bank behaviour are closely linked.

The notion of a monetary circuit is not new, and is as old as economics itself. It can be traced back to the work of Quesnay, and can be found in Marx, Schumpeter and Wicksell. Of course, it is also the foundation of Keynes, Kalecki, and Robinson, the latter too often overlooked by Post Keynesians (see Gnos and Rochon, 2003; and Rochon, 2004). In that tradition, the theory of the monetary circuit rests on the flow of money arising from debt and its circulation through the economy as it simultaneously traces the flow of goods. It exemplifies how the real and monetary sides of the economy are necessarily interdependent through the endogenous nature of money.

The division of society prevalent in Kaleckian macrotheories of income distribution forms the foundation of circuit theory. This class-based approach – or what Graziani (1990, p. 8) refers to as the 'relationship among macro-groups' – studies the relationship between banks, firms, and wage earners (although we can add the state (Parguez, 1997) and a central bank (Rochon and Rossi, 2004) without changing the analysis). Banks supply the much-needed credit to firms that undertake production and investment. As such, they determine the allocation of productive resources. Wage earners supply the intellectual and physical labour. This division helps us to understand the income distributive role of money, that is, the ability of capitalists to determine their own levels of profits through access to credit. As such, the ex nihilo creation of money is the result of the complexity of the relationship between three specific causal relationships: banks and firms (initial finance), workers and firms (final finance), banks and households (the demand for money). At heart is the notion that money is part of a circuit, and as such it is first created by credit, circulated, and destroyed. Hence, money exists to be ultimately destroyed, although households may decide at the end of the circuit to hold on to some money balances (which poses problems for the closure of the circuit).

While simplification requires us to deal exclusively with a single circuit, it is clear that many circuits exist simultaneously. While this is certainly true, the story of profits ought to be told within the confines of a single circuit. Can aggregate profits be explained, therefore, within a model where there is a single circuit, no government, and set within a closed economy? Let us assume the division of firms into consumption-goods and investment-goods firms. The monetary circuit begins with the firm's production and investment decisions. Planned production and investment are different from realised production and investment, and the difference is precisely the ability of firms to secure the proper amount of credit. As suggested by Keynes, the level of production is influenced by the expectations of effective demand, the level of which is determined by short-term expectations of proceeds. As for the factors that influence investment, the discussion is more ambiguous. We can, however, assume that investment decisions are based on expectations of the growth of effective demand over time; that is, the growth of markets in years to come.

Once production levels are determined, firms then set the wage level, employment, mark-up, and thus prices, where prices are set to generate sufficient proceeds over costs of production for the reimbursement of debt.

It is a central characteristic of the monetary circuit that credit is always required at the beginning of every period of production. Since initial credit must be reimbursed to the banks in the cancellation of debt, firms must either renew their credit with the banks or roll over their existing debt, even in a stationary system. Either way, this requires the tacit approval of the banks.

If the level of production is constant, firms receive constant revenues from the sale of their output. But the liquidity they receive must be reimbursed to the banks, which means that immediately after, even if firms desire to keep output constant, they must first obtain new credit. All that can be said is that a constant level of output requires a constant level of finance, but in no cases can it be suggested that in a stationary state the need for finance disappears. (Graziani 1985, p. 167)

Thus, given the general state of a lack of finance, it becomes imperative for firms to have access to credit. And as Eichner (1979) argues, *any* production *must* be accompanied by the emission of loans, this applies equally well to firms in both the investment-goods and consumption-goods sectors (Keynes, 1973a, p. 282).

In his finance motive articles, Keynes (1973a, p. 207) argues that 'planned investment – i.e. investment *ex ante* – may have to secure its "financial provision" *before* the corresponding saving has taken place' This is largely achieved through the extension of loans by commercial banks – hence banks are 'special' (Robinson, 1956, p. 10; Keynes, 1973a, p. 209), because of their ability to create money from their liabilities. As Parguez and Seccareccia (2000, p. 103) write, 'money appears when there exists a set of agents, which we shall call 'banks' (including the central bank), whose debts are accepted by all other agents in an economy as a means of payment to settle their own debt commitments'.

This discussion suggests that production is a process of debt creation (Seccareccia, 1988, p. 51) and 'bank credit is the primary mode of financing productive activity' (Seccareccia, 1996): firms cannot produce if they do not agree to enter into a debt contract with banks. Several debts are thus created: firms are indebted to banks for the amount of the initial finance, firms are also indebted to workers for their labour power, and banks are indebted to workers (or depositors) once wages have been paid out. As Graziani (1996, p. 143) writes, as soon as wages are paid, 'a triangular debt–credit situation, typical of any monetary economy, is thus created'. Hence, the hierarchy of debts corresponds to the hierarchy of agents discussed above. All debts are then settled with money: wages are paid in money, deposits when withdrawn are honoured in money, and bank debts are cancelled once firms reimburse a monetary value equal to the debt.

Money is the natural result of debt: it is credit-led and demand-determined. In this sense, money is endogenous and no excess supply of money exists. It is the result of double-entry accounting: debt being the asset of banks while money is its liability. As a result of debt, money is created only to be ultimately destroyed.

The role of banks is therefore crucial to the understanding of the theory of the monetary circuit, and is at the heart of the realisation of production plans, investment and profits. The creation of money is synonymous with the creation of incomes: the flow of money, incomes and production are intimately linked through bank credit.

While virtually all circuitists agree that wages and other costs of production are covered by bank credit, the subject of whether investment is financed by bank credit is at the heart of considerable debate among circuitists. Seccareccia (1988, 1996), Parguez (1996) and Rochon (1999) have all argued that investment is financed – or partly financed – by bank credit. Others, for instance Graziani (1990, pp. 12–14), claim that only wages are financed by bank credit. For Graziani, the question of investment financing arises only at the end of the circuit, allowing for growth in the subsequent period. They are financed as 'internal transactions' (Graziani, 1990, p. 12) within the non-financial business sector; that is, through retained earnings and the new issues market (see also Gnos, 2003). Otherwise, according to the author, it would represent a reinstatement of the natural rate hypothesis (although this is not correct if we assume, as do Post Keynesians and many circuitists, an exogenous rate of interest). Seccareccia (1996, p. 402) defends his position, noting that the 'assumption regarding bank credit going exclusively towards the financing of working capital, is highly questionable'.

Nell (1996) is even more restrictive, claiming that only a portion of the wages is financed by bank credit (the wages of workers in the investment-goods sector), with the velocity of money ensuring that the entire production of goods circulates, otherwise there would be too much money (see next section). The only relevant issue here is the role played by banks in financing the needs of all firms. There can be no production without a prior bank credit.[1]

Given the fact that bank deposits are part of any definition of money, money is created ex nihilo as soon as credit is granted to firms. Whereas money is endogenous, as in Post Keynesian theory, the analysis does not rest on the accommodative role of the central bank, nor on the nature of contracts, uncertainty and portfolio analysis. Production is what gives money its endogenous nature. But this initial increase in the money stock is only temporary; the final, observed increase in the stock of money is dependent on household behavior (the demand for money).

Once firms have formulated their demand for credit, they must have their demand validated by banks if production is to proceed. This supply of credit is not automatic. Banks will not meet all the demand for credit that is forthcoming at a given price. Banks also want to generate profits, but they also face an uncertain future and must incorporate that within their lending practices.

Banks are not passive players in the circuit. They are profit-seeking firms in the business of spelling a product – credit (the liabilities of which happen to be accepted as means of payment). The demand for credit is made at the initiative of the customers. Banks cannot lend if there are no customers willing to enter into debt.

Since banks are a part of the same uncertain economy as firms, uncertainty and expectations must be allowed to influence their decisions to extend credit. Given the inherent uncertainty regarding markets and effective demand, there always exists a risk that borrowers will be unable to repay loans; it becomes the banks' responsibility to evaluate this credit risk on an individual basis. Banks must seek creditworthy customers. In return, firms must be able to show that they are able to repay the loans. Firms' profits become the validation of their demand for credit. The role of the banks is to identify the creditworthiness of the firms and to compare these to the requirements needed to obtain a loan (Robinson, 1956, pp. 138, 231, 244). Banks are therefore interested in whether firms will be able to reimburse their loan and will therefore take into consideration several factors, including the economic environment and prospects for the industry, the quality of management, the past business relationship with the bank, the firm's ability to generate profits (dictated to a large degree by the banks themselves), the firm's net worth and collateral, the firm's ability to withstand transitory shocks, and certain key financial ratios, such as cash flows and debt/equity.

This does not imply – as has been erroneously suggested – that banks extend credit on demand. On the contrary, banks refuse credit to many customers – Keynes's 'fringe of unsatisfied borrowers.' But provided the customers' reasons for borrowing funds are sound and provided also that customers have sufficient assets or income collateral (creditworthiness), then they are granted loans virtually on demand.

The circuit ends when income is spread over the system in the form of consumption expenditures and saving. This last step represents the final financing of the initial loan. It occurs when commodities are brought to the market and sold at a price determined by the firm for the sole purpose of realizing profits. When goods are purchased, therefore, there is a transfer of money from households' accounts to the accounts of firms. Consumption becomes an income for the firm, which then reimburses previous loans – at which point money is destroyed. Le Bourva (1992, p. 454) has called this process 'alternating movements of creation and cancellation of money'. Firms therefore try to 'recapture' their outlays by selling their product to households. This is the 'reflux' principle.

In the simplified model, it is assumed that households do not save; they consume their entire income. If this is the case, then firms will be able to recoup all the initial outlays: income will be equal to expenditures. But in reality, households will save a portion of their wages. Because of savings, firms will be unable to recapture all the initial outlays and will not be able to repay the entire value of their debt to the banks and this poses a definite problem for the closure of the circuit. This is what Seccareccia (this volume) calls the 'Keynesian problem of insufficient reflux'. Because of household savings, firms are forced to emit financial securities on the financial market to try to capture a part of household saving. In this sense, saving will be divided into two components of wealth: liquid or hoarded saving and financial saving, which are used to purchase financial assets. It is here that the 'demand for money' as liquidity can pose a problem to firms. As Graziani (1990) made clear, in addition to the receipts from consumption, firms can capture a part of household saving by selling new securities to households. Money therefore flows back to firms through consumption and saving, that is, the part of saving that households do not hoard in their bank accounts: this is another source of final finance (see Keynes, 1973a, p. 221).[2]

At the end of the circuit, the final (observed) increase in the money stock is given by the quantity of saving that is hoarded by households. The final amplitude of these changes will depend on the saving behaviour of households. As such, changes in the 'stock' of money – as well as hoarded savings – are a residual of the system; that is, a result of the pattern of circulation of money. This point was well expressed. Lavoie (1992, p. 156) also defends this point: 'There is no difference between the outstanding amount of loans and the stock of money.'

These savings represent a net drainage on the overall system. Firms will not be able to reimburse the totality of their initial finance, implying that they will be permanently indebted toward the banks. If this is the case, how then can we close the system? Various solutions have been offered. They are related to the issue of profits, which is the subject of the following section.

The determination of profits

This section proposes to tackle one of the most contentious issues in the circuit approach; namely, the determination of macroeconomic or aggregate profits. Of course, the explanation of profits at the individual or micro level is not difficult to explain. Some firms are bound to extract from the market more revenue than they inject into it, while other will have deficits or even declare bankruptcy. At the micro level, therefore, there is competition among firms to extract more money than it initially injected. But it is the existence of profits at the aggregate level that is more difficult to explain.

Indeed, the problem is a simple one, as Zazzaro (2003, p. 233) explains, 'If in an economic system (closed to external exchange) the only money existing is what the banks create in financing production, the amount of money that firms may recover by selling their products is at the most equal to the amount by which they have been financed by banks.' One thing is certain, as Graziani (1996, p. 142) explains, 'the very formation of profits is explained by the presence of money'.

The conclusions are all too familiar: in a simple circuit where only wages are financed by banks and with households savings equal to zero, only consumption-goods producing firms make profits, which are equal to the wages of the workers in the investment-goods sector, as recognised by Robinson (1956, p. 75).

These profits are then used to purchase capital goods, which then become revenues for the firms in the capital-goods industry. Since their revenues are equal to their costs (wages), their profits are nil. Clearly, this is an unacceptable situation.

The situation, however, gets even more complicated as soon as we add interest payments on bank credit, as dictated by the exogenous rate of interest. In this more realistic situation, we see that even when firms in the consumption-goods sector spend their profits on accumulation, there cannot be sufficient proceeds to cover the costs of production in the investment-goods sector.

We can resolve part of this dilemma if we assume that the wages and expenditures of the banking industry are injected into circulation, as Robinson (1956) suggested. In this case, since bank profits are merely the interest on loans, firms would be receiving back the interest they paid to banks. But this does not solve the whole problem of profits. At best, firms in the capital-goods sector make zero profits.

The problem thus requires attention. How can we explain the creation of monetary profits in all sectors and hence at the macroeconomic level as well?

There have been several attempts at explaining the existence of aggregate profits. First, many have argued that profits can be explained by the inclusion of an external sector, say the state or an export/import sector. While the inclusion of the state may indeed lead to higher profits, it reminds us that the theory of the monetary circuit cannot explain profits in its most rudimentary form. This is not to say that government deficits do not help in generating profits, but as Nell (2002, p. 520) argues, 'it is necessary to show how the system can work without reliance on outside assistance'. Moreover, as Graziani argues (1994, p. 69, quoted in Zazzaro, 2003, p. 234), relying on the state to explain the existence of profits may open circuit theory to harsh criticism. In particular, it supposes that there is a need for a constant government deficit or, in the case of an open economy, to a permanent trade surplus (we can also assume that households get into debt and spend more than their income) (see also Seccareccia, 2003, p. 176).

A second approach consists of borrowing in advance the profits that firms will be making and injecting them into circulation; presumably, such profits would be built into wages. This is the Schmittian position advanced, for instance, by Renaud (2000) and Rossi (2001). According to Renaud (2000, p. 293), 'the endogenous realization of money profits in the monetary production economy is possible if business firms have the ability to spend in the present... the anticipated profits included in their supply price'. An obvious shortcoming of such an approach is that it assumes that firms spend their incomes before the beginning of the circuit and, indeed, before the realisation of their profits. Profits are formed in the goods market after production. Firms do not know, and cannot know, ex ante the value of their profits.

Of course, it also raises the question of the role of the banks: they lend in the hope that firms will generate profits which, taken individually, is not a guaranteed result. Why would banks therefore lend firms their profits before they are materialised? But more importantly, Gnos (2003, pp. 333–4) gave the most valid criticism: 'Unfortunately, the question cannot be settled in this way.... This is not sufficient to solve the problem under discussion: being anticipated, the formation of profits is not explained but presupposed.'

A third explanation consists in assuming the existence of a number of overlapping monetary circuits. This appears to be a solution that is shared by a great many circuitists and some Post Keynesians (see Smithin, 1997). The idea is that in the real world, firms do not borrow and reimburse their debt all at the same time. In this sense, Gnos (2003, pp. 332, 334) writes that 'The reality is that the start of production entails the superposition of different phases of the circuit (and so individual circuits)... Whatever the period of time we consider... firms again and again pay wages and sell goods, production processes overlapping one another, so that firms have no difficulty gaining profits out of wages provided buyers are prepared to purchase goods at prices exceeding factor costs.'

This explanation is interesting in the sense that it does not seek to explain how M becomes M' since there is no need to have $M' > M$. If there are several circuits overlapping each other, then there is always more money being injected at any one time than is being extinguished through the repayment of bank debt. According to Gnos (2003, p. 334), 'But in this case, neither the existence of a surplus in output nor in the money available in the economy needs to be presupposed...There is no need then to look for any additional quantity of money.'

A similar solution was proposed by Zazzaro (2003, p. 234) who adopts a Schumpetarian solution, where the real world is characterised by a dynamic market in which 'the economy undergoes an endless process of change that involves the entry of new firms, the start-up of new initiatives and failures of others.'

While interesting, both variations still do not solve the problem that was posed at the start: can profits be explained within a single circuit without having to resort to other circuits or outside sectors? Moreover, they rely essentially on a microeconomic explanation of what is a macroeconomic problem.

A fourth explanation would see the investment-goods sector divided into sub-sectors, where one sub-sector would purchase capital goods from the other. This is proposed, for instance, by Lavoie (1987). However, in the end, there would still be a sub-sector that would be unable to generate sufficient proceeds to pay back its initial debt. Nell (2002, p. 525) resolves this problem by assuming simply that there exists a sub-sector that does not require the purchase of capital goods: this 'machine-tool' sub-sector uses its own goods to produce its goods: 'It does not buy capital goods because it does not need them; it uses what it makes' – the production of commodities by means of its own commodities! This approach remains nonetheless rather unrealistic and seems to suit the theoretical conundrum without any reference to the real world.

A fifth and final solution is proposed by Nell (1996), who suggests that only the wages in the investment-goods sector need to be financed by bank credit. This minimalist approach, based on the needs of firms to minimise borrowing costs, can explain the circulation of the economy's entire output. Nell (2002) assumes that firms in the consumption-goods sector need not borrow to finance its production needs: it begins production and pays its workers only when workers in the investment-goods sector spend their income on consumption goods. Moreover, firms within the investment-goods sector extend credit to inter-sector firms. Through increases in velocity and inter sector credit, M can be turned into M' where all sectors realise profits in monetary terms.

Unfortunately, this solution has some flaws. First, if my interpretation is correct, it assumes that wages in the investment-goods sector are at least equal to those in the consumption-goods sector: otherwise, proceeds from the sale of commodities would not be sufficient to pay their own workers. Second, it assumes two important asymmetries. First, it assumes that firms in the investment-goods sector need to pay their workers now (by borrowing), while firms in the consumption-goods sector can somehow wait. Second, it assumes an asymmetry between the firms: some would be financed by bank credit and others would not qualify for bank credit but rather receive intersector credit. Nell (2002, p. 525, italics in original) recognises this asymmetry, but argues that 'the apparent asymmetry in monetary arrangements simply reflects a *real asymmetry*'. As Seccareccia (1996, p. 407) has argued, however, 'Why should firms in one sector provide private credit for purchases among themselves and, yet, require exchanges in money terms originating from bank credit with firms in the consumption goods sector?' This approach remains difficult to accept.

A common problem with all these explanations is that they rely on external conditions to generate profits. In other words, the simple model of the single circuit with no government in a closed economy seems to be unable to generate profits. Profits must be explained from within the circuit and from a realist account of markets. Only then can they be deemed truly endogenous to the monetary circuit.

With the inability of most approaches to explain monetary profits, the only remaining explanation that is consistent with both actual banking and entrepreneurial practices is where investment is also financed by bank credit. It allows for a symmetrical treatment of firms in all sectors and conforms to the real fact that firms *do* borrow bank credit to finance, at least in part, capital accumulation.

The standard way of proposing this approach is to assume that within a single period of circulation, banks cover the financing of working and fixed capital (see Seccareccia, 1996, 2003; Parguez and Seccareccia, 2000) that, once released into active circulation, would generate sufficient revenues for all firms in all sectors. The parallel relationship between the creation of money and the creation of income is maintained: the purchase of capital goods in simultaneously the creation of income in the investment-goods sector.

Many circuit writers reject this approach, and Graziani (1994, p. 277; see also Schmitt, 1996) has specifically argued against it. But Graziani assumes that firms would sell securities to households and use the proceeds to finance investment; what he calls final finance. However, as we will see below, there can be another interpretation of the role of financial markets and the reflux mechanism.

Seccareccia (2003) has shown that only when investment is included in bank credit can we arrive at a satisfactory explanation of monetary profits. There is a significant problem, however. The inclusion of investment financing through bank credit certainly explains the existence of profits in the investment-goods sector, but poses a definite challenge for firms in the consumption-goods sector. Can these firms receive sufficient proceeds to cover the cost of accumulation? To solve this problem, we can assume the existence of two parallel circuits: a production circuit and an investment circuit. These are *not* overlapping circuits but a single circuit divided into two reflecting different transactions. Each circuit is necessary for the reimbursement of debts and the generation of profits, but we can argue that the production circuit closes within the period of production, whereas the investment circuit typically will carry over a number of production circuits. In other words, it will be multiperiod reflecting the longevity and financing of capital goods. At the beginning of the circuit, firms borrow the necessary funds from banks to cover the costs of production, wages and raw material, as well as investment – or at least a portion of the cost of investment, where retained earnings from past production circuits can be used to finance the remaining portion.

At the beginning of the circuit, therefore, funds equalling the value of fixed and variable capital are released into circulation. These create an income for firms in all sectors. Profits are then easily explained. For firms in the consumption-goods sector, revenues will consist, as always, of goods sold to workers in their own sector, as well as to those in the capital-goods and banking sectors. The purchase of capital goods now represents revenues or proceeds for the firms producing them. These will be more than the cost of the wages in the investment-goods sector, and so profits will materialise in this sector as well.

As debt was incurred, debt must now be reimbursed. A potential problem arises, however, since the value of an investment tends to be very large. How can firms generate sufficient revenues to reimburse the whole of their investment? This is solved quite easily by assuming, as in the real world, that while firms need to reimburse their working capital at the end of a given period of production, they typically reimburse the investment over several periods. Indeed, firms often take years to pay back an initial investment. We can claim, therefore, that the investment circuit is multi-period: it amounts to several periods of production. Hence, profits are formed because incomes equalling the value of working and fixed capital are created (or a portion of the value of the fixed capital), while only a portion of the fixed capital needs to be reimbursed in any given period. As Messori and Zazzaro (2004, this volume) explain, 'a simple financial market whose function is to offer long-term (i.e. multiperiod) credit to firms for financing investment demand... makes possible the monetary determination of profits and the monetary payment of bank interest by the set of firms.'

It is thus possible, within a single period, to explain the generation of profits. There is no need for an external sector such as a government, or overlapping circuits, or other microeconomic explanations, such as bankruptcies. Rather, profits are explained at the macroeconomic level by a macroeconomic explanation. This said, governments and other explanations can still play a role, of course, but they do not *explain* profits. Government deficits can help to generate additional revenues and add to existing profits, but we can explain profits even without them.

Owing to interest, firms have an advantage to keep the number of periods small. In this sense, any additional profits owing, say, to government deficits, will be used to pay off existing debts. This is typical of a monetary economy of production.

As for the financial markets, they are, as Graziani said, never a source of fresh finance. Rather, firms need to capture household savings by issuing securities. Funds will flow back to firms to pay off their debt.

One of the advantages of this approach is the following: firms in the investment-goods sector are no longer dependent on the profits in the firms in the consumption-goods sector. Similarly, firms in the latter sector are no longer constrained by their profits: bank financing of investment has removed this unnecessary constraint.

Conclusion

The aim of this chapter was to acknowledge Graziani's rich intellectual legacy. While his writings have had a dramatic impact on the development of ideas within Post Keynesian and circulation approaches, it nonetheless led to considerable debate. One of the contentious issues that still needs to be resolved is the existence of profits. Whether the debate can ever be resolved, is another important question.

The chapter presented first a general overview of the theory of the monetary circuit, and then discussed some of the approaches to the problem at hand. A final solution was then presented that consisted in having banks finance investment, but where firms only need to pay back long-term credit over several periods of production. Undoubtedly it will also be a source of further debate, with the solution contained herein also critisised.

Notes

1. Post-Keynesians also have this debate. Moore (1988) assumes that only wages are covered by bank credit while Davidson (1972) assumes that investments are also born out of bank loans.
2. Liquidity preference is then consistent with the circuitist story, although it appears at the end of the monetary circuit. It is not a decision between consumption and saving, but a decision with respect to how to allocate total saving.

References

Davidson, P. (1972) *Money and The Real World* (New York: John Wiley & Sons).
Eichner, A. (1979) 'A Post Keynesian Short-Period Model', *Journal of Post Keynesian Economics*, 1 (Summer), pp. 38–63.

Gnos, C. (2003) 'Circuit Theory as an Explanation of the Complex Real World', in L.-P. Rochon and S. Rossi (eds), *Modern Theories of Money: The Nature and Role of Money in Capitalist Economies* (Cheltenham: Edward Elgar).

Gnos, C. and Rochon, L.-P. (2003) 'Joan Robinson and Keynes on Money, Relative Prices and the Monetary Circuit', *Review of Political Economy*, 15(4).

Graziani, A. (1985) 'Le débat sur le "motif de financement" de Keynes', *Economie Appliquée*, 38, pp. 159–75.

Graziani, A. (1990) 'The Theory of the Monetary Circuit', *Économies et Sociétés*, Série Monnaie et Production, 24, 6.

Graziani, A. (1994) *La teoria monetaria della produzione* ('Studi e Ricerche', 7) (Arezzo: Banca Popolare dell'Etruria e del Lazio).

Graziani, A. (1996) 'Money as Purchasing Power and Money as a Stock of Wealth in Keynesian Economic Thought', in E. Nell and G. Deleplace (eds), *Money in Motion* (London: Macmillan).

Keynes, J.M. (1973a) *The Collected Writings of John Maynard Keynes, Volume XIII: The General Theory and After, Preparation*, D. Moggridge (ed.), (London: Macmillan and Cambridge University Press).

Lavoie, M. (1984) 'Un modèle post-keynésien d'économie monétaire fondé sur la théorie du circuit', *Économies et Sociétés*, 18 (2), pp. 233–58.

Lavoie, M. (1987) 'Monnaie et production: une synthèse de la théorie du circuit', *Économies et Sociétés*, September, 9, pp. 65–101.

Lavoie, M. (1992) *Foundations of Post-Keynesian Economic Analysis* (Aldershot: Edward Elgar).

Le Bourva, J. (1992) 'Money Creation and Credit Multipliers', *Review of Political Economy*, 4 (4), pp. 447–66.

Moore, B. (1988) *Horizontalists and Verticalists: The Macroeconomics of Credit-Money* (Cambridge University Press).

Nell, E. (1996) 'The Circuit of Money in a Production Economy', in E. Nell and G. Deleplace (eds), *Money in Motion* (London: Macmillan).

Nell, E. (2002) 'On Realizing Profits in Money', *Review of Political Economy*, 14, 4, October, pp. 519–30.

Parguez, A. (1996) 'Beyond Scarcity: A Reappraisal of the Theory of the Monetary Circuit', in G. Deleplace and E. Nell (eds), *Money in Motion* (London: Macmillan).

Parguez, A. (1997) 'Government Deficits within the Monetary Production Economy or the Tragedy of the Race to Balance Budgets', unpublished.

Parguez, A. and Seccareccia, M. (2000) 'The Credit Theory of Money: The Monetary Circuit Approach', in J. Smithin, (ed.), *What is Money?* (London: Routledge).

Poulon, F. (1990) 'Graphe, crise et circuit keynésien', *Revue d'économie politique*, 90, (4), pp. 371–409.

Renaud, J.-F. (2000) 'The problem of the Monetary Realization of Profits in Post Keynesian Sequential Financing Model: Two Solutions of the Kaleckian Option', *Review of Political Economy*, 12, pp. 285–304.

Robinson, J. (1952) *The Rate of Interest and Other Essays* (London: Macmillan).

Robinson, J. (1956) *The Accumulation of Capital* (London: Macmillan).

Rochon, L.-P. (1999) *Credit, Money and Production: An Alternative Post-Keynesian Approach* (Cheltenham: Edward Elgar).

Rochon, L.-P. (2004) 'Joan Robinson on Credit, Money and Production: A Forgotten Contribution', in W. Gibson, (ed.), *Joan Robinson* (Cheltenham: Edward Elgar).

Rochon, L.-P. and Rossi, S. (2004) 'Banking in the Monetary Circuit', in M. Lavoie and M. Seccareccia (eds), *Central Banking in the Modern World: Alternative Perspectives* (Cheltenham: Edward Elgar).

Rossi, S. (2001) *Money and Inflation: A New Macroeconomic Analysis* (Cheltenham: Edward Elgar).

Schmitt, B. (1996) 'A New Paradigm for the Determination of Money Prices', in E. Nell and G. Deleplace (eds), *Money in Motion* (London: Macmillan).

Seccareccia, M. (1988) 'Systematic Viability and Credit Crunches: An Examination of Recent Canadian Cyclical Fluctuations', *Journal of Economic Issues*, March, 22 (1), pp. 49–77.

Seccareccia, M. (1996) 'Post-Keynesian Fundism and Monetary Circulation', in G. Deleplace and E. Nell (eds), *Money in Motion: The Post Keynesian and Circulation Approaches* (London: Macmillan).

Seccareccia, M. (2003) 'Pricing, Investment and the Financing of Production within the Framework of he Monetary Circuit: Some Preliminary Evidence', in L.-P. Rochon and S. Rossi (eds), *Modern Theories of Money: The Nature and Role of Money in Capitalist Economies* (Cheltenham: Edward Elgar).

Smithin. J. (1997) 'An Alternative Monetary Model of Inflation and Growth', *Review of Political Economy*, 9 (4), pp. 395–409.

Zazzaro, A. (2003) 'How Heterodox is the Heterodoxy of Monetary Circuit Theory? The Nature of Money and the Microeconomics of the Circuit', in L.-P. Rochon, and S. Rossi (eds), *Modern Theories of Money: The Nature and Role of Money in Capitalist Economies* (Cheltenham: Edward Elgar).

9
Central Banking in a Monetary Theory of Production: The Economics of Payment Finality from a Circular-Flow Perspective

Sergio Rossi[*]

Introduction

Payment finality – that is, 'the discharge of an obligation by a transfer of funds and a transfer of securities that have become irrevocable and unconditional' (Committee on Payment and Settlement Systems, 2003a, p. 496) – is crucial for the orderly working of modern economic systems. As a matter of fact, monetary transactions are the backbone of production and exchange, national as well as international. Payments equivalent to a country's annual GDP are presently made over a few working days within any national economy. The large volume and scope of payments at the time of writing imply that problems in their settlement could affect the financial sector and even the economy as a whole. Further, the implementation and transmission mechanism of a central bank's monetary policy also depends on the smooth functioning of domestic payment systems, and hence the issue of payment finality is of both private and public concern.

While the question of payment finality has been addressed by lawyers and central bankers, especially by those involved in the management and/ or supervision of settlement systems, it has received little attention from economists of any pedigree. Only in recent years has the economics profession begun to consider this question at both the theoretical and policy level. However, focus has been mainly, if not exclusively, on the importance of payment finality for non-bank agents (see, for example, Kahn and Roberds,

[*] The first draft of this chapter was presented at a conference in honour of Augusto Graziani held at the University of Sannio, Benevento, Italy, on 5–6 December 2003. The author would like to thank the discussant on that occasion, Giovanni Pavanelli, as well as Alvaro Cencini, Ghislain Deleplace, Claude Gnos, and Domenica Tropeano for their helpful comments and suggestions. The usual disclaimer applies.

2002, and Holthausen and Monnet, 2003). In particular, analyses focus on bank money and its role in facilitating exchange when the issue of payment finality has been settled by setting up a triangular payment structure in which a bank is the 'go-between' facing the payer and the payee. This framework, in fact, was put to the fore by monetary circuit theorists well before the attention it received from the economics profession. It is namely to be found in the work of a number of twentieth-century economists, led by authors such as Graziani in Italy, Parguez in France, and Lavoie and Seccareccia in Canada, who indeed trace their approach back to several founding fathers of our science such as Wicksell, Schumpeter, and Keynes, to quote only the most well-known of them (see Realfonzo, 1998). This approach has proven fruitful for explaining the nature of bank money and its credit-driven emission (see, among others, Graziani, 1990; Lavoie, 1996; Parguez and Seccareccia, 2000). Up to now, however, monetary circuit theorists have not devoted much attention to the role of central bank money in interbank payments; that is, for the settlement of debt within the banking system (see, however, Lavoie, this volume). This chapter aims to expand on this role in the latter framework by investigating the question of payment finality at the interbank level; that is, in the monetary circuit involving banks and the central bank at the top of them. As pointed out by Graziani (1990, p. 18), '[t]he role of the Central Bank is in fact of acting as a third party between single banks so far as their reciprocal payments are concerned'. Taking stock from the nature and role of bank money in the settlement of non-banks' debt, this chapter aims at explaining the nature and role of central bank money in the settlement of interbank debts within a closed economy. To be sure, the coexistence of central and commercial bank monies in modern capitalist economies is to be explained with reference to the same methodological approach, since the nature of modern money does not change when analysis switches from commercial to central bank money.

The structure of the chapter is as follows. The first section analyses the coexistence of central and commercial bank monies, and explains the money-purveying role of the settlement institution at the interbank level on the grounds of a circular-flow paradigm. Within this framework, the second section shows that a distinction exists between the money-purveying and the credit-purveying functions of central banks in domestic settlement systems. In this respect, the third section provides a few hints in order for the theory of the monetary circuit to expand on international monetary economics issues. Namely, it points out the need to set up an international settlement institution for cross-border transactions that involve central banks. The fourth section concludes this chapter.

The coexistence of central and commercial bank monies

Money is fundamental to the existence and functioning of national economies as these are based on production and exchange, be it in a closed- or open-economy framework. Without money, economic activity could not be measured, and values and prices could not be expressed in a social form necessary to homogenise and thus commensurate the thousands of goods and services produced in any dynamic market economy over any particular period. Yet, in any national economy there are several money issuers, namely, the central bank and the commercial banks making up the domestic banking system, each of them issuing its own means of payment. 'The multiplicity both of issuers of money and of payment mechanisms is a common feature in all developed economies' (Committee on Payment and Settlement Systems, 2003b, p. 1). As a result, central and commercial bank monies coexist in our economies, and an institutional mechanism must exist to make sure that ' "one dollar is one dollar", whatever form it takes (whether central or commercial bank money)' (p. 1). The 'singleness' of a currency is, in fact, a necessary (but not yet sufficient) condition for money to be the measure of value and the means of payment in the economic area where it is issued. The other condition is that money and payments are to be linked to production as the two faces of a single object. If there were no production, money could not exist and hence be the measure of value, but this issue lies outside the scope of the present chapter (see Rossi, 2003).

Commercial bank money is used by non-bank agents for the settlement of their debt on factor, goods, and financial markets as well. Note, however, that at this level fund 'transfers generally take place within organized "payment systems" where commercial and central bank money often complement each other in more complex chains of payments' (Committee on Payment and Settlement Systems, 2003b, p. 9). As a matter of fact, central bank money, in the form of notes and coins, may also be used by non-bank agents: the payer can pay for his purchases on any markets by surrendering to the payee a number of notes worth the amount of the transaction. Both commercial and central bank money (here in the form of notes and coins) are indeed means of final payment for the non-bank sector.

Now, in any national economy modern payment systems involve a great number of banks dealing with the settlement orders of non-bank agents. In fact, any transaction on any markets involves two agents and quite possibly two banks, each of the latter issuing its own means of payment in the form of commercial bank money. Because of the involvement of two banks, the notion of payment finality has been a crucial issue for central banks in the last decade or so, both on theoretical and practical grounds. In an environment of multiple banks, in fact, at any point in time a particular bank may be indebted to another bank within the banking system, as a result of the great number of incoming and outgoing payments initiated by and destinated to the non-bank sector (Lavoie, 2003, p. 516). The inflows and outflows elicited by monetary transactions require therefore that the banking system be complemented by a settlement institution providing payment facilities in order for the bilateral debt–credit relations at interbank level to be finally settled without systemic disruption or failure (Rochon and Rossi,

2004). As the Committee on Payment and Settlement Systems (2003b, p. 4) put it:

> While the role of the central bank as settlement institution is a long-standing one, in many cases this role only required the central bank to settle the relatively small net positions of commercial banks resulting from a netting procedure. Moreover, this occurred only once each day, at the end of the day. But with the introduction of newer, safer systems to handle the substantially increased payment system values, and in particular with the widespread adoption of real-time gross settlements (RTGS), where each payment is settled in real time throughout the day, central banks and central bank money have come to take on a much wider and more active role.

To expand on this point, let us consider a central bank facing two banks, B_1 and B_2, that are involved for the settlement of a monetary transaction between their non-bank clients, I and II. Suppose for example that a payment order of £x has to be settled in an RTGS system, which is the institutional form of most, if not all, large-value transfer systems existing at present. If the payer, I, and the payee, II, hold their accounts with the same bank, say B_1, the accounts concerned can simply be debited and credited by the latter, which issues its own means of payment in order for the final settlement between clients I and II to take place (in-house settlement). On the contrary, if both parties are not clients of the same bank, the payment involves two distinct banks, B_1 and B_2, each of them issuing its own means of payment and recording the result in their balance sheets as shown in Table 9.1.

As Table 9.1 shows, the final payment between the non-bank agents, namely, clients I and II, gives rise to a debt–credit relation between the paying and the receiving bank; that is, B_1 and B_2 respectively. In other words, B_2 acquires a commercial bank deposit created by B_1 as a liquid asset. B_1 is thus indebted to B_2 for an amount of £x as a result of the payment having occurred between client I (that is, the payer) and client II (the payee), who is finally paid by the latter bank.

Now, while the settlement of debt between the payer and the payee is done in bank money, the settlement of debt between banks is carried out in central bank money. As bank practitioners and actual practices indicate,

Table 9.1   The result of a payment between two clients of distinct banks

Bank B_1			Bank B_2		
Assets		Liabilities	Assets		Liabilities
Client I *(payer)*	£x	Bank B_2 £x	Bank B_1	£x	Client II *(payee)* £x

'banks do not accept bank money in interbank transactions, but ultimately require their claims to be settled in central bank money' (Deutsche Bundesbank, 1994, p. 46). The requirement of central bank money for the final settlement of interbank debt–credit relationships is usually explained by the need to control settlement as well as systemic risks that would exist and spread if the relevant payments were not finally paid using central bank money (see, for example, De Bandt and Hartmann, 2000, Heller and Sturm, 2003). In short, using central bank money to settle interbank transactions maintains stability and promotes efficiency of the financial system, which in turn enhances the allocation of resources, supports economic growth, and improves social welfare (Committee on Payment and Settlement Systems, 2003b, p. 8). As Graziani (2003, p. 63) points out, a monetary economy needs a central bank in order to prevent an unlimited expansion of credit by commercial banks, which could give rise to an inflationary increase of total demand by the public if banks moved forward 'in step'. This argument can be reinforced on analytical grounds, on account of the fact that each bank issues its own means of payment in the form of commercial bank money. The 'singleness' of money in any national economy is provided by the central bank, which homogenises the various means of payment issued by commercial banks by issuing its own means of payment (that is, central bank money) used to finally settle debts at interbank level.

In fact, as far as interbank settlements are concerned, the central bank (that is, the settlement institution) must create the number of money units needed to ensure that, in our stylised example, B₂ has no further claims against B₁ (Table 9.2).

At a technical level, the simplest case of interbank final settlements obtains when '[t]he paying and receiving banks are both direct participants in the interbank payment system and hold accounts at the settlement institution, and the settlement is effected by a debit from the account of the paying

Table 9.2 Central bank money as the means of interbank settlements

Bank B₁			Bank B₂		
Assets		Liabilities	Assets		Liabilities
Client I £x	Bank B₂	£x	Bank B₁ £x	Client II	£x
Bank B₂ £x	Central bank	£x	Central bank £x	Bank B₁	£x
Client I £x	Central bank	£x	Central bank £x	Client II	£x

Central bank		
Assets		Liabilities
Bank B₁ £x	Bank B₂	£x

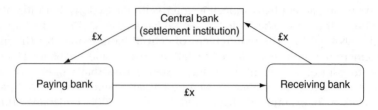

Figure 9.1   The circular flow of central bank money in the interbank market

bank and a credit to the account of the receiving bank' (p. 9). This case is shown in Figure 9.1.[1]

A sum of central bank money worth £x is created on Bank B_1's demand – hence the endogenous nature of central bank money – which uses it to settle its debt to Bank B_2. As a mark of payment finality, Bank B_2 acquires an equivalent central bank deposit at the settlement institution. As a result of the payment in central bank money, B_1 is now indebted to the central bank, for an amount of central bank money worth £x, and B_2 is entitled to an equivalent deposit at the central bank. So far, the payment between B_1 and B_2 has been finalised by an emission of central bank money. The creditor bank, B_2, has no further claims on the debtor bank, B_1. The credit–debt relationship is now defined with respect to the central bank.

The circular flow of central bank money and credit

The analysis in the previous section can be developed further if one distinguishes the money-purveying and the credit-purveying functions carried out by the settlement institution in the interbank market. Money and credit are indeed two separate things, at both commercial bank and central bank level. In fact, as the Committee on Payment and Settlement Systems (2003b, pp. 9–10) puts it, '[t]he payment [from the paying to the receiving bank (see Figure 9.1)] may either be financed with funds already on the account of the paying bank, or with credit provided by the settlement institution'. In the first case, a circuit of central bank money as depicted in Figure 9.1 can be observed, and the analysis provided in the previous section holds. In the second case, analysis is more complex since both central bank money and credit are involved.

In the latter case, which often occurs in the form of intraday credit, the settlement of interbank debt in fact elicits two distinct circuits of central bank money. The first circuit concerns the payment leg on the money market, where an imbalance between banks B_1 and B_2 is settled using central bank money. The second circuit concerns, in contrast, the payment leg in central bank money of a financial transaction on the credit market that is induced by the first circuit. To explain this induction let us recall that payment finality is 'the discharge of an obligation by a transfer of funds and a transfer of securities that have become irrevocable and unconditional' (Committee on Payment and Settlement Systems, 2003a, p. 496). As far as interbank settlements are concerned, this means that securities are to be transferred from the payer, say B_1, to the payee, say B_2, at the same time as the funds in central bank money are transferred from the paying to the receiving bank. In modern banking practice this principle is known as 'delivery versus payment'.[2]

Now, since the circuit of central bank money on the credit market is induced by the circuit on the money market, let us analyse them together (Figure 9.2).

The first circuit of central bank money, which in Figure 9.2 is represented anticlockwise, results from the money-purveying role of the central bank within the banking system: commercial banks need to ask the central bank in order for their reciprocal payments to be finally settled. The central bank is their settlement institution and guarantees monetary homogeneity within the domestic payment system (see p. 143). The second circuit of central bank money, which in Figure 9.2 is represented clockwise, occurs on the credit market when the paying bank, B_1, needs to ask for a credit to settle its debt with the receiving bank, B_2.

As regards this second circuit, two cases may be singled out.

The first case occurs when the debtor bank, say B_1, asks for and obtains a credit from the interbank market, represented in our stylised example by the creditor bank, B_2. For instance, B_2 may grant an intraday credit of £x to B_1, in order for the latter to settle the interbank transaction elicited by the payment occurring between non-bank agents I and II (see p. 143). In this case, the credit operation between the two banks involved may take the form of a daylight credit or a repurchase agreement, which as a general rule is fully collateralised and hence implies a transfer of securities from the borrowing to the lending bank to guarantee payment finality.[3] Since this transaction on securities requires payment, and since it occurs in the interbank market, the central bank has to provide the means of final payment in the form of a sum of central bank money that it creates on B_2's demand (which needs it to purchase the securities sold by B_1 in the interbank market).

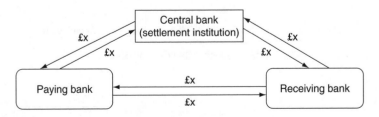

Figure 9.2 The two circuits of central bank money

As a result of this payment (see the clockwise circuit of central bank money in Figure 9.2), B_1 obtains a central bank deposit and can thus balance its account at the settlement institution.

The second case obtains when the debtor bank, B_1, does not find in the interbank market the funds necessary for final payment to the creditor bank, B_2.[4] This is where and when the so-called lender-of-last-resort facilities available at the central bank may be put to practical use. In short, the central bank might grant an intraday credit, also called daylight overdraft, to a debtor bank that neither has enough funds nor finds them in the interbank market. In this respect, the central bank acts as a lender-of-last-resort, and – as the phrase goes – creates the necessary credit in the process. Let us analyse this case more closely, to show that, in fact, the credit granted as a last resort by the central bank is not created by the latter, but results from its financial intermediation services through which it merely advances the result of an incoming payment that today's paying bank, say B_1, will obtain (the next working day or shortly thereafter) from any other bank participating in the domestic settlement system.

The central bank's financial intermediation between banks B_1 and B_2 can indeed be explained as a bilateral or a multilateral transaction on securities (Figure 9.3).

If and when B_2 decides to spend its central bank deposit, usually bearing no interest, for acquiring an interest-bearing asset, then the resulting financial transaction can be stylised as shown in the top part of Figure 9.3 (where B_1 may also be considered as the banking system as a whole). So, if B_2 buys those securities sold by B_1 directly, the financial transaction is bilateral because it implies a seller (B_1) and a purchaser (B_2) of the same securities. If, on the contrary, the securities sold by B_1 are purchased by the central bank –

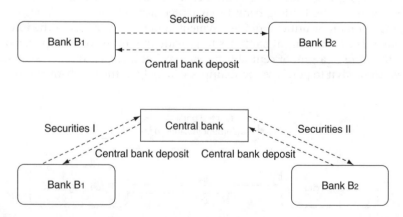

Figure 9.3   Bilateral and multilateral credit operations between banks

for instance, in the repo market –, as shown in the bottom part of Figure 9.3, then the financial transaction is multilateral in so far as a reverse repo between the central bank and B2 brings to the latter the same securities sold by B1 or other assets. In this second case, the central bank's explicit intervention in the financial market provides an institutional guarantee that commercial banks use eligible assets for the smooth functioning of the settlement system. (Note that in Figure 9.3 the circuit of central bank money is implicit in both stylised cases, and indeed exists in the form illustrated in Figure 9.1, but it is not drawn explicitly because it is not germane to the point discussed at this juncture.)

Be that as it may, the end result of these financial transactions on eligible assets shows that the money-purveying and the credit-purveying functions of the central bank have to be kept separate analytically. When the settlement institution creates a sum of central bank money for the final payment between two banks to be made, it does not necessarily enter into a credit operation with any of these banks. It is only when one of the latter banks does not find in the interbank market the funds it needs to clear its position towards the banking system as a whole, that the central bank intervenes by granting it a credit (say, in the form of a repurchase agreement), in order to reduce settlement and systemic risks and hence not to jeopardise the working of the whole payment system, the *conditio sine qua non* for production and exchange. In fact, even in this case the securities sold by B1 to the central bank are paid for with a central bank deposit owned by B2, which lends it to B_1 via the central bank (see the bottom part of Figure 9.3). As a result, in a monetary production economy the circuit of central bank money gives rise to the financial (real) flows depicted in Figure 9.4, where the monetary flows are implicit and look like those represented in Figure 9.2.

This analytical framework helps us conclude that the lender-of-last-resort facilities provided by a central bank are a twofold endogenous phenomenon involving both a money creation and a credit operation between the central bank and the domestic banking system. They involve, in fact, an emission of central bank money ensuring payment finality in the interbank market, and they also imply a fully collateralised credit operation to ensure the smooth working of the domestic payment system.

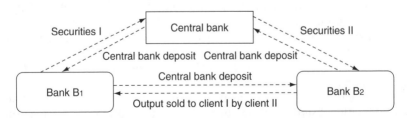

Figure 9.4 The real flows of a central bank's monetary circuit

Payment finality for cross-border transactions

Cross-border transactions are an essential component of modern open economies, be they advanced, emerging, or in transition, and their importance has been growing in line with the emergence of a globalised financial market. The issue of payment finality also applies therefore to cross-border transactions, and failure to settle them properly may have dramatic consequences for the countries involved. In fact, '[c]ross-border clearing and settlement requires access to systems in different countries and/or the interaction of different settlement systems' (Giovannini Group, 2002, p. i). From the perspective of systemic risk and central bank control, the settlement of cross-border transactions seems therefore more problematic than payment finality in domestic transactions.

At the time of writing, despite highly integrated financial markets, the international infrastructure for the settlement of cross-border transactions remains fragmented, and one may even say cacophonic. This represents a major limitation of international transactions, since they lack a sound monetary-institutional framework within which cross-border final payments can occur without destabilising effects on exchange rates, capital accounts, interest rates, and hence economic performance. The architecture of the cross-border payment systems available today could be significantly improved by the creation of a truly international settlement system integrating national systems within a significantly shorter time frame than that required for system unification, that is, creation of a world currency that for the time being remains highly utopian.

By applying a payment-versus-payment settlement mechanism,[5] the continuous linked settlement (CLS) system operated by the New York based CLS Bank as from 9 September 2002 represents the private-sector answer to globalised financial markets, and allows for the settlement of foreign-exchange transactions in some main currencies, including the US dollar, the yen, and the euro (see European Central Bank, 2003). In this framework, a number of central banks provide accounts and, in most cases, offer settlement services for CLS participating banks. What cross-border settlement systems are still lacking is a settlement institution for national central banks themselves that would homogenise the various national currencies by the emission of a supranational central bank money. As a matter of fact, recall that within any national economy the central and commercial bank monies that are used as means of payment are homogeneous owing to the existence of a settlement system headed by the national central bank, which guarantees payment finality by issuing its own means of payment at interbank level.

To allow for the final settlement of international transactions, therefore, an international settlement institution – a central bank of national central banks – has to be put into place, with the task of issuing a means of final payment for cross-border transactions that homogenises the various currencies involved in the international monetary economy. Without entering here in a debate that would lead us far beyond the scope of this chapter (see Rossi, 2004), let us merely point out that it would be relatively easy to issue electronic, interbank money at the international level, which would not be available to the public, each time that a central bank is implied for the settlement of a foreign transaction – initiated by and destinated to the non-bank sector across borders. This international money would exist only within the self-contained bookkeeping system linking the international settlement institution to the participating central banks. Private speculation on it would thus be mechanically avoided by the fact that this monetary unit could not leave the system that creates it, and hence could not enter into domestic circulation. This would be sufficient to make sure that the exchange rate between any participating national currency and this new, international monetary unit cannot be affected by private-market specula-tion, an issue that indeed might pose a problem for the CLS-based system as long as this system does not provide a means of final payment for the central banks involved in it as a result of cross-border transactions.

In short, the policy proposal that follows from a circular-flow analysis of payment finality as regards cross-border transactions calls for the creation of an international settlement system that replicates between countries the institutional architecture of the settlement systems existing within them at the time of writing. An international settlement institution would therefore act as a 'go-between' facing any two central banks involved by the final settlement of a cross-border transaction between two non-bank agents residing in two different countries (see Figure 9.5, where I.m.u. stands for the inter-national monetary unit).

Needless to say, analogously to what happens within any domestic settle-ment system, where the central bank carries out both a money-purveying and a credit-purveying function, at the international level the settlement institution (to be set up) will have money-purveying and credit-purveying roles that need to be distinguished in both theory and practice. In this respect, the contribution of monetary circuit theory is a further proof of its policy relevance in analysing and proposing a solution to important

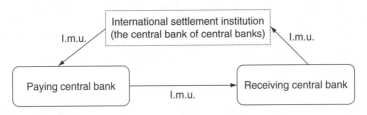

Figure 9.5 The circular flow of international central bank money

economic problems of modern capitalist societies. The theory of the monetary circuit has indeed a well-established tradition in economic analysis, and its perspectives are far-reaching. It has the potential to become the monetary theory of production and exchange of the twenty-first century, to equip policy makers with the necessary set of analytical tools to address the challenging issues of increasingly open economies – be they advanced, emerging, or in transition.

Conclusion

This chapter has focused on the issue of payment finality at interbank level in a closed-economy framework. Using a circular-flow paradigm, it has shown that any domestic settlement system is ultimately based on a central bank to homogenise the various bank monies issued within it. The distinction between money and credit at central bank level pointed out in this chapter has led us to the conclusion that the settlement institution for interbank transactions carries out two separate functions: it issues the means of final payment according to the endogenous-money view, and offers also financial intermediation services in the form of very-short-term central bank advances. As a hint to further analysis and policy agenda, the last section has raised the issue of payment finality at the international level, where cross-border transactions elicit the need for a means of final settlement between nations, represented in the international monetary economy by their central banks.

Notes

1. More complex payment arrangements may involve different tiers within and between which payments are made (see Committee on Payment and Settlement Systems, 2003b, pp. 10–11). This, however, would change neither our analytical framework nor our conclusions, and we may thus ignore it here.
2. The delivery-versus-payment mechanism is 'a link between a securities transfer system and a funds transfer system that ensures that delivery occurs if, and only if, payment occurs' (Committee on Payment and Settlement Systems, 2003a, p. 492).
3. Note in passing that 'in a credit transfer system with end-of-day final settlement, daylight credit is tacitly extended by a receiving institution if it accepts and acts on a payment order even though it will not receive final funds until the end of the business day' (Committee on Payment and Settlement Systems, 2003a, p. 490).
4. The reasons why a debtor bank fails to raise funds in the interbank market are not germane to the point at stake. They may be ascribed to an already too high leverage ratio of this bank, or to any other reasons linked to its creditworthiness that we do not pursue further here.
5. In a foreign-exchange settlement system, the payment-versus-payment mechanism 'ensures that a final transfer of one currency occurs if and only if a final transfer of the other currency or currencies takes place' (Committee on Payment and Settlement Systems, 2003a, p. 510).

References

Committee on Payment and Settlement Systems (2003a) *Payment and Settlement Systems in Selected Countries* (Basle: Bank for International Settlements).

Committee on Payment and Settlement Systems (2003b) *The Role of Central Bank Money in Payment Systems* (Basle: Bank for International Settlements).

De Bandt, O. and Hartmann, P. (2000) 'Systemic Risk: A Survey', *European Central Bank Working Papers*, 35.

Deutsche Bundesbank (1994) 'Recent Trends in the Deutsche Bundesbank's Cashless Payments', *Monthly Report*, 46, 8, pp. 45–61.

European Central Bank, 'CLS – Purpose, Concept and Implications', *Monthly Bulletin*, 5, 1, pp. 53–66.

Giovannini Group (2002) 'Cross-Border Clearing and Settlement Arrangements in the European Union', *European Commission Economic Papers*, 163.

Graziani, A. (1990) 'The Theory of the Monetary Circuit', *Économies et Sociétés* (Série 'Monnaie et Production', 7), 24, 6, pp. 7–36.

Graziani, A. (2003) *The Monetary Theory of Production* (Cambridge: Cambridge University Press).

Heller, D. and Sturm, A. (2003) 'The Role of the Swiss National Bank in the Electronic Payment System', *Swiss National Bank Quarterly Bulletin*, 21, 1, pp. 44–56.

Holthausen, C. and Monnet, C. (2003) 'Money and Payments: A Modern Perspective', *European Central Bank Working Papers*, 245.

Kahn, C.M. and Roberds, W. (2002) 'The Economics of Payment Finality', *Federal Reserve Bank of Atlanta Economic Review*, 87, 2, pp. 1–12.

Lavoie, M. (1996) 'The Endogenous Supply of Credit-Money, Liquidity Preference and the Principle of Increasing Risk: Horizontalism versus the Loanable Funds Approach', *Scottish Journal of Political Economy*, 43, pp. 275–300.

Lavoie, M. (2003) 'A Primer on Endogenous Credit-Money', in L.-P. Rochon and S. Rossi (eds), *Modern Theories of Money: The Nature and Role of Money in Capitalist Economies* (Cheltenham and Northampton: Edward Elgar), pp. 506–43.

Lavoie, M. (2005) 'On the Full Endogeneity of High-Powered Money: Lessons from the Canadian Case', in this volume.

Parguez, A. and Seccareccia, M. (2000) 'The Credit Theory of Money: The Monetary Circuit Approach', in J. Smithin (ed.), *What is Money?* (London and New York: Routledge), pp. 101–23.

Realfonzo, R. (1998) *Money and Banking: Theory and Debate (1900–1940)* (Cheltenham and Northampton: Edward Elgar).

Rochon, L.-P. and Rossi, S. (2004) 'Central Banking in the Monetary Circuit', in M. Lavoie and M. Seccareccia (eds), *Central Banking in the Modern World: Alternative Perspectives* (Cheltenham and Northampton: Edward Elgar), pp. 144–63.

Rossi, S. (2003) 'Money and Banking in a Monetary Theory of Production', in L.-P. Rochon and S. Rossi (eds), *Modern Theories of Money: The Nature and Role of Money in Capitalist Economies* (Cheltenham and Northampton: Edward Elgar), pp. 339–59.

Rossi, S. (2004) 'EMU and EU Enlargement: Lessons and Perspectives', in C. Gnos and L.-P. Rochon (eds), *Post Keynesian Principles for Economic Policy* (Cheltenham and Northampton: Edward Elgar), forthcoming.

Part III

The Monetary Circuit and Unemployment

10
Bank Mergers, Monopoly Power and Unemployment: A Monetary Circuit Approach

Guglielmo Forges Davanzati and Riccardo Realfonzo

Introduction

In the present macroeconomic debate there is widespread agreement between neoclassical scholars and supporters of the standard Keynesian theory concerning the following points:

(a) money supply is exogenous (depending on the autonomous decisions of the central banks);
(b) money can be significant only where it is required for keeping a stock of liquid wealth;
(c) income distribution reflects the marginal productivity of inputs.

These three principles are contrasted by the supporters of the monetary circuit theory. They maintain that:

(a) money supply is endogenous, depending on the demand for money by firms in order to finance production;
(b) money is significant not only as a store of value;
(c) income distribution depends on the bargaining power of agents.[1]

In this view, market configuration does not (only) depend on consumer preferences or on technologies but, above all, on the way money and credit are managed.

The main aim of this chapter is to analyse the effects of changes in the market structure of the banking sector on income distribution and employment. To do this, the basic theoretical framework will first be presented. A model will then be proposed in order to show that bank mergers and their consequences on the interest rate produce substantial effects on income distribution and employment, via changes in firm monopoly power, consequent changes in labour productivity and prices and allocation of income to consumption and savings. The chapter is organised as follows. The first section deals with the circuitist approach. In the second section the causes of bank mergers and the increase in firms' monopoly power are discussed, while the third section deals with their effects on income distribution and employment. The fourth section contains the main policy implications of the model and the fifth section focuses on the extension of the model to cases where savings are considered. The final section presents the conclusions.

The monetary circuit

The model takes three macro-agents into account: banks, which supply money; firms, producing goods; workers, who supply labour services.[2] The firm sector is divided into two sub-sectors: firms A produce consumer goods while firms B produce capital goods; both firms A and B require money for production purposes (the so called 'initial finance').

The working of the economy can be described as following sequential phases of monetary flows (see Figure 10.1):

1 Banks create money by financing both firms A and B. The inflow of money depends on money demand for initial finance. This, in turn, depends on the firms' decisions on employment and on the bargaining for the money wage.
2 Firms A and B buy labour services and pay money wages.
3 Assuming that workers' propensity to consume is equal to 1, workers (of both sectors) spend the whole wage bill on acquiring consumer goods. This implies that the whole amount of initial finance goes back to the firms A.
4 Firms A buy capital goods from firms B.
5 Firms A and firms B reimburse banks for the initial finance (money destruction).

It is necessary to stress that in such a model, the firms' decisions on production and employment depend on the level of the expected aggregate demand. In particular, the amount of production by firms A is set in the light of their forecast of aggregate demand for consumer goods. At the same time, firms B's production of capital goods depends on firms A's level of activity and consequent need for new capital goods for the next period (i.e. substitution of old worn out capital goods). In this theoretical framework, it is assumed that firms A in the period t use capital goods produced in the period $t-1$, and that the demand for finance by firms B in t is devoted to producing capital goods available in the period $t+1$.

Firms, as a whole, can collect an amount of money in the market for goods equal to the money wage bill advanced. Therefore, at the close of the

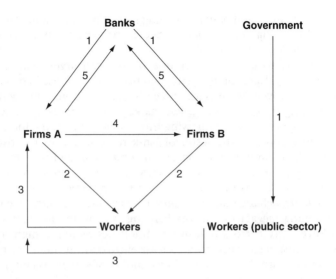

1 = initial finance
2 = payment of money wage
3 = purchasing of consumer goods
4 = purchasing of capital goods
5 = reimbursement of bank loans

Figure 10.1 The monetary circuit

circuit, they cannot pay money interest to banks except when – as in this model – public expenditure (or international trade) guarantees extra-money, via a deficit spending policy. It will be assumed that government employs workers, so that their wages increase the money wage bill and hence the demand for goods.

Increase in competition, bank mergers and firms' monopoly power

Within the theoretical framework of the circuitist approach, and in order to test the links between monopoly power in the bank and firm sector on employment and income distribution, the following remarks are in order.

The mark-up in the bank sector

It is a widespread idea that economies of scale (as well as scope economies) are the main determinants of the concentration ratio – and hence of the mark-up – in the banking sector. This idea appears to be supported by empirical evidence. It is suggested that the recent wave of bank mergers and acquisitions is due to the aims of exploiting scale and scope economies, and of implementing new information and communication technologies that need a large scale to be effective (see, among others, Schure and Wagenvoort, 1999).[3]

According to a different approach, one can argue that mergers and acquisitions in the banking sector, and hence the increase in bank monopoly power, are driven by changes in legal and institutional rules which induce the existing firms to create credit market entry barriers by increasing their size (see Dymski, 2000). Following this line of thought, the increase in bank monopoly power is the result of bank reaction to: (a) the risk of losing market shares; and (b) the increase in contestability of ownership structure control. Bank merger movements seems to reflect a global pattern of mergers and acquisitions in financial services. Furthermore, the introduction of technological change can be regarded as the outcome of the rise in competition among megagroups in the banking system. In fact, banks can try to reinforce entry barriers by using technologies requiring high fixed capital investments: in so doing, they increase entry costs. It should be noted that – by contrast with the view above – technological change is endogenous; that is, driven by banks' demand.

The effects of mergers and acquisitions on the interest rate have been widely explored in recent literature, both on the theoretical and empirical planes. The conventional wisdom – that once consolidation has been achieved, the banking industry will be more efficient – appears questionable. By contrast, it is argued that mergers and acquisitions, in that they produce an increase in monopoly power and do not involve scale economies, certainly have a positive effect on the interest rate. When scale and scope economies are in operation, the interest rate movement is ambiguous on the theoretical plane. On the one hand, technological changes reduce the operative costs of banks (above all, the cost of collection and processing of information), and, on the other hand, they increase banks' monopoly power, so that, in the first case, the interest rate should decrease, while in the second case the opposite happens. However, many empirical studies show that the overall result is an interest rate rise (see Dymski, 2000). Reasonably, banks fix the interest rate at a level that allows them to obtain the maximum amount of money profits, given their expectations of firm and worker behaviour in a context of uncertainty.

The industrial concentration ratio in the firm sector

We assume that the industrial concentration ratio in both the A and B sectors depends positively on the interest rate. Our argument is that the tendency of firms (A and B) to collude depends on bank monopoly power. The rationale for this argument is threefold. First, collusion can affect the price level: firms can try to maintain their profits unchanged by increasing prices and collusion allows them to do so. Second, when bank mergers occur and this determines an increase in the interest rate, firms can react by increasing their size, exploiting scale economies. This leads, in turn, to an increase in productivity and hence to higher profits with respect to a non-cooperative solution. Third, collusion may act as an effective device to increase firms' bargaining power in the money market, thereby moderating the bank tendency to raise interest. As a result, the more collusively banks behave, the more collusively firms (A and B) behave.[4, 5]

The following assumptions are put forward:

1 Bank monopoly power (α) (i.e. their tendency to merge and collude) depends on the changes in the legal and institutional setting – which can affect technological changes – and positively influence the money interest rate (i).

2 Firms monopoly power (β) (i.e. their tendency to collude) depends positively on the money interest rate and has a positive effect on productivity (a) or prices. For the sake of simplicity, firm technology is assumed to show constant returns, so that the aggregate production function is $Q_a = a_c N_c$ in the sector of consumer goods and $Q_k = a_k N_k$ in the sector of capital goods (where N_c and N_k is the number of workers employed). Firms A and B respectively operate in non-competitive markets, producing homogeneous consumption goods and homogeneous capital goods, and fix prices by adding a mark-up (q) on the average costs of production in order to obtain a target profit rate, money interest included. It is also assumed here that firms are able to obtain money profits and pay interest in money terms thanks to public expenditure (G) resulting from a deficit spending policy. Note that collusion in both the banking and firm sectors can hardly arise spontaneously, due to the individual agent incentive to behave non-cooperatively.[6] When collusion affects the price level, the incentive to defect depends on the possibility – on the micro level – of gaining market share at the expense of other firms. In other words, since a reduction in price is advantageous on the micro plane, insofar as it allows the market share to be increased, collusion is costly for the individual agent. Furthermore, the incentive to behave non-cooperatively is likely to go up as the price level rises. In fact, the higher the difference between the post-collusion price and the pre-collusion price, the more market share (and profit) the individual firm would obtain via defecting (i.e. by reducing prices).[7] Finally, firms are assumed to operate under uncertainty, so that they do not have complete information on the level of aggregate demand.

3 Neither capital nor labour mobility is assumed, so that both mark-ups (q_c, q_k) and wages (w_c, w_k) can be different in sectors A and B.[8] Similarly, labour productivity (a_c, a_k) can be different in the two sectors. On the other hand, the interest rate is equal in the two sectors.

4 Workers bargain for the money wage on the basis of adaptive expectations about the price level[9] and the unitary wage decreases as the unemployment rate increases, due to the decrease in workers' bargaining power. At the

start of the circuit, the unitary money wage (in both sectors) is settled by negotiation between firms and workers. Firms decisions on production (both of consumer and capital goods) and employment are determined by their expectations about the demand for consumer goods.[10] For the sake of simplicity, we assume that the propensity to consume is equal to 1 (we will remove this assumption in the section on interest rate, savings and employment).

Equations (1) and (2) respectively give the prices of consumer and capital goods:

$$p_c = (1+i)(w_c/a_c)(1+q_c) + \lambda(w_k/a_k)(1+q_k)(1+i)$$
$$= (1+i)[(w_c/a_c)(1+q_c) + \lambda(w_k/a_k)(1+q_k)] \tag{1}$$

$$p_k = (w_k/a_k)(1+q_k)(1+i) \tag{2}$$

Equations (1) and (2) mainly show that the price of consumer goods goes up in proportion to capital goods price rises (according to a technical coeffient λ, which is the share of capital goods that the individual firm uses) and interest rate rises. Firms react to the increase in the interest rate in order not to lose profits via collusion, with two possible results. First, they can try to maintain their profits unchanged by putting prices up. Second, they can exploit scale economies and therefore gain an increase in productivity.

It is worth noting that, for a given wage bill and public expenditure, firms are able to collect the same amount of money in the goods market whatever the price level is, and that money revenues go down in proportion to the fall in the money wage bill and/or public expenditure.

Monopoly power, interest rate and employment

Let us assume that in period t_{-1} the monetary circuit closed in a position of economic macroequilibrium with full employment.[11] This means that: (a) the money initially created by banks in order to finance production flowed back entirely to the banking system; (b) prices and bank interest rates are the same as the previous period; and (c) public expenditure G allows firms to repay banks for the money interest bill. We also assume that, at the start of the monetary circuit in period t, an external shock consisting of a change in the institutional and technological setting affects the banking sector by increasing bank monopoly power and hence the interest rate. Let us focus on the reaction of firms to the interest rate rise.

Collusion appears to be the most effective strategy in order not to lose profits. On the one hand, it increases firms' bargaining power in the money market and this reduces banks capability to increase the interest rate. On the other hand, collusion allows firms to exploit scale economies and hence to obtain higher productivity. The increased productivity allows them to produce

the same amount of goods – with respect to the previous circuit (i.e. before the increase in the interest rate) – with a lower level of employment. Possibly, firms may also react by increasing prices.
Therefore, two cases can result.

Case I. Interest and prices

As shown in sequence 1, firms can react to the increase in the interest rate by increasing prices (p). Given the level of demand for consumption goods in money terms ($wN+G$), firms cannot reimburse banks for the whole amount of the debt (i.e. $wN(1+i)$, and they accumulate unsold goods. In the ensuing period, this determines a decline in the quantity of consumer goods produced (S_{ct+1}) as well as capital goods produced and a reduction in employment in both sectors. At the same time, given the increase in the price level in the previous period, workers will claim an increase in money wages, which, in turn, will determine a further increase in the price level. For these reasons, a stagflation process occurs: notwithstanding the continuous decrease in firms' demand for finance, both the unemployment rate and the price level will increase. This process will gradually be stopped by the continuous decline in workers' bargaining power, due to the decline in employment.[12] Note that the increase in price negatively affects the real interest rate.

Institutional and technical $\rightarrow \uparrow\alpha \rightarrow \uparrow i \rightarrow \uparrow\beta \rightarrow \uparrow p \rightarrow \downarrow S_{ct+1} \rightarrow \downarrow N_{ct+1}$
changes (banking sector) $\qquad\qquad\qquad\qquad\qquad\qquad\qquad\qquad \downarrow$
$\qquad\qquad\qquad\qquad\qquad\qquad\qquad\qquad\qquad\qquad \downarrow D_k \rightarrow \downarrow N_k$

Sequence 1:   Interest rate, prices and employment

Case II. Interest and productivity

In this case, the overall result is described in sequence 2.

Institutional and technical $\rightarrow \uparrow\alpha \rightarrow \uparrow i \rightarrow \uparrow\beta \rightarrow \uparrow a_c \rightarrow \downarrow N_c$
changes (banking sector) $\qquad\qquad\qquad\qquad\qquad\qquad\qquad \downarrow$
$\qquad\qquad\qquad\qquad\qquad\qquad\qquad\quad \uparrow a_k \rightarrow \downarrow N_k$

Sequence 2:   Interest rate, productivity and employment

This sequence establishes that changes in the institutional and technological setting in the banking sector lead to an increase in the interest rate (i) – resulting from the increase in bank monopoly power(α). As a consequence, there are two effects:

1   Firms' incentive to collude (β) increases and this determines a growth in productivity (a_c). Given the level of demand for consumption goods in money terms ($wN + G$), firms are able to produce and sell an unchanged amount of goods with a lower level of employment (N_c). However, because of the reduction of employment, the money wage bill falls, with consequent reduction in the demand for consumer goods.

2   Since collusion also affects firms B, the same result occurs in the capital goods sector. The increase in productivity (a_k) allows firms B to produce the same amount of capital goods with a lower level of employment (N_k), given the demand by firms A for capital goods.

In this case, the effects of collusion on prices and employment are the following:

1   The price level remains unchanged if the increase in productivity is equal to the increase in the interest rate, given the mark-up and the unitary money wage. In other words, firms do not change prices where scale economies allow them to obtain an increase in productivity equal to the increase in the interest rate.

2   The reduction of employment allows firms to cut the average money wage, due to the decrease in workers' bargaining power, and the money wage bill. This would determine a decrease in the demand for consumer goods and hence a decrease in money profits. Since the level of production is not changed, and demand is lower, the increase in productivity – as in case I – determines solely the accumulation of unsold goods. In the ensuing production period, firms will produce a lower level of consumer goods, and will employ a lower number of workers. The difference between the outcome of cases I and II is basically that, in case II, the reduction in employment occurs in the present period, and the process of continuous decline of employment is faster. A possible counterbalancing effect is government intervention in paying unemployment benefits.

At this point, the following considerations are in order:

1   The increase in bank monopoly power generates two distributional conflicts: first, the conflict between bankers and industrial capitalists; second, the conflict between capitalists and workers.[13]

2   The negative effect of the increase in the interest rate on employment is not due – as in the standard Keynesian view – to a (direct) decrease in investments, but it is the outcome of the increase in productivity or of the increase in prices resulting from collusion among firms. In this theoretical framework, as Graziani (1994, pp. 83–4) points out, investments are not interest rate sensitive. In fact, in our assumptions, capital goods are

bought by firms of the consumption sector thanks to the revenue from the sale of consumer goods.[14]

Figure 10.2 shows the overall picture with reference to case I, on the simplifying assumption that firms are not distinguished into type-A and type-B. In quadrant (*a*), the money market is represented. Within a 'horizontalist' approach (see Moore, 1988), which is compatible with the approach of the monetary circuit according to which bank credit potential is theoretically unlimited, firms and banks bargain over the money interest rate, the bank sector being capable of producing money (M) without limits.

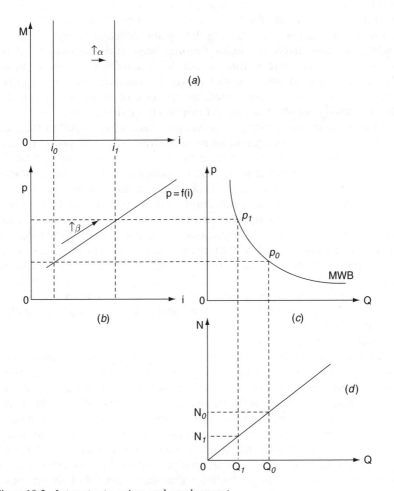

Figure 10.2 Interest rate, prices and employment

The shift from the i_0 to the i_1 line is due to the increase in bank monopoly power. In quadrant (b), the price–interest line, upward sloping, reflects the idea that the increase in the money interest rate induces firms to collude and, hence, to increase prices, or that total output declines for a given demand for consumer goods. The slope of the curve depends on firms' tendency to collude (i.e. the more they are ex-ante motivated to behave cooperatively, the less elastic the price-interest line will be). By contrast, the position of the price-interest line depends on wages and productivity: the higher the wage and/or the lower labour productivity, the more the price-interest line shifts upward.[15] Of course, this line starts with a positive value of p, which depends on the monopoly power firms enjoy in the case of competition in the banking sector (say, $i=i_0$). Quadrant (c) illustrates the market for goods, where the MWB curve is the money wage bill. This curve is a rectangular hyperbola, reflecting the equality $\mathrm{MWB}=wN+w_gN_g$, where w_g and N_g are respectively the unitary money wage and employment in the public sector (where wN, in turn, equals the 'initial finance'), and expresses the overall demand for consumer goods. In quadrant (d), the aggregate production function is represented: for the sake of simplicity, it describes the technology used by both the A firms and the B firms.

An increase in bank monopoly power (α) determines the shift of the i-line from i_0 to i_1. This generates an increase in firm monopoly power (β) and, therefore, in the prices of consumer goods, from p_0 to p_1, or a decline in output for a given demand for consumer goods due to bankruptcies or even a decrease in expectations, which leads – given the money wage bill – to a reduction in real wages and consumption (from Q_0 to Q_1) and, in the next period, to a decline of employment (from N_0 to N_1). Although the labour market is not included in the figure, one can demonstrate that the reduction of employment generates involuntary unemployment. The rationale for this lies in the difference existing between the actual real wage (w/p^*) and the expected real wage (w/p^e) since the latter is, in actual fact, the workers' reserve wage, and the outcome of bank–firm bargaining determines a condition where $w/p^*<w/p^e$, unemployed workers, who cannot find a job, are willing to work at the current real wage.

Figure 10.3 describes case II.

The increase in the rate of interest from i_0 to i_1 positively affects productivity, by means of collusion. In quadrant (b), the interest–productivity line, upward sloping, reflects the idea that the increase in the money interest rate induces firms to collude and, hence, to exploit scale economies. The slope of the curve depends on firms' tendency to collude (i.e. the more they are ex-ante motivated to behave cooperatively, the less elastic the price–interest line will be); by contrast, the position of the interest–productivity line reflects the position of the aggregate production function: the higher it is, the more the interest–productivity line shifts upward. This line starts with a positive value of a, which depends on the monopoly power firms

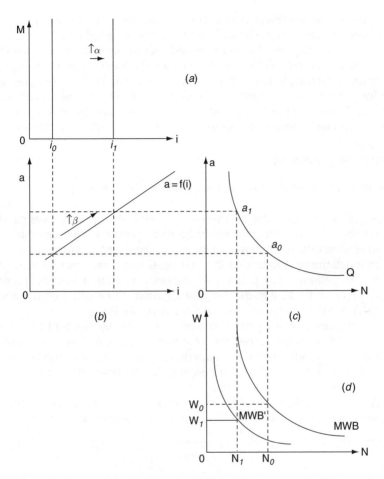

Figure 10.3 Interest rate, productivity and employment

enjoy in the case of competition in the banking sector (say, $i=i_0$). Quadrant (c) illustrates the relationship between productivity and employment, for a given level of output (Q). In quadrant (d) the labour market is described. The MWB curve is the money wage bill. This curve is a rectangular hyperbola, reflecting the equality $MWB=wN+w_gN_g$ (the overall demand for consumption goods).

An increase in bank monopoly power (α) determines the shift of the *i*-line from i_0 to i_1. This generates an increase in firm monopoly power (β) and, therefore, in productivity, from a_0 to a_1. Firms are now able to produce the same amount of goods (Q) with lower employment ($N_1 < N_0$) and, because of the decline of employment (in the present period), the unitary wage declines (from w_0 to w_1), and so does the money wage bill (MWB').

It is relevant to stress that in the period that we are considering (period t) the monetary circuit will close with: (a) the destruction of money initially created; (b) an increase in both productivity or prices and bank interest rate; and (c) involuntary unemployment. Because of the decrease in the money wage bill – and, hence, of the initial finance – at the close of the circuit firms may be able to reimburse money interests to banks, even for a higher rate of interest.[16]

Policy implications

The main policy implications of the model are the following:

1 A policy of regulation of the bank system aiming at increasing the number of banks and reducing the barriers to entry is an effective strategy in order to increase employment. In fact, as shown above, this policy, insofar as it determines a reduction in the interest rate, gives firms an incentive not to collude. This policy also implies a reduction in bank profits. However, according to the circuitist approach this result does not affect bank power to create money and finance production.
2 The increase in employment can also be achieved by means of a policy of deregulation of the market for consumer goods as well as of the market for capital goods. The more competitive markets become, the less firms can collude to exploit economies of scale, and hence the more employment goes up.
3 A policy of deficit spending by the state can increase employment. In sequence 3, the rationale for this argument is described.

$$\uparrow G \rightarrow \uparrow N_g \rightarrow \uparrow MWB \rightarrow \uparrow D_c \rightarrow \uparrow N_c$$
$$\downarrow$$
$$\uparrow D_k \rightarrow \uparrow N_k$$

Sequence 3: Public expenditure and employment

Given involuntary unemployment, the increase in public expenditure (G) increases employment in the public sector (N_g);[17] it will increase workers' aggregate income and, consequently, the demand for consumer goods. Production and employment in the consumer goods sector will increase. At the same time, given our assumption, production and employment in the capital goods sector will also increase. The increase in G allows firms to obtain their normal profits with a higher interest rate, so that they do not need to behave cooperatively.

Finally, note that – in this context – a policy of labour market deregulation is completely ineffective, and may be counterproductive for the purpose of increasing employment. In fact, a reduction in wages resulting from this policy determines solely a reduction in the demand for consumer goods and, therefore, in employment. Although the *individual firm* may view this strategy as convenient (insofar as it reduces costs), on the *macro plane* labour market deregulation cannot be seen as a socially rational choice (see Forges Davanzati and Realfonzo, 2004). However, this effect may be counterbalanced by the possible improvement in firms' expectations and, therefore, in labour demand, in view of the idea that labour market deregulation acts as an institutional shock.

Formally, the level of employment is determined as follows, by assuming that it is set at the level corresponding to the equality between supply and demand of consumer goods. For the sake of simplicity, only employment in the consumption sector is derived here. This is because, given the technical relationship that links the level of employment in sectors A and B (say, $0<\gamma<1$), employment as a whole is simply the sum: $N_c+\gamma N_c$. In the consumer goods sector, equation (3) holds in equilibrium:

$$aN^*p = wN^* + G \qquad (3)$$

where N^* is the full employment level in sector A. Equation (3) establishes the equality between aggregate supply and aggregate demand. By substituting equation (1) in the price level of equation (3), one obtains:

$$N = \frac{G}{w[(1+q)(1+i)-1]} \qquad (4)$$

In view of equation (4), N goes up in proportion to public expenditure, while it declines as the unitary wage, the mark-up and the interest rate increase.

Interest rate, savings and employment

Let us now relax the assumption of unitary propensity to consume. This allows us to analyse the effects of the increase in the interest rate on employment, through savings, by assuming that the initial condition is characterised by monetary equilibrium and full employment.

It is assumed that savings (S) positively depend on the money interest rate,[18] and that banks fix the interest rate of savings in order to obtain the maximum level of money profits given the interest on initial finance, in a context of uncertainty. Given the assumptions posed above, and considering this latter assumption, the following sequence holds.

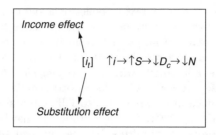

Sequence 4:   Interest rate, savings and employment

By assumption, the increase in the interest rate determines an increase in savings. The increase in savings corresponds (for a given money wage bill) to a decrease in the demand for consumption goods and, therefore, in employment. Furthermore – as will be shown – firms are now forced to operate in the financial market and this may determine two opposite effects on their profits (see below).

Since firms face a lower demand, in order to collect the initial finance and reimburse banks at the end of the circuit they need to operate in the financial market by issuing shares. For the buying of their securities to be profitable, they are forced to fix the interest rate above that fixed by banks (i_t in sequence 3). In so doing, as a consequence of the increase in the interest rate, firms are forced to further increase productivity (if they can) or to further increase prices. For the reasons above (pp. 160–6), this may lead to reduction in production and, hence, in labour demand. In a sense, the working of the financial market amplifies the negative effects of concentration in the money market. The more monopoly power banks have, the more firms are induced to issue shares, with higher rates of interest.

As Graziani (1994, p. 123) points out, issuing shares in the financial market may generate two further effects (see sequence 3): (a) an income effect (i.e. the increase in the demand for liquidity consequent to the increase in income) due, in turn, to the increase in interest rates (this outcome is negative for firms, since they collect a lower amount of money than when this effect is not in operation); and (b) a substitution effect, in that the increase in the interest rate provided by firms gives agents an incentive to buy securities and, hence, determines an increase in firms' overall revenues (i.e. the revenues obtained in the goods market plus that obtained in the financial market).

The main policy implication of this argument, which reinforces those commented upon previously in this chapter, is that a policy of regulation of the banking sector – insofar as it determines a reduction in the interest rate – allows firms to reduce the increase in the interest rate on securities, which, in turn, may reduce the intensity of the income effect without variations in the substitution effect. The overall result should be an increase in profits – due to the collection of more savings – with possible positive effects on labour demand.

Conclusion

Within the theoretical framework of the monetary circuit (see pp. 156–7), this chapter has focused on the effects of the increase in monopoly power in the banking sector on income distribution and employment. It has been shown that an increase in banks' monopoly power negatively affects employment. This occurs because firms can react to the money interest rate rise by colluding in order both to counterbalance the increased bargaining power of banks and to exploit scale economies. The consequent increase in productivity allows firms to produce an unchanged output with a lower number of workers, keeping their mark-ups constant. Firms can also collude in order to try to keep their profits unchanged by increasing prices.

The negative effect of an increase of bank monopoly power on employment is reinforced by taking the role of savings into consideration. In this case, the main outcome of the interest rate increase is a further reduction in the demand for consumer goods (because of the higher savings due to the interest rate rise) and, hence, in employment.

Finally, the basic policy implications of the model are: (a) the regulation of the banking sector and the deregulation of the firm sector; (b) the increase in public expenditure; and (c) the regulation of the labour market, in order to increase wages and hence consumption and employment.

Notes

1. A reconstruction of the history of this line of thought has recently been provided by Realfonzo (1998).
2. For the monetary circuit approach, see Graziani (1989); Lavoie (1992); Deleplace and Nell (1996); Parguez (1996); Realfonzo (1998).
3. The effects of a high banking market power on economic performance is the subject of a wide debate. On the one hand, some economists (see, for instance, Pagano, 1993) maintain that banking market power reduces equilibrium credit, thereby generating a negative effect on economic growth. On the other hand, others (see Petersen and Rajan, 1995) support the idea that banks with market power promote economic growth because they fund young firms, potentially endowed with higher return projects and more innovative technologies that would guarantee ever increasing profit-sharing opportunities for the banks.
4. A different and interesting view on the emergence of cooperative behaviours was proposed by Adam Smith (1976 [1776]): according to this view, agents tend to compete in contexts of 'relative scarcity' and to cooperate in contexts of 'relative plenty'. See Forges Davanzati (2002).
5. Bank monopoly power also affects market structure via possible bankrupcy and expectations. The increase in the interest rate reduces profits: as a consequence,

the less efficient firms would go bankrupt and firms as a whole are likely to experience a decline in their expectations on future profits.

6. This issue has recently been addressed in Earl (2002), where it is stressed that 'contractual ambiguity' is likely to give incentives for opportunistic behaviour and therefore to make inter-firm cooperation costly.

7. Even if, by means of collusion, firms *can* increase prices, they would find it convenient not to do so, because of the risk of workers' reaction and the consequent decline in labour productivity and/or in working hours. See Forges Davanzati and Realfonzo (2000).

8. Lunghini and Bianchi (2004) point out that – in a model of the monetary theory of production *where supply is given* – profit equalisation cannot logically be admitted, because profit equalisation requires capital mobility, which cannot be in operation if output has been previously determined.

9. Note that the assumption of adaptive expectation is explicitly taken into consideration by Keynes. In *General Theory*, when discussing the case of short-term expectations, he writes: 'it is sensible for producers to base their expectations on the assumption that *the most recently realised results* will continue, except insofar as there are definite reasons for expecting a change' (Keynes, 1991 [1936], p. 51, emphasis added).

10. The rationale for this assumption is that since workers do not buy capital goods, the employment (as well wages and profits) in sector B necessarily depend on the demand for capital goods in sector A, which, in turn, depends on the demand for consumer goods.

11. Where full employment is also reached via public expenditure.

12. However, this process of continuously rising wages and prices may not be in operation due to the reduction of employment, insofar as this decline determines a sudden decrease in workers' bargaining power and therefore a decrease in their money wages.

13. Lunghini and Bianchi (2003, p. 192) make a very similar comment.

14. In this context, given the assumption of propensity to consume equal to 1, the financial market is not in operation.

15. Since this line basically refers to firms A, an increase in the price of capital goods also shifts the price-interest line upward.

16. This basically depends on the amount of the increase of the interest rate in comparison with the decrease of the wage bill; that is, the more the wage bill is reduced – for a given (higher) rate of interest – the more likely firms are to be able to reimburse the money interest bill.

17. It is what Keynes called 'primary employment' (see Keynes, 1991 [1936], p. 113).

18. Note that the positive relationship between the interest rate and savings is assumed by Keynes in the *Treatise on Money*: 'In the case of saving, the effect of a change in the interest rate is direct and primary and needs no special explanation.' However, 'the amount of the effect may often be quantitatively small in practice, especially over the short period' (Keynes, 1989 [1930], p. 180).

References

Deleplace, G. and Nell, E.J. (eds) (1996) *Money in Motion* (Basingstoke: Macmillan).
Dueker, M.J. and Thornton, D.L (1997) 'Do Bank Loan Rates Exhibit a Countercyclical Mark-up?', *Federal Reserve Bank of St.Louis*, wp.004A.

Dymski, G. (2000) *The bank merger wave and the future of US banking,* http://iml.umkc.edu/econ/AFEE

Earl, P.E. (2002) *Information, Opportunism and Economic Coordination* (Aldershot: Elgar).

Forges Davanzati, G. (2003) 'Smith's theories of wages: towards the solution of a puzzle', mimeo.

Forges Davanzati, G. and Realfonzo, R. (2000) 'Wages, Labour Productivity and Unemployment in a Model of the Monetary Theory of Production', *Economie appliquée,* 4, pp. 117–38.

Forges Davanzati, G. and Realfonzo, R. (2004) 'Labour market deregulation and unemployment in a monetary economy', in R. Arena and N. Salvadori, *Money, Credit and the Role of the State* (Aldershot: Ashgate, pp. 65–74).

Graziani, A. (1989) 'The theory of the monetary circuit', *Thames Papers in Political Economy,* Spring.

Graziani, A. (1994) *La teoria monetaria della produzione* (Arezzo: Banca Popolare dell'Etruria e del Lazio).

Halevi, J. and Taouil, R. (1998) 'On a post-Keynesian stream from France and Italy: the Circuit Approach', mimeo.

Keynes, J.M. (1989 [1930]) *A Treatise on Money* (Cambridge University Press).

Keynes, J.M. (1936) *The General Theory of Employment, Interest and Money* (Cambridge University Press 1991).

Lavoie, M. (1992) *Foundations of post-Keynesian economic analysis* (Aldershot: Elgar).

Lunghini, G. and Bianchi, C. (2003) 'The monetary circuit and income distribution: bankers as landlords?', in R. Arena and N. Salvadori, *Money, Credit and the Role of the State* (Aldershot: Ashgate, pp. 152–74).

Moore, B. (1988) *Horizontalists and Verticalists: The macroeconomics of credit money* (Cambridge University Press).

Pagano, M. (1993) 'Financial markets and growth: an overview', *European Economic Review,* 37, pp. 613–22.

Parguez, A. (1996) 'Financial markets, unemployment and inflation within a circuitist framework', *Économies et sociétés,* 30 (2–3), pp. 163–92.

Petersen, M.A. and Rajan, R.G. (1995) 'The effect of credit market competition on lending relationship', *Quarterly Journal of Economics,* 90, pp. 407–33.

Realfonzo, R. (1998) *Money and Banking. Theory and Debate (1900–1940).* (Cheltenham: Elgar).

Schure, P. and Wagenvoort, R. (1999) 'Economies of scale and efficiency in European banking: new evidence', *European Investment Bank – Economic and Financial report,* 1.

Smith, A. (1976 [1776]) *An Inquiry into the Nature and Causes of Wealth of Nations* (London: Oxford University Press).

11
Circuit Theory and the Employment Issue

Claude Gnos *

The circuit is a time-honoured concept in economics. It can be traced back to the Physiocrats of eighteenth-century France, who viewed production as a circular process initiated by advances, that is, capital expenditures which are recouped when goods are produced and then sold. Ever since then, however, this conception, without being explicitly discarded, has been left on the sidelines. For instance, Schumpeter, Keynes, Kalecki and J. Robinson, to mention twentieth-century economists only, undoubtedly made allowance for the circuit but did not give it prominence.[1] In fact, the idea of making use of this conception as a research tool remained largely dormant until the late 1960s in France and Italy, when J. Le Bourva (1962), B. Schmitt (1966, 1984), A. Parguez (1975), A. Barrère (1979) and A. Graziani (1990, 2003) undertook to revive it. This undertaking has been largely inspired by Keynes's work and, just like the Anglo-Saxon Post Keynesians, circuitists have sought to set Keynes's heterodoxy opposite the neoclassical synthesis.

In its modern version, circuit theory refers to firms' successive outlays and receipts and the resulting formation and cancellation of money income. In this, it relates specifically to Keynes's principle of effective demand and finance motive. These references alone are sufficient to draw circuitists towards Anglo-Saxon Post Keynesians. Thus, a whole series of valuable essays, ranging from Lavoie (1984) to Rochon (1999a, b) and Fontana (2000), by way of Arena (1996), Arestis (1996), Deleplace and Nell (1996), Graziani (1996), Wray (1996), Chick (2000) or Parguez and Seccareccia (2000), has worked through the contributions of both schools of thought in search of mutual support. This chapter follows the same line of inquiry with respect to the employment issue.

The next section focuses on the way circuit theory helps account for the originality of Keynes's views on employment, in opposition to the so-called New Keynesian interpretation of it and in support of Post Keynesian

---

* Helpful comments by Alberto Giacomin, Sergio Rossi and Louis-Philippe Rochon are gratefully acknowledged. The usual disclaimer applies.

readings. The third section shows that circuit theory is central to the explanation of unemployment. The last section concludes.

How circuit theory accounts for the originality of Keynes's theory of employment

It is well-known that standard Keynesian economics, especially the New Keynesian version thereof, concentrates on wage and price rigidities. The theory holds that these rigidities prevent markets from clearing when there is a fall in nominal demand and so allow unemployment to occur. Actually, New Keynesians are on the same wavelength as Old Keynesians, who used to argue that the originality of Keynes's theory of employment resided in the perception that it was quantities instead of prices that adjusted. Their ambition is to enquire into the micro-foundations of wage and price rigidities:

> According to Keynesian economics, fluctuations in employment and output arise largely from fluctuations in nominal aggregate demand. The reason that nominal shocks matter is that nominal wages and prices are not fully flexible... The research program described here is modest in the sense that it seeks to strengthen the foundations of this conventional thinking, not to provide a new theory of fluctuations. In particular, its goal is to answer the theoretical question of how nominal rigidities arise from optimizing behavior, since the absence of an answer in the 1970s was largely responsible for the decline of Keynesian economics. (Ball, Mankiw and Romer, 1991, p. 149)

Post Keynesians are highly critical of this account of Keynes's theory:

> [T]he price rigidity New Keynesian program is of no help in understanding a *Keynesian* view on fluctuations in macroeconomic employment and output. Keynes rejected approaches which relied on methodological individualist perspectives focusing on output, labour and capital markets, because he believed they were inapplicable to analyses which attempt to understand movements in employment and output *as a whole*. (Rotheim, 1998, p. 52)

Rotheim refers notably to chapter 19 of *General Theory* where Keynes argues that the classical claim that 'a reduction in money-wages would stimulate demand by diminishing the price of the finished product, and will therefore increase input and employment' is grounded on the questionable assumption 'that the reduction in money-wages will leave demand unaffected', and so amounts to the undue transposition of an argument that is valid *ceteris paribus* for any given industry to industry as a whole (Keynes, 1936, pp. 257–9). Circuit theory undoubtedly supports this argument in highlighting the specific methodology of the principle of effective demand. Let us consider this issue in some detail.

According to standard Keynesian economics, the principle of effective demand comes within the standard theory of supply and demand. Employment is supposedly determined by a process of adjustment of aggregate supply and demand that is prevented from establishing full employment when wages and prices are sticky. Circuit theory challenges this interpretation. It emphasises that Keynes cast entrepreneurs in a crucial asymmetrical role, which is the hallmark of the 'monetary economy of production' he contrasted with the 'real exchange economy' described by neoclassical economists (cf. Keynes, 1973 [1933a, b]). The aggregate demand function is not a demand schedule as it is in the standard theory of supply and demand, representing decisions that buyers are prepared to make depending on prices when they enter the market (see Gnos, 2004). It in fact represents 'the proceeds which entrepreneurs expect to receive from the employment of N men' (Keynes, 1936, p. 25). It represents entrepreneurs' forecasts as to what the proceeds from sales of the goods they are considering producing and supplying in the market are going to be. As Keynes puts it, '*Ex ante* decisions in their influence on effective demand relate solely to *entrepreneurs*' decisions' (Keynes, 1973 [1937a], pp. 182–3).

According to Keynes, entrepreneurs' expected proceeds are to be linked to employment N. Why is it so? This is precisely where the circuit comes in: demand is fuelled by incomes formed in the payment of the wages of firms' employees. It is true that Keynes does not use the term 'circuit', but there is no doubt that the concept of the circuit underlies his analysis. In a draft of *General Theory*, written in 1933, he refers to Marx's formula, M-C-M', by which entrepreneurs part 'with money for commodity (or effort) in order to obtain more money' (Keynes, 1973 [1933b], p. 81). Later on, right at the beginning of chapter 3 of *General Theory*, he confirms his views in a way that is definitely close to the modern circuit theory.

Keynes explains that an entrepreneur meets two kinds of expenses when he invests funds in new production:

first of all, the amounts which he pays out to the factors of production (exclusive of other entrepreneurs) for their current services, which we shall call the *factor cost*... and secondly, the amounts which he pays out to other entrepreneurs for what he has to purchase from them together with the sacrifice which he incurs by employing the equipment instead of leaving it idle, which we shall call the *user cost*. Keynes, 1936. p. 23)

He then goes on to emphasise that entrepreneurs require that the proceeds from the sale of the goods produced not only reimburse the factor cost[2] incurred but also earn them a maximum profit: 'entrepreneurs will endeavour to fix the amount of employment at the level which they expect to maximise the excess of the proceeds over the factor cost' (pp. 24–5). He calls the corresponding proceeds which 'just make it worth the while of entrepreneurs to give that employment', 'the aggregate supply price of the output from employing N men' (p. 24). Although he is not fully explicit on this issue, Keynes on this occasion sketches a theory of distribution by which profits are a redistributed share of factor income, which is transferred from purchasers to firms. In effect, while factor cost, which forms factors' income,[3] is paid by entrepreneurs, profits (that is, entrepreneurs' income) are derived from the excess of prices over factor cost paid by consumers. Just as taxes on value added currently allow governments to capture some part of consumers' incomes, profits are thus an excess of prices over factor cost but do not form an additional income for the economy as a whole. This is precisely what makes up the hard core of circuit theory, which claims that the many-sided economic transactions performed by firms and households derive their significance from the successive formation and spending of factors' incomes – that is, wages[4] (see Gnos, 2003). In support of our interpretation, we may also highlight that Keynes already wrote along the same lines in his *Treatise on Money*, when explaining that the fall of the selling price of goods below their factor cost would mean a loss (that is, a negative profit) for entrepreneurs causing 'a transfer of wealth from the pockets of the entrepreneurs into the pockets of the general public' (Keynes, 1971 [1930], p. 159).

We are thus in a position to understand Keynes's principle of effective demand and his denial of any positive effect of wage and price flexibility on employment. On the one hand, we have confirmation that the income of the economy as whole, which is available to buy the goods produced, is dependent, for any level of wages, on the volume of employment N. It amounts to w x N, where w stands for the average level of wages. This is why, it should be noted, Keynes (1936, p. 44) could choose the wage-unit as an adequate yardstick for measuring income and output. Then, cutting wages by, say, 10 per cent means cutting demand in the same proportion: 'if the wage-unit changes, the expenditure on consumption corresponding to a given level of employment will, like prices, change in the same proportion' (p. 92). As we quoted from Keynes above, we may therefore deny 'that the reduction in money-wages will leave demand unaffected'. On the other hand, a decrease in prices is unable to increase the income available, and so the aggregate demand for goods. Its only possible effect concerns the way income as a whole is redistributed between workers and entrepreneurs. If wages are stable while prices are decreasing, then profits decrease.

All in all, the principle of effective demand does not deny the existence of markets and the correlated role of supply and demand in determining prices, and so in sanctioning production decisions made by entrepreneurs (their profits, and thus the profitability of their investments, depend on the amounts of money income holders spend on the goods produced). It claims, however, that the interplay of supply and demand in markets is not the ultimate feature of a monetary economy of production. Just as circuitists point out, supply and demand are predetermined by a macroeconomic constraint grounded in the asymmetrical relationship between entrepreneurs and their employees and the correlated circular flow of the wages that are formed when entrepreneurs invest money in the production of goods and that are spent when accruing back to entrepreneurs in purchases of the goods produced. The actual sequence starts with unilateral decisions made by entrepreneurs with reference to their expected costs and proceeds. In sharp contrast to what standard Keynesian economics claims, the employment entrepreneurs supply in this way is quite definitely not the outcome of an adjustment process that supposedly takes place in markets and allegedly generates unemployment in response to some exogenous fall in demand when prices and wages are inflexible.

Circuit theory at centre stage in explaining unemployment

Why does full employment not prevail in a monetary economy of production? The originality of Keynes's theory compared with the standard Keynesian interpretation of it, and the relevance of the reference to the circuit scheme are confirmed when we consider the causes of unemployment.

As Stiglitz (1973) points out, New Keynesians are not interested in examining why demand may fall short of supply. They assume that some exogenous fall (which they dub a 'shock') in nominal demand happens which, given price and wage rigidity, diverts output and employment from their equilibrium values. This story is clearly not consistent with Keynes's theory. As Keynes puts it: 'The essential character of the argument is precisely the same whether or not money-wages, etc., are liable to change' (Keynes, 1936, p. 27). Keynes's argument focuses on demand deficiency and its source. It is tied in with a possible discrepancy between the 'propensity to consume' and the 'inducement to invest'. As highlighted by circuit theory, the payment of wages forms the community's money income (including profits which are derived from wages), which fuels demand on goods markets. Part of this income is saved, and in greater proportions as individual incomes rise, which entails demand deficiency unless savings are borrowed by entrepreneurs who spend them on investment goods (that should be produced accordingly):

> The outline of our theory can be expressed as follows. When employment increases, aggregate real income is increased. The psychology of the community is such that when aggregate real income is increased aggregate consumption is increased, but not by so much as income. Hence employers would make a loss if the whole of the increased employment were to be devoted to satisfying the increased demand for immediate consumption. Thus, to justify any given amount of employment there must be an amount of current investment sufficient to absorb the excess of total output over

what the community chooses to consume when employment is at a given level. For unless there is this amount of investment, the receipts of the entrepreneurs will be less than is required to induce them to offer the given amount of employment. (Keynes, 1936, p. 27)

It is true that Keynes's argument features prominently in standard Keynesian textbooks, but there the propensity to consume and the inducement to invest are seen simply as determinants of the aggregate demand function that features in the adjustment process we referred to earlier, and that is at variance with Keynes's conception of the principle of effective demand.

Contrary to standard Keynesians, Post Keynesians highlight Keynes's originality. They endorse his viewpoint with respect to the effect of excessive saving on employment:

> The basic message of Keynes's principle of effective demand is that (for a given level of entrepreneurial investment spending) too great a demand for saving in the form of liquid assets can prevent 'saved' (that is, unutilized or involuntarily unemployed) real resources from being employed to expand the economy's stock of productive facilities. The unemployment problem is basically always a liquidity problem. (Davidson, 2002, p. 25)

Post Keynesians usually relate the excess of saving to the fact that holding savings in the form of money (or more generally in the form of liquid assets) is one way of coping with the uncertainty that characterises the economic future. As regards the way to improve employment, different views are currently expressed. For instance, Wray considers persistent government deficits – which Keynes did not require – as a necessary condition of growth and full employment: 'Given usual private sector preferences regarding net saving, economic growth requires persistent government deficits' (Wray, 1998, p. 75). Davidson is more moderate. He calls first on central banks to provide liquidity at very low nominal interest rates, and then, if still necessary, on the government to support private entrepreneurial initiative by running a capital account deficit (Davidson, 2002, p. 254).

The reference to the circular flow of wages uncovers an additional source of unemployment. This point has been raised by Schmitt (1984, 1996) who looks closely at how firms finance their spending on investment goods.

To make the point, let us first suppose that firms borrow amounts deposited by income holders with banks. This is consistent with the rationale of income spending outlined by Keynes (1936). The community's income, Y, may either be spent on consumption goods (C) or saved ($Y = C + S$). When borrowing S to buy investment goods (I), firms allow the saved income to be spent on goods, so that the whole income is spent on the whole set of goods produced in the current period ($C + S = C + I$). Firms have to sell the goods they produce at a price that will repay them factor costs (wages), yield a profit (out of which they will be able to pay interest and dividends), and amortize the sums of money spent on equipment. The correlated amortization fund may be used to pay back the borrowed money income to lenders, who then dispose anew of their income (in fact, they dispose of an income currently earned by firms from sales, which firms transfer to them) that they may spend on consumption goods or lend again to firms. When firms reinvest these funds, this simply means that the initial loan has been (implicitly) renewed.

Suppose now that firms make use of the profits they earn in the current period to buy investment goods instead of redistributing them to their owners (shareholders) or to lenders. At first sight, this case is in no way different from the case we have just examined. There is a difference, however. When borrowing redistributed profits or any income saved by its holders, firms become indebted to lenders. Not so when they use the profits they earn from the sale of current output directly. There is therefore a 'short-circuit' so to speak: with regard to firms as a whole (that is, when we abstract from inter-firm purchases which are what the purchases of investment goods by firms actually are) investment goods are ipso facto appropriated by firms when the latter pay wages to the workers producing these goods. This is namely apart from the general case where firms have to borrow money in order to pay for wages and then have to sell the produced goods in markets to income holders in order to get their money back. In the general case, firms may of course buy goods, but, as highlighted by Keynes, they have to borrow the corresponding income from income holders (including shareholders and lenders benefiting from the redistributed profits). In the case under examination, on the contrary, while paying for wages firms do not become indebted and thus immediately appropriate the produce of the workers they employ (it stands for a net asset in their books). As a consequence, the workers get a purely nominal income; that is, an income to which no goods correspond. If we assume that wages paid in the consumption goods sector amount to £150 and wages paid in the investment goods sector amount to £50, we have to conclude that the £200 wage bill paid in the whole allows income holders to buy only the consumption goods produced (£150) instead of the whole output. The investment goods were directly bought by firms when the latter paid for wages. As Schmitt puts it, the wages paid in the investment goods sector 'are completely empty of all purchasing power, that is, devoid of any output' (Schmitt, 1996, p. 102). This means that an inflationary gap is created (cf. Rossi, 2001). Now, this inflationary gap may have a harmful consequence on employment.

To check this latter point, suppose that, observing a decline in their rate of profit (or an increase in interest rates), firms decide not to reinvest the funds they obtain from amortization. These funds may then be redistributed to firms' owners, or lent on financial markets as is common practice. The crucial issue is that no goods produced correspond to these funds: firms get back the 'empty' wages they paid to workers. Then, two possibilities are at hand. These funds (be they redistributed or not to firms' owners) may be borrowed by other firms which spend them on the payment of wages. This is actually the less harmful alternative with regard to employment since the available cash then finances new production. Alternatively, the cash may be spent in goods markets by firms' owners, or borrowed from them by households to finance the purchase of currently produced consumption goods. Then, we observe a double-sided situation. Spending 'empty' wages no doubt feeds inflation. Simultaneously, since this cash is made available through a cut in investment, it shrinks employment. In this way, circuit theory allows us to account for stagflation (see Schmitt, 1984, and Cencini, 1996), which was considered in the 1970s to be in contradiction with Keynesian economics. Of course, though, the inflation gap identified here may be concealed insofar as price increases may be cancelled out by an increase in the overall productivity of production processes (more goods are then on sale at unchanged unit prices). The inflationary gap remains, however, and more importantly so does the involuntary unemployment caused by the withdrawal of investment. Let us insist that inflation and unemployment would not occur if firms were to invest funds they borrow from income holders. In this latter case, the amortization funds yielding from sales would correspond to wages captured from workers, the purchasing power of which is defined by goods currently produced. The withdrawal of investment would allow these funds to be spent on consumption goods: employment would not shrink, the production of consumption goods would simply have taken the place of the production of investment goods.

To deal with this dysfunction of capital accumulation, Schmitt argues for a reform of the way the banking system manages monetary and financial flows, the objective of which would be to avoid any direct compensation between the payment of wages and the spending of profits (Schmitt, 1996). It should be noticed that this does not mean that firms should be prevented from ploughing back profits into business, but that flows in banks' books should be accounted for in such a way that the formation of 'empty' wages would be prevented.

Conclusion

While propounding the concept of a monetary economy of production or entrepreneur economy, Keynes did not deny the role of markets, in which goods are supplied and purchased by income holders. This role is indeed crucial because entrepreneurs cannot avoid the sanction of markets and so have to adapt the employment they supply to their expectations regarding the demand for the goods they plan to produce. A monetary economy of production has some originality, however. This is a claim we have highlighted here while showing that the principle of effective demand is based on a macroeconomic feature which amounts to the circuit of money wages that are successively formed in the payment of factor costs and then spent on goods. In doing so, we have been able to support the Post Keynesian dismissal of the standard Keynesian interpretation of Keynes's theory of employment which is used to reduce the determination of employment to the interplay of aggregate supply and demand functions in markets and to impute unemployment to price and wage rigidities. We have also been able, then, to show that the reference to the circuit of wages reveals an original source of unemployment, which relates to the process of capital formation and so supplements Keynes's theory of demand deficiency and its Post Keynesian developments.

Notes

1. On Robinson and the circuit, see Gnos and Rochon (2003).
2. As suggested by Keynes, we will disregard user cost here: 'The reader will observe that I am deducting the user cost both from the *proceeds* and from the *aggregate supply price* of a given volume of output, so that both these terms are to be interpreted *net* of user cost; whereas the aggregate sums paid by the purchasers are, of course, *gross* of user cost' (Keynes, 1936, footnote 2, p. 24).
3. 'The factor cost is, of course, the same thing, looked at from the point of view of entrepreneur, as what the factors of production regard as their income' (Keynes, 1936, p. 23).
4. 'It is preferable to regard labour, including, of course, the personal services of the entrepreneur and his assistants, as the sole factor of production, operating in a given environment of technique, natural resources, capital equipment and effective demand' (Keynes, 1936, pp. 213–14). Circuit theory confirms the validity of Keynes's claim. While the payment of wages forms new incomes, the purchase of capital-goods amounts to spending current incomes the amortization of which, together with interests and dividends paid to firms' creditors, firms will derive from sales, that is, from wages spent on consumption goods.

References

Arena, R. (1996) 'Investment decisions in circuit and Post Keynesian approaches: a comparison', in G. Deleplace and E. Nell (eds) *Money in Motion: the Post Keynesian and Circulation Approaches* (London and New York: Macmillan and St. Martin's Press), pp. 417–33.

Arestis, P. (1996) 'Post-Keynesian economics: towards coherence', *Cambridge Journal of Economics*, 20, pp. 111–35.

Ball, L., Mankiw, G. and Romer, D. (1991) 'The New-Keynesian Economics and the Output-Inflation Trade-Off', in G. Mankiw and D. Romer (eds) *New Keynesian Economics*, 1 (Cambridge, MA: MIT Press), pp. 147–211.

Barrère, A. (1979) *Déséquilibres économiques et contre-révolution keynésienne* (Paris: Economica).

Cencini, A. (1996) 'Inflation and deflation: the two faces of the same reality', in A. Cencini and M. Baranzini (eds) *Inflation and Unemployment. Contributions to a new macroeconomic approach* (London: Routledge), pp. 17–60.

Chick, V. (2002) 'Money and effective demand', in J. Smithin (ed.) *What is Money?* (London and New York: Routledge), pp. 124–38.

Davidson, P. (2002) *Financial Markets, Money and the Real World* (Cheltenham, UK and Northampton, USA: Edward Elgar).

Deleplace, G. and Nell, E. (1996) *Money in Motion: the Post Keynesian and Circulation Approaches* (London and New York: Macmillan and St. Martin's Press).

Fontana, G. (2000) 'Post Keynesians and Circuitists on money and uncertainty: an attempt at generality', *Journal of Post Keynesian Economics*, 23, (1), pp. 27–48.

Graziani, A. (1990) 'The theory of the monetary circuit', *Économies et Sociétés* (Série 'Monnaie et Production'), 24,(6), pp. 7–36.

Graziani, A. (1996) 'Money as purchasing power and money as a stock of wealth in Keynesian economic thought', in G. Deleplace and E. Nell (eds) *Money in Motion: the Post Keynesian and Circulation Approaches* (London and New York: Macmillan and St. Martin's Press).

Graziani, A. (2003) *The Monetary Theory of Production* (Cambridge University Press).

Gnos, C. (2003) 'Circuit theory as an explanation of the complex real world', in L.-P. Rochon and S. Rossi (eds) *Modern Theories of Money* (Cheltenham, UK and Northampton, USA: Edward Elgar).

Gnos, C. (2004) 'Is Ex ante–Ex post Analysis Irrelevant to Keynes's Theory of Employment?', *Review of Political Economy*, (forthcoming).

Gnos, C. and Rochon, L.-P. (2003) 'Joan Robinson and Keynes: finance, relative prices and the monetary circuit', *Review of Political Economy*, 15,(4), pp. 483–91.

Keynes, J.M. (1971 [1930]) *A Treatise on Money*, in *The Collected writings of John Maynard Keynes*, vol. V (London: Macmillan).

Keynes, J.M. (1936) *The General Theory of Employment, Interest and Money* (London: Macmillan).

Keynes, J.M. (1973 [1933a]) 'A monetary theory of production', in *The Collected Writings of John Maynard Keynes*, XIII (London: Macmillan Press), pp. 408–11.

Keynes, J.M. (1973 [1933b]) 'The distinction between a co-operative economy and an entrepreneur economy', in *The Collected Writings of John Maynard Keynes*, XXIX (London: Macmillan Press), pp. 76–106.

Keynes, J.M. (1973 [1934]) 'Poverty in Plenty: is the Economic System Self-Adjusting?', in *The Collected Writings of John Maynard Keynes*, XIII (London: Macmillan Press), pp. 485–92.

Keynes, J.M. (1973 [1937a]) 'Ex post and ex ante', in *The Collected Writings of John Maynard Keynes*, XIV (London: Macmillan), pp. 179–83.

Keynes, J.M. (1973 [1937b]) 'The "ex-ante" theory of the rate of interest', *Economic Journal*, in *The Collected Writings of John Maynard Keynes*, XIV (London: Macmillan), pp. 215–23.

Lavoie, M. (1984) 'Un modèle post-keynésien d'économie monétaire fondé sur la théorie du circuit', *Économies et Sociétés*, 59, 1, pp. 233–58.

Le Bourva, J. (1962) 'Création de la monnaie et multiplicateur du crédit', *Revue Economique*, 13(1), pp. 29–56.

Parguez, A. (1975) *Monnaie et macroéconomie* (Paris: Economica).

Parguez, A. and Seccareccia M. (2000) 'The credit theory of money: the monetary circuit approach', in J. Smithin (ed.) *What is Money?* (London and New York: Routledge), pp. 101–23.

Rochon, L.-P. (1999a) 'The creation and circulation of endogenous money: a circuit dynamic approach', *Journal of Economic Issues*, 33(1), pp. 1–21.

Rochon, L.-P. (1999b) *Credit, Money and Production: An Alternative Post-Keynesian Approach* (Cheltenham and Northampton: Edward Elgar).

Rossi, S. (2001) *Money and Inflation. A New Macroeconomic Analysis* (Aldershot: Elgar).

Rotheim, R.J. (1998) 'New Keynesian Macroeconomics and Markets', in R.J. Rotheim (ed.) *New Keynesian Economics/Post Keynesian Alternatives* (London: Routledge), pp. 51–70.

Schmitt, B. (1966) *Monnaie, salaires et profits* (Paris: Presses Universitaires de France).

Schmitt, B. (1984) *Inflation, chômage et malformations du capital* (Albeuve, Switzerland and Paris: Castella and Economica).

Schmitt, B. (1996) 'Unemployment: Is there a principal cause?', in A. Cencini and M. Baranzini (eds) *Inflation and Unemployment. Contributions to a new macroeconomic approach* (London and New York: Routledge), pp. 75–105.

Stiglitz, J.E. (1973) *Economics* (New York: W.W. Norton).

Wray, L.R. (1996) 'Money in the circular flow', in G. Deleplace and E. Nell (eds) *Money in Motion: the Post Keynesian and Circulation Approaches* (London and New York: Macmillan and St. Martin's Press), pp. 441–64.

Wray, L.R. (1998) *Understanding Modern Money* (Cheltenham, Northampton: Edward Elgar).

Part IV
Money, Inflation and Distribution

12
Non-Credit Money to Fight Poverty

*Biagio Bossone and Abdourahmane Sarr**

Introduction

While finance plays an important role in supporting economic growth, financial institutions have a limited reach in low income countries. This is because underdeveloped financial infrastructures, inadequate collateral, weak contract enforcement, and low participation in payments systems expose banks to high liquidity and credit risks. Circuit analysis shows how banks enable a monetary production economy to function and grow by creating and allocating money through lending to support demand and production. When lending is hindered by structural impediments, economic growth is constrained.

This chapter proposes to reform the way money is created by institutions that provide payments services in poor countries from a lending based system to a gift-to-demand depositors based system. The aim is to overcome the lack of domestic demand caused by low bank credit. Being gift-based, the proposed system would foster participation in payments systems and lower liquidity risks. It would also overcome financial infrastructure problems by eliminating the need for credit risk analysis for financial institutions that provide payments services only.

In this new gift based circuit route, liquidity is key to a bank's survival. Distributed liquidity creates demand for firms' output which in turn finances production through retained earnings and capital market financing. If appropriately designed, with monetary policy ensuring price stability, the system could help growth in low income countries.

* The authors wish to thank participants at the 5–6 December 2003 Benevento conference in Italy on the Monetary Theory of Production in honour of Augusto Graziani. The opinions expressed in this paper are the authors' only and do not necessarily coincide with those of the institutions with which they are associated.

The proposal relies on the postulate that payments services providing banks that enjoy stable demand deposits which make money creation possible with low liquidity risk do not have to allocate this newly created money through loans. Had the regulator confined these institutions to the provision of payments services, while retaining the potential they have to create money, the only necessary criteria for such institutions to continue operating would be that they guarantee deposit liquidity. In fact, a single bank in a cashless world could create deposits at will within the constraints of monetary policy without worrying about liquidity risk.

In the following, the first section points to the problems that limit the role of finance in low-income countries. The second section presents our alternative model of finance and discusses its operational features, the underlying policy framework, and the transition to it. The final section discusses the expected effects of the proposed system on the real and financial sectors. It also contrasts the system's allocation mechanism with conventional banking and argues that the system can stimulate domestic demand in poor countries and help offset the constraint on external demand caused by international trade barriers on basic goods.

Finance for growth: what works and what does not

While research shows that financial intermediation plays an important role in supporting growth, it also indicates that the growth-finance relationship is nonlinear (Kahn and Senhadji, 2000) and that finance may not be as effective for growth in low-income countries (Berthelémy and Varoukadis, 1996). Two factors may explain this phenomenon. One is the presence of threshold effects in the growth-finance dynamics, whereby agents need to reach some minimum wealth before they can access financial services. It may take a considerable time before financial development makes a significant impact on growth in low income countries. The other feature is the predominant role that banking has in low-income economies where financial infrastructure is poor and the public prefers deposit- and loan-contracts to other financial instruments. The limited impact of finance on growth may have to do with the limited ability of banks to serve low-income agents (Bossone *et al.*, 2003).

Let us see how banks support economic activity and why they may fail to do so.

Banks as 'circuit starters'

The monetary circuit approach has systematically studied the links between bank money and production, and the features of a monetary production economy. The circuit sequence can be stylised as follows (see also Figure 12.1):

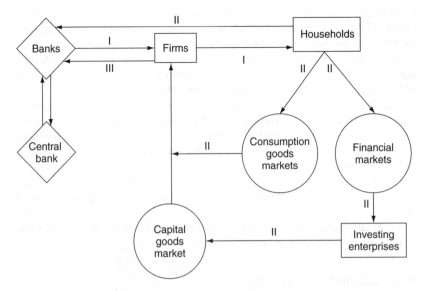

Figure 12.1   Flow of funds in the circuit model

1 At circuit-start (stage I), banks create money (initial finance) to fund the labour inputs of consumption and capital goods producers. Firms request loans on the basis of expected demand that existing production capacity can satisfy. All transactions take place on banks' books.

2 In the interim phase (stage II), household labour incomes (from the initial finance) are spent on consumption goods and savings. Investing firms bid for household savings by issuing securities (final finance) to purchase capital goods. All firms' expected demands are validated.

3 At circuit end (stage III), firms use sales proceeds to pay off bank debt. Money originally created is destroyed and the circuit is closed. Firms that fail to sell all output seek to borrow from the capital market in order to repay banks or ask banks to rollover their outstanding debt. If firms fail to raise the money, they exit the market while banks write off the corresponding net losses.

The main elements of the circuit approach that relate to our discussion are the following:

Banks mobilise real factors by lending new liabilities (demand deposits). Such liabilities, when issued, are only partially supported by existing real resources and are backed only ex post as the stream of newly produced output (made possible by them) comes to the market. Economic activity can expand faster and at a lower real resource cost when banks lend new money to firms, since they can create inside money ex nihilo.

Banks and financial markets play distinctive roles. The former creates additional liquidity to finance production (and consumption), while the latter allocates the existing liquidity from investors to fund-users.

Large deposit market shares facilitate bank money creation. Other things equal, a bank's larger deposit base increases its redeposit capacity and increases the number of payments settled within its own books. Also, through a larger deposit base, a bank may increase its lending, while facing a lower probability of losing deposits to other banks, and a higher probability that deposits will flow back to its books from other banks as a result of payment activity. This reduces the bank's liquidity needs and the associated costs (Bossone, 2003).

We discuss next how structural impediments in low-income countries may hinder the role of banks as circuit starters.

Why banks may not succeed

Several factors limit the impact of banking on growth in low-income countries. First, since banks are liable for the money they lend, borrowers must have initial endowments that banks hold as collateral and liquidate to cover deposits when needed. In low-income countries, borrowers generally do not possess the required collateral. Alternatively, financial statements can prove cash flows and substitute for collateral, but many small borrowers do not have reliable financial statements. Second, the legal system is often unable to support banks in seizing collateral.

Third, the liquidity available to banks for lending depends on a large and diversified base of depositors, with independent cash flows. Independent flows allow banks to minimise the liquidity risk that would otherwise require long-term deposit funds or a very large redeposit capacity. Without these two elements, banks have to keep high levels of liquidity idle, which constrain their lending capacity. Banks in poor economies do not have a sufficient depositor base because most people do not participate in the banking system. In many instances, this is caused by unaffordable account maintenance fees and results in essentially cash-based economies.

Fourth, in many low-income countries the lack of scale economies and a limited banking sector competition contribute to generating substantially larger lending-deposit interest rate spreads than in advanced economies. Seigniorage makes access and financial deepening more difficult.

Fifth, banks lend to firms when these face market demand that can be satisfied profitably. In poor countries, weak demand leads banks to regard most domestic loan proposals as not creditworthy. When banks lend to governments, on the other hand, the political process determines how the money is spent, often with undesirable consequences.

Finally, transaction costs for accessing bank loans are too high for many potential borrowers, while administration costs make small loans uneconomical to banks.

Finance to fight poverty: a proposal

The arguments above suggest that conventional finance cannot do enough to foster growth in low-income countries. We propose a system that is based on money that is created and distributed to individuals on a nonlending basis. Our system aims to broaden access to financial resources and promote financial deepening; generate non-inflationary purchasing power without rising private-sector debt and output growth;

Banks' money creation power derives essentially from their payment function, since deposit flows largely net out in their books and depositors do not withdraw funds all at the same time. We propose to separate the money creation and lending function in order to overcome the lack of credit risk management infrastructure in poor countries.

Conventional banks are replaced with special payment institutions, hereafter called Deposit Creating Institutions (DCIs). DCIs collect non-interest bearing deposits, provide deposit transfer services, and distribute new deposits to individual depositors on a nonlending basis, under criteria to be discussed below. In the noncredit money system (NCMS), banks and nonbank financial intermediaries fund their assets exclusively by issuing nondemandable instruments. All individuals, firms and intermediaries need to hold DCI accounts if they want to receive/transfer deposits for payments or use demandable deposits as financial assets.

This section discusses the technical aspects of our proposal.

Operations of DCIs

The DCIs are not allowed to extend credit. They earn revenues from fees charged on payment services. Their fee income is the reason investors would want to start a DCI.

DCIs hold part of their assets as central bank reserves and liquid securities. The remainder consists of liquidity that they distribute to individual depositors. They augment the deposit balances of each individual depositor by a proportion of the depositor's average holdings over a reference period. The liquidity distributed is reported on the asset side of the DCI balance sheet for record keeping purposes and gives rise to new deposit liabilities, as loans do (see Table 12.1).

Table 12.1   The balance sheet of a DCI

Assets		Liabilities	
RR	10	DD	100
LA	20	Debt	20
DL	90	Equity	20
FA	20		
Total	140	Total	140

RR = Reserve requirements (10%)
LA = Liquid assets
DL = Distributed liquidity (loans in a conventional bank)
DD = Demand deposits
FA = Fixed assets
Debt + Equity = LA + FA = DCI effective capital
Liquid assets other than reserve requirements and free reserves
can only be held using non-demand deposit liabilities.

The proportion of deposit balances a DCI distributes is a strategy variable determined by the DCI itself. Different DCIs can apply different rates to different types of depositors. DCIs need to determine the amount of noncredit money they can distribute without running into liquidity problems. In the absence of an interest rate mechanism, the deposit distribution rate is one of the instruments available to DCIs to compete in the market for deposits.

The DCIs modulate deposit distribution with a view to attracting depositors and to expand their payment business. They face a tradeoff between the benefits derived from maximising the rate of deposit creation by running the smaller reserves possible and the benefits that arise from accumulating large capital and reserves. Liquidity management is therefore key in determining their competitiveness.

The liquidity distributed takes the form of deposits issued on the accounts of depositors and is additional to the deposits outstanding at the time of distribution. Deposits are convertible into cash and foreign exchange on demand by holders. Depositors can use their balances to finance any type of transaction.

DCIs decide whether and when to distribute liquidity. If deposits are unstable or decrease, and the DCI deems it unsafe to distribute liquidity, then distribution does not take place.

In the NCMS, solvency ceases to be a criterion for sound DCIs while liquidity is key. The capital of a DCI equals its fixed assets plus its own liquid funds (Table 12.1). Hereafter, we call primary liquidity the funds that the DCI is required to hold in the form of cash, central bank reserves, and liquid securities, as well as any funds that it holds in excess of requirements. DCIs may purchase private and government securities on their own behalf only with their own capital. Given the asset structure of a DCI, its primary liquidity coincides with its total assets net of physical assets.

DCIs need primary liquidity to comply with regulatory requirements, settle payments to other DCIs, and meet cash demand from customers. Primary liquidity is a key factor of competition in the NCMS. DCIs that are more capitalised can take more liquidity risk and distribute more inside money, thereby attracting depositors from other DCIs. By expanding its redeposit capacity, a DCI economises on the use of (costly) primary liquidity since its share of 'on us' payments increases relative to its competitors. Also, a larger redeposit capacity enables a DCI to distribute new deposits with a higher probability of attracting them back to its own books.

Exit of a failed DCI

A DCI fails when it runs out of primary liquidity and is unable to settle its payment obligations. Since DCIs are subject to a reserve requirement (see next section), a payment settlement failure happens when a DCI loses primary liquidity to the point where it cannot comply with its requirement.

This situation may result from competition or from depositor runs. Competition may be such that deposits are attracted to DCIs offering better services and move out of less competitive DCIs. The process may go on until the weakening DCI becomes unable to settle deposit outflows with its reserves. In fact, when the market perceives the continued deterioration of the DCI's liquidity position, the anticipation of further liquidity depletion may precipitate a run from depositors and accelerate the DCI's default in the payment system.

However, DCIs are less subject to insolvency and, therefore, less exposed than conventional banks to the risk of runs. This is because of the way a DCI failure can be handled. Once a DCI has run out of primary liquidity and has exploited all options to raise the needed reserve balances, it is allowed to fail and thus exits the system. A DCI exiting the system is left with its fixed assets since, as indicated, the liquidity distributed to depositors does not bear DCI claims attached and does not give rise to DCI demandable debt obligations. Thus, only the fixed assets of a failed DCI can be liquidated to repay its (nondeposit) debt. Upon failure, the deposit liabilities of the failed DCI are allocated to the surviving DCIs with net open credit positions outstanding vis-à-vis the failed institution. The allocation can be done on a pro-rata basis relative to the capital of each surviving DCI. Obviously, in the post-allocation period, depositors are free to transfer their deposits to other DCIs or to use them when and as they wish.

Since DCI liabilities are not matched by real claims on DCI books, their allocation to other DCIs does not require full collateralisation with performing assets. The only necessary and sufficient condition for the allocation not to undermine public confidence in the receiving DCIs is that the latter have enough primary liquidity to maintain their required ratios via-à-vis their larger post-allocation liabilities.

Now, if there are no leakages to currency, this condition is satisfied by construction. In the event of leakages to currency, however, the actual reserve ratio of the leaking DCIs can drop below the required level and the affected DCIs may find themselves unable to settle obligations. In the case of failure(s), the allocation of the liabilities to surviving DCIs would cause their actual reserve ratio to drop below requirement: a portion of the allocated liabilities would be uncovered by existing reserves. Any such reserve shortage would have to be supplemented through recapitalisation. The needed injection of funds, however, would likely cost less than under a comparable case of bank failure where all the bank's uncovered liabilities would have to be written off, matched with restructuring bonds, or refunded by government.

The exit of a failed DCI, however large, would not trigger systemic reactions since depositors would have their deposits immediately transferred to surviving DCIs. Deposit insurance would reinforce deposit safety without creating standard moral hazard issues since deposits are not lent.

In the event of a run on all DCIs simultaneously, the public sector could in principle let all DCIs fail, order the transfer of all deposits to a central institution, and keep the payment system alive allowing deposit transfers to be executed with only a fractional reserve base.

The system would not be sustainable in the case of a run on the currency, but the consequences would not be different than under conventional banking.

Monetary policy in the NCMS

DCIs are required to hold a minimum reserve-to-deposit ratio with the central bank. Prudentially, DCIs can also be required to hold a minimum ratio of liquidable securities which would be equivalent to a capital requirement since DCIs cannot buy securities with the public's deposits. Individual DCIs can exceed the required ratio(s) based on their own prudential criteria. They could also be subject to maximum distributed liquidity exposures to single or connected depositors as banks are with respect to loans to such entitities.

Like in conventional banking, a minimum reserve requirement determines the maximum deposit creation by the DCIs.

The central bank issues reserves and determines the reserves stock that is consistent with its output forecasts and inflation objective. Reserves injections and withdrawals are effected through open market operations (OMOs) with nonDCI intermediaries. In order to avoid distorting DCI market competition, the central bank may not lend either to DCIs or to other private sector agents. In particular, the central bank may not provide reserves to support the expansion of individual DCI balance sheets or to relieve DCIs from liquidity pressures. Recall that liquidity is a key factor of competition in the system and that, unlike conventional banks, a DCI cannot be temporarily illiquid since illiquidity indicates that it is being competed off the market by more efficient DCIs. Therefore, in the NCMS the central bank is never confronted with the option of extending financing to an illiquid but otherwise solvent DCI: any central bank lending to illiquid DCIs would alter DCI market competition.

In order to facilitate payment settlements, however, the central bank may sell reserves to DCIs against securities or can make reserves available to DCIs overnight or for very short time windows on a collateralised basis and at penalising fees. DCIs can raise liquidity in the money market using their own assets and use the room provided by reserve requirement averaging. Since all intermediaries hold accounts with DCIs, OMOs with nonDCIs are reflected immediately on the reserves balances held at DCIs and, indirectly, on the supply of deposits.

The central bank, thus, controls the overall liquidity of the economy through reserve requirements and the supply of reserves to the financial market. It does not have an interest rate policy since this would interfere with DCI market competition for primary liquidity (see above) through potential liquidity support to meet an interest rate target. Interest rates are determined in the financial market and, as such, they also reflect monetary policy decisions and credibility. In turn, the central bank may use market interest rates as an indicator of the economy's liquidity conditions and as a guide for policy making.

For a given velocity of money circulation, the distribution rate of noncredit money in the aggregate approximates nominal GDP growth. However, if velocity falls as the real demand for transactions balances increases with the new system, a higher distribution rate can be achieved without inflationary consequences. Also, during the transition to the NCMS (see below), a higher distribution rate is necessary to replace the deposits that are destroyed when existing bank loans are repaid, thus avoiding deflationary gaps.

Transition to the NCMS

The activities and balance sheets of DCIs must be kept separate from nonDCIs. To this end, DCIs can be dedicated entities, specialised subsidiaries of financial holding companies, or fire-walled departments within multi-product financial companies.

In moving from conventional banking to the NCMS, each bank would have to choose between being a DCI or a nonDCI. Banks willing to become DCIs sell their loans to nonbank financial institutions. Other banks can transform themselves into financial companies that either control DCI and nonDCI subsidiaries or run separate fire-walled DCI and nonDCI departments. Every nonDCI is allocated the assets of the transforming bank and issues non-demandable debt liabilities or offers investors to voluntarily exchange nondemandable debt instruments for demand deposits at market conditions.

In the absence of nonbanks willing to buy conventional bank loans, or in the event the market does not finance nonDCI subsidiaries (departments), a process of bank debt unwinding can be set up by letting old loans mature and by allowing DCI depositors to use distributed liquidity to accelerate bank debt repayment. Appendix I illustrates the transition process with a numerical example.

Economic effects of the NCMS

What would be the effects of the NCMS on the real and financial sectors? Note first in the following stage-sequence and in Figure 12.2 the alterations that the system would bring to the circuit process:

1   At stage I, DCIs distribute liquidity to depositors. Firms use internal resources or access trade finance facilities to start production. The financial market block in Figure 12.2 comprises both short-term and long-term intermediaries and intermediation facilities.
2   In stage II, depositors and wage earners spend their money on consumption and savings in financial assets. Firms producing consumption goods capture part of DCI liquidity as revenues. Firms wishing to invest use retained earnings and issue nondemandable securities to savers to purchase or finance the production of capital goods. Firms producing capital goods finance production with nondemandable securities.

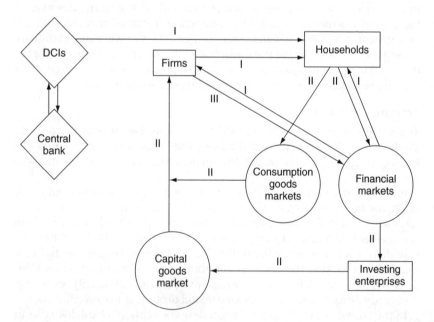

Figure 12.2   Flow of funds in the NCMS

3 At stage III, the trade finance fund is reconstituted as part of sales revenues and its resources are carried over to the next round. The new circuit route does not require that money created be destroyed, it continues to be recycled in the system. Firms can use part of liquidity captured in revenues to purchase production factors for the next production round.

The sequence shows that the DCIs would be the new circuit starters and that the new flow-of-funds structure would be consistent with the circuit process achieving closure.

Effects on the real economy

The NCMS would create and distribute purchasing power to the public more broadly and at a lower cost than is possible under conventional banking, with no need for financial infrastructure to support money creation other than through an efficient payment system. Also, the NCMS would grant the attendant seigniorage back to the public, thereby averting accumulation of private debt due to bank rents.

A larger and more convenient creation of purchasing power, as well as broader access to it, would generate more aggregate demand accompanied by price rises for the goods in higher demand. This would stimulate production and production finance (Bossone and Sarr, 2002). Local firms could plan production based on larger and more predictable demand than under conventional banking. In sectors producing profitable goods, higher output would be accompanied by more capital accumulation. Money injection and incomes formation would generate savings, and second round effects would trigger new liquidity distribution.

Consumption financed by noncredit money would increase the demand for the goods preferred by those who have access to new liquidity. In countries with high poverty and dependency ratios, consumption concentrates mostly on goods with a large content of local resource inputs (including low skill labour), such as food, clothing, garments and footwear, and housing and related expenses. If, as a result of participating in the NCMS, depositors were distributed new purchasing power, spending would increase mostly in those basic sectors, inducing relative price rises that would attract production factors.

Through employment and relative price rises in basic goods, the poor would capture liquidity. The new money wages paid out would enable their earners to enter the NCMS and start accumulating resources.

The incentive structure built in the liquidity distribution mechanism would have two dynamic effects. First, the perception of the benefits associated with accumulating larger balances may lead depositors to postpone decisions to spend the newly distributed liquidity and to intensify their work or job-search efforts in an attempt to enhance their own saving capacity. Second, easier access to finance may induce entrepreneurial individuals to accumulate purchasing power and invest it in new businesses.

Effects on the financial system

The expansion of noncredit money and the separation of money creation from lending would enhance financial stability and deepening. The DCIs would run no credit risk and face a low liquidity risk. Also, the illiquidity or insolvency of nonDCI intermediaries would not affect the liquidity of deposits.

NonDCI intermediaries could not rely on insured demand liabilities and, therefore, all their liabilities would have to be priced at levels that reflect their true creditworthiness. Moreover, since no intermediary's failure would affect the payment system, or have systemic ripples through deposit runs, public intervention would be unnecessary to salvage failing institutions. Finally, the separation of the payment system from credit would eliminate the need for capital requirements based on complex credit-risk evaluations.

DCIs would be easier to monitor than conventional banks since primary liquidity ratios are readily observable. Such transparency would enable supervisors and market players (depositors, DCI shareholders, and investors in DCI shares) to monitor the DCIs efficiently.

By competing for customers, the DCIs would likely have a stronger and more rapid impact than conventional banks on financial deepening and access to financial resources in poor economies. Agents who typically use cash would have a way to increase their purchasing power by converting cash into deposits. Through liquidity distribution, more individuals would sooner reach the wealth threshold beyond which they could afford to participate in the financial system.

By being net fund providers, the DCIs would foster the formation of a broader depositor base. Since average deposit balances would be used to determine depositor shares for liquidity distribution, individuals would want to be paid in deposits. Similarly, individuals would tend to prefer businesses that offer noncash payment facilities so as to minimise their cash handling.

Allocation of financial resources in the NCMS

The NCMS features an allocation mechanism of financial resources that is alternative to that of conventional banking. Under conventional banking, inside money is allocated through lending and thus requires credit-risk management infrastructure and capabilities. The NCMS, instead, relies on consumption and investment spending directing funds to successful firms (with internal finance and trade finance funding production). Spending drives up the relative price of desired goods (in a context where monetary policy ensures overall price stability). Successful firms capture liquidity through higher revenues and profits, thus attracting production factors. In the NMCS, demand and the price mechanism are the primary allocation criteria for newly created funds.

In the market for loanable funds, the price mechanism does not function well because high interest rates create asymmetric information problems that lead banks to resort to credit rationing (Stiglitz and Weiss, 1981). These information problems can only be mitigated by a well developed credit-risk management infrastructure; precisely what is lacking in poor countries and demands considerable time and resources to create. On the other hand, in the NCMS, direct investments by recipients of distributed funds (either depositors or firms through retained earnings) reduce the moral hazard inherent in lending by increasing the equity stake of borrowers in the financial market.

Achieving growth despite international trade barriers

The NCMS may enable poor economies to grow out of their poverty trap even in the presence of barriers to the international trade of their products. With free international trade of basic goods (e.g. agriculture), loans and investments are expected to flow from the developed economies to the low income countries with a comparative advantage in the production of these goods. If the proceeds from trading these goods internationally are enough to enable recipient countries to repay the loans and to remunerate investments adequately, their economies can become integrated in world trade (the global circuit of major currencies), with external demand being the driving factor.

The current world trade environment, however, makes this outcome unattainable. By creating domestic purchasing power, which can be spent on local output in the context of an appropriately valued exchange rate, the NCMS would complement the external demand model. Non-credit money would allow local circuits of production to develop, and domestic capital to accumulate, even in the presence of trade barriers that limit access of basic goods to markets in advanced economies.

Appendix I

Transition to the NCMS

We assume an economy with a single bank, no currency in circulation, and no financial assets other than demand deposits used for payments. In such a system, the bank cannot convert itself into a nonDCI by selling loans to nonbanks or individual depositors, since there are no surplus funds. The bank will need to separate its loan business from its payment services business by creating two separate departments – a DCI and a nonDCI, as explained below.

Step 1. The original bank is split in two departments

The bank has demand deposits (DD) in liabilities and loans (L) in assets. It does not have reserves, implying that all payments net out on its books. When the bank is split into a DCI and a nonDCI department, the former inherits the demand deposits, while the latter inherits the loans. Since the loans were the assets backing the demand deposits, the DCI now holds an asset against the nonDCI department (Capital K).

Original bank		New financial institution			
		DCI department		NonDCI department	
Assets	Liabilities	Assets	Liabilities	Assets	Liabilities
100 L	100 DD	100 K	100 DD	100 L	100 K

Step 2.1 Depositors repay loans by 10

When depositors repay their loans by 10, they make a transfer from their accounts to the account of the nonDCI department at the DCI department (recall that all transaction accounts are held at DCIs). The loan stock at the nonDCI declines by 10 and the nonDCI now holds 10 in liquid assets (LA) in the form of DCI demand deposits. At this point, if the nonDCI were expected to continue its operations, it could use the 10 units to lend funds again. That way, the balance sheet would remain as above. The nonDCI would be identical to a conventional nonbank institution intermediating investment funds (in this case, it would be capital owned by the DCI), while the DCI only deals with the payment system.

If, instead, the bank is transitioning to a specialised DCI, the DCI department offsets the nonDCI liability by 10 when the loan is reimbursed. The balance sheets shrinks to 90 as a result.

New financial institution			
DCI department		NonDCI department	
Assets	Liabilities	Assets	Liabilities
90 K	90 DD	90 L	90 K

In the absence of new deposits created by the DCI, the balance sheet shrinks to zero as loans are repaid, with deflationary effects. New money needs to be created as a result.

Step 2.2 The DCI department creates and distributes money

The DCI department creates money (distributed liquidity DL) both to off-set the deposit destruction that occurs as loans are repaid (10 in the above example) and to accommodate expected nominal GDP growth. Assuming nominal GDP growth of 10 per cent, the DCI needs to distribute $20 = (10 + .10*100)$. This represents a 20 per cent distribution rate. If we had assumed that all loans were repaid in this period, then the DCI would need to replace 100 in deposits and create 10 to accommodate GDP growth. The balance sheet of the new institutions would be as shown below. When the loan repayment process is completed, the new money distributed would equal nominal GDP growth every year (unless the velocity of money decreases because of increased demand for inside money for transactions purposes).

New financial institution			
DCI department		**NonDCI department**	
Assets	Liabilities	Assets	Liabilities
110 DL	110 DD	0	0

References

Berthelémy, J.C. and Varoudakis, A. (1996) *Financial Development Policy and Growth*, Development Centre Studies, Long-Term Growth Series (Paris: Organisation for Economic Co-operation and Development).

Bossone, B., Mahajan, S. and Zahir, F. (2003) 'Financial Infrastructure, Group Interests, and Capital Accumulation', *IMF Working Paper 03/24* (Washington: International Monetary Fund).

Bossone, B. (2003) 'Thinking of the Economy as a Circuit', in L.-P. Rochon and S. Rossi (eds), *Modern Theories of Money. The Nature and Role of Money in Capitalist Economies* (Northampton: Edward Elgar), pp. 142–72.

Bossone, B. and Sarr, A. (2002) 'A New Financial System for Poverty Reduction and Growth', *IMF Working Paper 02/178* (Washington: International Monetary Fund).

Freeman, S. (1996) 'Clearing House Banks and Banknote Over-Issue', *Journal of Monetary Economics*, 38, pp. 101–15.

Kahn, M.S. and Senhadji, A.S. (2000) 'Financial Development and Economic Growth: An Overview', *IMF Working Paper 00/209* (Washington: International Monetary Fund).

Stiglitz, J.E. and Weiss, A. (1981) 'Credit Rationing in Markets With Imperfect Information', *America Economic Review*, 71, pp. 393–410.

13
Towards a Non-Conventional Circuit Approach: Credit, Microcredit and Property Rights

*Lilia Costabile**

In the circuit approach, as developed by Augusto Graziani (1980, 1988, 1996, 2004), credit plays a fundamental role, as firms open up the monetary circuit by buying the services of labour, in exchange for the money which they receive as credit from the banking system. Graziani's approach assumes that the banking sector adopts conventional principles, thus ensuring that some agents have privileged access to credit, while others undergo severe 'credit rationing'.

Microcredit schemes, such as those implemented by the Grameen bank in Bangladesh, adopt non-conventional principles and, by so doing, weaken or abolish the credit constraint faced by producers not owning physical wealth to offer as collateral. These principles are illustrated by Muhammad Yunus in his book *Vers un monde sans pauvreté* (1997; Italian translation, 1998).

In this chapter, I propose the idea of a 'non-conventional' circuit approach that combines the insights form Graziani's model with those from Yunus's microcredit scheme. In order to explore the basic motivations and features of the 'non-conventional' circuit approach, I start by offering a brief account of the story which, in 1974, inspired Yunus's microcredit project. I next impose on this story the alternative 'tests of legitimacy' proposed by some current streams of economic and philosophical thought. The purpose is to discover the analytical and normative approach that may have motivated Yunus's project. In the next section I offer my interpretation of the effects of conventional banking principles on what I define as the 'property rights constraint'. Finally, in the last section, I combine the insights from Graziani's circuit model with the non-conventional approach to banking, and argue that, in addition to relieving poverty by redistributing income, the credit mechanism may be

---

*This chapter is an abridged version of a paper delivered at the Conference in Honour of Augusto Graziani.

instrumental to a general project to redistribute property rights, thus affecting the basic nature of the economic system.

Sufia's story

In his book *Vers un monde sans pauvreté*, Muhammad Yunus tells us the story of Sufia Begum, one of the women whom he met in the village of Jobra, near the University of Chittagong in Bangladesh, during the terrible famine in 1974.

Sufia earned her livelihood by making bamboo stools. Yunus informs us of the specific conditions of Sufia's work: every day she borrowed the equivalent of 22 cents of a dollar from the *paikar* (i.e. the merchant). With this money she bought the raw materials (bamboo) necessary for a day's work. At the end of the day, she sold the stools to the merchant, and earned the difference between the value of her daily product, as agreed upon between her and the merchant, and the value of the raw materials. This difference, the daily compensation for her work, would amount to two cents, barely enough to provide food for one person, but insufficient to feed her family, let alone to provide decent clothing and basic education for her three children (Yunus, 1997, p. 19). As Yunus explains, Sufia had not enough money (that is, 22 cents) to buy the straw elsewhere. This circumstance enabled the merchant both to appropriate the stools, and to fix her daily compensation at the level just necessary to cover the price of the raw materials, plus a little amount necessary to keep her alive, and in need of his money.

The first thing to note is that, interestingly, in this story deprivation was not the result of lack of employment, but stemmed from the nature of the contractual relation in which the deprived person was involved. Secondly, the connection between work and credit is worth exploring. The merchant, by providing Sufia with credit, was able to 'command' her daily labour and become the owner of its product. Thus, although formally an 'independent worker', Sufia was involved in a sub-category of what economists call the 'employment relation'.

For the purpose of alleviating the situation of poor people at Jobra, Yunus started his micro-credit programme, whereby Sufia, and other people like her, were given the credit necessary to buy capital assets (in Sufia's case, the bamboo) in order to start their own business, become independent of the merchants, and achieve a higher standard of living.

In the following sections, I propose an enquiry into the reasons motivating Yunus's decision to act, and his choice of the credit channel as the appropriate instrument. Although they might seem quite obvious at first sight, these reasons are interesting to investigate. Obviously, he was motivated by the notion that there was something unacceptable in the situation discovered at Jobra, something that needed to be changed. But, as we will see, this notion is not so obvious as may seem at first sight. Sufia's situation would have appeared acceptable, or not requiring interference, if judged by the standards of some modern economic and philosophical theories.

To illustrate this point, in the next section I propose an exercise in interpretation: the relation between Sufia and the merchant will be explored in the light of the alternative analytical arguments and normative criteria proposed by alternative streams of modern economic and philosophical thought.[1] These alternative approaches will be ranked in ascending order; namely, from those imposing less demanding principles of legitimacy to those founded on more demanding normative criteria, until the approach, or the approaches, able to motivate Yunus's project are found.

Conventionalism, libertarianism, welfarism, and the capability approach

Conventionalism

The weakest among alternative principles of justice is that proposed by conventionalism, which I will explore through the writings of Robert Sugden (1986). The tests of legitimacy imposed by this approach are not very demanding.

First, conventionalism does not require that the situation is evaluated from an economic point of view. It is irrelevant, for instance, whether the economic system in which Sufia and the merchant happen to live is characterised by feudal or capitalist property rights. Also irrelevant is the nature of the employment relation that binds them together, as well as the structure of the labour, credit and product markets in which they operate. Secondly, conventionalist ethics is bound by its very nature not to object to existing conventions, whatever these might be, because it regards the mere fact that a convention has been established as a sufficient condition for its ascent to the role of a moral norm. Conventionalist ethics is, indeed, relativist. People are expected to follow the rule that everyone else in that community respects, but if a different rule is followed in the community, then everybody is expected to follow this alternative rule. Whatever the initial situation, that situation is the only legitimate point of view from where we are entitled to make moral judgements. Rights and obligations are 'matters of convention' (Sugden, 1986, p. 175).

Sufia's situation would probably pass the conventionalist test of legitimacy, both on analytical and on normative grounds.

From an analytical point of view, this approach, if anything, has a presumption in favour of inegalitarian property rights, for their asserted superior degree of 'salience'. The idea here is that established conventions of property emerge as salient, and therefore as a solution towards which the competing parties are attracted, because they exploit a particular asymmetry between them. More precisely, 'they exploit an existing association between claimants and objects. Such conventions inevitably tend to favour possessors, since to be in possession of something is to have a very obvious association with it' (Sugden, 1986, p. 89). In other words, in this model, property rights are established on a 'first-come, first served' basis.[2]

From the normative point of view, no grounds for an intervention in favour of Sufia can be found in this approach. What we find, instead, is a recommendation that the existing property rights are not violated since, according to this view, 'conventions by which people resolve disputes come to have the status of moral rights and obligations'. Consequently, 'any government that tries to overturn these conventions must expect its actions to be viewed as morally wrong – as illegitimate invasions of individuals' rights' (Sugden, 1986, p. 176). Sugden's conclusion is that 'the morality of spontaneous order is conservative' (Sugden, 1986, p. 177).

Libertarianism

Procedural justice, proposed by libertarians, implies some more demanding criteria of justice than conventionalist morals. A formulation of the libertarian approach, proposed by Nozick in the 1970s, relies on the notion that the 'principle of voluntary exchange' (market transactions) and voluntary transfers (gifts, charity, bequests, and so on) is what makes a distribution of holdings legitimate. The first principle of justice states that 'a distribution is just if it arises from another just distribution by legitimate means' (Nozick, 1974, p. 151). The basic idea is that what makes the established distribution of holdings legitimate is simply the 'just' and voluntary nature of its generating process.

This principle of justice also implies that only an examination of the whole chain of prior transactions can tell us whether the current distribution of holdings is legitimate. But this process of 'backward examination' sooner or later brings us to the stage when an 'original acquisition' of previously unheld things occurred.

This observation leads us to the second condition required for a distribution to be 'just' in Nozick's sense – namely, 'the principle of justice in the original acquisition of resources' – stating that a system of property rights, established by an act of private appropriation of previously unheld things, is legitimate if 'enough and as good is left to others'. According to this approach, private property rights are conducive to greater productivity and efficiency, thus enabling the 'appropriator' to compensate the excluded persons with an amount of resources at least equal to what they would get in the absence of the appropriation. Hence, private property is legitimate from a moral point of view; in other words, private property is conducive to greater social welfare.

We can now attempt an evaluation of Sufia's story according to Nozick's 'entitlement approach' and related tests of legitimacy. Suppose some illegitimate means (e.g. theft or violence) were adopted by the merchant and/or by any previous owner in the chain of ownership transfers. Under these circumstances, the employment relation between Sufia and the merchant would suffer from an 'original sin', and would have to be 'undone'. By contrast, under the alternative assumption, that the merchant's money was acquired by legitimate means, the relationship between Sufia and the merchant would pass Nozick's 'principle of justice in the original acquisition of resources'.

Nozick's second requirement is the 'principle of justice in transfers'. Since the relationship under examination is based on a voluntary exchange between the legitimate owners of, respectively, the money and the labour services, Nozick's second test is also respected.

Thus, we seem to be entitled, within the boundaries of the libertarian approach, to deduce that Sufia's rights are not being violated, even if her compensation is at mere subsistence. The consequences concerning the health, education, quality of life of Sufia and her children, in absolute terms as well as in comparison to the conditions of people born in more fortunate circumstances, are also not regarded as sufficient to impose a reconsideration of the 'legitimacy argument' in favour of private property. The paradox of the libertarian approach is that, for all its stress on people's rights, it completely ignores welfare rights (Hausman and MacPherson, 1996, p. 130–1).

The 'entitlement approach' would definitely object to any violation to the 'principle of justice in the original acquisition of resources'. Under given circumstances, it could even ask for a general 'rectification' of the system of property rights, in order to undo past injustices. But, according to this approach, the present reality of the 'employment relation' between Sufia and the merchant does not entail any current violation of economic or moral principles, given the voluntary nature of the exchange occurring between them. Therefore, it passes the libertarian test of legitimacy.

Welfarism

Economists raised in the welfarist tradition would enquire whether the economy under investigation is Pareto efficient. Their approach may imply a severe condemnation of the relationship between Sufia and the merchant, and may thus lead us to call for far-reaching economic reform. However, as will be argued below, this normative approach suffers from severe limitations.

Under competitive conditions, equilibrium wage and employment levels are on the labour supply curve. This implies that exchanges on the labour market are voluntary, and that workers' utility is maximised. Moreover, in perfect competition, each potential borrower faces an infinitely elastic credit supply, implying that he or she can borrow any desired amount at the current interest rate. The usual interactions between demand and supply bring both the credit and the labour markets to their equilibrium condition.

However, Sufia's situation must imply a departure from perfect competition. A welfarist economist may adduce one of the following reasons, depending on which market is considered as non-purely competitive:

1 The merchant is a monopolist in the credit market at Jobra. Consequently, in equilibrium, the average cost of lending is lower than its price (the interest rate). This circumstance has a twofold implication: first, the merchant earns a positive profit, or rent, which will not be eliminated by competition;

secondly, the equilibrium is inefficient, since the amount of credit granted to the villagers is lower than in perfect competition.

2 In Bangladesh, as in other less developed countries, the labour supply should be described as a horizontal line with intercept equal to the height of the subsistence wage. At this real wage, the labour supply is unlimited (Lewis, 1953). The merchant maximises profits by demanding Sufia's work up to the point where her marginal productivity equals the exogenously given subsistence wage. By so doing, he earns a positive rent.

3 The merchant is a monopsonist in the labour market at Jobra. Hence, both employment and the wage level are lower than the corresponding competitive levels. The difference between the competitive wage and the current wage is a measure of 'Pigouvian exploitation'.

Rent extraction is not compatible with the long-run equilibrium of a competitive economy. In the latter type of economy, other merchants would compete for extra-profits by demanding Sufia's work at a higher real wage, until these extra-profits are absorbed into higher costs. Similarly, other lenders would enter the credit market, thus establishing a competitive equilibrium that, in a production economy, will normally reflect the underlying forces of productivity and thrift. In the long run, no surplus would survive, and Sufia would reap the whole fruits of her productivity. Since the economy under examination does not satisfy the conditions of perfect competition, poverty, 'exploitation' and inefficiency should be remedied by a reform of the credit and labour market, thus ensuring that rents are washed out by the restored competitive process.

The problem with this normative approach is that there is no guarantee that Sufia, the weak trading partner, would be immune from poverty in a restored perfectly competitive economy, where every agent is paid according to the marginal product of the factor that he or she owns. In fact, the market distribution depends entirely on the initial distribution of assets. Because an agent's income is the product of that marginal product times the amount of the factor he or she owns (and, moreover, the marginal product of a factor itself depends on the level of output and the initial distribution of assets), a poorly endowed agent would not be safe from poverty and deprivation in a pure competitive world (Varian, 1979, pp. 140–1).

Thus, social justice (and even the far more limited objective of preventing one of the agents from starving) may require that the Pareto distributive principle is violated, by redistributing income or resources away from the rich agent and in favour of the poor. By so doing, the rich would be made worse off, but, in a world of limited resources, that is exactly what we want, in order to restore some degree of distributive justice.

The capability approach

By focusing on her standard of living and the quality of her life, the capability approach provides interesting insights into Sufia's condition. Standard of living can be defined as 'personal well-being related to one's own life' (Sen, 1987, p. 29). The conditions of a person's life, on which her well-being depends, include both the set of her 'functionings' and the set of her capabilities.

Functionings are the characters of the lifestyle that a person actually leads, or 'different aspects of living conditions' (Sen, 1987, pp. 36–7). Seen in a slightly different perspective, functionings are what a person actually achieves (Sen, 1992, pp. 31–3), such as being well nourished, or being decently dressed, or 'living a life free from cholera or smallpox' (Sen, 1987, p. 104), being literate, reading literature and poetry, 'having self-respect, preserving human dignity, taking part in the life of the community' (Nussbaum and Sen, 1993, Introduction, p. 3).

No less important than these actual functionings, according to Sen, are the 'real opportunities' a person has regarding the life he or she may lead. It is important to stress that, while in the traditional economic approach only 'achievements' (e.g. the levels of utility, or the amounts of goods chosen) would enter an evaluation of the agent's living standard, in Sen's approach the opportunities open to that agent are an essential component of his or her living standard.

Thus, by making freedom a constituent part of a person's living standard, the capability approach parts company with traditional economic analysis. Moreover, Sen's famous, severe evaluation of Pareto efficiency as a criterion of social justice marks still another significant departure from the traditional welfarist approach, and suggests that Sen would have objected to the employment relation between Sufia and the merchant, but not merely on efficiency grounds.[3]

The gulf between the capability approach and the other lines of thought discussed above is even wider. Despite the importance that it gives to freedom, the capability approach is very different from libertarianism, since it interprets freedom as substantive freedom. In fact, the 'enabling' function of freedom (as opposed to its procedural aspects) is now regarded as one of its basic, if not its basic, character. With regard to Sufia's story, for instance, Sen would probably argue that her capability set is very restricted indeed, since she has no choice but to accept a contractual relation with the merchant, and it merely enables her to achieve the 'functionings' of working hard and living in misery with her children. Hence, although both Sufia's and the merchant's procedural rights are respected, she, and the society they both inhabit, enjoy very little substantive freedom.

Finally, Sen repeatedly objects to accepting 'traditions' as a foundation for, and guarantee of, social justice (Nussbaum and Sen, 1992, p. 4). This suggests that the capability approach would not justify Sufia's situation on conventionalist grounds, and would probably advocate that action be taken in order to abolish the conventions causing Sufia's absolute and relative deprivation.

Thus, our analysis of alternative arguments concerning economic justice can be concluded by observing that the capability approach, by taking the standard of living as a baseline, and by insisting that both absolute and relative deprivations should be removed, is certainly the most severe and demanding approach to social justice among those reviewed thus far.

In my opinion, Yunus may well have been motivated by a vision similar to that endorsed by Sen, with regard to the ethical and economic problems plaguing Jobra, the Bangladesh economy and, perhaps, the world as a whole. Nevertheless, I think that we should also focus on some further aspects of Sufia's story. In order to change her living standards, Yunus took actions aiming to allow her to leave the employment relation, and remove the property right constraint that was impeding both her access to the instruments required for production, and her full control over the product of her work. Abolishing absolute and relative deprivation, and establishing a just distribution of capabilities may, in some cases, require that this type of constraint be removed.

Microcredit and its reasons

In the days following his first meeting with Sufia, Yunus discovered that 42 families were indebted with merchants for a total amount of 856 *taka*, the equivalent of 27 dollars, and worked for them under contracts similar to Sufia's. A whole village was starving for a debt amounting to a total of 27 dollars (Yunus, 1998, p. 21).

Yunus explicitly makes clear that the villagers were not poor 'because of their stupidity or laziness'. On the contrary, they worked all day, performing complex physical activities (Yunus, 1998, p. 21). Why, then, did they not have access to the goods and services that would ensure a decent standard of living for themselves and their families? Simply because they did not own the bamboo or other productive assets used for performing their work.

Moreover, they were too poor to obtain credit. In Yunus's own words, people in Jobra were poor because 'the financial structures in our country were not prepared to help them in enlarging their economic basis. It was a problem of structures – not one of people' (Yunus, 1998, p. 21). In other words, because the villagers were poor, they also faced a severe financial constraint. Since, under these circumstances, they could not own the required capital assets, their constrained, if voluntary, choice was – and could not be otherwise – to borrow from the merchant, thereby entering an employment relation with him, at whatever terms the (implicit or explicit) contracts would fix.

Yunus started his micro-credit project, whereby the villagers were given enough money to buy whatever capital assets they needed in order to start-up their own activities. Some considerations may be drawn from Yunus's investigation and from the rationale behind his credit scheme.

1. Firstly, what motivated Yunus to start his project at Jobra was the extreme poverty of the villagers, which caused the death of many of them in the extreme event of famine, but was an endemic condition even in normal times. In the course of his investigation, he discovered that the causes of poverty were deeply rooted in the credit and labour markets, and in the underlying system of property rights prevailing in Bangladesh.

By excluding some people from the ownership of productive assets, the system of property rights and institutions (including financial institutions) also creates a separation between them and the 'necessaries of life'. Once this double separation is established, the conditions for the existence of an employment relation are established too, since these people's command over the goods and services necessary for their survival and well-being must now be mediated by such a relation. This limits their autonomy, by placing them under the control of others, who are entitled to decide the organisation of work, the product mix, and the distribution of income – possibly within the limits set to their bargaining power by some external constraints (see below).

The specific contractual relations that these voluntary exchanges bring into existence may vary: in fully developed market economies, wage contracts prevail. By contrast Sufia, formally an independent worker, is tied to the merchant by a debt–credit relation. She has no access to bank credit because the bank is not interested in the only 'collateral' she could offer as a guarantee: her ability to work. By contrast, the merchant is ready to offer her his money, since he is interested in commanding the specific product of her work at a minimum price, thus maximising his returns over the capital advanced. Under these circumstances, the merchant, a monopolist in the credit market, faces a very inelastic demand curve, given the lack of substitutes and the workers' absolute necessity to borrow. If he borrows the money from the banking sector, his cost curve reflects the passive interest which he pays on these borrowings. Alternatively, he may lend Sufia part of the proceeds from the sale of her stools, at virtually zero cost to himself. In either case, he earns the difference between the price of credit that she pays and the cost of credit to himself. Total profits absorb virtually the whole value of the borrower's product, except for the share of her wage, set at the level necessary in order to keep the 'wheel' of exploitation spinning. Sufia must adjust her work effort in order that the value of her product enables her to pay for the bamboo, the merchant's share, and to keep herself alive.

In spite of the different contractual relations, the underlying motivations are the same in Jobra as in developed market economies: the employers' purpose is to control the employees' work-effort and the value of their product; for the workers, the purpose is to re-establish a link between their work and the instruments of production, in order to gain access to the 'necessaries of life'. Thus, a voluntary exchange between labour and capital occurs because, as Joan Robinson appropriately noted, there is only one thing worse than being exploited by a capitalist: not to be so exploited by any.

2. Secondly, once the employment relation is actually established, the workers' access to the necessaries of life becomes possible, but – given that they lack direct control over productive assets – it also becomes dependent on the contracts that they are able to strike with their contractual counterpart. This brings us towards the realm of bargaining theory, with bargaining powers set unequal by the unequal degree of command over productive assets.

Within these limits, the parties' bargaining power may find further determinants in the economic and institutional features of the country in which they happen to live. Thus, for example, in the conditions described by Yunus, the villagers' bargaining power is so restricted – it is practically nil – that their compensations are at the mere subsistence level. The reason why Sufia and her fellow villagers cannot get a higher compensation for their work is that many other people would be willing to take their place if they were to refuse the conditions dictated by the merchant, since everybody's next best alternative is to starve. Under these circumstances, they have no bargaining power and, consequently, wages – according to Yunus's appropriate remark – are just sufficient to keep workers alive and in need of the merchants' money. Under these circumstances, wages are determined by pure market forces.

By contrast, in more advanced economies – as with many western economies – workers' bargaining power may be enhanced, even at less than full employment; for example, by unemployment benefits, which raise their 'outside options'.

3. In spite of this major difference – 'backward' and 'developed' economies share some basic elements in the structure of property rights (as was stated above, by assigning different 'bundles of rights' over productive assets to different people) – these systems also establish the necessity of the 'employment relation', as an intermediary between some agents and the means of their subsistence and well-being, thus limiting their autonomy.

This basic character of the 'employment relation' in modern market economies is obscured, in some streams of economic analysis, by the sometimes implicit, but crucial, assumption that workers have full choice between dependent and independent work, which does not hold in reality (Marglin, 1986 [1974]; Graziani, 1993).

Yunus's story brings to the forefront the issue of the differential control of productive assets. Any existing inequality in the distribution of income between workers and their 'merchants' is the product of this more basic inequality.

4. Our fourth consideration concerns changing property rights. How do property rights change? Again, different schools of thought provide different answers. According to the 'spontaneous order' school, property rights, like other institutions, change as the result of spontaneous evolution; other authors predict that they change if and when they come into conflict with economic efficiency, or if the underlying system of costs and benefits changes. However, some may argue that property rights may also change as a result of rational choice and, in some cases, as a result of an ethical project. The very fact that

Yunus started his project, as well as his efforts to devise a rational poverty-relief scheme, may be regarded as evidence that the latter approach to institutional change inspired the lines along which he acted.

Consistent with his finding that Sufia's poverty was the result of her employment relation, what Yunus did was to help her to quit: she would thus be freed from the necessity to make a contract with the merchant, and offered an alternative way to earn the 'necessaries' of life. What was obstructing this freedom was her lack of ownership of the capital assets (the bamboo). Yunus tried to remove this obstacle by enabling her to buy the required means of production. Starting on a small scale, he was trying to introduce some element of change in the existing system of property rights.

His solution was different from those recommended by other schools of thought, some of which would have recommended that the spontaneous order of established conventions should not be interfered with or, alternatively, would have made changes subordinate to the proven inefficiency of existing property rights. What motivated Yunus to act was not Pareto inefficiency (indeed, weakening or abolishing the merchant's control over Sufia's labour certainly made him worse-off), but a concern with both the standard of living and the autonomy of the working population.

Microcredit and the circuit approach

Our final point concerns the role of credit as a means of redistributing capital assets and changing property rights. In order to analyse this point, it is helpful to recall some basic features of Graziani's model of the economic circuit, where credit plays a fundamental role.

Firstly, Graziani argues that, in a market economy with production, different social groups may be distinguished by their differential access to bank credit. By virtue of their access to credit, entrepreneurs command an amount of purchasing power that is independent of their income; by contrast, workers' purchasing power is constrained by, and equal to, their incomes (Graziani, 1988, pp. XXVII–XXVIII). Entrepreneurs open up the monetary circuit by 'buying' labour in exchange for the money that they receive as credit from the banking system. By contrast, workers are not in a position to express any demand until some firm decides to hire them (see Graziani's argument on firms' autonomy, as opposed to the lack of autonomy of wage earners).

Secondly, given that workers' budget constraint is determined by their money wage and by the price level of consumption goods (which, in turn, is determined on the goods market), it follows that the maximum amount of consumption that workers can attain is equal to the amount of consumption goods produced by the firms in the opening phase of the circuit (though workers may decide to consume less). Thus, entrepreneurs' autonomy also extends to the composition of output and, through this channel, to the determination of real wages (though Graziani accepts that workers may defend real wages via the instruments of 'social contracting') (Graziani, 1988, p. xxxii). The 'opening phase of the circuit' is in many ways the fundamental one. This is so, basically, because it is at this stage that a trilateral relationship comes into existence: a debt–credit relationship between the firms' sector and the banking sector, and a buyer–seller relationship between firms and workers in the labour market (Graziani, 1988, pp. xix–xxi).

Now, the question is: can we interpret the relationship between Sufia and the merchant, as well as Yunus's micro-credit scheme, in the light of these insights from the circuit model? My answer is yes, for the following reasons.

What Graziani's entrepreneur and the merchant at Jobra have in common is their being 'mediators' between the worker and the materials needed for production. Their role as mediators is made possible by their command over purchasing power, which they use to command labour either directly in the labour market, or indirectly through lending. The similarity between them becomes clearer if we assume, for argument's sake, that the merchant, like the entrepreneur, acquires his command over purchasing power via the banking system. Under this assumption, both the circuit model and the Bangladesh economy work with a tripartite class scheme (banks, firms and workers).In the circuit model, this tripartite class scheme is adopted in order to provide a description and an interpretation of the working of market economies. This purpose also explains why the circuit model concentrates on the principles of conventional banking, whereby credit is only granted to some categories of people: presumably, those who own wealth to serve as collateral.[4] But, setting aside this interpretative purpose, there is no logical necessity why the circuit scheme should assume either a tripartite class structure or conventional banking principles. In principle, credit may be granted to any category of people, whether or not they own collateral to serve as a guarantee.

Similarly, in Yunus's approach, there is no logical necessity or practical reason why banks should apply conventional principles, thus reproducing such a tripartite class-structure. Yunus decided to lend money to poor people not owning any collateral, thus enabling them to exit any inconvenient employment relation.

In the non-conventional circuit, the bank lends credit directly to the producers; that is, to people using their own work effort to make goods and services. With this credit, they are enabled to buy the materials and start their production processes, finally selling their products and paying back the loan and interest to the bank. This is exactly what the Grameen Bank did in Bangladesh and, later, in many other countries. The credit channel was not used for the purpose of reproducing the employment relation, but for the opposite end of abolishing it. Thus, while workers' autonomy is established by virtue of this scheme, also a bigger share of the fruits of their effort accrues to them.

The final result of this lending scheme depends upon the banking sector's objectives and what it decides to do with the interest payments on its lending. The Grameen Bank devotes its distributive share to the purpose of expanding the area of independent work at the expense of direct or indirect employment relations. Obviously, the Grameen Bank experience is not yet strong and pervasive enough to change the established system of property rights in Bangladesh, let alone in the world as a whole. The non-conventional circuit theory is still to be born. Nevertheless, the hope is that all those involved in the two projects combine their practical and theoretical skills to make progress in this direction.

Notes

1. Other relevant approaches, such as those developed by Alchian and Demsetz, North, Hodgson are dealt with in Costabile, 1998 (see also Costabile 1995).
2. The illustrating example is the convention, ruling on the Yorkshire coast up to the 1930s, whereby property rights over driftwood were assigned to the first person to go to a stretch of shore after high tide and collect the wood.
3. 'An economy can be optimal in this sense [i.e. Pareto efficient] even when some people are rolling in luxury and others are near starvation as long as the starvers cannot be made better off without cutting into the pleasures of the rich ... In short, a society or an economy can be Pareto optimal and still be perfectly disgusting' (Sen, 1970, p. 22).
4. Even though the circuit approach is not explicit on this point, there must be some reason underlying the asymmetry referred to at the beginning of this section. Why do some people (entrepreneurs) have access to bank credit while others (the workers) are discriminated against? The reason usually adduced is that only those people who have collateral to serve as a guarantee are granted credit by the banking system. The circuit approach must either implicitly adopt this explanation, or assume some other selection process (e.g. a random one).

References

Costabile, L. (1995) 'Institutions, social custom and efficiency wages models: alternative approaches', *Cambridge Journal of Economics*, October, pp. 605–23.
Costabile, L. (1998) 'Ordine spontaneo ordine negoziato? Conflitti e risoluzione dei conflitti nella nuova teoria economica delle istituzioni', in A. Amendola (ed.), *Istituzioni e mercato del lavoro* (Naples: ESI).
Graziani, A. (1980) 'Malthus e la teoria della domanda effettiva', Introduction to L. Costabile, *Malthus. Sviluppo e ristagno della produzione capitalistica* (Turin: Einaudi).
Graziani, A. (1988) 'Il circuito monetario', in Graziani e Messori (eds), *Moneta e Produzione* (Turin: Einaudi).
Graziani, A. (1993) *Teoria economica. Prezzi e distribuzione*, 3rd edn (Naples: Edizioni Scientifiche Italiane).
Graziani, A. (1994) *The Monetary Theory of Production* (Cambridge University Press).
Graziani, A. (1996) *La teoria del circuito monetario* (Milan, Jaca Books).
Hausman, D.M. and McPherson, M.S. (1996) *Economic Analysis and Moral Philosophy* (Cambridge University Press).

Kymlicka, W. (1990) *Contemporary Political Philosophy: An Introduction* (New York: Oxford University Press).

Lewis, A.W. (1953) 'Economic Development with Unlimited Supplies of Labour', *Manchester School of Economic and Social Studies*, May.

Marglin, S. (1986) 'What do bosses do? The origins and functions of hierarchy in capitalist production', in L. Putterman, *The Economic Nature of the Firm* (Cambridge University Press), pp. 269–78 (originally in *The Review of Radical Political Economy*, 6, 1974).

Nozick, R. (1974) *Anarchy, State and Utopia* (New York: Basic Books).

Nussbaum, M. and A. Sen (eds) (1993) *The Quality of Life* (Oxford: Clarendon Press).

Sen, Amartya (1987) 'The Standard of Living', The Tanner Lectures, Clare Hall, Cambridge 1985, with contributions by John Muellbauer, Ravi Kanbur, Keith Hart, Bernard Williams (Cambridge University Press).

Sen, Amartya (1970) *Collective Choice and Social Welfare* (San Francisco: Holden Day).

Sen, Amartya (1993) 'Capability and well-being', in M. Naussbaum and A. Sen (eds), *The Quality of Life* (Oxford: Clarendon Press).

Sugden R. (1986) *The Economics of Rights, Co-operation and Welfare* (Oxford: Basil Blackwell).

Varian, H.R. (1979) 'Distributive justice, welfare economics, and the theory of fairness', in F. Hahn and M. Hollis (eds), *Philosophy and Economic Theory* (Oxford University Press) (originally in *Philosophy and Public Affairs*, 4, 1974–5, pp. 223–47).

Yunus M. in collaboration with Alan Jolis (1997) *Vers un monde sans pauvreté*, Edition Jean-Claude Lattès (Italian translation, *Il banchiere dei poveri*, Milan, Feltrinelli, 1998).

14
Monetary Theory of Production and Disequilibrium Inflation

Elie Sadigh

Introduction

Present-day studies of inflation concentrate largely on price-rise inflation, which is measured by comparing changes in the general level of prices from one period to another. Monetarists and Keynesians are the main protagonists in this domain.

Monetarists offer an arithmetical explanation (transactions equation) for price-rise inflation. They claim inflation is caused when the money supply increases proportionately faster than output, with an attendant fall in the purchasing power of money. But this claim is meaningless because money has no purchasing power. In this view, it is impossible to differentiate between the spending of income and the spending of money on the products market.

Keynesians measure inflation by studying changes in the cost of production (which determine the source of demand) from one period to another. Such comparisons are of no analytical interest. Changes in nominal wages affect neither distribution between income and profits (the level of profits remains unchanged from one period to another) nor the working of the economy insofar as monetary equilibrium is respected.

Both of these approaches to inflation should be abandoned as they are of no analytical value. They may be usefully replaced by the study of disequilibrium inflation within the framework of the monetary theory of production, of which Augusto Graziani is one of the most eminent exponents. This theory marks the beginning of a new era in economic research and notably in respect of the determination of inflation. This chapter will show that inflation affects the smooth running of the wage economy, imposing unwarranted and even illegitimate levies on the purchasing power of income holders.

Inflation defined only as an increase in the general level of prices

Inflation defined as the increase in the level of prices is often taken as a benchmark for indexing wages to changes in prices. But to perform such an

217

indexation and to ascertain whether such indexation really does maintain the purchasing power of production factors, the source of which lies in production and changes that are dependent on growth in output, it is essential to know the cause(s) of price-rise inflation. To study the scope and limits of inflation thus defined, we have to draw a distinction between transactions-equation inflation, cost-push inflation and demand-pull inflation, which are the different forms of inflation studied by most economists.

Transactions-equation inflation

Monetarist theory is interested in changes in the purchasing power of money, which is why it is led to compare the general level of prices for two different periods. It connects the cause of the variation in the purchasing power of money with changes in the money supply relative to the quantity of goods traded, which is of no great interest. It would be more judicious to seek out the cause(s) of these changes. At any rate, it is this last point that has preoccupied most economists who have taken an interest in this form of inflation.

The causes of variations in the money supply were a concern of the mercantilist authors in their time. Jean Bodin in the sixteenth century attributed such increases primarily to the entry of gold and silver from the Americas, and sought to show that the purchasing power of money was inversely proportional to the quantity of precious metals a country held. Some authors also attributed price rises to monetary transformations, meaning that more money was minted with the same quantity of bullion, thereby increasing the quantity of money in circulation.

This was the starting point of a controversy that led to what came to be known in the nineteenth century as the 'quantity theory' of money, by which the 'value' or purchasing power of money, of whatever form, is determined by the quantity of it in circulation, this value being inversely proportional to the quantity of it compared with output.

Quantity theory is used to study price changes in a trading economy and the transactions equation is the tool for investigating such changes. By definition, that tool actually intercedes at the level of transactions, and, in a trading economy, any variation in the quantity of money does not alter the actual purchasing power of the traders. Monetarists make use of this same tool to study inflation in a wage economy. So, the question is whether or not this tool can be used to determine during which transaction the money supply increases in a wage economy. In other words, it is a question of whether or not, in a wage economy, the transactions equation can determine what it is that causes the increase in the money supply, which in turn generates the rise in prices or during which transaction the economy is monetised.

Milton Friedman, one of the leaders of the Monetarist School of the second half of the twentieth century, claimed that 'Inflation is a disease, a dangerous and sometimes fatal disease, a disease that, if not checked in time, can destroy a society, as it did in China.' (1993; p. 191). As Friedman concentrates on inflation in the twentieth century, he has to take an interest in the causes of inflation in a wage economy. Overcoming this 'dangerous disease' meant first knowing what caused it. Does Friedman successfully identify its causes? It is important to know whether the analytical tools he uses enable him to identify the true causes of inflation, which he defines simply by the increase in the general level of prices. In fact, those tools do not, because the determination of price increases by the transactions equation does not reveal the cause(s) of the increase in the money supply that gives rise to inflation in a wage economy, and precisely because Friedman determines inflation by this transactions equation. Indeed, the transactions equation deals only with what happens on the products market; that is to say, with the relation between the quantity of money and the quantity of products. It is therefore unable to indicate the cause(s) of the increase in the quantity of money involved in transactions. Although the increase in the money supply does not alter the actual purchasing power of the immediate producers in a trading economy, which limits the point of inquiring into the cause of such changes, on the other hand, this is not true of a wage economy, where knowledge of the origin and the use of money is essential if the ills that befall the wage economy are to be overcome. So, to determine the causes of inflation in a wage economy, it is necessary to know what causes the increase in the money supply; whether it is the nominal increase in wages of the production factors, variations in profit levels, the creation of money in exchange for the entry of foreign currencies, monetary financing of the government's budget deficit, or the monetary financing of investments. In fact, the transactions equation cannot determine the origin of the increase in the money supply. Therefore, the determination of inflation by the transactions equation in a wage economy, as it is unable to determine what causes the increase in the money supply, cannot be of any help in overcoming inflation, which Friedman considers a dangerous disease. We notice that, even if Friedman considers inflation to be a dangerous disease, he fails to identify its cause(s), and is therefore unable to prescribe any remedies liable to prevent its effects. So, even if some causes of inflation can be determined ex post, this, by definition, does not allow any forestalling of the harmful consequences, which have already wrought their effects.

Cost-push inflation

Most Keynesians essentially study two forms of inflation: cost-push inflation and demand-pull inflation. We need to find out whether the study of these two forms of inflation precludes the consequences of inflation as stated by Friedman, or whether its objective is simply to determine price-rise inflation.

Cost-push inflation is defined quantitatively or tautologically: it is brought about by the increase in the cost of production. However, this analysis is superior to the previous case in that, by taking costs as the basis for inflation, it determines right from the production stage the amount of money monetising production. Accordingly, it does not need to take into account changes in productivity, because, whatever the changes in productivity, the payment of production factors represents the monetary value of output. So, if changes in wages are proportional to changes in productivity, none of this has any effect on price levels, all else being equal. This account of inflation, however, remains silent about how revenues are shared between wages and profit. Consequently, the cost of aggregate supply being determined by the wages of production factors, the increase in money wages, which outstrips rises in productivity, brings about a rise in the level of prices. It is because this determination of the rise in price levels cannot take account of the true distribution between wages and profit that we need to add 'all else being equal'. In this case, an increase in money income, without any increase in output, does not spell an improvement in the purchasing power of income holders as a whole. This raises the question of whether incomes should be index-linked if inflation arises solely from the increase in nominal wages.

Scope and limits of demand-pull inflation

While cost-push inflation is easy to define, the same is not true of demand-pull inflation when studied in a situation of monetary equilibrium. Let us dismiss from the outset the explanation by which demand-pull inflation arises from an imbalance between the supply of goods (which is assumed to be insufficient) and consumer demand. It is important to realise that what is meant by inflation is an increase in the general level of prices and not an increase in the price of any one product. Therefore, this definition of demand-pull inflation is meaningless. In fact, aggregate demand being based on aggregate supply or on wages representing the monetary value of output, income holders cannot demand more than they can afford on their income. The limit on demand is determined by the income created in the course of production, which income itself represents the monetary value of the output of each period; that is, the monetary value of aggregate supply. Consequently, in spending solely that income that was created in the course of production, it is impossible for demand to exceed actual production. In other words, an imbalance between the supply of goods and consumer demand, which is the basis of income, is meaningless in a situation of monetary equilibrium. Ultimately, in a situation of monetary equilibrium, demand-pull inflation would amount to cost-inflation. Where monetary equilibrium is achieved, the source of demand lies only in the income created in the course of production, so it is the nominal increase in production costs that causes the increase in nominal demand; monetary equilibrium means that the value of aggregate demand is equal to the value of aggregate supply.

Monetary disequilibrium inflation

Disequilibrium inflation means that the value of aggregate demand exceeds the value of aggregate supply (Schmitt; 1975). Under this definition, inflation is not determined by comparing changes in prices between two different periods, but by comparing the values of aggregate supply and demand for the same period. Such comparison reveals the decline in the actual purchasing power of the income of the production factors. The problem lies in why the value of aggregate demand exceeds that of aggregate supply and who benefits from the loss of purchasing power of the production factors.

The monetary theory of production provides a definition of monetary equilibrium. Equilibrium means that the spending of the income created in the course of production takes up its counterpart, which is the output for the period. The determination of the value of output right from the production stage in the act of paying production factors determines the quantity of money that must monetise the output of each period. This quantity is determined at the production stage by means of workers' wages. So, any money entering the economy that is not related to workers' wages generates an inflationary imbalance. Accordingly, the monetary value of aggregate demand diverges from the monetary value of aggregate supply. This is the definition itself of monetary disequilibrium.

Now, it is clearly worthwhile studying disequilibrium inflation because it can shed light on two important points. First, it reveals the loss in the actual purchasing power of workers' incomes. Second, it can be used to demonstrate not only that it is not income, created by virtue of production, that exerts a purchasing power over the output of the period, but also that other amounts of money, spent on the products market, effect an unwarranted levy on the purchasing power of income holders. The amount of this unwarranted levy is equal to the excess of the monetary value of aggregate demand over the value of aggregate supply. But this still leaves open the question of what is the source of this unwarranted levy that generates the inflationary imbalance.

It is important to notice that profit created in the context of monetary equilibrium should not be considered as an unwarranted levy on the purchasing power of the production factors. Profit is the main source of capital formation, which is essential in financing the economic development that will increase the purchasing power of the production factors in future periods. So, it is not profit itself that must be brought into question but its appropriation by those agents who are not directly involved in production.

By starting from the definition or the tautology (tautology because production is the source of the income) by which the wages of the production factors represent the monetary value of production of the period, the quantity of money which monetises output is determined right from the production stage; it follows that any money that does not enter the economy by means of such payments generates a monetary imbalance. Some economists argue that the excess of money is necessary, either to revive the economy (monetary financing of the government's budget deficit proposed by some Keynesians) or to facilitate the formation of capital (this is Schumpeter's case). That last requirement follows from the fact that these economists fail to account for profit in monetary equilibrium (cf. Schumpeter, 1935).

Consequences of disequilibrium inflation

We know that production is the source of all income and that, as production factors are the cause of production, their monetary wages represent the value of production. So, in a situation of monetary equilibrium, products are sold solely through spending the income created in the course of production. In this case, it is market price that determines the actual distribution between wages and profit. The relation of equivalence established during production between wages and output allows us to say that, when disequilibrium inflation occurs, one of the fundamental laws of the wage economy is breached, the law by which only the spending of the income created during the production process must take up the output of each period.

Some Keynesians and Schumpeter, in proposing to kick-start the economy and to finance investments by the creation of money, argue that banks should create a 'purchasing power' that is not derived from production. These economists assign a role to banks which breaches the ground rules for determining the formation of purchasing power in a wage economy. We know that in a wage economy, monetary purchasing power can be created only as the counterpart of production, and through the remuneration of production factors. So, by giving the banking system the capacity to create 'purchasing power', these economists make the banks responsible for starting an inflationary imbalance and for an unwarranted levy on the purchasing power of production factors. This situation is worsened since, under the present system, the capital financed by the money newly created, like capital financed by normal profits, is appropriated by agents who are not directly involved in production, thus becoming a source of income for owners.

In addition, disequilibrium inflation allows firms to make net monetary profits, in that firms as a whole recover more than the amount that allowed them to monetise production. In the banking system as it presently works, net monetary profit (inflationary profit) may be used in either of two ways: in paying the production factors or on the products market. These two ways of spending net or inflationary monetary profit have different consequences. In this chapter, we shall concentrate on the second case.

Spending of inflationary profit on the products market

This way of spending monetary profit gives rise to inflationary profits. Where public investments are financed by the creation of money, the disequilibrium-inflation process is renewed throughout the period the government remains in debt to the banking system. In other words, throughout the period of indebtedness, an unwarranted levy is made on the purchasing power of the production factors when inflationary profit is spent on the products market. This levy is cumulative, growing each time the government finances public investments through the creation of money. So, disequilibrium inflation allows firms to levy a part of workers' purchasing power during the period of the banking system's monetary loan to the government. This situation is particularly unfair in that, in the case of private firms, the inflationary profit is appropriated by agents other than the workers, who are the cause of production and, under the present system, capital constitutes a source of income that is levied on the workers' income.

Keynesians justify the financing of public investments through monetary creation by arguing that it promotes an upturn in the economy, the aim of which is to reduce unemployment. They think that inflationary profit makes entrepreneurs optimistic, prompting them to increase their investments. For a given technology, the increase in investment generates an increase in demand for labour, and therefore an increase in output. Keynesians see only the 'positive' effect on output and employment levels in this economic recovery policy. This 'positive' effect persists over time through the expenditure of inflationary profit on the products market, which expenditure finances investments. This way of financing the budget deficit imposes an unwarranted levy on workers' purchasing power where the inflationary profit is distributed and spent on the consumer products market. Finally, inflationary profit may be used to pay production factors, which may bring about insufficiency in aggregate demand and lead to the opposite effect from that sought by these economists.[1]

How to explain the relative poverty of workers, who are however the cause of production, compared with the opulence of owners of the means of production

Inflationary financing of private investments becomes a source of social injustice to the detriment of workers' purchasing power. This is because the working of the banking system, as it stands, favours unjustified levies on workers' purchasing power, for the banking system does not always comply with the rule of money creation in a wage economy.

It has been seen that, in a wage economy, money newly created must go to paying the production factors. As production factors are the cause of production, their remuneration represents the monetary value of output determined in its realisation. Any money that does not enter the economy by way of payment of the production factors gives rise to an inflationary imbalance and entails a levy on part of the purchasing power of the production factors. It is true that a money loan spent on the product markets by firms runs up a debt of firms to the banking system. To repay their debt, firms simply have to agree, explicitly or implicitly, on the level of profit that they wish to make. Thus, they manage to pay their debts, after having levied a part of the purchasing power of the production factors. This situation is a significant cause of social injustice and it is one of the causes of the workers' relative poverty compared with the wealth of those who benefit from the creation of money that they spend directly on the products market. Acceptance of Schumpeter's proposal removes any limit to this unwarranted levy. If the banking system has the means to create just one money unit that does not enter the economy by way of the remuneration of production factors, it can satisfy all demand for money that is not intended for monetising production in the act of wage payment, and that does not come from the savings of private individuals. In this way, a class of agents who are not involved in production grows richer at the expense of those who are involved in production. This explains the puzzle of how the class that is not involved in production can obtain more 'purchasing power' than the class that is involved in production, and is its direct cause.

Let us recapitulate to clarify the steps in this process of unwarranted levy, which is a cause of social injustice. As production factors are the cause of production, their monetary remuneration represents the value of output of each period. It is in this act that money turns into a monetary income or into legitimate purchasing power over the output of the period. The amount of this remuneration determines the amount of money which monetises and measures output. So, the spending on the products market of the income formed in the course of production by way of the remuneration of the production factors signifies the disposal of the product of the period.

Conversely, any newly created money that is spent directly on the products market, without being channeled into the remuneration of the production factors, does not turn into an income, and so it is analytically distinct from monetary income. Once it has been injected into the economy to be spent on the products market, such money imposes an illegitimate levy. Although, analytically, such money can be distinguished from monetary income, both tend to be identical for the sellers on the products market. Sellers are unable to differentiate demand whose source is monetary income from demand whose source is newly created money that has not become income by way of remuneration of the production factors. As we have seen, the money that has no real counterpart in the economy exercises an illegitimate purchasing power through a levy on the purchasing power of the production factors. This follows from the fact that the banking system is accorded a power to which it is not entitled. In creating money, banks do not create any purchasing power, even if the money created exercises a purchasing power on the products market. The legitimate purchasing power is created by firms in the act of paying workers.

The two propositions below, which follow from the previous developments, are absolutely not contradictory:

Proposition 1: Banks, by creating money, do not create any purchasing power.

Proposition 2: The spending on the products market of money newly created by banks, exerts a purchasing power.

Proposition 1 is true because, by definition, production is the source of all income. Without production there is no income. Now, it is not because banks create money that they create output. If we accept the creation of money to be synonymous with the creation of purchasing power or of wealth, we reach the absurd conclusion that a country grows wealthier in proportion as its banking system creates more money. This assertion misses the point that it is production that is the cause of enrichment and the source of all income. Without production, there is no income, no purchasing power. So, in simply creating money, banks do not create wealth and so they do not create purchasing power.

Proposition 2 is also true. As has been seen, it follows from the fact that, first, production has already been realised, and second, once the money is injected into the economy, sellers cannot tell whether it represents monetary income or money that has no counterpart in the economy. That situation is brought about by the inherent defect in the working of today's banking system, which does not make the creation of money dependent solely upon the remuneration of production factors.

Monetary imbalance can exist alongside stable prices

Proponents of the dominant theory think that the economy works harmoniously if the general level of prices remains stable. Now, we are going to demonstrate that the persistence of a monetary imbalance, which is a cause of unwarranted levies, is not incompatible with price stability.

An example helps to shed light on this situation. Suppose that in period T1, the amount of money which monetises production through pay is 100 MU (money units) for 100 PU (product units). In a situation of monetary equilibrium, the spending of the income formed in the course of production (100 MU) means the disposal of all the products made in the period (100 PU). Suppose now that the banking system creates 100 MU and lends them to firms that finance their purchases on the products market (Schumpeter's proposition). The income holders, by spending all their income (100 MU), get 50 PU, and firms, by spending their monetary loan (100 MU), get 50 PU. We observe that in T1, firms get 50 PU thanks to the monetary loan that is granted to them by the banking system. In other words, in this case, the purchase of products by firms, which is financed by newly created money, gives rise to an inflationary imbalance. The output of the period, instead of being disposed of for 100 MU, is sold for 200 MU. The level of prices in T1 is 2 MU = 1 PU. In this example, the value of the aggregate supply is 100 MU and the level of the aggregate demand is 200 MU, so there is an inflationary imbalance.

Suppose that in T2 the same amount of money (100 MU) is given over to pay that monetises production (100 PU), and that the same amount of money (100 MU) is loaned (renewal of monetary credits) by banks to firms to be spent on the products market (or that the firms that made inflationary profits spend them on the products market). We observe that in T2 the level of the prices is the same as in T1 (2 MU = 1 PU) and that the monetary imbalance persists. Although we can determine a monetary imbalance analytically, we observe that the general level of prices as it is established does not allow us to determine the monetary imbalance or disequilibrium inflation; so it does not allow us to observe the actual loss of the workers' purchasing power, allowing us to denounce the unwarranted levy made on the purchasing power of the production factors. In others words, a constant general level of prices does not necessarily mean that there is no monetary imbalance, that there is no inflationary imbalance, or that there is no unwarranted levy on the purchasing power of the production factors. This example shows that a part of the national product can be appropriated by firms through monetary loans from banks.

Conclusion

The neoclassical analysis fails to determine during production the amount of money necessary and sufficient for the monetisation of the wage economy. Consequently, it is unable to explain the working of the wage economy and, therefore, it cannot remove the causes of unwarranted or illegitimate levies. It has been seen that the spending of inflationary profit brings about a further inflationary profit that is the cause of an unwarranted levy on the purchasing power of the production factors, and this for the whole period in which firms run up monetary debts. To remove any possible occurrence of disequilibrium inflation that generates social injustice, a reform of the banking system is absolutely essential. Such a reform would compel the banking system to comply with the principle of money creation, a necessary principle in a wage economy, and according to which newly created money is intended to monetise production by way of the payment of workers.

Note

1. The consequences of spending profits in this way are studied in *Crise et dépense du profit* (Sadigh, 1994).

References

Barrère, A. (1976) *Controverses sur le système keynésien* (Paris: Economica).
Barrère, A. (1981) *La crise n'est pas ce qu'on croit* (Paris: Economica).
Barrère, A. (1985) *Keynes aujourd'hui* (Colloque international de Paris I), coordonné par A. Barrère (Paris: Economica).
Barrère, A. (1986) 'La crise de surinvestissement', in *Théories de la crise et politiques économiques* (Paris: Du Seuil).
Benetti, C. (1987) 'La théorie de la monnaie-marchandise chez Marx', in *Cahiers d'Economie Politique : Histoire de la pensée et de la théorie* (Paris: Anthropos).
Friedman, M. (1970) *Inflation et systèmes monétaires* (Paris: Calmann-Lévy).
Friedman, M. (1971) 'La théorie quantitative de la monnaie, nouvelle formulation', in *Théorie monétaire* (Paris: Dunod).

Elie Sadigh   227

Friedman, M. (1993) *La monnaie et ses pièges* (Paris: Dunod).
A. Graziani (1980) '*Malthus e la teoria della domanda effettiva*', in L. Costabile, *Malthus, sviluppo e ristagno della produzione capitalistica* (Turin, Einaudi), pp. VII–LV.
A. Graziani (1987) '*Economia keynesiana e teoria del circuito*', in Gandolfo e F. Marzano (a cura di), *Keynesian Theory, Planning Models, and Quantitative Economics* (Milan: Giuffré), pp. 57–76.
Gurley, J.G. and Shaw, E.S. (1973) *La monnaie dans une théorie des actifs financiers*, (Paris: Cujas).
Hahn, F. (1984) *Monnaie et inflation* (Paris: Economica).
Hayek, F.A.V. (1985) (ed.) *Prix de production* (Paris: Calmann-Lévy) (Collection Agora).
Hayek, F.A.V. (1941) *The pure theory of capital* (University of Chicago Press).
Hicks, J.R. (1956) *Valeur et capital* (Paris: Dunod).
Jevons, W.S. (1909) *La théorie de l'économie politique* (Paris: Giard et Brière).
Kaldor, N. (1985) *Le Fléau du monétarisme* (Paris: Economica).
Kalecki, M. (1965) *Théorie de la dynamique économique*, traduction française (Paris: Gauthiers-Villars).
Keynes, J.M. (1943) *Proposals for an International clearing union* (London: Macmillan).
Keynes, J.M. (1971) *Théorie générale de l'emploi, de l'intérêt et de la monnaie* (Paris: Payot).
Keynes, J.M. (1971) *Treatise on money*, Collected Writings, V and VI (London: Macmillan).
Myrdal, G. (1950) *L'équilibre monétaire* (Paris: Genin).
Nurkse, R. (1953) *Problems of capital formation in underdeveloped countries* (Oxford University Press).
Patinkin, D. (1972) *La monnaie, l'intérêt et les prix* (Paris: Presses Universitaires de France).
Sadigh, E. (1978) *Monnaie, Revenu, Capital* (Université de Dijon).
Sadigh, E. (1994) *Crise et dépense du profit* (LATEC, CNRS-Université de Bourgogne).
Sadigh, E. (1998) *La théorie économique dominante: un siècle d'imposture* (Paris: L'Harmattan).
Sadigh, E. (1999) *Principes de l'économie salariale* (Paris: L'Harmattan).
Sadigh, E. (2001) *Du libéralisme ou de la loi du plus fort à l'économie politique* (Paris: L'Harmattan).
Sadigh, E. (2002) *Valeur, prix et capital* (Paris: L'Harmattan).
Sadigh, E. (2003) *Etude économique et géopolitique du développement* (Paris: L'Harmattan).
Schmitt, B. (1975) *Théorie unitaire de la monnaie, nationale et internationale* (Paris: Castella, Suisse).
Schmitt, B. (1977) *L'or, le dollar et la monnaie supranationale* (Paris: Calmann-Lévy).
Schumpeter, J. (1935) *Théorie de l'évolution économique* (Paris: Dalloz).
Walras, L. (1976) *Eléments d'économie politique pure* (Paris: Librairie générale de droit et de jurisprudence).
Wicksell, K. (1954) *Value, Capital and Rent* (London: Allen & Unwin).

Part V

Monetary Circulation and Economic Policy

15
What is Wrong with the Euro Area Monetary Model?

Philip Arestis and Malcolm Sawyer

Introduction

The creation of the euro has also created a euro area of countries with a single currency and a single monetary policy, but with no other euro area level macroeconomic policies. The fiscal policies of the national governments are supposedly constrained by the Stability and Growth Pact (SGP), which places an upper limit of 3 per cent of GDP on government deficits and a balance or small surplus on the government budget over the course of the business cycle. In this chapter, we argue that the monetary policy of the euro area is firmly based on what has been termed the 'new consensus' in macroeconomics (NCM). This new consensus stands in contrast with the monetary theory of production (and Graziani's many contributions, including Graziani, 1994, 2003), where 'understanding of the workings of an economic system can only be acquired if the economy is analysed from the outset as *a monetary economy*' (Graziani, 1989, p. 1). Three of the key features of the NCM-based euro-area monetary model involve the classical dichotomy, the neutrality of money and the relevance of Say's Law: and clearly each of those features is rejected by the monetary theory of production.

Theoretical underpinnings of the EMU model

The economic model underlying the 'new' consensus can be summarised in three equations (see, for example, Arestis and Sawyer, 2004):

$$Y^g_t = a_0 + a_1 Y^g_{t-1} + a_2 E (Y^g_{t+1}) - a_3 [R_t - E_t (p_{t+1})] + s_1 \tag{1}$$

$$p_t = b_1 Y^g_t + b_2 p_{t-1} + b_3 E_t (p_{t+1}) + s_2 \text{ (with } b_2 + b_3 = 1) \tag{2}$$

$$R_t = RR^* + E_t (p_{t+1}) + c_1 Y^g_{t-1} + c_2 (p_{t-1} - p^T) \tag{3}$$

where Y^g is the output gap, R is nominal rate of interest, p is inflation, and p^T is the inflation target, RR* is the 'equilibrium' real rate of interest (that is, the rate of interest consistent with zero output gap which implies from equation 2 a constant rate of inflation), and s_i (with $i = 1, 2$) represents stochastic shocks.

Equation (1) is the aggregate demand equation; equation (2) is a Phillips curve; and equation (3) is a monetary policy operating rule. There are three equations and three unknowns: output, interest rate and inflation. Equation (1) is the result of intertemporal optimisation of a utility function, while the traditional IS emerges from the interaction of aggregate demand and output. There are both lagged adjustment and forward-looking elements; the model allows for sticky prices (the lagged inflation term in the Phillips-curve relationship) and full price flexibility in the long run. The term $E_t\ (p_{t+1})$ in equation (2) signals central bank credibility. Where a central bank credibly signals its intention to achieve and maintain low inflation, then this term indicates that it may be possible to reduce current inflation at a significantly lower cost in terms of output than otherwise. The operating rule implies that 'policy' becomes a systematic adjustment to economic developments rather than an exogenous process. Also, it contains no stochastic shock, implying that monetary policy operates without random shocks. It contains the neutrality of money property, with inflation determined by monetary policy (that is, the rate of interest), and equilibrium values of real variables are independent of the money supply. The final characteristic is that money has no role in the model; it is merely a 'residual' (for further discussion, see Arestis and Sawyer, 2003).

This model views the economy as essentially stable, though subject to shocks. It is assumed that the level of demand that arises from the 'equilibrium' real rate of interest (RR*) is consistent with a zero output gap.

We postulate that the economics of the EMU can be understood as based on the following elements:

(a) The market economy is viewed as essentially stable, and that macro-economic policy (particularly discretionary fiscal policy) may well destabilise the market economy. Markets, and particularly the financial markets, make well-informed judgements on the sustainability of economic policies, especially so in the current environment of open, globalised, capital and financial markets.

(b) Monetary policy has emerged as one of the key components of government macroeconomic policy. It is perceived as a flexible instrument for achieving medium-term stabilisation objectives: it can be adjusted quickly in response to macroeconomic developments. Indeed, monetary policy is the most direct determinant of inflation, so much so that in the long run the inflation rate is the only macroeconomic variable that monetary policy can affect.

(c) Monetary policy can be used to meet the objective of low rates of inflation. However, monetary policy should not be operated by politicians but by experts (whether banks, economists or others) in the form of an 'independent' central bank. Indeed, those operating monetary policy should be more 'conservative'; that is, place greater weight on low inflation and less weight on the level of unemployment than the politicians (Rogoff, 1985). Politicians would be tempted to use monetary policy for short-term gain (lower unemployment) at the expense of long-term loss (higher inflation). An 'independent' central bank would also have greater credibility in the financial markets and be seen to have a stronger commitment to low inflation than do politicians.[1]

(d) Credibility is recognised as paramount in the conduct of monetary policy to avoid problems associated with time-inconsistency. This is an argument that reinforces the requirement of central bank independence. It is argued that a policy that lacks credibility because of time inconsistency is neither optimal nor feasible. The only credible policy is the one that leaves the authority no freedom to react to developments in the future, and that even if aggregate demand policies matter in the short run in this model, a policy of non-intervention is preferable. It is precisely because of the time-inconsistency and credibility problems that monetary policy should be assigned to a 'credible' and independent central bank.

(e) There is explicit acknowledgement that low and stable inflation is monetary policy's primary long-term objective. This improves communication between the public and policy makers and provides discipline, accountability, transparency and flexibility in monetary policy.

(f) The level of economic activity fluctuates around the NAIRU, and unemployment below (above) the NAIRU would lead to higher (lower) rates of inflation. The NAIRU is a supply-side phenomenon closely related to the workings of the labour market.

(g) The essence of Say's Law holds; namely, that the level of effective demand does not play an independent role in the (long-run) determination of the level of economic activity, and adjusts to underpin the supply-side determined level of economic activity (which itself corresponds to the NAIRU). Shocks to the level of demand can be met by variations in the rate of interest to ensure that inflation does not develop (if unemployment falls below the NAIRU).

Institutional framework

The institutional policy framework, within which the euro has been introduced and will operate, has three key elements that relate directly to monetary and financial policy. First, the ECB is the only effective federal economic institution. The ECB has the one policy instrument of the rate of interest (the 'repo' rate) to pursue the main objective of low inflation. A quantitative definition of price stability has been adopted in the form of, in effect, a 0–2 per cent target for the annual increase in the Harmonised Index of Consumer Prices (HICP) for the euro area. The ECB has adopted a 'two-pillar' monetary strategy to achieve this target through the policy instrument of interest rate. The 'first pillar' is a commitment to analyse monetary developments for the information they contain about future price developments. This is the quantitative reference value for monetary growth, where a target of 4.5 per cent of M3 has been imposed. The 'second pillar' is a broadly based assessment of the outlook of price developments and the risks to price stability. This broad range of indicators includes: the euro exchange rate; labour market indicators, such as wages and unit labour costs; fiscal policy indicators; financial market indicators, such as asset prices.

Second, the ECB and the national central banks are linked into the European System of Central Banks (ESCB) with a division of responsibility between them. The ECB has the responsibility for setting interest rates in pursuit of the inflation objective, and the national central banks has responsibility for regulatory matters.

Third, the ECB is intended to be independent of the EU Council and Parliament and of its member governments. Thus, there is a complete separation between the monetary authorities, in the form of the ESCB, and the fiscal authorities, in the shape of the national governments comprising the EMU. It follows that there can be little coordination of monetary and fiscal policy. Indeed, any attempt at coordination would be extremely difficult to implement. For, apart from the separation of the monetary and fiscal authorities, there is also the requirement, cited elsewhere in this chapter, that national governments (and hence the fiscal authorities) should not exert any influence on the ECB (and hence the monetary authorities). Any strict interpretation of that edict would rule out any attempt at coordination of monetary and fiscal policies.

The ECB at present stands as the only body that can implement economic policy at a European Union (EU) level. The ways in which the ECB operates is crucial for the economic health of the EU, but it suffers from two major shortcomings; namely its undemocratic and unrepresentative nature, and the objective that it has been set. Hence, we argue that the ECB should be changed in two significant ways: the membership of the board of directors should be broadened and the directors made directly answerable to the European Parliament, and the objectives set for it reformulated to include growth and employment, not merely price stability.

The monetary theory of production view

The monetary theory of production runs counter to this NCM analysis and casts many doubts on its validity, and we focus on three aspects here.

First, the monetary theory of production is based on a very different analytical perspective, which rejects Say's Law, the classical dichotomy and neutrality of money. There would then be no strong case for thinking that the level of economic activity will gravitate (whether quickly or slowly) to the supply-side equilibrium (corresponding to the NAIRU). There cannot be the separation between the real and monetary sides of the economy as postulated in the NCM, and the activities of the monetary authorities will have long-lasting real effects.

In particular, it would be anticipated that variations in the rate of interest would have an impact on the level of investment (and thereby future productive capacity) and on the exchange rate. Monetary policy in the form of interest rates is viewed as operating through the effect of the level of economic activity and thereby on the rate of inflation. Insofar as interest rate changes are effective in influencing the pace of economic activity, they can be seen to do so through exchange rates (and thereby on demand for import and exports) and through investment. In the long run this sequence of events could very well affect output, both its level and growth.

Second, there is a range of reasons for thinking that monetary policy will have a differential impact across regions and countries. As the UK Monetary Policy Committee (of the Bank of England) recognises (see Monetary Policy Committee, 1999), monetary policy 'sets one interest rate for the economy as a whole and can only take account of the impact of official rate changes on the aggregate of individuals in the economy' (p. 7). Monetary policy is undifferentiated in that a single official rate applies. But there are differences in financial structures between countries in the euro area, and in particular differences in the extent of variable rate and fixed rate borrowing and in the effect of interest rate changes on economic activity. The effects of interest rate changes will be far from uniform across euro area countries. An interest rate rise may succeed in slowing down economic activity in some countries but not in others; it may have little effect on inflation in some, but act to speed it up in others.

The interest rate impacts on the distribution of income, most notably between borrowers and lenders. The interest rate has differential effects across regions, and the setting of a single interest rate for the euro area cannot deal with the different economic conditions of regions and the different institutional arrangements that lead to different effects of a given interest rate change.

Third, the monetary theory of production would challenge the essentially monetarist two-pillar strategy of the ECB, that monetary policy can only affect inflation, and that money is used as a reference value implying that money is exogenous and controllable, and suggests that inflation can be controlled by monetary policy without any harm to the real side of the economy. The idea that money is endogenously created within the private sector would suggest that the stock of money adjusts to inflation, generated on the real side of the economy, and that monetary policy in the form of interest rates can have effects on the real side of the economy. Further, it should also be recognised that monetary policy through the manipulation of interest rates may not be an effective way of guiding the economy, and the effects of interest rate changes on economic performance are highly indirect and uncertain, and as such difficult to predict. It is also the case that interest rates form a cost (to borrowers) and hence increases in interest rates raise costs and thereby prices.

Doubt is thus cast on the effectiveness of interest rate policy in the relatively closed EU economy, specifically in terms of the inflation objective. Insofar as interest rate policy can influence the pace of inflation, it does so through suppressing the level of aggregate demand, which in turn may well have detrimental effects on investment and the creation of productive capacity. By creating unemployment, the lower level of aggregate demand may have long-lasting effects on labour market participation as some of the unemployed lose skills and withdraw from the labour market. When monetary policy (in the form of interest rate changes) is seen as an aggregate demand policy (through which it is presumed inflation can be controlled), it should be compared with the alternative policies. In particular, fiscal policy may well be a more powerful policy weapon to move the level of aggregate demand as compared with monetary policy.

Effectiveness of interest rate changes

The case for monetary policy as envisaged in the NCM analysis rests on the idea that interest rates can have a significant impact on the level of aggregate demand, which in turn has a significant impact on the rate of inflation. But it also asserts that the impact of interest rates will be short-lived and will not affect the supply side of the economy. In this section we review some evidence, which suggests that those propositions are not empirically maintained. Interest rates are likely to influence investment expenditure, consumer expenditure, asset prices and the exchange rate. This view is well illustrated by the Bank of England (1999) analysis of the transmission mechanism of monetary policy, where they view a change in the official interest rate as influencing the market rates of interest, asset prices, expectations and confidence and the exchange rate, which in turn influences domestic and external demand, and then inflationary pressures. In addition, and as already argued, interest rate changes can also have distributional effects, whether between individuals or between economic regions.

The effectiveness of interest rate changes can be judged to some degree through simulations of macroeconometric models. The simulations reported in Bank of England (1999, p. 36) for a 1 percentage point shock to nominal interest rates, maintained for one year, reaches a maximum change in GDP (of opposite sign to the change in the interest rate) of around 0.3 per cent after five to six quarters.[2] The Monetary Policy Committee (1999) puts it aptly: 'temporarily raising rates relative to a base case by 1 percentage point for one year might be expected to lower output by something of the order of 0.2% to 0.35% after about a year, and to reduce inflation by around 0.2 percentage points to 0.4 percentage points a year or so after that, all relative to the base case' (p. 3).[3] The cumulative reduction in GDP is around 1.5 per cent over a four-year period. Inflation responds little for the first four quarters (in one simulation inflation rises but falls in the other over that period). In years 2 and 3 inflation is 0.2 to 0.4 percentage points lower; the simulation is not reported past year 3 (in these simulations interest rates are changed over a year). There are limits as to how far interest rates can be manipulated; and this, of course, has some reflection in reality. For example, there are clear limits on how far interest rates in one country can diverge from those elsewhere (and models often impose some form of interest rate parity). A recent review of the properties of the major macroeconometric models of the UK indicates that 'the chief mechanism by which the models achieve change in the inflation rate is through the exchange rate' (Church *et al.*, 1997, p. 92). Since much of the effect of interest rate changes comes via the exchange rate, these results for the UK may well be greater than comparable results for the euro area would be since the UK economy is much more open than the euro area. The effects of an exchange rate change will be much smaller on the EU economy, which trades relatively little with non-EU economies, than on, say, the Dutch economy where imports and exports amount to over 50 per cent of its GDP. The relatively closed nature of the EU in terms of international trade (with imports and exports amounting to less than 10 per cent of GDP) means that variations in the exchange rate of the euro will have much less impact on prices than in more open economies.

The claim that monetary policy is an effective and powerful tool for macroeconomic management depends on a range of assumptions. One of the assumptions is that variations in the rate of interest have substantial effects on aggregate demand and thereby on the rate of inflation. In this section, we seek to summarise the results of some recent simulations undertaken by others based on macroeconometric models.

In their work on the impact of monetary policy in the euro zone, Angeloni *et al.* (2002) argue that:

> VAR and structural model analyses for the euro area confirm sizeable and plausible monetary policy effects on output and prices. In the VARs, an unexpected increase in the short-term interest rate temporarily reduces output, with the peak effects occurring after roughly one year. Prices respond more slowly, hardly moving during the first year and then falling gradually over the next few years. Again, these VAR properties are similar to those reported for the US. The structural models of the US and the euro area broadly confirm this picture. (p. 21)

Table 15.1   Effects of monetary policy change

100 basis point increase for two years	EMM		AWM	
	Year 1	Year 3	Year 1	Year 3
Effective exchange rate	1.6	0.0	1.6	0.0
Consumer prices	−0.09	−0.31	−0.15	−0.38
GDP	−0.22	−0.31	−0.34	−0.71
Consumption	−0.12	−0.19	−0.27	−0.54
Investment	−0.34	−1.22	−0.81	−2.96

Notes: EMM (Eurosystem Macroeconometric Models of National Central Banks) calculations;
AWM (ECB area-wide model) calculations;
Year 1 and Year 3 refer to yearly average deviations from baseline.
Source: Angeloni *et al.* (2002, Table 2).

The estimated effect of a one standard error monetary policy shock
(approximately 30 basis points) on prices is 0.00 in year 1 and −0.07 per cent in
year 3 with a decline in output in year 1 of 0.15 per cent and 0.05 in year 3.[4]
In Table 15.1, we provide some results from simulations with macroeconometric models based on their table 2. These results indicate that a 1 percentage
point hike in the rate of interest held for two years leads to prices lower
by between 0.3 to 0.4 per cent after three years, and hence that the rate of
inflation over those three years is around 0.1 per cent per annum lower than
it would have been otherwise. As far as we are aware no statistics are available
by which we can judge whether this should be regarded as a statistically
significant reduction. In any event, we would judge these reductions as
relatively small. It can also be noted that the effects on investment are larger
than the effects on consumption expenditure, and one implication of this is
that monetary policy can have long-lasting effects in that the size of the
capital stock is affected.

These authors also provide some comparisons between the euro area and
the USA. They report the effects of a 50 basis points short-term interest
change on a range of economic variables. The effects are reported after one
year and three years (that is, variations for quarter 4 and quarter 12 relative
to a baseline). They give the semi-elasticity multipliers, and these are summarised in Table 15.2.

The general impression from this table is that the results for the USA are not
dissimilar from those for the euro zone, though the effects of interest rate
changes on investment appear more muted in the USA.

Van Els *et al.* (2001) report results for the euro area countries, where 'The
monetary policy shock was a two-year increase of the short-term policy
interest rate by 1 percentage point from 2001Q1–2002Q4. From and including
2003Q1 a return to baseline values was assumed' (p. 22). A footnote adds

Table 15.2 Impact of changes in interest rates

	Effects after 1 year			Effects after 3 years		
	Euro area EMM	Euro area AWM	US FRB-US	Euro area EMM	Euro area AWM	US FRB-US
CPI	–0.02	–0.03	–0.05	–0.15	–0.21	–0.57
GDP	–0.11	–0.24	–0.14	–0.49	–0.63	–0.52
Consumer expenditure	–0.10	–0.25	–0.17	–0.38	–0.62	–0.64
Investment expenditure	–0.59	–0.68	–0.17	–2.43	–2.07	–1.08

Note: FRB-US: Federal Reserve Board, USA.
Source: Angeloni *et al.* (2002, Table 3).

that 'this meant that the experiment was a temporary one, as a permanent change in the nominal interest rate would force most models onto an explosive path'. Furthermore, 'the exercise on national models is conducted on the basis that the change in monetary policy has taken place simultaneously in all euro area countries' (p. 8). They find that:

Two stylised facts appear to be at variance with the traditional view of the monetary transmission mechanism, namely the low elasticity of the cost-of-capital in estimated spending equations and the high degree of amplification, i.e. the empirical evidence that though central bank's actions induce relatively small and transitory movements in open market interest rates, nevertheless they have large and persistent effects on the purchase of long-lived assets, such as housing or production equipment. (p. 10)

Moreover, in figure 6.1 of Van Els *et al.* (2001), a summary is provided of the common assumptions underlying the response pattern of the euro exchange rate vis-à-vis non-euro countries along with the long-term interest rate (10 year bond). These exercises suggest that the interest rate increase implies an appreciation of the euro exchange rate, with respect to non-euro currencies, of 1.6 per cent on average in the first year and 0.6 per cent in the second. The figure shows a peak appreciation in the exchange rate of 2 per cent and a decline back to zero into the tenth quarter. The long-term rate peaks at 0.2 per cent during quarter 1, gradually declining back to no increase in quarter 9, when the short-term rate returns to a zero increase.

The authors find substantial differences between countries of the euro zone, which is relevant for the operation of a single monetary policy. They conclude that at one extreme there are countries, like Germany, Benelux and Finland, where a policy tightening is effective in curbing inflationary pressures at mild costs in terms of output losses, while there are other EMU countries, in particular Greece and Portugal, where the increase in interest rates engenders a marked contraction in economic activity and only a modest restraint on price developments. The remaining countries are located in-between, though somewhat closer to the core region. (p. 48)

Further, 'the distribution of the national responses of investment is very wide, with maxima ranging between −0.3 per cent for Germany and France and −3.6 per cent for Italy and Ireland' (p. 39). Although it is generally implicit, this chapter also indicates the role of unemployment in dampening down inflation. 'The impact of the monetary policy shock on unemployment is a crucial element in the process of monetary policy transmission on prices in the medium and long term'. (p. 39)

The overall conclusions that Van Els *et al.* (2001) draw from these results are on the following lines:

> In terms of the impact of monetary policy on output, a 1 percentage point rise in short-term interest rates is found to have a maximum aggregate effect in NCBs [National Central Bank] models of −0.4 per cent after 2 years. The maximum aggregate effect on prices is also −0.4 per cent but in this case it occurs 2 years later, reflecting the fact that in most of the models prices react more slowly and largely in response to changes in economic activity. The dominant channel of transmission in the first two years − both in terms of its impact on output and on prices − is the exchange rate channel. However, in terms of the impact on output, from the third year of the simulation onwards the user cost of capital channel becomes dominant. (p. 52)

The tables in the Annex of the Van Els *et al.* (2001) paper give results by country and for prices, GDP, consumption, investment and unemployment, A summary of these results is given in Table 15.3.

The rather small effect of the interest rate change on the rate of inflation is again apparent, with a substantial effect on the level of investment. The way the results are presented suggest that output rises back to its benchmark level a few years after the interest rate policy is switched off. But this means that for a two-year increase in interest rates of 1 percentage point, there is a loss of output that is never recovered and the cumulative loss of output is equivalent to 1.1 per cent of annual output (summing line for GDP in first part of Table 15.3). For unemployment, the created total of unemployment is equivalent to 0.6 per cent of a workforce year. In the case of the price level, there is, within the forecast period, a reduction in the price level; in the aggregate model this amounts to around 0.4 per cent. But the rate of inflation is

Table 15.3 Effects of 1 percentage point increase in interest rate sustained for 2 years

Aggregate (based on national models)

	2001	2002	2003	2004	2005
GDP deflator	−0.04	−0.20	−0.35	−0.43	−0.41
Inflation*	−0.04	−0.16	−0.15	−0.08	+0.02
GDP	−0.22	−0.38	−0.31	−0.14	−0.02
Private consumption	−0.12	−0.23	−0.19	−0.06	0.01
Investment	−0.34	−1.04	−1.22	−0.80	−0.39
Unemployment	0.04	0.11	0.17	0.17	0.11

*Percentage point change in inflation: not calculated in original paper, own calculations from preceding line.

AWM (area wide model)

	2001	2002	2003	2004	2005
GDP deflator	−0.10	−0.31	−0.44	−0.57	−0.76
Inflation**	−0.10	−0.21	−0.13	−0.13	−0.19
GDP	−0.34	−0.71	−0.71	−0.63	−0.57
Private consumption	−0.27	−0.58	−0.54	−0.43	−0.37
Investment	−0.81	−2.37	−2.96	−2.63	−2.42
Unemployment	0.10	0.39	0.58	0.62	0.58

**Percentage point change in inflation: not calculated in original paper, own calculations from preceding line.
Source: Van Els *et al.* (2001, Annex).

not permanently affected in the aggregate model; by year 5 inflation is back to the benchmark level. Much of the effect on inflation comes through the exchange rate. Presumably when the interest rate policy is reversed, the exchange rate effect is reversed, leaving no permanent effect on inflation from that channel.

Conclusions

The general conclusions we draw from this discussion are twofold. First, having noted the key role ascribed to monetary policy within the euro area and the absence of fiscal policy, we have cast doubt on the effectiveness of monetary policy in terms of responding to recession and as a means of controlling inflation. Second, since interest rate policy has a range of effects (e.g. on investment, exchange rate and distributional effects), the objectives of monetary policy should reflect that. The objectives of monetary policy should be recast to include growth and high levels of employment alongside inflation. But since monetary policy may be a weak instrument for the control of inflation, other policy measures are required.

Notes

1. See Forder (2000) for an extensive discussion and critique of the notion of credibility.
2. The precise figures depend on assumptions concerning the subsequent responses of the setting of interest rates in response to the evolving inflation rate.
3. The precise figures depend on assumptions concerning the subsequent responses of the setting of interest rates in response to the evolving inflation rate.
4. The VAR estimates are taken from Peersman and Smets (2001). Their Graph 1 indicates that the upper 90 per cent confidence interval on prices is at or above zero (compared with the base case); that is, prices may not decline at all.

References

Angeloni, I., Kashyap, A., Mojon, B. and Terlizzese, D. (2002) 'Monetary transmission in the euro area: where do we stand?', *European Central Bank Working Paper Series*, 114.

Arestis, P. and Sawyer, M. (2003) 'Does the stock of money have any significance?', *Banca Nazionale Del Lavoro Quarterly Review*, 56, 225, pp. 113–36.

Arestis, P. and Sawyer, M. (2004) 'Can monetary policy affect the real economy?', *European Review of Economics and Finance*, 3(3), pp. 9–32.

Bank of England (1999) *Economic Models at the Bank of England* (London: Bank of England).

Church, K.B., Mitchel, P.R., Sault, J.E. and Wallis, K.F. (1997) 'Comparative performance of models of the UK economy', *National Institute Economic Review*, 161, pp. 91–100.

Forder, J. (2000) 'The Theory of Credibility: Confusions, Limitations, and Dangers', *International Papers in Political Economy*, 7(2), pp. 3–40.

Graziani, A. (1989) 'The theory of the monetary circuit', *Thames Papers in Political Economy*, Spring, pp. 1–26.

Graziani, A. (1994) *La Teoria Monetaria della Produzione* (Rome: Banca Popolare dell'Etruria e del Lazio).

Graziani, A. (2003) *The Monetary Theory of Production* (Cambridge University Press).

Monetary Policy Committee (1999) *The Transmission Mechanism of Monetary Policy* (London: Bank of England).

Peersman, G. and Smets, F. (2001) 'The Monetary Transmission Mechanism in the Euro Area: More Evidence from VAR Analysis', ECB Working Paper no. 91 (Frankfurt am Main: ECB).

Rogoff, K. (1985) 'The Optimal Degree of Commitment to an Intermediate Monetary Target', *Quarterly Journal of Economics*, 100(4), pp. 1169–89.

Van Els, P., Locarno, A., Morgan, J. and Villetelle, J.-P. (2001) 'Monetary policy transmission in the euro area: what do aggregate and national structural models tell us?', *European Central Bank Working Paper Series*, 94.

16
Circulation Approach and Applied Economics: Monetary Duality in Cuba

*Ghislain Deleplace**

This chapter is an exercise in applied economics, concentrating on circular flows. It is trivial to mention that the monetary theory of production is centrally concerned with the analysis of circular flows in a market economy. By contrast with the mainstream approach, which understands such an economy exclusively in terms of real supply and demand, the circulation approach focuses on the monetary flows generated by economic activity. My contention is that circular flows are not simply one of the various aspects which characterise this approach, together with, for example, endogenous money, the bank rate of interest or producers sovereignty. It is the core of the monetary theory of production, and an author may happen to be closer to this theory even if he deals only with real magnitudes, than another author who deals with monetary magnitudes, but from an allocation standpoint. To put it in a provocative way: Sraffa might be closer to Graziani than Kaldor.

The origin of the chapter is my old concern with monetary duality; that is, the question: what happens when two monies circulate side by side in an economy? When all the monetary flows are homogenised by being measured in the same unit of account, one deals with a closed economy; the exchange of currencies is then only introduced when one extends the model to an open economy, and it takes place at the borders of this economy. But the analysis of the relation between liquidity, monetary stability and convertibility may take advantage of the study of particular cases, in which the various domestic circular flows imply more than one currency, with an exchange rate appearing inside the economy itself. This situation is made still more complex when different exchange rates coexist in the same economy. Not

* I thank Emiliano Brancaccio for his comments on a previous version of the chapter, but release him from any responsibility in the views expressed here. I thank Nathalie Sigot for her expertise in drawing the figures.

only the circulation approach may then be used for applied economics, but also applied studies may contribute to a better theoretical understanding of circular flows. This double link is here explored on the basis of the Cuban case, where two currencies circulate side by side (the US dollar and the national peso), and are exchanged for each other at two different rates, one for firms and one for the population.

The chapter is organised in four sections. The first section raises the issue of monetary duality and discusses some fundamentals of the circulation approach, concerning the relation between the unit of account, circular money flows, and convertibility. The second section presents the specificity of the Cuban monetary regime, which combines strict exchange controls with a double monetary duality (two legal tender currencies, with two different exchange rates between them). The third section studies the viability and the stability of this regime, and shows that it generates an endogenous tendency to the depreciation of the national currency, which will make it difficult in the future to achieve the official objective of replacing the dollar by a convertible peso. The final section draws some conclusions, at the applied level (the irreversibility of the dollarisation process, even when it is strictly controlled) and for the circulation approach (the necessity of appropriate proportions between wages and the aggregate value of consumer goods).

The issue of monetary duality

History

The issue of monetary duality may be approached from two different angles: historical and theoretical. To assess its historical relevance, I shall limit myself to a few examples of cases amply documented in the literature. One example is provided by the sixteenth century, when domestic and foreign coins legally circulated side by side in most European countries. The legal value of both kinds of coins, expressed in the national unit of account, was determined by their intrinsic weight in metal, but, in addition, domestic coins bore a seigniorage which gave them a higher circulating value per unit of weight than their foreign counterparts. The consequence was the generalisation of higher 'voluntary' (commercial) values of foreign coins, which explained a great part of the inflation process, independently of the well known inflows of precious metals from America (see Boyer-Xambeu, Deleplace and Gillard, 1994).

Another example of monetary duality was bimetallism, in which gold and silver coinages issued by the same state coexisted. This monetary regime was the most common in the eighteenth century, and, according to Wilson, 'the worldwide orthodoxy in the earlier nineteenth century consisted in bimetallism in its many variants' (Wilson, 2000: ix). In this regime the unit of account was defined in two different standards (gold and silver), with two corresponding kinds of coins endowed with legal tender. For example, in France in the middle of the nineteenth century the unit of account, the French franc, was defined either as 0.29 grams of pure gold or as 4.5 grams of pure silver, which implied a monetary ratio of 15.5. The corresponding standard monies were on the one hand the twenty-francs coin, containing 6.45 grams of gold 900/1000 fine, and on the other hand the one-franc coin, containing 5 grams of silver 900/1000 fine. This relation between one single unit of account and two standard monies assessing its definition in two distinct but strictly connected standards could be checked at any time at the mint, where the kilogram of pure gold was monetised in twenty-francs coins at the fixed price of 3444.44 francs and the kilogram of pure silver in one-franc coins at the fixed price of 218.89 francs. As is well known, the central theoretical debate about bimetallism in the nineteenth century was about its viability. Some authors contended that the legal monetary ratio (15.5, in the case of France) could not be sustained, and that bimetallism fatally degenerated in 'alternate monometallism', one coined metal disappearing from circulation during one period and the other one during the next period. Other authors considered that bimetallism was viable, especially if, as the Banque de France did consistently, the bank of issue was allowed to put a premium on the coined metal that was demanded against its notes.

A last historical example refers to the coexistence of a state currency and a private money, such as the British sovereign and the Bank of England note in the nineteenth century, a model widely imitated in the gold-standard era (see, e.g., Bordo, 1999). Fierce monetary debates occurred in the first half of the nineteenth century, from the bullion controversy to the currency-versus-banking controversy, around the conditions under which a private (bank) money could 'represent' the state (metallic) currency, without creating monetary instability. This leads from history to theory.

Theory

From a theoretical point of view, the issue of monetary duality is linked with two main distinctions: on the one hand, between the unit of account and the means of payment; on the other hand, between central money and private money.

In a monetary economy, all transactions are measured in a common unit of account and executed by a means of payment. The uniqueness of the unit of account is a definitional feature of a monetary economy, in contrast with a barter economy in which each transaction is measured in its own unit. Although they are related, the unit of account and the means of payment are two distinct features. This was clear in old monetary regimes when two different names were used in practice to designate them (e.g. the pound sterling and the sovereign), but it is no less true today: a dollar written on a price-list is not the same thing as a dollar printed on a Federal Reserve banknote. This distinction allows several forms of the means of payment to circulate side by side (e.g. coins, bank notes, bank deposits), provided their values are all expressed in the same unit of account. Even in a *fiat money* regime, where the bank note is not convertible in any standard, the coherence of the monetary regime requires that all these domestic instruments of payment be convertible against one another; that is, exchangeable at the legal par. If they are not, so that private exchange rates appear for some of them, the uniqueness of the unit of account is no longer guaranteed, because prices of the same purchase contract or debt contract differ according to the particular instrument of payment used in the transaction. Usually, the convertibility between these various instruments is guaranteed by the central bank acting as an issuer of a central-bank money and a clearing house of bank deposits.

Therefore, the distinction between the unit of account and the means of payment is related to the distinction between central money and private money. The main concept is here convertibility, whose relevance is not restricted to foreign exchange or to a metallic-standard regime, although its relation with the stability and the liquidity of the economy is different according to the regime. For the metallic-standard regime, the issue of convertibility has been extensively studied by the monetary literature of the nineteenth century (see Deleplace, 2004). Either excess liquidity created by banks jeopardised the capacity of the central bank to maintain the monetary stability consistent with convertibility, or a depreciation of the unit of account provoked by an adverse foreign balance exposed the central bank to convertibility problems, which it tried to alleviate by restraining its credit, hence imposing liquidity problems on the economy. The currency-versus-banking controversy showed that two main solutions could be imagined: either a separation between the issuing and banking activities of the central bank, with a 100 per cent metallic backing of the additional note issue (currency principle), or a discretionary policy by the central bank of its discount rate, aimed at making credit more expensive without squeezing it (banking principle). In both cases, the purpose was to regulate credit (through quantity rationing or price adjustment), in order to prevent a situation of overbanking inconsistent with the maintaining of convertibility.

In a *fiat money* regime, the link between stability and convertibility seems to be broken, because the stability of the unit of account is usually assessed (through a general price index) in terms of a conventional basket of commodities, against which money is not convertible at the central bank. But there is still a link between liquidity and convertibility. The continuity of the payments system implies the compensation between bank deposits, which requires the conversion (at a fixed price) of this private bank money into central-bank money; this is of the same nature as, in a mixed regime of metallic specie and convertible notes, the conversion (at a fixed price) of the private bank money (the bank note) into the legal tender money (the coin). Again, the viability of the monetary regime is only guaranteed if liquidity problems faced by commercial banks do not jeopardise this convertibility between bank deposits and the legal tender currency, making it difficult for the central bank to maintain the stability of the unit of account.

The study of the issue of monetary duality therefore implies a need to explore the concept of convertibility: if this concept has been central in the history of monetary thought for nearly five centuries, the monetary theory of production certainly has something to say about it. The relation between pure theory and applied economics can be used both ways here: the circulation approach helps to understand the functioning of observed examples of convertibility, and, reciprocally, the study of these cases contributes to the deepening of the circulation approach.

The specificity of the Cuban monetary regime

Economic duality

The present study is about a case of partial dollarisation at the time of writing, the Cuban economy.[1] By contrast with a market economy, in which the various means of payment can be used in all markets, a separation here is legally imposed between the markets in which one unit of account and the corresponding means of payment (the dollar) are enforced, and the markets in which the other unit of account and the other corresponding means of payment (the national currency) are enforced.

At first sight, the main feature of the Cuban economy is its duality: there are two currencies (the US dollar and the 'national peso'), two domestic exchange rates between them (one for the firms and one for the population), two exchange regimes (with fixed and floating rates, respectively), two productive sectors (the 'emerging' sector and the 'traditional' sector), two kinds of property in these sectors (state and private), two domestic markets for goods (one in the US dollar and one in the 'national peso'), two price regimes (an administrative price regime and a market one), two banking sectors (one for firms and one for the population), two ways for the population to have access to the dollar (one legal and one illegal). The situation, however, is still more complex: firstly, these various pairs do not overlap, so that one cannot separate two homogenous sub-economies; secondly, a third element often complements each pair, so that arbitrage possibilities are generally more triangular than bilateral, if not multilateral.

Legal tender and convertibility: a monetary duality

In fact there are not two but three legal currencies that may be owned and used in circulation: the 'national peso' (*moneda nacional*), the US dollar and the 'convertible peso' (*peso convertible*).[2] None of them – including the US dollar – is endowed with external convertibility, because neither individuals nor firms are free to transfer abroad any currency, even on a current account.[3] Inflows of foreign currency generated by exporting firms are centralised and allocated by the state; as for individuals, they may keep dollars legally obtained through family transfers from abroad (*remesas*) or personal activity (*por cuenta propria*).

Inside Cuba, the three currencies are not freely interchangeable, either against one another, or as a means of payment in domestic transactions, or as a store of wealth in bank saving accounts. No exchange market exists for the firms (*personas juridicas*), who obtain from the state and return back to it the quantity of each currency required and generated by their activity. Individuals (*personas naturales*) have access to what the central bank (*Banco Central de Cuba*, or BCC) calls 'a regime of limited convertibility, implemented through institutional channels' (BCC, 2001, p. 32).[4] In all the exchange counters of the state bank CADECA, dollars may be sold for pesos at a fixed exchange rate and in unlimited quantities; in only some of these exchange counters, convertible pesos may be obtained against pesos at a slightly higher exchange rate,[5] and in quantities limited to one hundred convertible pesos per person per day. Strictly speaking, the peso is therefore not convertible in dollars, but it is convertible, with limitations, in a currency issued by the BCC at par with the dollar. In domestic transactions involving firms, two mutually exclusive spheres coexist, even if a particular firm may belong to both of them. When the output is sold in convertible currency (dollar or convertible peso), the firm has to purchase its inputs from other firms in the same way; when its sales are in pesos, it may purchase the inputs in pesos, unless dollars are required, which are then provided by the state. In all firms, wages are paid in pesos; firms selling in convertible currency may only distribute bonuses in that currency, in fixed limits. For the transactions of the population, two kinds of markets coexist, which are strictly separated according to the means of payment. In what Cubans usually call 'shoppings' (officially TRD, for *tiendas recaudadoras en divisas*), the goods are paid for in convertible currency (dollar or convertible peso, taken at par), and in ordinary stores goods are paid for in pesos. The same holds in the tourism sector and for a legally fixed list of services – catering (*paladares*), lodging (*casas particulares*), and so on – that individuals are allowed to sell, some of them in convertible currency, others in pesos. Finally, separate accounts are held in banks for each of the three currencies, and a different interest rate is served to individuals on fixed-term deposits, the highest on the peso and the lowest on the dollar, with an intermediate rate on the convertible peso. This means that, even though the convertible peso and the dollar are perfect substitutes as means of payment, they are not considered so as stores of value, since it is necessary to induce the population to save in the former currency rather than the latter.

Exchange rates: an exchange duality

The Cuban monetary system is not only characterised by the coexistence of a (domestically) convertible currency (the dollar or the convertible peso, taken at par) and a partially convertible one (the 'national peso'), but also by the coexistence of two exchange rates between them, one for firms and one for the population. With a few exceptions, all the exchange operations between *personas juridicas* (firms and administrations) are made at the official one-to-one rate. As seen above, *personas naturales* (individuals, including persons selling services of their own) may sell dollars against pesos and buy convertible pesos with pesos at CADECA, at an administered exchange rate that is significantly higher (it has never fallen below 19 pesos since this 'informal' exchange market was introduced). Besides, black-market exchange rates complement the 'official' and 'informal' rates, but in recent years they did not depart much (at least in Havana) from the CADECA rates, showing a rather good integration of the exchange market, whether 'informal' or illegal.

If the official rate is ruled by a fixed exchange regime, there is some ambiguity about the exchange regime which regulates the 'informal' rate. The state bank CADECA is part of the group 'Nueva Banco', and is thus formally distinct from the central bank (BCC). It returns to the BCC the dollars purchased from the population and it receives from BCC the convertible pesos sold to the population. Officially, these convertible pesos are issued with a 100 per cent backing by dollars (which makes this regime resemble a currency board), and the CADECA rate is determined by the supply and demand of convertible currency against pesos from the population. In fact, this rate does not vary from day to day, and its evolution shows successive plateaux, suggesting that it is administered. Hidalgo, Tabares, and Doimeadios (2002, p. 23) speak of a dirty-floating regime (*regimen de flotacion sucia*), but they only mention a situation of net purchases of dollars by the BCC, leading between 1996 and 2001 to fluctuations constrained by an 'implicit band' of 19–23 pesos per dollar (*ibid.*, pp. 24–5). There is in official or research papers no indication of net sales of convertible currency by the BCC since the depreciation of the peso in 2001, either through the use of reserves or the issuance of unbacked convertible pesos. The question of the asymmetrical or symmetrical character of this dirty-floating regime, and accordingly of a strict or loose currency board, is then left open.

Viability and stability of monetary duality in Cuba

A simple pattern of circulation

Many puzzles already show up in the monetary theory of production, when all the monetary flows are expressed in the same unit of account and executed by a unique means of payment. So, it is necessary to simplify the pattern of monetary flows in order to focus on the particular problems raised by monetary duality in Cuba. I shall here concentrate on the monetary flows between firms and households, the banking sector being reduced to the central bank acting as an exchange bureau. I shall also ignore flows among firms and make

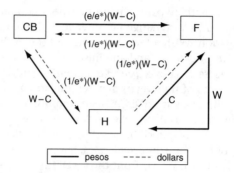

Figure 16.1   Pattern of circulation without private resources in dollars

the assumption that all wages are spent in consumption (no savings out of wages). These assumptions should be relaxed in a further stage of the research, allowing the introduction of the banking sector with its various functions.

Let us call W the wages paid by firms to households in pesos (I shall neglect the bonuses paid by some firms in dollars), and C the amount of earned pesos spent in the goods-markets in pesos. Under the assumption of no savings out of wages, $(W-C)$ is then the amount of pesos exchanged at the central bank by households for an amount of dollars equal to $(1/e^*)$ $(W-C)$, with e^* the exchange rate of the dollar for the population. These dollars are spent in the goods-markets in dollars, and the receipts are exchanged at the central bank by firms for an amount of pesos equal to (e/e^*) $(W-C)$, with e the exchange rate of the dollar for the firms. Figure 16.1 shows the corresponding pattern of circulation (with CB being the central bank, F firms, and H households).

The central bank is a simple intermediary in the circulation of dollars: it supplies to households the dollars that it obtains from firms. What about the firms? Their budget constraint in pesos reads:

$$W \leq C + (e/e^*)(W-C) \qquad (1)$$

Hence:

$$(W-C)(e^*-e)/e^* \leq 0 \qquad (2)$$

In the Cuban case, where $C < W$ and $e^* > e$, this constraint cannot be fulfilled, and, as a consequence, state subsidies to firms are necessary in pesos.

Viability

This simple case shows that this pattern of circulation is not viable without exogenous resources in dollars. This had been understood by Cuban authorities who, when legalising the dollar, allowed households to obtain own resources in hard currency, through family transfers or personal services. Let us call R these private resources, and assume provisionally that they are all spent in the goods-markets in dollars, where they fuel additional receipts in dollars for the firms. Figure 16.2 shows the new pattern of circulation.

The central bank captures the totality of the private resources in dollars through the goods-markets in dollars. The budget constraint of the firms in pesos becomes:

$$W \leq C + e\left[(1/e^*)(W - C) + R\right] \qquad (3)$$

Hence:

$$(W - C)(e^* - e)/e^* \leq e\,R \qquad (4)$$

This condition means that for firms the proceeds in pesos of the additional receipts originating in the private resources in dollars may compensate the loss incurred because of the lower exchange rate imposed on them. There is a maximum value e_{MAX}^* of the exchange rate for the population which is consistent with budget equilibrium of the firms:

$$e_{MAX}^* = e\,(W - C)/[(W - C) - e\,R] \qquad (5)$$

For $e_{MAX}^* > e^* \geq e$, firms are making profits, and for $e^* > e_{MAX}^*$ they are making losses, which call for state subsidies.

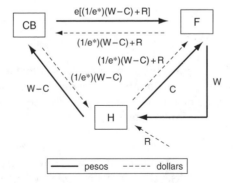

Figure 16.2 Pattern of circulation with private resources in dollars totally spent in dollars

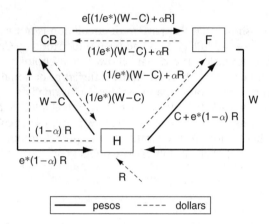

Figure 16.3   Pattern of circulation with private resources in dollars partly spent in dollars

Let us now consider that households, instead of spending their total resources in dollars in the goods-markets in dollars, may prefer to do it in proportion α, and exchange a proportion $(1-\alpha)$ for pesos at the central bank. It is rational to do so when the same goods are available in the markets in pesos at a lower price than in the markets in dollars (at the ruling exchange rate e^*). The pattern of circulation is now given by Figure 16.3.

Nothing changes for the central bank: it still captures the totality of R, in proportion α through the goods-markets in dollars (*via* firms), and $(1-\alpha)$ through foreign exchange operations with households. For firms, however, the budget constraint now reads:

$$W \leq C + e^*(1-\alpha)\,R + e\,[(1/e^*)(W-C) + \alpha\,R] \qquad (6)$$

Hence:

$$(W-C)\,(e^*-e)/e^* \leq R\,[e^*\,(1-\alpha) + e\,\alpha] \qquad (7)$$

The situation of the firms is made easier by the fact that a proportion $(1-\alpha)$ of the private resources in dollars now generates receipts in pesos for them at the exchange rate e^* (obtained by the households) instead of the lower e (imposed on the firms). One may check that if $\alpha = 1$, condition (7) is reduced to (4).

Now that households as a whole are both supplying and demanding dollars against pesos at the central bank, it may be interesting to focus on the value of e^* that would clear these private foreign exchange transactions, without any active intervention of the bank. Let us call this value e^{**}, which is given by:

$$e^{**} = (W - C)/R (1 - \alpha) \tag{8}$$

Subtracting the left-hand side of (6) (i.e. the wage-cost in pesos of total production) from the right-hand side (i.e. the total receipts in pesos by firms) gives the profits Π of the firms in pesos, which, for $e^* = e^{**}$, are:

$$\Pi = e R \tag{9}$$

This result is not surprising: because e^{**} clears the 'informal foreign exchange market' for the population, all private resources in dollars are channelled to the central bank through the goods-markets in dollars and, after the conversion in pesos at the exchange rate e, they provide firms with additional money-receipts, above the reflux of the wage-cost. But this also means that the pattern of circulation is viable even with an exchange duality; that is, two different exchange rates, one for the firms (e) and one for the households (e^*). The level of e^* given by (8) is not the only one that is consistent with a given e and the values of the parameters W, C, R and α. A more precise study of condition (7) is necessary to determine the viability zone of the pattern of circulation (see Deleplace, 2003). But this particular example with $e^* = e^{**}$ shows that the uniqueness of the exchange rate is not a necessary condition for the viability of partial dollarisation, which is consistent with the administrative fixing of at least one of the two exchange rates (here, e).

Stability

If monetary duality in Cuba is viable, can it be stable in the long run? The available studies show a steady progress of dollarisation during the past few years, up to levels (more than 70 per cent of inter-firm sales and nearly 60 per cent of sales to the population) that are steadily increasing. From 1996 to 2002, the yearly growth rate of sales in hard-currency stores has been on average four times the GDP growth rate (Hidalgo and Doimeadios, 2003; Marquetti, 2003). This means that households tend to increase the amount of earned pesos that they exchange for dollars at the central bank or in the black market, and also the proportion of their private resources in dollars that they spend directly in the goods-markets in dollars. In equation (8), both $(W - C)$ and α tend to increase, and this pushes e^{**} upwards; that is, they create a long-term tendency to the depreciation of the peso.

This result, however, seems to be contradicted by the observation that, as noted above, the exchange rate of the dollar for the population has remained fairly stable during this period of expanded dollarisation, at least until the end of 2001 (and, even then, with a slight increase from 23 to 26–27 pesos to the dollar). The explanation of this surprising stability lies in the fact that, from the very beginning, actual e^* had been administered by the central bank at a level significantly higher than the market-clearing rate e^{**} (maybe twice as high, since the deviation from the domestic purchasing power parity is around this magnitude; see Deleplace, 2003). Therefore the (hidden) increase in the market-clearing exchange rate of the dollar e^{**} did not reflect in the central-bank rate e^*. To put it another way, the initial deliberate undervaluation of the peso had opened a margin for a depreciation that would be inescapable when dollarisation spread out, but unobservable in the central-bank rate.

Conclusion

At the applied level, the study of the pattern of circulation that illustrates monetary duality in Cuba leads to an ambivalent conclusion. On the one hand, this kind of partial dollarisation combined with a centrally-controlled economy appears to be viable. The coexistence of two units of account and two means of payment in separate goods-markets is consistent with two different exchange rates (one for firms, one for the population) and positive profits for firms, under the double condition of exogenous resources in dollars and arbitrage opportunities for households. On the other hand, the dollarisation process generates by itself an endogenous tendency to the depreciation of the national currency (the 'national peso'), which will make it difficult in the future to achieve the official objective of replacing the dollar with a convertible peso and exposes Cuba to the risk of a complete and irreversible dollarisation.

The role devoted in the model to the behaviour of households may seem at odds with the monetary theory of production, which stresses producers' sovereignty instead of consumers' sovereignty. However, the fact that the share of production and consumption transacted in dollars steadily increases in Cuba, in spite of the attractive exchange rate for the dollar offered to the population by the central bank, shows that consumer choices are in fact constrained by the behaviour of firms, which direct an ever greater part of their production to the markets in dollars. When an arbitrage option exists for households, they take advantage of it, and this explains why part of the private resources in dollars are exchanged for pesos; but this is a secondary phenomenon.

The main implication of this study in applied economics for the monetary theory of production is this: when the money flow generated by the payment of wages is not consistent with the money aggregate value of consumer goods, this results in monetary instability. This inconsistency is the consequence of the fact that all wages are paid in pesos, while a growing part of production is supplied by firms against dollars, and the instability takes the form of the depreciation of the national currency vis-à-vis the dollar. But this conclusion has a more general character, which is rooted in the long-standing tradition stressing the necessity of appropriate proportions in the pattern of monetary circulation.

Notes

1. A more detailed analysis of the dollarisation process in Cuba may be found in Deleplace (2003); see also Kildegard and Orro Fernandez (1999), CEPAL (2000), Ritter and Rowe (2000); Hidalgo, Tabares, and Doimeadios (2002), Marquès-Pereira and Théret (2002), Marquetti (2002, 2003), Hidalgo and Doimeadios (2003).
2. From now on, the term *peso* will designate the 'national peso', to be distinguished from the (literally speaking) *convertible peso*.
3. There is an exception for foreign or jointly-owned companies, which may transfer abroad the dollars they earn under particular conditions.
4. One also finds the term 'informal exchange market' to designate these 'institutional channels'; the 'informality' comes from the fact that the exchange rate in this 'market' is not the 'official' one applied to firms.
5. In March 2003, the buying price of the dollar by CADECA was 26 pesos and the selling price of the convertible peso was 27 pesos.

References

Banco Central de Cuba (2001) *Informe economico 2000* (La Habana: BCC).
Bordo, M.D. (1999) *The Gold Standard and Related Regimes* (Cambridge University Press).
Boyer-Xambeu, M.-T., Deleplace, G. and Gillard, L. (1994) *Private Money and Public Currencies. The 16th Century Challenge* (Armonk, New York: M.E. Sharpe).
CEPAL (2000) *La economia cubana. Reformas estructuralesy desempeño en los novenia* (Mexico: Fondo de cultura economica).
Deleplace, G. (2003) 'A Model of the Dollarised Cuban Economy', mimeo, 20th Symposium on Banking and Monetary Economics, Birmingham University (Paris: LED).
Deleplace, G. (2004) 'Monetary Stability and Heterodoxy: A History of Economic Thought Perspective', in R. Arena and N. Salvadori (eds), *Money, Credit, and the Role of the State. Essays in Honour of Augusto Graziani* (Aldershot: Ashgate), pp. 45–62.
Hidalgo, V. and Doimeadios, Y. (2003) 'Dualidad monetaria en Cuba: causas y implicaciones de politica economica', mimeo (La Habana: Universidad de La Habana).
Hidalgo, V., Tabares, L. and Doimeadios, Y. (2002) 'El debate sobre regimenes cambiarios en economias dolarizadas: el caso de Cuba', in O. Everleny (ed.), *Cuba: reflexiones sobre su economia* (La Habana: Universidad de La Habana), pp. 15–64.
Kildegard, A.C. and Orro Fernandez, R. (1999) 'Dollarization in Cuba and implications for the future transition', *Cuba in Transition*, 9, pp. 25–30.
Marquès-Pereira, J. and Théret, B. (2002) 'La couleur du dollar. Enquête à La Havane', *Critique internationale*, 17, pp. 81–103.
Marquetti, H. (2002) 'Cuba: el nuevo patron de crecimiento de la industria manufacturera', in O. Everleny (ed.), *Cuba: reflexiones sobre su economia* (La Habana: Universidad de La Habana), pp. 119–57.
Marquetti, H. (2003) 'Dolarizacion de la economia cubana: Impacto y perspectivas', mimeo (La Habana: Centro de Estudios de la Economia Cubana).
Ritter, A.R. and Rowe, N. (2000) 'Cuba: From "Dollarization" to "Euroization" or Peso-ReConsolidation?', mimeo (Ottawa: Carleton University).
Wilson, T. (2000) *Battles for the Standard* (Aldershot: Ashgate).

17
Lessons from Asset-Based Financial Systems with Zero-Reserve Requirements*
Marc Lavoie

Although Augusto Graziani has devoted a large number of his works to the notion of endogenous money, there is little to be found about the behaviour of the central bank. This in itself is not surprising, since most writers of the circuit school have paid no attention to the role of central banks. Most analyses of the monetary circuit are set within a kind of pure Wicksellian economy, closed and without a government. The links between commercial banks and the central bank, as well as the interdependence between the decisions of the central bank and the non-financial sectors, are thus left aside.

By contrast, post-Keynesian writers, in particular American ones, have devoted a great deal of attention to the relationships between the central bank and the commercial banks, in particular to the question of reserves – compulsory reserves and reserve-constrained economies. One could speculate at length on the causes of this divergence, but I will bring forth here what seems to me an obvious explanation.

Most circuit writers come from two countries that, according to the distinction made by Hicks (1974), are based on overdraft financial systems – Italy and France. 'The overdraft economy is defined by a double level of indebtedness: that of the firms to the banks and of the banks to the central bank' (Renversez, 1996, p. 475). We are concerned here about the latter link, whereas Graziani and circuit writers in general are concerned with the former. A large proportion of the assets of these overdraft central banks are made up of claims over their domestic banking sector – the advances made to commercial banks. Before the advent of the euro and the European Central Bank, claims on banks by the Bank of France represented about 70 per cent

---

* This chapter has benefited from the financial assistance of C-FEPS, the Center for Full Employment and Price Stability, located at the University of Missouri in Kansas City. The author thanks Kevin Clinton, Marina Colonna and Warren Mosler for their comments.

of its total domestic claims, while the claims on banks by the Bank of Italy represented about 15 per cent of its total domestic claims. In terms of overall central bank assets, claims on banks represented 25 per cent and 10 per cent respectively. As one would expect, advances to credit institutions still play a large role in Euroland. Lending to banks in the consolidated financial statement of the Eurosystem still represents between 25 and 30 per cent of its total assets.

When circuit theorists were developing their ideas, it was quite obvious to all that overdraft financial systems imply that the supply of high-powered money is endogenous, and responds to the needs of demand. In France, commercial banks hardly held any Treasury bills. The only means to acquire banknotes or compulsory reserves was to borrow them from the central bank, as had been shown in detail by Le Bourva (1992 [1962]). The central bank thus had to provide the required high-powered money through the discount window, but at the interest cost of its choice. Since the supply of high-powered money is so obviously endogenous and demand-led under these conditions, this would explain why circuit authors paid little attention to it. Indeed, in Graziani's own work, when he discusses the balance sheet of commercial banks, Graziani (2003, p. 93) assumes that banks carry no treasury bills and have debts towards the central bank.

I have argued previously that the supply of high-powered money in the so-called financial market economy (or asset-based financial system) is just as fully endogenous as it is under overdraft systems (Lavoie, 1992, p. 169). I made the claim that 'the logic of a monetary production economy is such that the consequences of an overdraft economy also apply to an economy with open market operations... whatever the actual financial institutions' (Lavoie, 1992, p. 179). My claim then was that Anglo-Saxon monetary systems, dominated by asset-based financial systems, had more complex institutional features that hid the reversed causality and the essential mechanism of the endogenous supply of high-powered money.

The prevailing view, however, among mainstream 'overdraft' economists, and implicitly among some members of the so-called Post Keynesian structuralist approach, is that while the supply of high-powered money is endogenous in an overdraft economy, it is not the case in an asset-based economy. Renversez (1996, p. 475), for instance, claims that the functioning of the monetary system in an overdraft economy is 'different from that achieved under the control of the central bank in the financial market economy.... The intervention of the central bank is discretionary in the financial markets economy, but it is obligatory in the overdraft economy'.

The purpose of this chapter is to take advantage of the institutional changes that arose within the North-American financial systems in the 1990s, which help to cut through the complexities of asset-based financial systems. The new procedures put in place by the Federal Reserve System and the Bank of Canada illustrate quite clearly, to those who are not blinded by mainstream textbook presentations of central banking, the endogenous nature of the supply of high-powered money. They show that short-term interest rates are the exogenous variable under the control of central banks. The central banks do not, nor can they, control any monetary aggregate. The supply of high-powered money, even in Anglo-Saxon countries with asset-based financial systems, is fully endogenous, in the revolutionary sense defined by Rochon (1999, p. 63).

I start by describing the Canadian monetary system. This will then be compared to the situation occurring in the US. The comparison will allow us to understand why some American Post Keynesian authors came to believe that the federal funds rate was not really under the control of the Federal Reserve, and why they thought the central bank could somehow constrain the amount of reserves.

Zero-reserve requirements at the Bank of Canada

Prior to 1991, Canada had a textbook monetary system. Commercial banks faced reserve ratios on their deposits, advances to banks at the discount window were strongly discouraged, and open market operations by the Bank of Canada were frequent. Discussions on the possibility of implementing monetary policy with highly reduced reserve and even zero-reserve requirements started in September 1987 (Bank of Canada, 1987, 1991). A first step towards this process was implemented in 1991, when the frequency of advances or loans to commercial banks became unrestricted (with the appropriate collateral) and left to a new price mechanism designed by the staff at the Bank of Canada. While bank deposits at the Bank still did not pay interest, advances that lasted through the averaging period were costed at twice the discount rate. The purpose of such a move was to insure that the opportunity cost of holding excess reserves was about equal to the opportunity cost of central bank advances (relative to returns on alternatives).

It was known however that this new system was only a transitory one. Compulsory reserve requirements were progressively diminished, until they were completely dismantled in mid-1994 (Clinton, 1997, p. 14). The focus of monetary policy moved away from the treasury bill rate, towards the overnight rate. A 50 basis points operating band for the overnight rate was put in place in 1994, and in 1996 the Bank rate was set at the upper end of the operating band, to provide more clarity as to the intentions of the Bank (Lundrigan and Toll, 1997–98, p. 36). A second round of discussion took place in 1995, when the present system, dealing with electronic large-value payments, was designed (Bank of Canada, 1995). It was implemented in 1999. The term 'reserves' was struck out and replaced by the expression 'settlement balances' (in the USA, they are called 'clearing balances'). An official target overnight rate was put in place. This rate is in the middle of the operating band. Its upper limit is the Bank rate (the discount rate), at which commercial banks can borrow settlement balances (reserves); its lower limit is the rate on positive settlement balances – the rate paid on bank deposits at the central bank.

In Canada, as in New Zealand, the amount of high-powered money is now limited to the amount of banknotes held by the general public or in the vaults of commercial banks. There are no compulsory reserves. In addition, one can say that there are virtually no reserves of any kind. Bank deposits at the Bank of Canada are normally zero. This in itself should help to demonstrate that the supply of high-powered money is fully endogenous. High-powered money in these countries is only made up of banknotes (issued by the central bank). Besides extraordinary situations such as the one that occurred in Argentina in 2001–02, it is difficult to imagine that the supply of bank notes through automatic teller machines would be restricted by the central bank. Whenever commercial banks need banknotes to feed their machines, as a result of the demand for banknotes arising from their customers, they are being provided by the central bank. Indeed, as noted by a researcher at the Bank of Canada, 'withdrawals of bank notes from the central bank are made as needed by the clearing institutions' (Clinton, 1991, p. 7).

The operations of the settlements system

In Canada, as in many other countries, banks and other direct clearers are required by law to settle their payment obligations on accounts at the Bank of Canada (Goodlet, 1997). If there were no transactions with the public sector, or with the foreign exchange fund, the level of net settlement balances would always be zero. Since any debit for a bank corresponds to a credit for some other bank, the net amount of settlement balances in this pure credit economy cannot be any different from zero. By contrast, the gross amount of settlement balances would vary according to the dispersion in incoming and outgoing payment flows between banks. A given amount of transactions can give rise to widely different amounts of gross settlement balances.

However, as has been emphasised recently by members of the neo-chartalist school, the situation is modified when government transactions are entered into the clearing system, or when the central bank intervenes on foreign exchange markets (Mosler, 1997–98; Wray, 1998; Bell, 2000; Bell and Wray, 2002–3). As is well known, when the central bank purchases foreign currency to keep the exchange rate fixed, this adds to the reserves or the settlement balances of commercial banks. Similarly, when governments pay for their expenditures, by making cheques on their central bank account, which are later deposited at banks, these transfers add to reserves. By contrast, when private agents pay their taxes by writing a cheque to the government, this transaction withdraws reserves or settlement balances from the financial system once the cheque is deposited in the government account at the central bank. Similarly, when banks acquire banknotes, this reduces their settlement balances.

The Bank of Canada normally acts in such a way that the level of settlement balances in the financial system by the end of the day is exactly equal to zero. 'To maintain the level of settlement balances at zero, the Bank must neutralize the net impact of any public sector flows between the Bank of Canada's balance sheet and that of the financial system' (Howard, 1998, p. 59). To achieve this, the Bank transfers government deposits in and out of its own accounts, towards or from, government deposit accounts held at various commercial banks.

The Bank effects such neutralisation late in the afternoon, after all settlement transactions with the government are completed. When the Bank makes its final cash management decisions, it knows with perfect certainty the amounts that need to be transferred between government accounts at the Bank and government accounts at commercial banks to achieve complete neutralisation of the public sector flows. In addition, early in the morning, when most of the clearing transactions occur, the Bank offers open-market operations (in the form of overnight repos or reverse repos, called sale and repurchase agreements and special purchase and resale agreements in Canada), at the target rate, to keep the market overnight rate on target. This often has the effect of promptly neutralising government flows. For instance, on a day when tax receipts are high (a drain on the system liquidity), the Bank will be providing central bank credit from the outset.

In terms of standard terminology, one could say that these transfers of government deposits and open-market operations are part of the 'defensive' operations of the Bank of Canada. As Eichner *et al.* (1985, p. 101) put it, 'this is the neutralising component of a fully accommodating policy'. I argue that it cannot be otherwise. There is an overall demand for high-powered money, exactly equal to the demand for banknotes, to which the central bank responds by providing the precise amount being demanded. The extent and the importance of these 'defensive' operations are nothing new. Prior to the implementation of the new procedures, the Bank already knew with a good degree of accuracy the amount of defensive operations that were required (Clinton, 1991, pp. 7–8).

The determination of the overnight interest rate

There are two substantial changes between the new procedures and the previous ones. First, banks are given the opportunity to get rid of their surplus settlement balances, or to wipe out their negative settlement balances (their day overdraft at the Bank of Canada), by being able to have a last go on the overnight market in the evening, when they know with certainty what their clearing balances are (this is the so-called pre-settlement period). This allows banks to have day overdrafts only, and to avoid the discount window. Secondly, the central bank now knows with perfect certainty not only the amount of settlement balances being supplied but also its demand.

Previously, when compulsory reserves were still required and averaged through the month, the daily demand for settlement balances by the banks could vary, with the Bank being unable to predict the changes. This was because the daily demand for reserves was responsive to interest rates.

This reflected mainly two factors: 'First, that uncertainty about the results of the clearings creates a precautionary demand to hold reserves in excess of minimum requirements; and second that reserve averaging allows the banks some flexibility in respond to expected changes in overnight rates' (Clinton, 1991, p. 9). If overnight rates were expected to move up in the future, the demand for reserves would move up, in an attempt to accumulate excess reserves that could be depleted at a later stage of the averaging period, when their cost would be higher. This made the overnight rate fluctuate, as demand moved around the demand for settlement balances expected by the Bank of Canada, and hence the amount of non-borrowed reserves supplied by the Bank. Any adjustment had to be carried through either by changes in borrowed reserves or in changes in the overnight interest rate.

None of this, or very little of it, occurs with the new rules. The new procedures ensure a determinate demand for settlement balances. First, banks need not play any games about expected clearing positions or about future expected overnight rates as there are no averaging provisions anymore, since no amount of reserves need to be held. Secondly, the Bank has put in place 'incentives that motivate the banking system to target zero settlement balances at the central bank' (Clinton, 1997, p. 4). As already pointed out, there is symmetry in the opportunity cost of being in an overdraft position vis-à-vis the central bank and in holding a reserve deposit at the Bank. Overnight rates, repos rates and treasury bill rates are normally in the mid-range between the Bank rate on overdrafts and the rate paid on deposits at the central bank. This mid-range is the target overnight rate, publicly announced by the central bank. This encourages banks to rely on the overnight market to obtain or get rid of their excess settlement balances.

The overall demand for settlement balances is thus equal to zero, in normal circumstances, since no surplus-clearing bank will desire to keep its surplus balances as deposits at the central bank, while no deficit-clearing bank will rely on advances that can be granted on demand by the Bank of Canada, since settlement balances can be borrowed or lent at a rate that is somewhat half-way in between the rates that could be obtained from the Bank. In the worst of circumstances, the overnight rate cannot be any higher than the Bank rate, for otherwise deficit banks would prefer to get central bank advances. Similarly, the overnight rate cannot fall any lower than the rate on deposits at the central bank for, otherwise, surplus banks would all put their surplus balances on the accounts of the Bank of Canada. Supply of and demand for settlement balances would readjust to each other.

Clinton (1997, p. 11) argues that in normal times both the supply and the demand for settlement balances are given by a vertical line arising from the zero level of settlement balances. 'Since equality of demand and supply is represented by the intersection of two vertical lines (at zero quantity), on any given day the precise overnight rate at which the market settles is indeterminate within the 50-basis-point operating band. The actual rate will be influenced by a variety of technical factors, such as the size and distribution of clearing imbalances among the banks'.

The overnight rate of interest could thus be any rate within the operating band. In a truly competitive market, however, one would expect the overnight rate to be right in the middle of the operating band. If the target overnight rate is set as the mid-point of the operating band, there is thus some likelihood that it will be exactly realised. Under non-competitive conditions, or if some banks are viewed as less credit-worthy than others, the overnight rate might be different from the target set by the Bank of Canada. For instance, if deficit-clearing banks happen to be the less credit-worthy, there is a chance that the overnight rate would exceed the mid-range point. Also, if a single bank holds positive settlement balances, while all others are in a negative position, the surplus-clearing bank may take advantage of its monopoly status and the overnight rate could be higher than the target overnight rate.

In reality, it turns out that the overnight market rate is systematically equal to the target rate set by the Bank of Canada. With the new procedures, tied to zero-reserve requirements, near-perfect certainty on the demand for settlement balances and absolute control over the supply of settlement balances, the Bank is able to control the overnight rate to the tune of one basis point. Over the course of sixty days preceding the writing of chapter, the overnight rate was either exactly equal to its target, or one basis point below it, except one day, when if was off by four basis points. When target rates are changed, overnight rates move instantaneously to their new position. For instance, on 3 September 2003, the target rate was moved down from 3.00 per cent to 2.75 per cent. On the same day, the actual overnight rate dropped to 2.75 per cent.

Another feature worth noting is that overnight rates change in response to target rates without central banks having to add or subtract any amount of settlement balances. This has been noted for other countries as well, under the name of 'open-mouth operations' (Guthrie and Wright, 2000). In the Canadian case, the Bank of Canada keeps targeting zero settlement balances, even when a new rate is announced. The associated changes in the rates of the overnight credit and deposit facilities at the central bank are sufficient to enforce the new rate on the interbank money market. In general, there is no specific need to intervene on the repos market. The target rate set by the central bank, with its operating band, provides an anchor to the financial system. The anchor is credible because the Bank of Canada has the capacity to enforce it. If the overnight rate were to wander away from the target, the Bank could get it back on track.

The above analysis clearly shows that reserves are fully endogenous. The Bank of Canada supplies high-powered money by fully responding to the demand for it; that is, by providing banknotes whenever banks require them. The fact that no reserves are required anymore, and that cost incentives have been put in place that encourage banks to hold neither positive nor negative settlement balances, makes the endogeneity of high-powered money very clear. In addition, it is quite flagrant that the control variable of central banks is the overnight rate of interest. The Bank of Canada sets the target overnight rate, and the actual overnight rate adjusts to it within the day, either right on the dot, or one or two basis points above or below it. As Wray (1998, p. 107) correctly concludes, 'the Canadian system makes central bank operations more transparent – reserves are not a lever to be used to control the money supply. The Bank of Canada intervenes to keep net settlement balances at zero, an operation that by its very nature must be defensive.'

This is precisely the argument that I wish to make. In the case of the overdraft economy, it is undeniable that reserves are being provided on demand by the central bank. It is not so obvious in an asset-based financial system. But in systems such as the Canadian one, which is an asset-based financial system, the veil of open market operations is superseded by the transparency of the zero-reserve requirements. It becomes nearly as evident that the day-to-day role of the central bank is to provide on demand the required level of high-powered money. High-powered money is a fully endogenous variable, while the overnight rate is the exogenous interest rate, determined by the target rate set by the Bank of Canada. Within such a system commercial banks cannot be reserve-constrained.

The case of the American financial system

The argument that I wish to make here is that the American financial system obeys the same logical requirements that rule overdraft economies or financial systems with zero-reserve requirements. Some Post Keynesians pointed out long ago that open market operations had little or nothing to do with monetary policy. For instance, Eichner *et al.* (1985, p. 100) start their article by making the following statement: 'It is usually assumed that a change in the Fed's holdings of government securities will lead to a change, with the same sign attached, in the reserves of the commercial banking system. It was the failure to observe this relationship empirically which led us, in constructing the monetary-financial block of our model, to try to find some other way of representing the effect of the Fed's open market operations on the banking system.' That other way is that 'the Fed's purchases or sales of government securities are intended primarily to offset the flows into or out of the domestic monetary-financial system' (Eichner, 1987, p. 849).

Throughout most of its history, the Federal Reserve System has acted on the premise that its main role in the financial system is to conduct 'defensive' operations, since the monetary base is an endogenous variable beyond its direct control. Even when the Fed had monetary targets, these targets were implemented through the estimation of a money demand function; this estimate led the Fed to target unannounced federal funds rates, and the game was to guess the Fed's target overnight rate. In 1987, the Fed reverted to official federal funds rate targeting, and that rate became publicly announced in 1994. In the USA, as in Canada, there has been a move towards greater transparency, removing the scaffolding that hid the true monetary operations of the central bank. As Mosler (2002, p. 419) points out, 'the Federal Open Market Committee's target has been the focus of activity under previous Fed policies as well, and the difference is that prior to 1994 the target rate was known only within the Fed, whereas currently it is disclosed to the general public'.

It is now much more obvious that the Fed is mainly pursuing 'interest maintenance operations' (Mosler, 1997–98, p. 170; Wray, 1998, p. 87). Again, neo-chartalist Post Keynesians have made this quite clear over the last years. For instance, Wray (1998, p. 115) claims that 'Fed actions with regards to quantities of reserves are necessarily defensive. The only discretion the Fed has is in interest rate determination'. Similarly, Mosler (1997–98, p. 170) writes that 'as a practical matter, the Fed can only react to required legal reserve imbalances that threaten to alter the targeted federal funds rate. The Fed does not have the option to act proactively to add or drain reserves to directly alter the monetary base.'

Still, in the USA there have been important fluctuations in the overnight rate, relative to the federal funds rate target. Taylor (2001, p. 36) reports that the standard deviation of the spread between the federal funds rate and its target has been 18 basis points over the 1998–2000 period. Similar deviations between the target rate and the actual overnight rate have been observed with the new European Central Bank. Nonetheless, over the last years, the average federal funds rate is virtually equal to its average target rate.

In view of these results, it is easier to understand why some American Post Keynesians are reluctant to recognise that reserves are fully endogenous and that interest rates are set exogenously by central banks. In the USA, as in Europe, the central banks do not appear to have full control over the shortest of the rates – the overnight rate. Interest rates under the control of the central bank do not appear to be truly exogenous. Their levels seem to depend on the interaction between the demand for and the supply of reserves. It should be noted that this feature of the American system was underlined by the major proponent of exogenous interest rates. In his book, Moore (1988, p. 124) wrote that 'the federal funds rate is predetermined within a small range, ordinarily within fifty or sixty basis points ... It is not *directly* set by the Fed ... It is ... disingenuous and misleading to declare that the funds rate is now "market-determined". Market forces are really attempting to forecast the behavior of the Fed itself.'

My interpretation of all this is the following. The Fed is pursuing essentially defensive operations, just like the Bank of Canada. The difference is that the Fed does not have perfect information about the drains on reserves that must be compensated for, nor does it have perfect information about the daily or even hourly demand for free reserves or for discount window borrowing; as a result, the Fed cannot perfectly equate supply to demand at the target funds rate (or at the actual rate). As Sellon and Weiner (1997, p. 18) put it, 'the size of a daily surplus or shortage in the settlement system depends, in large part, on the central bank's ability to estimate settlement bank demand for settlement balances'.

One cause of this is the averaging provisions, that encourage banks to speculate about daily or even hourly evolutions of the federal funds rate, by modifying their demand for reserves. The markets try to anticipate changes in the target rate, and they try to anticipate the evolution of the federal funds rate around the target rate. As pointed out by Mosler (2002, p. 420), 'this is in sharp contrast to the notion often supported by the media that market rates, rather than anticipating Fed action, contain information as to where the Fed should target the federal funds rate'. In the USA, over the reserve-averaging period, the Fed supplies high-powered money on demand, as in overdraft economies or in zero-reserve financial systems, but it is unable to do so perfectly on a day-to-day basis. In other words, the apparent 'non-defensive' operations arise inadvertently.

Conclusion

After a long intermission, central bankers are coming back to the view that movements in money aggregates or in the monetary base contain no useful information for monetary policy; they are a sideshow – 'a meaningless abstraction', as Albert Wojnilower (1980, p. 324) once put it. The new proced-ures put in place in Canada are particularly enlightening. Central banks do not attempt to control the monetary base. The latter is entirely demand-determined. The monetary operations of central banks are entirely defensive. Their purpose is precisely to ensure that the supply of high-powered money is exactly equal to its demand, at the target interest rate of their choice. The central bank may also intervene in specific markets, besides the repo market, to make sure that interest rates in certain specific markets are in line with the target overnight rate. Monetary operations are always interest rate maintenance operations.

Thus, one must distinguish between 'defensive' and 'accommodating' behaviour. In my opinion, central banks pursue defensive operations at all times, as emphasized by the neo-chartalist authors. On the other hand, central banks can be accommodating or not. When they are, they will peg the interest rate, whatever the economic conditions (or they might reduce it). When they are not accommodating – that is, when they are pursuing 'dynamic' operations as Victoria Chick (1977, p. 89) calls them – central banks will increase interest rates. As shown above, to do so, they need simply announce a new higher target overnight rate. The actual overnight rate will gravitate towards this new anchor within the day of the announcement. No change whatsoever in the supply of high-powered money is required. 'Money is in some sense endogenous whether central banks are dynamic or not' (Lavoie, 1984, p. 778).

References

Bank of Canada (1987) 'Discussion paper on the implementation of monetary policy in the absence of reserve requirements', September 29, Bank of Canada.

Bank of Canada (1991) 'The implementation of monetary policy in a system with zero reserve requirements', *Bank of Canada Review*, May, pp. 23–31.

Bank of Canada (1995) 'A proposed framework for the implementation of monetary policy in the Large Value Transfer System environment', Discussion Paper I, Bank of Canada.

Bell, S. (2000) 'Do taxes and bonds finance government spending?', *Journal of Economic Issues*, September, 34 (3), pp. 603–20.

Bell, S. and Wray, L.R. (2002–3) 'Fiscal effects on reserves and the independence of the Fed', *Journal of Post Keynesian Economics*, Winter, 25 (2), pp. 263–72.

Chick, V. (1977) *The Theory of Monetary Policy* (Oxford: Parkgate Books).

Clinton, K. (1991) 'Bank of Canada cash management: the main technique for implementing monetary policy', *Bank of Canada Review*, January, pp. 3–32.

Clinton, K. (1997) 'Implementation of monetary policy in a regime with zero reserve requirements', Working Paper 97–8, Bank of Canada.

Eichner, A.S. (1987) *The Macrodynamics of Advanced Market Economies* (Armonk: M.E. Sharpe).

Eichner, A.S., Forman, L. and Groves, M. (1985) 'The demand for money further reconsidered', in A.S. Eichner (ed.), *Toward a New Economics: Essays in Post-Keynesian and Institutionalist Theory* (London: Macmillan), pp. 98–112.

Goodlet, C. (1997) 'Clearing and settlement systems and the Bank of Canada', *Bank of Canada Review*, Autumn, pp. 49–64.

Graziani, A. (2003) *The Monetary Theory of Production* (Cambridge University Press).

Guthrie, G. and Wright, J. (2000), 'Open mouth operations', *Journal of Monetary Economics*, 46 (2), pp. 489–516.

Hicks, J. (1974) *The Crisis in Keynesian Economics* (Oxford: Blackwell).

Howard, D. (1998) 'A primer on the implementation of monetary policy in the LVTS environment', *Bank of Canada Review*, Autumn, pp. 57–66.

Lavoie, M. (1984) 'The endogenous flow of credit and the Post Keynesian theory of money', *Journal of Economic Issues*, September, 18 (3), pp. 771–98.

Lavoie, M. (1992) *Foundations of Post-Keynesian Economic Analysis* (Aldershot: Edward Elgar).

Le Bourva, J. (1992) 'Money creation and money multipliers', *Review of Political Economy*, 4 (4), pp. 447–66.

Lundrigan, E. and Toll, S. (1997–98) 'The overnight market in Canada', *Bank of Canada Review*, Winter, 27–42.

Moore, B.J. (1988) *Horizontalists and Verticalists: The Macroeconomics of Credit Money* (Cambridge University Press).

Mosler, W. (1997–98) 'Full employment and price stability', *Journal of Post Keynesian Economics*, Winter, 20 (2), pp. 167–82.

Mosler, W. (2002) 'A critique of John B. Taylor's 'Expectations, open market operations, and changes in the federal funds rate', *Journal of Post Keynesian Economics*, Spring, 24 (3), 419–22.

Renversez, F. (1996) 'Monetary circulation and overdraft economies', in G. Deleplace and E.J. Nell (eds), *Money in Motion: The Post Keynesian and Circulation Approaches* (London: Macmillan), pp. 465–88.

Rochon, L.P. (1999) *Credit, Money and Production: An Alternative Post-Keynesian Approach* (Cheltenham: Edward Elgar).

Sellon, G.H. and Weiner, S.E. (1997) 'Monetary policy without reserve requirements: case studies and options for the United States', *Federal Reserve Bank of Kansas City Economic Review*, 82 (2), pp. 5–30.

Taylor, J.B. (2001) 'Expectations, open market operations and changes in the federal funds rate', *Federal Reserve Bank of St. Louis Review*, July–August, 83 (4), pp. 33–48.

Wojnilower, A.M. (1980) 'The central role of credit crunches in recent financial history', *Brookings Papers on Economic Activity*, (2), pp. 277–326.

Wray, L.R. (1998) *Understanding Modern Money: The Key to Full Employment and Price Stability* (Cheltenham: Edward Elgar).

18
Interest Rates, Interest Spreads and Monetary Circulation: Theoretical Framework and Empirical Implications for Macroeconomic Performance

*Mario Seccareccia**

Introduction

Traditional neoclassical macroeconomics confers an important position to interest rates in determining macroeconomic activity but pays little attention to the possible role of interest spreads. In contrast, as Augusto Graziani (1987, p. 25; 2003, p. 123) makes it abundantly clear, the relation among subsets of the vast array of interest rates in a modern monetary economy may be of critical significance, especially since these rates pertain to different aspects of the process of monetary circulation. Indeed, as soon as one adopts a circuitist perspective where credit relations are crucial and where, inter alia, the distinction, made famous by Graziani (1987), between *initial* and *final* finance, becomes relevant, suddenly the relations among the various rates associated with the flux/reflux process take on new meaning and offer insights that were hitherto inconceivable within traditional macroeconomic analysis. The object of this chapter is to discuss how some of these interest rates are envisioned within the framework of the monetary circuit, and what theoretical and empirical implications changes in both levels and interest spreads could have on macroeconomic performance.

* With the usual disclaimer applying, the author would like to thank Carlo Giannone, Marc Lavoie, Warren Mosler, Alain Parguez and Louis-Philippe Rochon for their very helpful comments.

Brief historical digression: Wicksell's model of monetary circulation and some original insights from Robinson to Nell

The monetary circuit approach has its historical antecedents in the works of nineteenth-century banking theorists and of Marx. However, it is in the writings of Wicksell that the logic of that framework was best articulated, especially with regards to the role that interest rates and, more precisely, interest spreads played in the flux/reflux process. With the obvious exception of Keynes in *Treatise on Money*, Wicksell's work primarily influenced a large number of continental writers in Austria and Germany, such as Schumpeter and Neisser (see Graziani, 2003).

Unfortunately, with the success of the 'bastard Keynesian' interpretation of *General Theory*, much of the postwar revival of the theory of monetary circulation belongs to Robinson (1956) who, in her *Accumulation of Capital*, was to reintroduce almost single-handedly some important key characteristics of Wicksellian analytics within a strictly Keynesian–Kaleckian framework in which firms, workers, banks and rentiers interact during both the financing stage and period of circulation (Graziani, 1989). One of the crucial implications of introducing banks as the sole purveyors of liquidity within a circuitist perspective, recognised by Robinson, is that the proceeds of firms would never be sufficient for the reflux to the banks in the form of principal plus interest, unless the banking sector itself (or the state) becomes a source of additional liquidity at least equal to the net flow of interest payments. As Graziani (1989, p. 626) shows, such recognition of the possible imbalance that could arise between firms and banks in the reflux process was of great theoretical significance, but Robinson did not pursue the analysis much further. While offering numerous intuitions relating to the theory of monetary circulation, Robinson did not fully explore the consequences of her insights, especially with regards to what is now commonly referred to as the closure of the monetary circuit.

A number of other writers in the early postwar years, such as Le Bourva and Schmitt in France, followed in Robinson's footsteps in investigating important features of the circulationist perspective. However, the work of understanding the 'short-circuiting' that could occur during the flux/reflux process was left, among others, to Nell (1967), who pointed to the part played by the interest spread in Wicksell's theory of the monetary circuit. For instance, in a four-class economy in which workers, entrepreneurs, capitalists, and bankers interact, he explains the dilemma of what within the modern literature on monetary circulation is commonly referred to as the problem of the closure of the monetary circuit. Describing credit relations among bankers, entrepreneurs and capitalists in accordance with Wicksell's original model of monetary circulation, and defining M as bank credit advances and r, the rate of interest on these loans to entrepreneurs, he argues that at the end of the production process the settling of all liabilities may not be possible:

For the banks do not have any more money than *M* [that is advanced to entrepreneurs]... Only *after* the entrepreneurs have paid them interest will they have *M + rM*; but the capitalists must have *M + rM before* the entrepreneurs pay, for the entrepreneurs cannot pay the bank unless the capitalists have bought their goods. [Emphasis in original] (Nell 1967, p. 392)

Pointing to the problem of the reflux, he shows how the timing in the payment of interest can lead to general bankruptcy where, for example, banks may be forced to foreclose on entrepreneurs. While an analysis of the unfeasibility of paying interest within a credit-money economy can be traced, for instance, to the theoretical 'underworld' of such heterodox writers as Major Douglas, the articulation of this problem within a sophisticated Wicksellian framework belongs to Nell (1967) by pointing to the role played by the interest spread between the loan and deposit rates in the monetary reflux. It is to this issue that we shall now turn by exploring the macroeconomic implications of such interest rates within the perspective of Graziani's analysis of monetary circulation.

Financial implications of the interest spread: Graziani's analytics

Graziani's research (1987, 1990, 2003) follows the path established by this earlier work and specifies an economy in which there are three sectors: households (who supply their labour and may hold financial assets), firms (who, as a group, engage in production by hiring labourers via bank credit) and banks (who supply credit requirements based on the creditworthiness of the borrowing firms). For the purpose of the analysis, we shall consider a closed economy and we shall abstract from the direct role of the state. Assuming a consolidated business sector and abstracting from other complications discussed elsewhere as to what exactly needs to be financed (Seccareccia, 1996), at the starting phase of the production cycle, business enterprises require short-term (or initial) finance that will allow them to purchase necessary working capital needed to undertake production which, for the consolidated business sector, can be reduced to the payment of wages (M). However, once production is completed and firms begin to sell their products during the circulation phase, the 'reflux' process of the monetary circuit begins, thus allowing firms to reimburse previously incurred short-term debts with banks.

As in Robinson (1956) and Nell (1967) previously discussed, the reflux to banks, equal to the principal of the loans, M, plus interest, rM, would appear at first glance as a pure macroeconomic Ponzi system, since unless firms also borrow the interest rM, they would never be able to pay back the principal *plus* interest. In reality, however, banks are not only advancing M to firms but a sum equal to $(1 + i)M + Y_b$, where i is interest on deposits and Y_b is the flow of non-interest payments made to households whose income depends on the banking sector.

Although various scenarios are possible (some having been discussed in Seccareccia, 1996, 2003), it is clear, that abstracting from the Keynesian problem of household liquidity preference, the circuit would come to a closure when the reflux $[(1+r)M=(1+r)Y]$ is equal to the efflux $[(1+i)M+Y_b]$. That is to say:

$$(1+r)M=(1+i)M+Y_b \tag{1}$$

Or simply:

$$(r-i)=Y_b/M \tag{1'}$$

Graziani (1987) is very clear about the 'short-circuiting' potential arising from the interest spread $(r-i)$. In initially abstracting from the role of Y_b (where $Y_b=0$), he writes:

> If $r=i$, receipts of firms are…equal to their debt towards banks. The situation is different if, as it is most likely to be the case, $r>i$. In this case, even if wage earners spend the whole of their incomes, firms will never be able to repay their debt. A possible way out is given by the fact that banks themselves pay wages to their own employees who spend their incomes on consumption goods or on the financial market, thus adding to the receipts of firms without adding to their outlays. Another way out consists in the possibility that banks spend on the market profits originating from the difference between r and i. If this is the case, what in fact happens is that firms are paying their interest debt partly or wholly in kind, by selling goods or securities to banks. (Graziani 1987, p. 32)

He then adds: 'If, r being greater than i, banks do not pay wages high enough or refrain from spending their profits, firms are unable to repay their debt.' (Graziani 1987, pp. 32–3). Indeed, as was also pointed out in Seccareccia (1996, p. 411), *ultimately* the closure of the circuit arises either voluntarily or involuntarily on the part of firms. The first of these possibilities, referred to by Graziani (1987) but also originally pointed out by Robinson (1956, pp. 249–50), is when Y_b, which includes wages and salaries of bank employees and management as well as dividends paid out regularly to bank shareholders, is fully spent and is equal to $(r-i)M$. In such an 'equilibrium' situation (to use Graziani's (1987) expression), firms would be able to acquire the required reflux for the reimbursements of principal and interest. On the other hand, if in the 'financial disequilibrium' situation Y_b is less than $(r-i)M$, that is to say, that the spread is too high relative to the net flow of spending from the financial sector, then banks would be foreclosing on the least creditworthy firms in the corporate sector, with accompanying losses on the part of such firms and/or banks equal to Graziani's 'financial disequilibrium' gap. This is not to suggest that foreclosing is a necessary immediate outcome. Individual banks can, for quite some time, continue to extend credit to the financially strapped firms but only at the cost, ultimately, of compromising their own bank-specific financial viability. As Graziani (2003, p. 31) concludes, 'There seems to be no way out: either a debt equal to the interest payments remains unsatisfied, or interest is paid in kind.'

It can be seen from equation (1') above that, for a given outstanding debt M, any variation in the interest spread, $(r-i)$ that is not accompanied by a concomitant movement in Y_b would quickly transform a financial equilibrium state into a disequilibrium one. Because of the stickiness in the payment of wages and dividends both in the economy at large and in the banking sector in particular, one can assume Y_b to be relatively stable over the business cycle. Assuming that i would be less responsive to central bank changes in, say, the overnight rate than r, it follows that as the labour market overheats in relation, for instance, to some assumed NAIRU, interest spreads (or bank mark-ups) would be moving pro-cyclically, thereby impacting positively on business debt. This is because, as r rises, neither i would rise proportionally, especially if banks hold some form of local monopoly vis-à-vis their depositors, nor would Y_b rise as quickly, because of wage stickiness as well as the possible institutional rigidity in the payment of dividends to bank shareholders.

Real interest rates, debt and macroeconomic performance: some further Grazianian insights

An important consequence of the above analysis is that, as long as Y_b and the deposit rates, keep up with movements in the loan rates, and there is no tendency for overall propensities to consume to change, there would be no negative consequences on firms' ability to extinguish their debts. Moreover, as he has shown at various times (see Graziani 1990, 2003), since interest is both a cost to firms as well as source of revenue, as long as private sector propensities to consume and to invest out of national income do not vary, then profits would not be affected by changes in interest rates on the securities issued by firms in the financial markets. While that may be the case when we assume that all of household income is consumed, such a result would not hold when one adopts a more realistic assumption of positive *and* differential saving propensities between workers and rentier households. If the latter is so, then, to the extent that higher interest rates are reflected in real interest rate changes in the bond market and, therefore, in a distribution of income that becomes more favourable to rentiers whose propensities to save are generally higher than wage earners, the consequence would be to slow overall growth of effective demand.

What would be the consequences of real interest rate changes in the Grazianian framework? Let us start with the situation where nominal rates are kept constant despite the appearance of inflation $(\Delta P/P)$, so that real interest rates decline. In the case in which inflation, arising, say, from wage increases triggered at the beginning of period by very tight labour markets, is financed fully within the banking system, firms in the non-financial business sector will initially be borrowing overall labour income Y_w plus an additional amount that would rise commensurate with the inflation rate ($\Delta P/P$). That is to say, the beginning-of-period 'efflux' to the non-financial business sector, M_F, is now the original wage bill, Y_w, plus the inflation rate, $\Delta P/P$ (which is assumed to be equal to the beginning-of-period change in nominal wage rates):

$$M_F = Y_w \, (1 + \Delta P/P) \tag{2}$$

Assuming no changes in propensities to consume and nominal loan and deposit rates are constant at r_0 and i_0 respectively and, for simplicity, Y_b is also initially taken as given, then at the end of the period, the reflux, M_R, to the banking sector ought to be:

$$M_R = Y_w \, (1 + r_0) \, (1 + \Delta P/P) \tag{3}$$

which would be equal to $Y_w \, (1 + i_0)(1 + \Delta P/P) + Y_b$. In this context, Graziani (2003) argues that, since prices facing producers will be rising at the same rate, overall effect on the flux/reflux process would be neutral, even though, as we can infer, real rates ($r_0 - \Delta P/P$) would have declined. Hence, in an inflationary environment, 'financial equilibrium' would be consistent with real rates falling concomitantly with the rise in prices. Moreover, in the simplest classical case in which household propensity to save is equal to zero, aggregate effective demand would not be affected. However, what if we were to assume a more realistic case in which the propensity to save out of rentier income is higher than that for wage earners? In this situation, the overall flow of aggregate demand from the household sector would now have risen somewhat, since the rentier share would be lower as a result of the fall in real interest rates.

What if, instead of allowing real rates to decline, the central bank, believing in the Fisher rule, acts to protect rentier income by keeping real interest rates constant at their initial level when inflation was zero? By targeting a constant real rate, it ensues that, since the nominal loan rate would now be $r_0 + \Delta P/P + r_0\Delta P/P$, overall bank debt by firms would be growing exponentially when defined on the basis of the beginning-of-period benchmark interest rate r_0:

$$M_F = Y_w \, (1 + r_0)(1 + \Delta P/P)^2 \tag{4}$$

Indeed, he writes:

> Inflation, if defined as a continuous increase in money prices, brings about in itself a proportional increase in the bank debt of firms. If an

increase in the rate of interest proportional to the inflation rate is added to the increase in the amount of debt, the annual financial burden falling on firms is increased in money terms by an amount equal to twice the inflation rate. In real terms, the financial burden of the firms is increased in proportion to the inflation rate. (Graziani 2003, p. 141)

Although, in the strict logic of his analysis, such an inference may be unobjectionable, Graziani (2003) concludes that not only debts would explode with the constant real rate, because of the compounding effect of the inflation rate, but also that business profits would be squeezed, because their revenues will be rising less quickly than their costs.

However, the latter conclusion would only be so if rentiers do not spend all of their interest income. In the special case where they would, it is not intuitively obvious why that conclusion would hold. This problem notwithstanding, certainly in the more realistic case where rentiers' propensity to save is high relative to that of wage earners, it follows that any central bank rule that seeks to adjust nominal interest rates to the inflation rate would have a positive effect on business costs relative to revenues and could have a negative impact on growth. Furthermore, as long as r, i and Y_b all grow in tandem with the inflation rate, $\Delta P/P$, it is not clear why Graziani (2003, p. 141) would conclude that: 'inflation produces a redistribution of profits from the firms to the banks, which implies a decline in industrial profits and an increase in financial profits.' Unless there is an asymmetry in the way inflation affects r, i and Y_b so that it could lead, say, to an increase in interest spread and thus to a change in the flux/reflux relation, it is not evident why this should raise bank profits at the expense of industrial profits. It is only when central banks seek to stabilise real interest rates at a high level or, perhaps even more importantly, in the situation witnessed during the late 1970s and 1980s, where central banks targeted *rising* real rates, that this would put further upward pressure on the growth of private debt and squeeze business profit. However, this would not necessarily favour bank profit, but primarily rentier income, unless the interest spread is positively affected, or other elements of bank revenues not addressed in this framework, such as the prices of financial services, also increase.

Some empirical insights on the effects of changes in interest spreads and real interest rates

Historically, mainstream economists, who at times even confound the rate of interest with the rate of profit, have had little to say about how changes in interest spreads can impact on economic activity, with the possible exception of those inspired by the neoclassical loanable funds approach. In more recent times, the empirical analysis of interest spreads has become somewhat more popular ever since mainstream writers, such as Bernanke, made use of spreads to predict the evolution of industrial production historically. However, followers of Bernanke, such as Barran, Coudert and Majon (1995), who have employed interest spreads for predictive purposes, have looked primarily at the spread between public and private sector returns, as indicator of default risk, on private debt in order to make inferences about the evolution of private sector macroeconomic performance.

To our knowledge, no one has employed the loan/deposit spread for such predictive purposes. In those few other cases where the spread between the lending and deposit rates has been employed, such as in Shan and Morris (2002), the spread has been interpreted as an indicator of 'financial efficiency' in the development process. Still others who directly study the banking sector and seek to explain sources of bank profits (see, for instance, Smith 1999) do inevitably examine these spreads but not to provide any analysis of their consequence on macroeconomic performance. Writers rarely focus on what heterodox economists, especially Post Keynesians, would identify the spreads between the loan and deposit rates to be (i.e., indicators of bank mark-ups, along the lines first put forth by Rousseas (1986), that can affect overall expenditure flows). In this section, we shall try therefore to address this question empirically, first, by looking at some measures of interest spreads, and then evaluating how they relate to the behaviour of output growth and business debt.

Reliable data on spreads between lending and deposit rates are not readily available for the purpose of making reasonable cross-country comparisons. For instance, consistent series from the International Monetary Fund (IMF) can be obtained for several countries, but such data are neither particularly reliable nor available for sufficiently long historical periods. Indeed, even if they are reliable, the competitive structure of banking differs greatly from one country to the other, and sources of bank revenues vary a great deal both across countries and intertemporally (for instance, in Canada, bank revenues used to be derived primarily from their interest spreads, while nowadays about half of their revenues come directly from charging service fees to the public (see Smith 1999, 18)).

For this reason, in order to illustrate the general *cyclical* evolution of interest spreads across the G-7 countries (with the exception of the United Kingdom, where data produced from the IMF was somewhat disjointed), the time series for the remaining six countries in the G-7 needed to be prefiltered in order to provide a common basis for comparison. Hence, data for Canada, France, Germany, Italy, Japan and the USA for the period 1978–2001 were first detrended using the popular Hodrick–Prescott procedure in order to capture the cyclical fluctuations in the detrended interest spread series. These detrended data for the six countries in the G-7 are illustrated in Chart 1 below.

Because we have graphed the deviations from their respective trends, the various series are depicted as gravitating around the zero value in Chart 18.1. While there is much noise in the series, especially since the six

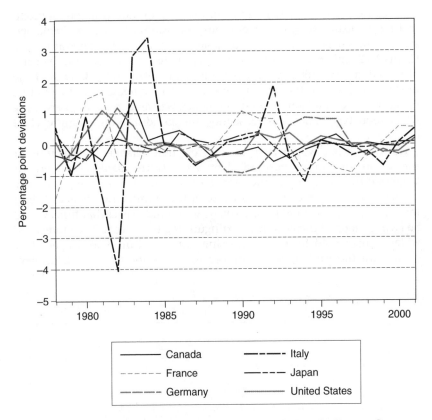

Figure 18.1 Interest spreads: deviations from HP trend (Canada, France, Germany, Italy, Japan and the USA 1978–2001)
Source: IMF, *International Financial Statistics* (various issues).

countries' banking systems may have not suffered similar shocks during those 24 years, what is remarkable is that the positive deviations from trend tend generally to be clustered around three sub-periods: the early 1980s, the early 1990s and, possibly, though less clear, around 2000–01. These sub-periods broadly coincide with periods when most Western economies slowed down significantly, especially during the first two sub-periods as central banks sought to fight inflation by raising interest rates, both nominal and real.

For purposes of econometric testing, lengthier time series were available in Canada for the complete half-century between 1950 and 2002. Out of the array of interest rate series that are readily available from Statistics Canada, two that were deemed most representative of the loan/deposit rates were chosen: the chartered banks' prime lending rate (roughly approximating the loan rate, r, in our previous discussion) and the checkable personal savings deposit rate (to approximate a 'representative' deposit rate, i). Charts 18.2 and 18.3 depict this particular interest spread for both the complete period 1950–2002 and for the sub-period 1970–2002. Because of the relative stickiness of the deposit rate series, this interest spread would be rising when central bank interest rate policy was tightening and narrowing when monetary policy was loosening, thereby displaying strong cyclical behaviour.

However, what would be the effect of these changes in the interest spread on short-term business debt vis-à-vis the banking sector? As suggested by the theory of the monetary circuit, when r-i rises, as during the late 1970s and late 1980s, because of the asymmetric impact of tight monetary policy on r and i respectively, we should expect that firms would be facing a more difficult time in extinguishing their debts. Therefore, as r-i widens, this would force an increasing number of firms to deepen their debts with the banking sector just to remain aloof. Chart 18.2 displays

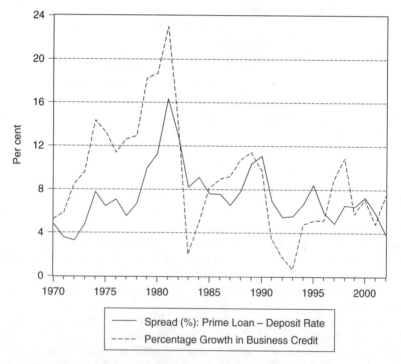

Figure 18.2   Interest spread and growth in short-term business credit (Canada, 1970–2002)
Source: Statistics Canada, CANSIMI, Series B2325, B14020 and B14035.

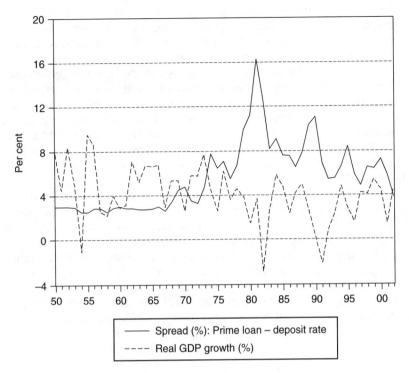

Figure 18.3 Interest spread and real GDP growth (Canada, 1950–2002)
Source: Statistics Canada, CANSIM 1, Series B14020, B14035, D14442, and CANSIM II, V1992067.

some Canadian evidence that is compatible with this hypothesis for the period 1970–2002, for which data on short-term business credit was available. The evidence does reveal a generally strong positive correlation between these two series.

Does this growing indebtedness that would be squeezing business revenues and profitability also slow down overall growth? Evidence presented in Chart 18.3 for the entire period between 1950 and 2002 for Canada would suggest that, except for the very early postwar years, during which the interest spread had remained low and remarkably stable, since the late 1960s any movement in the interest spread tended to be met generally with an opposite co-movement in real GDP growth. Hence, as businesses were struggling to meet their financial obligations because of a growing *r-i*, it would seem that firms would be seeking to cut back on production and investment. As Chart 18.3 suggests, rising interest spreads do appear to be associated with deteriorating macroeconomic performance – a result that seems to be consistent with the theory of the monetary circuit.

Although a graphical depiction of such relations does dramatise the importance of interest spreads in possibly affecting both business indebtedness to the banking sector and overall macroeconomic activity, would this conclusion stand up to more rigorous econometric testing? Moreover, while a bivariate relation between interest spreads and, say, real GDP growth can be inferred visually from a two-dimensional graph, when evaluating the impact of an additional variable, say, the level of real interest rates, traditional regression analysis would be more appropriate. Consequently, simple regressions were run on both the growth in short-term business debt and on real GDP growth, as dependent variables, and interest spread and the level of real interest rates as explanatory variables. These results are presented in Tables 18.1 and 18.2.

Table 18.1 offers some strong empirical support for the part played by both interest spreads and real interest rates in explaining the behaviour of business short-term indebtedness to the banking sector. Indeed, when examining the t-ratios (found in parentheses below the estimated coefficients), our r-i variable was consistently significant in explaining short-term business indebtedness and the coefficient held the correct sign. Hence, as already shown in Chart 18.2, as r rises in relation to i, firms are forced to fall deeper into debt, much as in a Minskian Ponzi scenario. In much the same way, our real interest rate variable was also strongly significant in impacting on short-term debt. The variable chosen was the long-term (10 years and over)

Table 18.1 Regression results: rate of growth of business short-term credit correlated with interest spread and real long-term rates

Dependent variable	Constant term	Interest spread	Real long-term rates	Adj. R^2	D.W.	AR(1)
Growth in	0.8367	1.1192		0.3507	0.4823	
Business Credit	(0.410)	(4.276)*				
Growth in	0.7750	1.1766		0.7093	1.4355	0.7632
Business Credit	(0.265)	(4.366)*				(5.748)*
Growth in	15.1104		−1.2287	0.3551	0.9233	
Business Credit	(9.578)*		(−4.315)*			
Growth in	13.1925		−0.8104	0.5363	1.8027	0.5894
Business Credit	(5.447)*		(−2.067)*			(3.951)*
Growth in	6.8829	1.1396	−1.2509	0.7438	1.4653	
Business Credit	(4.445)*	(6.931)*	(−6.970)*			
Growth in	6.0345	1.1309	−1.0607	0.7513	1.8112	0.3429
Business Credit	(2.972)*	(4.946)*	(−3.842)*			(1.521)

N.B.: The asterisk (*), adjacent to the t-ratios in parentheses, indicates acceptance at the 5 per cent level of significance, and AR(1) is the autoregressive factor in adjusting for first-order autocorrelation.

Table 18.2 Regression results: rate of growth of real gross domestic product correlated with interest spread and real long-term rates

Dependent variable	Constant term	Interest spread	Real long-term rates	Adj. R^2	D.W.	AR(1)
Real GDP	6.0007	−0.3435		0.1569	1.8993	
Growth	(8.892)*	(−3.267)*				
Real GDP	5.8212	−0.3220		0.1292	1.9713	0.0401
Growth	(8.145)*	(−2.912)*				(0.284)
Real GDP	4.9573		−0.2155	0.0339	1.7771	
Growth	(7.806)*		(−1.680)*			
Real GDP	4.3696		−0.0931	0.0182	1.9362	0.1641
Growth	(5.431)*		(−0.578)			(1.071)
Real GDP	6.3320	−0.3154	−0.1174	0.1550	2.0287	
Growth	(8.313)*	(−2.882)*	(−0.941)			
Real GDP	6.1678	−0.3067	−0.1015	0.1201	1.9719	−0.017
Growth	(7.909)*	(−4.946)*	(−0.763)			(−0.11)

N.B.: The asterisk (*), adjacent to the t-ratios in parentheses, indicates acceptance at the 5 per cent
level of significance, and AR(1) is the autoregressive factor in adjusting for first-order autocorrelation.

corporate bond yield less the rate of change in the Consumer Price Index. It
was felt that this variable would capture well the role played by rentier
income and, moreover, it was assumed *not* to create any possible problem of
multicollinearity arising from using, say, an identical proxy (such as *i*) for
both the interest spread and the real rate of interest in a regression equation.
While the statistical evidence was also quite strong, the sign was opposite of
that which one might infer from Graziani's analysis of the adoption of the
Fisher rule previously discussed and about the postulated positive effect that
constant and/or growing real rates would have on business debt. As evidence in
Table 18.1 suggests, because of a growing real burden of servicing their
long-term debt, business firms would be seeking to cut their overall indebtedness with the banking sector.

Table 18.2 presents the results of our simple regression analysis when using
real output growth as the dependent variable. When subjected to the same
econometric specification, the empirical results were far less robust, especially
with regards to the statistical significance of the real interest rate variable,
which although having the expected sign, it never passes standard threshold
levels of statistical significance except, marginally, for one of the specifications
shown in Table 18.2. On the other hand, as suggested by the theory of the
monetary circuit, the interest spread continued to play a significant role, in
this case, in affecting negatively overall output growth. As to the real interest
variable, a possible explanation for the weak negative coefficient may be the

simple fact that, while higher real interest rates are a burden on business profits, they are also a source of greater sales proceeds. As long as rentier propensity to consume is positive, then the overall effect might be quite mitigated because of these partially offsetting factors.

As is confirmed from our results displayed in Tables 18.1 and 18.2, especially when looking at the adjusted R^2, interest spreads and real interest rates are far from being the sole factors in determining both business indebtedness and output growth. After all, we have abstracted from analysing the important role played by government and the foreign sectors, which in the case of Canada are both very critical to the macroeconomic health of the economy. However, for heuristic purposes, the results can serve to highlight the possible relevance of at least one key variable – the interest spread – which is not normally considered to be of any relevance in explaining macroeconomic performance within the traditional literature.

Before concluding, there is one last issue that needs to be addressed. Obviously, statistical correlation does not necessarily mean causation. For instance, it could just as well be that both the interest spread and the growth rates of output and business debts are influenced by some unknown third variable that affects, say, aggregate output growth, with the latter then impacting on the interest spread, especially if the lending rate, r, is assumed to be more responsive to demand pressures than the deposit rate, i. While one cannot exclude this possibility completely, our view of the causal process starts with the exogenous decision of the central bank in targeting some base interest rate, such as the overnight rate in Canada or the federal funds rate in the USA. Once such a key interest rate fluctuates, the complete array of interest rates would then be affected, including the loan and deposit rates. These changes, in turn, would lead to fluctuations in the interest spread and then business indebtedness and, ultimately, they could also affect output growth, as partially inferred from our statistical evidence in Tables 18.1 and 18.2. To address this question of a reverse causality to that specified in our above-mentioned hypothesis, one possible solution would be to run some standard Granger causality tests that would at least seek to identify the temporal profile of the underlying relation between, say, interest spread and output growth. The results of applying Granger causality tests with different lags between our interest spread variable and real GDP growth are presented in Table 18.3.

Since the evidence overwhelmingly rejects the null hypothesis $H_0{}^*$ that the interest spread does not 'Granger cause' real GDP growth on the basis of one to three-year lags and not the competing hypothesis ($H_0{}^{**}$), this would suggest that, in the Granger sense, variations in the interest spread could have caused changes in real GDP growth, as the circuit approach would advise, but not the reverse as the competing hypothesis would indicate.

Table 18.3   Granger causality tests: interest spread and real GDP growth

Period 1950–2002 (53 Observations)	H_0*		H_0**	
Number of lags	Calculated F-values	Reject*** Yes/No	Calculated F-values	Reject*** Yes/No
1	21.9891	Yes	2.49583	No
2	12.9507	Yes	1.18456	No
3	7.21214	Yes	0.40037	No

Notes:
H_0*: 'Interest Spread does not Granger Cause Real GDP Growth.'
H_0**: 'Real GDP Growth does not Granger Cause Interest Spread.'
***: Using critical F-values at the 5% level of significance.

Conclusion

The key contribution of the theory of the monetary circuit has been to provide a more comprehensive framework that allows researchers to capture the complex realities of a monetary economy. Of central significance to the monetary circuit framework is the flux/reflux mechanism by showing why money is fundamentally the result of an endogenous process in which, under the watchful eye of the state, two key actors, firms and banks, interact in generating credit flows needed to finance productive activity in a monetary economy. The logic of that interaction ultimately has macroeconomic consequences. An important element of that interaction which has been highlighted in the works of Augusto Graziani is the constellation of interest rates that forms the basis for the various interest rate spreads or mark-ups. The spread between the loan rate and deposit rates constitutes a key element, since it not only can shape effective demand but it could also set the conditions for the reconstitution of the monetary circuit. Our empirical analysis does somewhat substantiate the role that this key bank mark-up could play in explaining corporate indebtedness to the banking sector and, to some extent, macroeconomic performance. Although much further empirical research is necessary, for those wishing to establish a new macroeconomics founded on Post Keynesian and circuitist theories, the interest spread would certainly deserve a more prominent position than it is generally accorded within the economics literature.

References

Barran, F., Coudert, V. and Majon, B. (1995) 'Taux d'intérêt, spreads, comportement bancaire: les effets sur l'activité réelle', *Revue économique*, 46, pp. 625–34.

Graziani, A. (1987) 'Keynes's Finance Motive', *Économies et sociétés*, 21, pp. 23–42.
Graziani, A. (1989) 'Money and Finance in Joan Robinson's Works', in G.R. Feiwel (ed.), *The Economics of Imperfect Competition and Employment: Joan Robinson and Beyond* (New York University Press), pp. 613–30.
Graziani, A. (1990) 'The Theory of the Monetary Circuit', *Économies et sociétés*, 24, pp. 7–36.
Graziani, A. (2003) *The Monetary Theory of Production* (Cambridge University Press).
Nell, E.J. (1967) 'Wicksell's Theory of Circulation', *Journal of Political Economy*, 75, pp. 386–94.
Robinson, J. (1956) *The Accumulation of Capital* (London: Macmillan).
Rousseas, S. (1986) *Post Keynesian Monetary Economics* (Armonk, N.Y.: M.E. Sharpe).
Seccareccia, M. (1996) 'Post Keynesian Fundism and Monetary Circulation', in G. Deleplace and E.J. Nell (eds), *Money in Motion: The Post Keynesian and Circulation Approaches* (London: Macmillan Press), pp. 400–16.
Seccareccia, M. (2003) 'Pricing, Investment and the Financing of Production within the Framework of the Monetary Circuit: Some Preliminary Evidence', in L.-P. Rochon and S. Rossi (eds), *Modern Theories of Money* (Cheltenham: Edward Elgar), pp. 173–97.
Shan, J., and A. Morris (2002) 'Does Financial Development "Lead" Economic Growth?', *International Review of Applied Economics*, 16, pp. 153–68.
Smith, R.T. (1999) *Money in the Bank: Comparing Bank Profits in Canada and Abroad*, Commentary 124 (Toronto: C.D. Howe Institute).

Appendix: Augusto Graziani's Selected Publications*

Books

(1957) *Sviluppo economico e produttività del capitale*, Naples, Jovene.
(1961) *La teoria delle scelte negli investimenti pubblici*, Naples, Jovene.
(1965) *Equilibrio generale ed equilibrio macroeconomico*, Naples, ESI.
(1969) *Lo sviluppo di un' economia aperta*, Naples, ESI.
(1975) (ed.) *Crisi e ristrutturazione nell' economia italiana*, Turin, Einaudi.
(1981) *Teoria economica* (2 vols; 5th edition 2001), Naples, ESI.
(1988) (ed. with M. Messori) *Moneta e produzione*, Torino, Einaudi.
(1989) *The Theory of the Monetary Circuit*, Thames Papers in Political Economy.
(1989) *L'economia italiana dal 1945 a oggi*, 3rd edition, Bologna, II Mulino.
(1992) *Problemi e metodi di politica economica*, 4th edition, Naples, Liguori.
(1992) (ed. with R. Realfonzo), *La teoria del credito e della circolazione* by Marco Fanno, Naples, ESI.
(1994) *La teoria monetaria della produzione*, Banca dell'Etruria, Collana Studi e Ricerche, Arezzo.
(1997) *I conti senza l'oste* (Collected articles from various journals), Turin, Boringhieri.
(2000) *Lo sviluppo dell'economia italiana*, 2nd edition, Turin, Boringhieri.
(2003) *The Monetary Theory of Production*, Cambridge University Press.

Chapters in books

(1982) L'analisi marxista e la struttura del capitalismo moderno, in *Storia del marxismo*, 4th vol. Turin, Einaudi.
(1987) Economia keynesiana e teoria del circuito, in G. Gandolfo and F. Marzano, eds, *Keynesian Theory, Planning Models, and Quantitative Economics*, Milan, Giuffrè.
(1996) Piero Sraffa's Vision of the Capitalist Process, in P. Zarembka, ed., *Latest Developments in Marxist Theory, Research in Political Economy*, vol. 15.
(1988) The Financement of the Economic Activity in Keynes's Thought, in H. Hageman and O. Steiger, eds, *Keynes's General Theory Nach Fünfzig Jahren*, Berlin, Duncker & Humblot.
(1988) Le teorie del circuito e la *Teoria generale* di Keynes, in A. Graziani and M. Messori, eds, *Moneta e produzione*, Turin, Einaudi.
(1989) Money and Finance in Joan Robinson's Works, in G.R. Feiwel, ed., *The Economics of Imperfect Competition and Employment*, New York, MacMillan.
(1991) Export-led Growth. The Italian Experience, in C. Bianchi and C. Casarosa, eds, *The Recent Performance of the Italian Economy*, Milan, F. Angeli.

---

* Please note that the complete list of Augusto Graziani's publications covers about 300 items. What follows includes only some of the main titles.

(1991) Nuove interpretazioni dell'analisi monetaria di Keynes, in J.A. Kregel, ed., *Nuove interpretazioni dell'analisi monetaria di Keynes*, Bologna, Il Mulino.

(1992) Production and Distribution in a Monetary Economy, in H. Brink, ed., *Themes in Modern Macroeconomics*, London, Macmillan.

(1992) A. Graziani, in P. Arestis and M. Sawyer, eds, *A Biographical Dictionary of Dissenting Economists*, Aldershot, GB, E. Elgar.

(1993) Money as Purchasing Power and Money as a Stock of Wealth, in H.-J. Staderman and O. Steiger, eds, *Der Stand und die Nächste Zukunft der Geldforschung*, Berlin, Duncker & Humblot.

(1994) Monetary Circuits, in P. Arestis and M. Sawyer, eds, *The Elgar Companion of Radical Political Economy*, Elgar.

(1996) Money as Purchasing Power and Money as a Stock of Wealth in Keynesian Economic Thought, in G. Deleplace and E. Nell, eds., *Money in Motion. The Post Keynesian and Circulation Approaches*, Macmillan, 1996.

(1998) A Note on Hayek's Macroeconomic Equilibrium, in F. Michon, ed., *L'économie: une science pour l'homme et la société*, Paris, Publications de la Sorbonne.

(1998) Nota sulle decisioni di investimento in Keynes, in N. De Vecchi and M.C. Marcuzzo, eds, *A cinquant' anni da Keynes*, Milan, Unicopli.

(1998) The Independence of Central Banks. The Case of Italy, in P. Arestis and M. Sawyer, eds, *The Political Economy of Central Banking*, Cheltenham, Elgar.

(1999) Comment on J.A. Kregel, 'Instability, Volatility, and the Process of Capital Accumulation', in G. Gandolfo and F. Marzano, eds, *Economic Theory and Social Justice*, London, Macmillan.

(1999) L'economia del Mezzogiorno nel contesto internazionale, in M. De Benedictis and F. De Filippis, eds, *M. Rossi Doria e le trasformazioni del Mezzogiorno d'Italia*, Manduria, Lacaita.

(2001) The Third Way. Italian Experiments, in P. Arestis and M. Sawyer, eds, *The Economics of the Third Way. Experiences from Around the World*, Cheltenham, Elgar.

(2002) New Lines of Research in Monetary Economics, in S. Bhoem, C. Gerke and H.D. Kurz, eds, *Is There Progress in Economics?*, Cheltenham, Elgar.

(2002) The Investment Decision in Keynes' Thought, in P. Arestis, M. Desai and S. Dow, eds, *Money, Macroeconomics, and Keynes*, London, Routledge.

(2002) The Relevance of Economic Ideas of the Past, in S. Nisticò and D. Tosato, eds, *Competing Economic Theories*, London, Routledge.

(2003) Finance Motive, in J.E. King, ed., *The Elgar Companion to Post Keynesian Economics*, Cheltenham. Elgar.

(2003) Microéconomie et Macroéconomie: A qui la priorité?, in P. Piegay and P.L. Rochon, eds, *Théories monétaires postkeynésiennes*, Paris, Economica.

(2004) Behind Globalization, in B. Greve and J. Jespersen, eds, *Globalization and Welfare*, Roskilde University Press.

(2004) La politica monetaria della Banca centrale europea, in R. Cagliozzi, ed., *Economia e politica dell'allargamento dell'Unione europea*, Turin, Giappichelli.

Journal articles

(1978) The Mezzogiorno in the Italian Economy, *Cambridge Journal of Economics*, 2.

(1978) Il Trattato della moneta di J. A. Schumpeter, *Note economiche*, 1.

(1983) Interesse monetario e interesse reale, *Studi economici*.

(1984) The Debate on Keynes's Finance Motive, *Economic Notes*, March.

(1984) Moneta senza crisi, *Studi economici*, 24.

(1986) Schumpeter's Political Writings, *Economic Notes*, 3.
(1987) Efficiency Criteria at the Micro- and Macro Levels, *Rivista Internazionale di Scienze Economiche e Commerciali*, 10.
(1987) Keynes's Finance Motive, *Economie et Société*, 9.
(1989) J.A. Schumpeter and Italian Economic Thought in the Inter-War Period, *Studi economici*, 1.
(1990) Activitad bancaria: Intermediacion contra creacion de dinero, *Coyuntyura Agropecuaria*, 4.
(1990) La théorie du circuit et la théorie macroéconomique de la banque, *Economie et Sociétés, Série Monnaie et Production*, 6.
(1991) La théorie keynésienne de la monnaie et le financement de l'économie, *Economie appliquée*, 1.
(1991) The Italian Economic Journals and Some Major Turning Points in Economic Theory, *Economic Notes*, 1.
(1992) La Banca come controllore di efficienza dell'impresa, *Studi economici*, 3.
(1993) M. Fanno's 'Production Cycles, Credit Cycles, and Industrial Fluctuations': An Introduction, *Structural Change and Economic Dynamics*, 4, 2.
(1994) Real Wages and the Loans–Deposits Controversy, *Economie appliquée*, 1.
(1997) The Marxian Theory of Money, *International Journal of Political Economy*, 27, 2.
(1997) Let's Rehabilitate the Theory of Value, *International Journal of Political Economy*, 27, 2.

Introduction to books

(1980) Malthus e la teoria della domanda effettiva, Introduction to L. Costabile, *Malthus, sviluppo e ristagno della produzione capitalistica*, Turin, Boringhieri.
(1981) Introduction to J.A. Schumpeter, *Il processo capitalistico*, Turin, Boringhieri (Italian edition of *Business Cycles*).
(1988) La partita a scacchi, Introduction to D.N. McKoskey, *La retorica dell'economica*, Turin, Einaudi.
(1997) Introduction (with R. Realfonzo) to G. Del Vecchio, *Lineamenti di teoria monetaria*, Torino, Utet.

Index

accommodating central bank
  behaviour 266–7
accommodationist approach 7–8
adjustment process 175, 178
advantage of circulation 76
Agger, E.E. 60
aggregate demand 175, 178, 231–2, 236
Ahmed, S. 56
'alternative theories of the rate of
  interest debate' of 1937 71–3
American School of qualitative credit
  theory 5
Angell, J.A. 59
Angeloni, I. 237–8, 239
anticipated profits, spending 132
Arena, R. 23, 29, 36, 83, 173
Arestis, P. 8, 173, 231–2
asset-based financial systems 15–16,
  257–68
  Canada 258–64, 266
  USA 264–6
Auerbach, R.D. 60

Backhouse, R. 53
Bagehot, W. 61
Ball, L. 174
Banco Central de Cuba (BCC) 248, 249
Bangladesh 203, 204, 208, 210–11,
  214, 215
Bank of Amsterdam 56
Bank of Canada 15, 258–64, 266
  determination of overnight interest
    rate 261–4
  operation of settlements system 260–1
  zero-reserve requirements 15, 259–60
Bank of England 61, 62–3, 236–7
Bank of France 257–8
Bank of Italy 257–8
bank money 70–1, 71–2, 95–6
  coexistence of central and commercial
    bank monies 140–4
bank rate 85
bankruptcies see failures
banks/banking sector 45–6, 54
  banks as creators of money 4–5
  creation of credit 54–7, 102–3;
    see also endogenous money
  creation of purchasing power 222;
    creation of money and 224–5

credit see credit
evolutionary approach to
  development stages of money and
  banking 5
finance for growth 188–91; banks as
  circuit starters 189–90; why
  banks may not succeed 190–1
government expenditure and 8–9
mergers 13, 155–71; increase in
  competition and firms' monopoly
  power 157–60; interest rate,
  savings and employment 167–9;
  monopoly power, interest rate and
  employment 160–6; policy
  implications 166–7
bargaining power 212
Barger, H. 61
Barran, F. 276
Barrère, A. 173
Bell, S. 9, 260
Bellofiore, R. 2, 7, 31, 50, 51
Bendixen, F. 4
Bernstein, E.M. 59, 60
Berthélemy, J.C. 188
Bianchi, C. 170
bimetallism 244–5
Bodin, J. 218
Boianovsky, M. 27
bonds, interest rate on 101, 105
Bordo, M.D. 245
Bossone, B. 7, 121, 188, 190, 197
Boughton, J.M. 59
Boyer-Xambeu, M.-T. 244

C-M-C economy 2–3
CADECA 248, 249
Canada
  financial system 15–16, 258–64, 266
  interest spreads 16, 276–83
Cannan, E. 55, 58
capabilities 208–10
capitalist evolution 45–9, 49–50
cash deposits 96
Cawthorne, D.R. 59, 61
Cencini, A. 6, 7, 25, 180
central banks/banking 13, 139–51
  asset-based systems 15–16,
    257–68; Canada 258–64, 266;
    USA 264–6

circular flow of central bank money
and credit 144–7
coexistence of central and commercial
bank monies 140–4
control of high-powered money 62,
62–3
credibility 232, 233
independence 233, 234
NCMS 194–5
payment finality for cross-border
transactions 148–50
see also under individual names
central money *see* state money
CEPAL 255
Chandler, L. 59, 60, 61, 62
chartalism 4
Chick, V. 54–5, 56, 173, 266
Chiodi, G. 26
Church, K.B. 237
circuit starters, banks as 189–90
circuit theory *see* monetary circuit
circuitist school 6–7
circular flow (Schumpeter) 27–31
class, social 30–1
tripartite scheme 214
classical economics, restoration of 91–2
Clinton, K. 259, 260, 261, 262–3
closure of the monetary circuit 270–1,
272
realisation of monetary gross
profits 12, 111–23
CLS Bank 148
Cochran, J.A. 61
collateral 68–9, 73–5, 76, 190
Committee on Payment and Settlement
Systems 139, 141, 142, 143, 144,
145, 150
competition 86
bank mergers and firms' monopoly
power 157–60
NCMS 193
welfarism 207–8
Congdon, T. 53
consumer sovereignty 34
consumption 130, 238–41
continuation analysis 8
continuous linked settlement (CLS)
system 148, 149
control 61–2
conventionalism 205–6
convertibility 246–7
Cuba: 'convertible peso' 247–8, 249;
legal tender and 247–8
Costabile, L. 7, 215
cost-push inflation 219–20
Cottrell, A. 6

Coudert, V. 276
credibility 232, 233
credit
banks and creation of 54–7, 102–3;
creation vs 'lending on' 56–7
circular flow of central bank money
and 144–7
creation and collateral 68–9
creation of DCIs 199–200
and innovation 31, 45–6
interest spreads and 278–9, 280–1
microcredit *see* microcredit
real interest rates and macroeconomic
performance 273–5
Schumpeter on finance, innovation
and capitalist evolution 45–7
theory of monetary circuit 127–30
credit inflation 68
creditworthiness of firms 129–30
Crick, W.F. 57, 58, 59, 60–1
cross-border transactions 148–50
Crowther, G. 55, 57, 61
Crowther's Fact 55–6
Cuba 15, 243–55
economic duality 247
exchange duality 248–9, 252–3
monetary duality 247–8, 249–54;
pattern of circulation 249–50;
stability 253–4; viability
251–3
Currie, L. 55
Curtis, M. 57, 59, 60
cyclical movements 49–50

Dahlberg, A. 4, 5
Dalziel, P. 8
Dangel-Hagnauer, C. 29
Davenport, H.J. 5, 58
Davidson, P. 6, 136, 178
daylight credit 144, 145–6, 150
de Viti de Marco, A. 4–5
De Vroey, M. 112, 120, 121
debt titles 70–1, 71–2
defensive central bank behaviour 264,
264–6, 266–7
deficit spending 166
Deleplace, G. 6, 23, 169, 173, 244, 246,
254, 255
delivery versus payment
mechanism 144–5, 150
demand deficiency 177–8
demand deposits 190
creation of DCIs 199–200
demand for money 99–100, 103–4
demand-pull inflation 219, 220
Demsetz, H. 73–4

deposit-creating institutions
  (DCIs) 191–201
  creation and distribution of
    money 200–1
  economic effects of NCMS 196–9
  exit of failed 193–4
  monetary policy 194–5
  operations of 191–3
  transition to NCMS 195–6,
    199–201
deposit multiplier 54, 57–60
  flexible 48
  what starts it off 59–60
depositor runs 193–4
deposits 54, 85
  mechanism of generating 54–7
deregulation
  bank system 166, 168–9
  consumer goods and capital goods
    markets 166
  labour market 167
Deutsche Bundesbank 143
Dijon–Fribourg group 7
dirty-floating regime 249
disequilibrium 41, 44, 47, 272–3
  existence of monetary disequilibrium
    alongside stable prices 225–6
disequilibrium inflation 14, 217–27
  consequences of 222–6
  monetary 220–1
Doimeadios, Y. 249, 253, 255
dollarisation, partial in Cuba 247–54
Dow, S. 6, 8, 99
Dowrie, G.W. 55, 61
dual theory of prices 43
Dupont, F. 121
Dymski, G. 158

Earl, P.E. 170
economic development 27–31, 45–7,
  49–50
economic duality 247
  see also monetary duality
economic rationality, individual 10–11,
  23–38
  Schumpeter 23–4, 27–31, 35
  von Mises 23–4, 31–5, 35
  Wicksell 23, 24–7, 35
effective demand 9, 127, 174–7
egoism 28–9
Eichner, A.S. 127, 261, 264
Ellis, H.S. 53
employment
  circuit theory and 13,
    173–83; accounting for the
    originality of Keynes's theory

of employment 174–7; explaining
  unemployment 177–80
  determination of level 167
  monopoly power, interest rate
    and 160–6
  savings and 167–9, 178
employment relation 14, 203–16
encompassing view of functions of
  money 10
endogenous money 5, 11, 53–66, 128,
  129, 155, 258–9
  banks and creation of credit 54–7
  Canada 264
  contemporary debate on MTP 6, 9
  deposit multiplier 57–60
  role of reserves 60–3
energetic egoism 29
entitlements 206–7
entrepreneurs 30, 31, 49–50, 68
  Keynes's theory of employment 175–7
entrepreneurs and promoters 33–4
equilibrium 41, 112, 221, 272
  as systemic order 112, 120–1
European Central Bank (ECB) 148,
  233–4, 265
European Monetary Union (EMU) 14–15,
  231–42, 257–8
  effectiveness of interest rate
    changes 236–41
  institutional framework 233–4
  MTP view 234–6
  theoretical underpinnings of EMU
    model 231–3
European System of Central Banks
  (ESCB) 234
evenly rotating economy (ERE) 31–5
evolutionary approach 5
ex post real wage 42–3
exchange rates
  exchange duality in Cuba 248–9,
    252–3
  monetary policy in EMU 237, 238,
    239, 241
exogenous money 98–9, 155

factor cost 175–6
failures
  DCIs 193–4
  firms 118–19, 120
fallacy of composition 58
Fanno, M. 4, 5
Federal Reserve 61–2, 258–9, 264–6
Festré, A. 29, 31, 33, 35
fiat money regimes 246–7
Ficek, K.F. 59
Figuera, S. 7

final finance 85, 134
financial instability 117–18
financial market 43, 190
  separation from money market 10
financial resources, allocation of 198–9
financial systems
  asset-based 15–16, 257–68
  effects of NCMS on 198
  overdraft-based 257–8
firms
  creditworthiness 129–30
  failures 118–19, 120
  industrial concentration ratio 158–60
  profits *see* profits
flux/reflux mechanism 270–1, 271–2
Fontana, G. 2, 6, 7, 8, 173
forced savings 42
Forder, J. 242
Forges Davanzati, G. 7, 167, 169, 170
Forstater, M. 9
France 245, 257–8, 276–7
Frazer, W.J. 59, 61
freedom 209
Friedman, M. 62, 218–19
functionings 209

Garis, R.L. 5
GDP/output
  EMU model 236–7, 238–41
  growth and interest spread 279–80,
    281–3
Germany 276–7
Gerrard, B. 2
Gillard, L. 244
Giovannini Group 148
Gloria-Palermo, S. 29
Gnos, C. 7, 84, 126, 128, 132, 133,
  175, 176, 181
Goldfeld, S.M. 59, 61–2
Goodhart, C.A.E. 62
Goodlet, C. 260
government deficits 132
government expenditure 8–9, 166
Grameen Bank 214–15
Granger causality tests 282–3
Graziani, A. 2, 3, 5, 6, 7, 9, 10, 23, 25,
  26, 83, 92, 93, 111, 112, 113, 118,
  120, 121–2, 125, 126, 127, 128, 130,
  131, 132, 134, 136, 140, 143, 162,
  168, 169, 173, 203, 212, 213–14,
  217, 231, 257, 258, 270
  defence of Joan Robinson 85–6,
    90, 91
  history of economic analysis 39–51;
    Keynes's *A Treatise on Money* 42–4;
    Schumpeter on finance, innovation

    and capitalist evolution 45–7;
    Wicksell's *Interest and Prices* 40–2
  interest spreads 269, 271–3
  model of monetary circuit 112–14,
    116
  real interest rates, debt and
    macroeconomic
    performance 273–5
growth
  achieving despite international trade
    barriers 199
  finance for 188–91
Gunning, J.P. 32
Gurley, J.G. 56, 59
Guthrie, G. 263

Hahn, L.A. 4, 5, 85
Hall, M.J.B. 63
Hanson, J.L. 61
Harcourt, G. 92
Harmonised Index of Consumer Prices
  (HICP) 234
Harrod, R.F. 57, 59
Hart, A.G. 55, 57
Hawtrey, R.G. 61, 71
Hayek, F. 48
hedonistic egoism 28–9
Heinsohn, G. 72, 75, 79
Helfferich, K. 4
Hicks, J.R. 67, 71, 74, 87, 121, 257
Hidalgo, V. 249, 253, 255
high-powered money, control of 62,
  62–3
Holthausen, C. 140
horizontalist approach 7–8
Horwich, G. 73
Howard, D. 261
Howells, P.G.A. 8
Humphrey, T.M. 55, 57–8

income distribution 126
  Keynesian theory vs circuit
    theory 155
  non-marginalist theory of 10
  relative poverty of workers compared
    with owners of means of
    production 223–5
individual economic rationality *see*
  economic rationality, individual
industrial concentration ratio 158–60
inflation 14, 43, 46, 97–8
  barrier 88–9
  circuit theory and
    unemployment 179–80
  defined only as an increase in the
    general level of prices 217–20

inflation – *continued*
  disequilibrium   *see* disequilibrium
    inflation
  EMU model and   232, 233, 235–6,
    237–41
  real interest rates, debt and
    macroeconomic
    performance   274–5
initial finance   85
innovation   29–30, 45–7
interbank settlements *see* payment
  finality
interest rates   11, 67–81
  bank mergers   158; monopoly power
    and employment   160–6; savings
    and employment   167–9
  changes in Keynes's analysis   12,
    95–107; *The General Theory*
    98–102; *A Treatise* vs *The General
    Theory*   102–5; *A Treatise on
    Money*   95–8
  EMU   233–4, 235–6; effectiveness
    of interest rate changes
    236–41
  interest spreads and monetary
    circulation   16, 269–84; effects of
    changes in interest spreads and
    real interest rates   275–83; real
    interest rates, debt and
    macroeconomic
    performance   273–5
  1937 debate on 'alternative theories of
    the rate of interest'   71–3
  overnight   *see* overnight interest
    rate
  own capital and collateral   73–5
  and price level   97–8, 161, 163–4
  property paradigm   75–8
  Schumpeter's and Keynes's criticism of
    the neoclassical theory   67–8
  source of money in Schumpeter's and
    Keynes's theories   68–71
interest spreads   16, 269–84
  effects of changes in interest
    spreads and real interest
    rates   275–83
  financial implications   271–3
international settlement
  institution   148–50
intraday credit   144, 145–6, 150
investment
  EMU area   238–41
  financing   111–12, 115–18, 128–9,
    134–5, 178–80
  financing public investments through
    monetary creation   222–3

interest rates and   101–2, 105–6
  savings and   43–4, 67–8, 73, 101–2,
    105–6
investment circuit   135
investment-goods sector   133–4
Italy   257–8, 276–7

Jaffee, D.M.   74
Japan   276–7
Jobra, Bangladesh   203, 204, 210–11
justice, principles of   205–10

Kahn, C.M.   139–40
Kahn, M.S.   188
Kalecki, M.   173
Kanatas, G.   74, 75
Kaufman, G.C.   62
Kent, R.F.   59
Keynes, J.M.   6–7, 11, 55, 58, 76, 77–9,
  87, 120, 121, 127, 130, 140, 170,
  178–9
  changes in analysis   12, 95–107;
    money in *The General Theory*
    98–102; money in *A Treatise on
    Money*   95–8; *A Treatise* vs
    The General Theory   102–5
  circuit theory and Keynes's theory of
    employment   173, 174–7, 177–8,
    178–9, 181
  criticism of neoclassical theory of rate
    of interest   67–8
  Graziani and *A Treatise on Money*   42–4;
    The General Theory and   48–9
  legacy and MTP   1–3
  1937 debate on 'alternative theories of
    the rate of interest'   71–3
  source of money   69–71
Keynesian economists   217, 219–20,
  222, 223
Kildegard, A.C.   255
King, D.   62
Klein, J.J.   59
Knapp, G.F.   4, 70

labour market deregulation   167
Laidler, D.   31, 55, 58
Laughlin, J.L.   5, 55–6, 60
Lavoie, M.   6–7, 8, 24, 84, 130, 133, 140,
  141, 169, 173, 258, 267
Le Bourva, J.   6, 130, 173, 258, 270
leadership   29–30
Leaf, W.   58
Leijonhufvud, A.   23, 32, 78–9
lender-of-last-resort facilities   146–7
lending, types of   57
'lending on'   56–7

Lewis, A.W. 208
libertarianism 206–7
Lindahl, E. 27
liquidity 192–3, 194–5
liquidity preference 71–2, 72, 101,
  105, 106
liquidity premium 71–2, 72, 77, 78
living standards 208–9
loanable funds 72, 73
Lombra, R. 63
long term 87–9, 91–2, 115–18
low-income countries 190–1
  financing growth in 191–6
  see also microcredit; non-credit money
  system
Lugli, L. 4, 5
Lundrigan, E. 259
Lunghini, G. 170

M-C-M' economy 2–3, 175
'machine-tool' sub-sector 133
MacKinnon, K. 121
Macleod, H.D. 56
macro approach to analysis 9
Majon, B. 276
Mankiw, G. 174
marginal productivity 26
Marglin, S. 212
mark-up in bank sector 157–8
market rate of interest 97, 103, 105
Marguès-Pereira, J. 255
Marquetti, H. 253, 255
Marshall, A. 56
Marshall, R.H. 59
Marx, K. 2, 175, 270
material reproduction, systems of 75
McKenna, R. 5, 58
Meade, J.E. 62
means of payment 10, 245–6
mediators 214
Meigs, A.J. 59, 62, 63
Messori, M. 7, 114, 118, 121
Meulen, H. 5
microcredit 14, 203–16
  and the circuit approach 213–15
  and its reasons 210–13
  origins of Yunus's programme 204
  principles of justice and 205–10
Midland Bank School 5
Mills, R.C. 60, 61
Minsky, H.P. 6, 112, 117, 118
Mireaux, E. 5
Mises, L. von 11, 48, 50–1
  contribution to circulation
  approach 23–4, 31–5, 35
Mishkin, F.S. 62

monetarism 62, 217, 218–19
monetary circuit 5, 149–50, 156–7,
  270–1
  alternative perspectives within circuit
  theory 11, 39–51
  central banking *see* central banks/
  banking
  circuit approach and
  microcredit 213–15
  closure of *see* closure of the monetary
  circuit
  and employment 13, 173–83;
  accounting for the originality of
  Keynes's theory of
  employment 174–7; explaining
  unemployment 13, 177–80
  existence of monetary profits 12–13,
  125–38
  Graziani's model 112–14, 116
  overlapping monetary circuits
  132–3
  realisation of monetary gross
  profits 12, 111–23
monetary duality 15, 243–55
  Cuba 247–54; stability 253–4;
  viability 251–3
  issue of 244–7; history 244–5;
  theory 245–7
monetary economy 1–2
monetary policy
  EMU 231–3, 235–6, 241;
  effectiveness 236–41
  in NCMS 194–5
Monetary Policy Committee 235, 237
monetary theory of production
  (MTP) 1–19
  contemporary debate on 6–10
  history of and Joan Robinson's
  contribution 11–12, 83–94
  Keynes's legacy 1–3
  traditions of in Keynes's time 3–5
  view and EMU 234–6
money of account 70, 76–7
money-base theory 59, 63
money market 10
money multiplier 11, 62, 63
money proper 70, 76–8
money-wage economy 2–3
Monnet, C. 140
monopoly power 157–60
  interest rate and employment 160–6
Moore, B.J. 6, 136, 163, 265
Morris, A. 276
Mosler, W. 9, 260, 265, 266
multilateral transaction on
  securities 146–7

NAIRU   233
'national peso'   247–8
    see also Cuba
natural rate of interest   97–8, 101–2,
    103, 105
Nell, E.J.   6, 23, 26, 129, 132, 133–4,
    169, 173, 270–1
neo-chartalists   8–9
neoclassical theory   25, 67–8, 87–8
neutral economy   2
neutral rate of interest   102, 104, 105
neutralisation of government
    flows   261
'new consensus' in macroeconomics
    (NCM)   15, 231–4
New Keynesians   174, 177
Newlyn, W.T.   62
Nogaro, B.   54
nominalism   4
non-credit money system (NCMS)
    13–14, 187–201
    allocation of financial resources
        198–9
    economic effects of   196–9
    effects on real economy   197
    finance to fight poverty   191–6
    monetary policy in   194–5
    transition to   195–6, 199–201
non-redeemable money   77
notes, creation of new   90
Nozick, R.   206–7
Nussbaum, M.   209

Ohlin, B.   71, 74
open-market operations   261, 264–6
open-mouth operations   263
original acquisition of resources,
    principle of justice in   206, 207
Orro Fernandez, R.   255
output   *see* GDP/output
overlapping monetary circuits   132–3
overdraft financial systems   257–8
overnight interest rate
    Canada   259–60;
        determination   261–4
    USA   265
own capital   73–5
owners of the means of
    production   223–5

Pagano, M.   169
Palley, T.I.   8
Pareto efficiency   207–8, 209
Parguez, A.   7, 84, 86, 90, 93, 112, 126,
    127–8, 134, 140, 169, 173
Patinkin, D.   47–8

payment finality   13, 139–51
    circular flow of central bank money
        and credit   144–7
    coexistence of central and commercial
        bank monies   140–4
    for cross-border transactions   148–50
payment-versus-payment settlement
    mechanism   148, 150
Pearce, I.   59
Peersman, G.   242
Pesciarelli, E.   29
Pesek, B.P.   56
peso   247–8
    see also Cuba
Petersen, M.A.   169
Peterson, J.M.   59, 61
Phillips, C.A.   55, 57, 58
Phillips curve   231–2
Physiocrats   173
Pigou, A.C.   91
policy
    implications of bank merger
        model   166–7
    monetary   *see* monetary policy
Pollin, R.   7
'Ponzi' (ultra-speculative) financial
    regime   117–18
possession   73–5, 78
post-chartalists   8–9
post-classical paradigm   24
Post Keynesian school   6–8, 174, 178,
    264
Poulon, F.   7
poverty   13–14, 211
    finance to fight   191–6
    relative poverty of workers compared
        with owners of means of
        production   223–5
    see also microcredit; non-credit money
        system
Prather, C.L.   57
prices
    firms' monopoly power   159, 160
    inflation defined only as an increase in
        general level of   217–20
    interest rate and   97–8, 161, 163–4
    Keynes's theory of employment
        174–7
    monetary imbalance existing
        alongside stable prices   225–6
primary deposits   59–60
primary liquidity   192–3
private money   245, 246
procedural justice   206–7
production circuit   135
production function   87, 92, 159

productivity
  marginal 26
  monopoly power and 159, 161–2,
    164–6
profits 86, 89–90
  employment and 175–6
  existence of monetary profits within
    the monetary circuit 12–13,
    125–38; determination of profits
    131–6
  inflationary profit 222; spending on
    the products market 222–3
  realisation of monetary gross
    profits 12, 111–23; financing of
    investment demand 115–18;
    monetary profits and firms'
    failures 118–19; profit realisation
    in kind 112–15
progressing economy (PE) 31–5
promoters 33–4
property 73–5
  property paradigm as an alternative
    theory of the rate of interest
    75–8
  property rights constraint and
    credit 14, 203–16
property premium 69, 75–8
public expenditure 8–9, 166
public investments, financing through
    monetary creation 222–3
purchasing power 197, 222, 224–5
pure credit model 3, 40–2

quantity theory of money 218

Rajan, R.G. 169
rational choice 212–13
real balance effect 47
real-exchange economy 1–2
real-time gross settlements (RTGS) 142
real-wage economy 2
Realfonzo, R. 2, 3, 4, 5, 7, 16, 26, 48,
    140, 167, 169, 170
reflux 130, 270–1, 271–2
Renaud, J.F. 121, 132
Renversez, F. 257, 258
representative money *see* state money
reserve requirements 194
  zero-reserve requirements 15,
    259–60, 264
reserves 54
  change in 59
  role 60–3
resource allocation 198–9
Reus, E. 121
reverse causation 62–3

Ritter, A.R. 255
Ritter, L.S. 61
Roberds, W. 139–40
Robertson, D.H. 3–4, 5, 61, 71, 72–3
Robinson, J. 127, 129, 131, 173, 211,
    270, 271, 272
  contribution to MTP 11–12, 83–94
Rochon, L.-P. 7, 16, 84, 93, 121, 126,
    128, 141–2, 173, 181, 259
Rogoff, K. 233
Romani, P. 29
Romer, D. 174
Rossi, S. 6, 7, 8, 16, 126, 132, 141–2,
    149
Rotheim, R.J. 174
Rousseas, S. 276
routine 28
Rowe, N. 255

Sadigh, E. 7, 226
Salvadori, N. 83
Santarelli, E. 29
Sarr, A. 197
Sause, G.G. 59
Saving, T.R. 56
savings
  and employment 167–9, 178
  forced 42
  and investment 43–4, 67–8, 73,
    101–2, 105–6
savings deposits 96
Sawyer, M. 231–2
Sayers, R.S. 60, 61
Say's Law 233
Schmitt, B. 7, 14, 36, 121, 134, 173,
    178, 179, 180, 220, 270
Schumpeter, J.A. 3, 4, 5, 11, 49–50, 53,
    56, 72, 78, 79, 118, 121, 140, 173,
    221, 222
  contribution to circulation
    approach 23–4, 27–31, 35
  criticism of neoclassical theory of rate
    of interest 67–8
  Graziani and Schumpeter on finance,
    innovation and capitalist
    evolution 45–7
  source of money 68–9
Schure, P. 158
Schwartz, A. 62
Scott, R.H. 60
Seccareccia, M. 7, 31, 90, 112, 127–8,
    132, 134, 140, 173, 271, 272
seigniorage 244
self-financing 120
Sellon, G.H. 266
Sen, A. 209, 215

Senhadji, A.S. 188
sequential analysis 9
settlement systems
Canada 260–1
payment finality 13, 139–51
Shan, J. 276
Shapiro, E. 60
shares, issuance of 168
Shaw, E.S. 56, 59
short term 87–8
Silber, W.S. 61
single-period analysis 8
sixteenth century 244
Skidelsky, R. 55, 96
Smets, F. 242
Smith, A. 169
Smith, H.M. 59
Smith, P.F. 62
Smith, R.T. 276
Smithin, J. 6, 121, 132
social justice
approaches to 205–10
workers' poverty relative to owners of
means of production 223–5
social leadership 29–30
Soto, H. de 79
sovereignty of the consumer 34
Speight, H. 59
spontaneous order 212, 213
Sraffa, P. 85, 88
stability 246–7
Cuba 253–4
Stability and Growth Pact (SGP) 231
Stadermann, H.-J. 68, 69, 70, 72, 74, 76
stagflation 180
state money 70–1, 95–6, 246
coexistence with private money 245
state subsidies 250, 251
Steiger, O. 68, 69, 70, 72, 74, 75, 76, 79
Steuart, J. 74, 76
Stiglitz, J.E. 74, 177, 199
Stockholm School 3
store of wealth 10, 99–100, 155
structuralist approach 7–8
Struthers, J. 59
subsidies, state 250, 251
Sugden, R. 205–6
Swanson, R.B. 59
systemic order 120–1

Tabares, L. 249, 255
Taylor, W.G.L. 4, 5
Tchernava, P. 9
technological change 158
Théret, B. 255
Thomas, L.B. 59

Thomas, R.G. 59
thriftiness 86
time 89
Tobin, J. 62
Toll, S. 259
Torto, R. 63
Townshend, H. 57, 59, 60
trade barriers, international 199
trade finance fund 197
transactions-equation inflation 217,
218–19
tripartite class scheme 214

Uhr, C.G. 27
ultra-speculative ('Ponzi') financial
regime 117–18
uncertainty 89
fundamental 9–10
unemployment 98, 100
EMU area 240, 241
explaining using circuit theory 13,
177–80
unit of account 245–6
United States of America (USA) 238,
239, 264–6, 276–7
unwarranted levies 223–4, 225–6
user cost 175

Van Els, P. 238–41
Varian, H.R. 208
Varoukadis, A. 188
Vernengo, M. 7
viability of partial dollarisation 251–3
voluntary exchange and transfers 206,
207

wage and money system 3–4
Wagenvoort, R. 158
wages
bank mergers 159–60, 164, 165–6
circuit theory and employment
174–7, 178–80
ex post real wage 42–3
Walker, E.R. 60, 61
Walker, F.A 54
Weil, P. 56
Weiner, S.E. 266
Weiss, A. 74, 199
welfarism 207–8
Whittlesey, C.R. 57
Wicker, E.R. 59
Wicksell, K. 3, 4, 5, 11, 27–8, 48, 50–1,
140, 270
contribution to circulation
approach 23, 24–7, 35
Graziani and *Interest and Prices* 40–2

Wilson, T. 244
Withers, H. 4, 5, 56
Wojnilower, A.M. 266
workers, relative poverty of 223–5
Wray, L.R. 6, 8, 55, 173, 178, 260, 264, 265
Wright, J. 263

Yohe, W.P. 59, 61
Yunus, M. 203, 204, 210, 210–13, 214

Zazzaro, A. 112, 121, 131, 132, 133
zero-reserve requirements 15, 259–60, 264